History and the Public Sphere

History and the Public Sphere
Essays in Honour of John A. Murphy

Edited by

TOM DUNNE

and

LAURENCE M. GEARY

CORK UNIVERSITY PRESS

First published in 2005 by
Cork University Press
Youngline Industrial Estate
Pouladuff Road, Togher
Cork
Ireland

British Library Cataloguing in Publication Data
A CIP catalogue record for this book is available from the British Library
A CIP record for this publication is available from the Library of Congress

ISBN 1-859-392-1

Typeset by Tower Books, Ballincollig, Co. Cork
Printed by ColourBooks Ltd., Baldoyle, Co. Dublin

www.corkuniversitypress.com

Contents

SECTION 1

John A. Murphy

Introduction

THE EDITORS

The tradition of honouring a distinguished Professor Emeritus with a festschrift or collection of essays by former students and colleagues reflects the sense of a community of scholarship that is still (or should be) the true mark of a university. However, in the case of John A. Murphy, Professor of Irish History at University College Cork from 1971 to 1990, we honour a major contribution, not just to scholarship, but to the wider community. Through his membership of Seanad Éireann (the second chamber of the Irish Dáil or parliament), where he served as a vocal independent for ten years (1977–83, 1987–92), and through his extensive journalism, media appearances and public lectures, John A. has played a leading role in Irish public life, particularly during the crucial and traumatic period of the Troubles in Northern Ireland. His own often difficult and public journey from the traditional Catholicism and republican nationalism of his west Cork background to the secular humanism and pluralism he has championed for many years not only mirrored but helped to shape crucial aspects of Irish public opinion generally.

His trenchant, but often humorous, critique of the myths and shibboleths of physical-force republicanism and its fellow travellers focused the radical insights of a major revolution in Irish historical scholarship on the contemporary scene, and brought them to wider notice with the skills of a natural communicator. He played a key, perhaps even a crucial, role in the slow re-education of Irish public opinion in the complexity of Irish history and politics, which was a necessary foundation for the Northern Ireland peace process and the Good Friday Agreement. He will, no doubt, before long, be the subject rather than a practitioner of historical research, and for that reason we have gone beyond the usual listings of publications, and included details of his Seanad and other public speeches, his contributions to the press and radio, and, in particular, his lively and influential columns for the *Sunday Independent*. All show a scholarly mind grappling courageously and often controversially with the most fundamental problems of his society, and offer an important example of the application of academic values to the public sphere.

John A. Murphy also played a prominent political role in his university, particularly as a member of the governing body of University College Cork from 1983 to 1998, and of the Senate of the National University of Ireland from 1983 to 1998. His experiences in these arenas also influenced his many contributions on educational issues in the Irish Senate. His great love of UCC, which he first entered as a first-year undergraduate in 1945, was particularly evident in his very fine history, *The College*, published for its 150th anniversary. His services to the National University were part of what was recognized in its award of an honorary Doctorate in Literature, in 2001. We include the encomium delivered on that occasion by Seán Ó Coileáin.

However, those who worked with John A. in what were then UCC's three history departments, his postgraduates and the undergraduates who flocked to his lectures knew that the public figure was always subordinated to his core roles as academic colleague, supervisor and teacher – in all of which he excelled. His contribution to the discipline of History at UCC was significant and distinctive. He was proud of the department he had built up and of the range of talents he had drawn into it. He was a supportive Head and played a key role in the development of what he called at his retirement presentation,'the best history school on this island'. Despite his extensive public commitments, he always took a full teaching load, supervised more than his share of postgraduates and was always accessible to students. An inspired teacher, his most important monument, perhaps, is the largely invisible one of the respect and affection of generations of students, to whom he communicated some of his own historical curiosity, critical spirit and flair for language. This is represented here in the contributions by former postgraduates, Maurice Bric, Liam Irwin, Maura Cronin and Larry Geary, but also, appropriately, by a Paul Durcan poem, and an essay on the media and politics by Eoghan Harris.

While John A., like many of his generation, felt that, in a period of rapidly escalating student numbers, he often had to give priority to teaching over research, he made several major contributions to Irish historical scholarship, particularly in the areas of settlement and society in seventeenth-century Munster, religion and politics in nineteenth-century Ireland, the formation of the modern Irish state, and many aspects of Irish nationalism. These are detailed in his list of scholarly publications. His *Ireland in the Twentieth Century* is a classic, still the best introduction to the subject, and full of original insights, which, according to his former colleague Joe Lee, 'will inform historical research well into the next century'. These research interests are also reflected in this volume by new work on the Munster presidency, O'Connell, Young Ireland, Catholicism, the Land War, Parnell and cultural nationalism.

Also represented here is another of his distinctive contributions – the development and strengthening of links with Irish scholarship in America. John A. spoke at some of the early meetings of the American Committee of

Irish Studies, introduced by his friends Emmet Larkin, Larry McCaffrey, and later Jim Donnelly, who were among its founders and guiding spirits. In return, he helped to bring these fine historians into the Irish mainstream. Still a regular visitor to the United States (not least to visit his daughter Cliona, another of our contributors, and Professor of History at the University of California at Bakersfield), John A. has been Visiting Professor at Loyola University Chicago (1974), James Madison University, Virginia (1979), Boston College (1984–5) and Colby College, Maine (1987). With his friend, the late Sean Lucy, John A. also founded the first Summer School of Irish Studies in 1979, at UCC, where it still flourishes.

However, this brief outline of a distinguished academic and public career is only part of the story of John A., as he is widely and affectionately known – a title of respect as much as a name, and an indicator of his remarkable rapport with a wide public. He is also a wise, complex and passionate man, with strong convictions and opinions and formidable moral courage. He has a great gift for friendship – but also the ability to generate hostility. Few are neutral about him. He is a great character, an original, a colourful and charismatic figure who can enthral with a passionate rhetoric, amuse with a barbed wit, then charm with a remarkable repertoire of song in that distinctive tenor voice. Ruth Dudley Edwards and Úna O'Donoghue attempt in our opening essay to capture this larger-than-life personality as well as tell his story. His former colleague at UCC and great *uileann* piper Tomás Ó Canainn, brings together John A.'s passion for traditional music and his interest in the Irish-American connection. His gift for friendship across generations of historians and public figures is also reflected in the contributions by J.J. Lee, Owen Dudley Edwards and Conor Cruise O'Brien.

This festschrift thus seeks to go beyond the academic, and to pay tribute, however inadequate, to the much wider role and importance of a remarkable man, who in recent times has been combining historical scholarship with his love of singing. In a remarkable *tour de force* in Irish and English, he has been enthralling audiences in Ireland and America with his lavishly illustrated lectures on 'The Political Song in Modern Irish History'. Now, if he can only be persuaded to make a few CDs, a whole new career beckons!

Tom Dunne
Laurence M. Geary

Honoris Causa

DELIVERED BY PROFESSOR SEÁN Ó COILEÁIN, 11 MAY 2001

The encomium recommending John A. Murphy to the National University of Ireland for the award of an Honorary D.Litt.

John Augustine Murphy was born in Macroom on 17 January 1927. The world in which he grew into boyhood was far from the dreary stereotype of Irish life of the period. Not far removed in family background and rural hinterland lay the newly respectable Irish language. It would come to town on fair days and with visiting relatives; at school Eibhlín Dubh's lament for Art Ó Laoire would light up the placenames and history of the area and fire the imagination. At home there was music and song, ranging from Verdi and Schubert to the nationalist ballads of Thomas Davis and T.D. Sullivan. And the young John A. would devour the novels of Charles Dickens. In retrospect, it would seem to have been an ideal nurturing for one who would become a standard bearer for political and cultural pluralism. The songs might change but the song would remain, as would his love of literature and literary quotation. The Irish language itself would remain a constant presence in his life, being the medium of a good part of his writing from *Stair na hEorpa* [*History of Europe*] to his article on 'Seán Ó Ríordáin' and providing him with insights (as, for instance, in its barbed yet familiar anti-clericalism) that he would use to good effect in seminal essays such as 'Priests and People in Modern Irish History' and 'Daniel O'Connell and the Gaelic World'.

He entered UCC (then a college of fewer than 1000 students) on a county council scholarship, one of only three available, in October 1945. That it was the centenary year of the founding of the Queen's Colleges was scarcely noted by the authorities; fifty years later the publication of John A. Murphy's *The College* would be the central event of the sesquicentennial celebrations of a more mature and self-confident institution. But UCC had its figures of national importance in 1945 and of these he came into contact with three in particular: Daniel Corkery, James Hogan and, in a very different way, Alfred O'Rahilly. He never quite warmed to Corkery and would later come to reject him. But where Corkery stifled, James Hogan, Professor of History, perhaps the most remarkable scholar produced by that remarkable department, liberated and inspired, ranging freely in his lectures over the whole history of ideas.

John A. Murphy, described by Hogan as the best student he ever had, graduated with a First Class Honours BA and first place in both History and Latin in 1948. His MA research, the results of which were published in a series of articles in the *JCHAS*, was on Lord Inchiquin, Murrough O'Brien, called in Irish 'Murchadh na dTóiteán', and regarded by tradition as a byword for national and religious apostasy. This was followed by work on Justin MacCarthy, Lord Mountcashel, commander of the first Irish Brigade in France, 'the prototype Wild Goose'. From there his work extends into the twentieth century – his *Ireland in the Twentieth Century*, published in the Gill History of Ireland series, has achieved classic status.

Recalled from the diocesan seminary at Farranferris, where he had taught for the pervious decade, John A. Murphy became assistant lecturer at UCC under Hogan in 1960, and was appointed Professor of Irish History in 1971, a position he held until his early retirement in 1990. His contribution to History at UCC is second to none, and that in a department which is itself second to none. He was an inspiration to an entire generation of students, particularly to those many who carried out postgraduate research under his direction, drawing on his wide expertise and on a great fund of human understanding which extended both to subject and student.

History to John A. Murphy was more than an academic discipline: it was his life and he lived it and he made it part of the lives of others. His interest in regional and local history; his work with the Cork Historical and Archaeological Society, whose Journal he edited from 1964 to 1979 and to which he made many significant contributions by article and review; his radio lectures in the Thomas Davis series; his continuing engagement in public debate on issues critical to the future of this country, having played no small part in shaping its present by his courageous and incisive commentary – these are all of a piece. As is, indeed, his membership of Seanad Éireann (on which he served from 1977 to 1983 and again from 1987 to 1992), of the governing body of UCC and of the Senate of the National University. Knowledge, wisdom, ideas, the very joy of living – these were things not to be hidden away but to be communicated, and there has scarcely ever been a better communicator.

Lord Chesterton once said that 'Nobody should tamper with a University who does not love it well'. John A. Murphy loves every limestone step of the old College stairs hollowed by successive generations of students, every knotted uneven floorboard of this Aula Maxima, where he and his wife to be, Cita, danced in the days and nights of their student courtship. He has written the history of the College, but he has also been part of that history for more than one-third of its existence, still the same eager student of its triumphs and of its foibles. In honouring him, the National University, in a very profound sense, honours itself.

A Personal Appreciation

J.J. LEE

John A. and I were colleagues at UCC, he as Professor of Irish History and I as Professor of Modern (i.e. non-Irish) History, from my arrival in 1974 until his retirement in 1990. UCC actually contrived to have three Departments of History during that period, there being also a Department of Medieval History (under the headship of Professor John G. Barry until his death in 1989), operating on the basis of a common budget, before their merger into a single department in 1993. Connoisseurs of institutional inanities will not need to be told that an arrangement that had sufficed to half-choke the publication potential of even so productive a scholar as Oliver MacDonagh, my own immediate predecessor, could serve as a classic case-study of the ethos of university decision-making in an era where otherwise incomprehensible institutional structures reflected the primacy of personal relations, which were even more central to decision-making then than now. MacDonagh, incidentally, would duly resume major publication once he succeeded in extricating himself from the institutional coils of UCC to escape to Australia in search of conditions more conducive to research, writing and sanity.

I would, of course, have known John A.'s name long before my own appointment to Cork. Professor of Irish History at UCC since 1971, he had already a high reputation as a contributor to the study of the last four centuries in a series of sharply etched scholarly articles and profiles that revealed his particular gift for the probing incision, in the framework of the synoptic overview, that would become familiar from 1975 to a wider public through his *Ireland in the Twentieth Century,* which still rewards the closest reading for its sharpness of observation and felicity of formulation. But I had actually come to know his name much earlier still. His two-volume textbook, *Stair na hEorpa,* [*History of Europe*] stretching over the centuries, had descended like manna on me as a secondary school student in the late fifties. The art of textbook writing for pre-university level is an extraordinarily demanding one, little appreciated by those who have never attempted it. It was clear to even an unformed mind that here was someone with a striking talent for vivid, succinct presentation, a talent that would be equally impressive in English as in Irish.

Hugely gifted on paper in both languages – interspersed with the telling Latin phrase, sadly increasingly incomprehensible to younger audiences in their growing ignorance of classical European civilization – he undoubtedly is. But unlike some gifted stylists, not excluding that honorary Corkman, Edmund Burke, his voice is as seductive as his pen. It counts among the great joys of UCC that it gives such frequent opportunity of relishing the melodious cadences of one of the finest lecturers it could be anyone's privilege to hear, as he laces the fruits of independent thinking with sardonic wit. Nor is the reference to melody fortuitous. He can pepper his delivery with not only reference to, but performance of, song and poem. No one who heard, in Cork or Boston, his recent lecture, 'The Political Song in Modern Irish History', could ever forget his penchant for illustrating his presentation with participant performance, exuberantly enjoying himself while entrancing his audience. Nor could anyone at Merriman the year John A. could not be there, because of his heart-bypass operation, but endorse the good wishes for not only his full recovery, but for his return in full voice. As the announcer lamenting his absence put it, 'tis awful hard to get that man not to sing'. Happily he returned from his operation not only with mind and pen as sharp as ever, but with voice as sweet as ever, to continue to enthral a further generation of listeners. I was reminded of how far his renown extended at a dinner at the University of North Carolina at Chapel Hill recently, to celebrate the launching of an Irish Studies programme there, when his name came up and the mere mention that I had known him for thirty years reduced an envious company to reverential silence – allowing me to bask with becoming modesty in the warm glow of fame by association!

John A. is so much his own man that no one should claim credit for having put anything into his head, but I do remember suggesting to him on one of our trips to Limerick in the mid Seventies, when UCC had been entrusted by the National University with the grave responsibility of chaperoning Mary Immaculate, that he should stand for the Senate – recollecting in particular, if memory serves me right, a virtuoso lecture he gave on the subject 'Irish and Catholic', on the RTÉ Irish Identity series, a year or two before. This had brought home to a television audience his flair as an expositor, with not only his refreshingly iconoclastic way of looking at history, but that combination of conviction, clarity and command of language that, without ever compromising standards, showed a rare ability to lift viewers up to him rather than speak down to them. I do not flatter myself that I can claim credit for first broaching the idea, for I'm sure it was a thought that must have occurred to many others too, but I hope it is not too self-indulgent to feel a certain sense of proprietary, if vicarious, pride in having encouraged entry into political life of one of the most distinguished contributors to parliamentary debate in modern Ireland.

In that debate, as well as in his numerous columns in the *Sunday Independent* and elsewhere, he has been a resolute and robust critic of the IRA and Sinn Féin, so that some might label him a revisionist historian, Irish style. Indeed, he has himself identified himself with the doyen of revisionism, Conor Cruise O'Brien, with his 'sense of irreverent fun in life and literature (co-existing with a philosophical bleakness) and with the dismissal of sacred cows and political correctness, as when he exposed the pretentiousness of Yeats or refused to let the anti-apartheid movement be his conscience'.[1] One can see why John A. would cherish this association, for it adds up to the same type of irrepressible personality that makes him such engaging company. But the qualities listed do not in themselves add up to those that make a great historian, as distinct from a powerful polemicist, though those qualities can no doubt add to the gaiety of historical scholarship. A necessary, if not sufficient, precondition for candidature for inclusion in the ranks of the great historians – or indeed of any historians – is respect for the evidence, especially inconvenient evidence, making all appropriate allowance for the limits of, and problematics attaching to, the idea of evidence. If some of John A.'s ideological positions do indeed correspond closely to those popularly associated with revisionists, he has always been too independent-minded, or so it seems to me at any rate, to subscribe fully to the values at the core of revisionism, or to indulge in the unscholarly use of evidence, inherent in the imposition of the perspectives of the present on the past. Given that even historians devoted to the primacy of scholarly values, much less revisionists, can often succumb to the temptation, this deserves special recognition in any circumstances, and all the more so given the intensity of his own commitment to the causes he champions so eloquently in the present.

My impression, then, is that John A. has been far more successful than his estimable friend Conor Cruise in guarding against the temptation to approach history as simply a projection backwards of the polemics of the present. As the past is not for him simply an extension of the present, he offers fewer hostages to critical fortune than the vigour of his polemics in the present might lead one to assume, and his historical work therefore seems likely to survive when the passions of the present subside. It is difficult to envisage the later Cruise O'Brien, for instance, achieving the mature balance of John A.'s masterly survey of nineteenth- and twentieth-century Irish history in *The Encyclopedia of the Irish in America*,[2] in which he distils the ripe fruits of decades of inquiry and reflection in a more judicious spirit than one has come to associate with his great contemporary.

That one should contemplate such a comparison is of course instantly to acknowledge the stature of John A. himself, for how many names could be invoked in the same breath with that of Conor Cruise O'Brien? No more resounding accolade could be given to an Irish intellectual of even that gifted generation.

Message from Conor Cruise O'Brien

It is a source of peculiar satisfaction to me to contribute to John A. Murphy's festschrift. In a sense the invitation closes a cycle for in 1998 John A. Murphy contributed to my own festschrift, *Ideas Matter*. He contributed an essay entitled 'Myself and "The Cruiser"'.

Our backgrounds are, as he notes, and of which he is always acutely aware, significantly different. His whole education was in Catholic schools in Co. Cork and then in University College Cork, then formally Catholic in ethos, though not in technical affiliation. I attended a secular school that was nominally neutral, but substantially Protestant in ethos and went on to attend Trinity College Dublin, which Catholics were then permitted to attend only with the permission of the Ordinary of the Diocese, John Charles McQuaid. The permission was not as yet a formal requirement as it later became, but it was understood to be needed. I went up to Trinity without applying for permission and was thus in a sense cut off from the Church, and popularly deemed to be formally excommunicated.

So John and I started off far apart. Indeed, John was seen in some quarters as the man destined to put me down. As he records in his own essay, the late Tomás Ó Fiaich, then President of Maynooth College and afterwards Cardinal Primate, promising John his first preference vote in the elections for Seanad Éireann in 1977, remarked, 'Well, now, any man who can put Conor in his box . . .'

Yet it was never quite like that, though sometimes it felt a bit like it. John had been a warm supporter of mine in the Congo crisis in 1961, as he records in his essay. We have always remained friends and the friendship has withstood strains that were sometimes severe enough. I thought I gained some insight into the strains during a meeting in Cambridge in (I think) the mid Seventies. The convenors were concerned at the gains which the Provisionals appeared to be making in the Republic of Ireland (and were in fact making). John and I had been invited as prominent Irish people who were known to be opposed to this trend.

Several of our hosts were Old Etonians and some of them sounded condescending to those outside the fold. I was familiar enough with this phenomenon, always slightly irritated by it but disposed to ignore it. But John, as our meeting went on, was infuriated by it. Towards the end, as he rebuked our hosts for absolute failure to understand Ireland, he almost began to sound like a Provo himself, and began to look rather balefully at me for failure to back him up.

In the main Irish controversies of the day, especially in relation to the North, John and I basically remained on the same side, though with significant differences in emphasis. The differences came most strongly to the surface in a contribution of John's to a debate in *The Crane Bag* in 1977–8. Having said some generous things about my earlier contributions to the debate, John went on to make the severest comments he has ever made about me. He said: 'Having compelled us to ask questions, he provided no real answers. His pronouncements became increasingly abrasive and intolerant; those who disagreed with him he tended to see as conniving at subversion. Moreover his magisterial tone became pedantic and supercilious and this considerably diminished the force of the message he wished to convey.'

In retrospect, I acknowledge the force and truth of John's criticism and especially of his last sentence. I think I am unlikely to lose a certain tendency to acerbity in the heat of controversy, but at least the memory of John's weighty criticisms will always be there to put me on my guard against this dangerous tendency.

The controversies between us continued but became more good humoured as time went on. John recalls 'a Trinity College Historical Society Inaugural where Conor (as President of the Society) was in the chair. The old spark ignited when Conor (as President of the Society) shouted "Shame" at a point I made. "Observe", I said to the audience, "the admirable impartiality of the chair." Both of us enjoyed the moment, I think.'

We did indeed.

Canon James O. Hannay Pays a Return Visit to the Old Rectory, Westport, County Mayo, October 8, 2000

PAUL DURCAN

The lines are fallen unto me in pleasant places;
yea, I have a goodly heritage.

The Old Rectory has long since passed out of the hands of the Church of Ireland.
In 1982 it was purchased by young Seamus Walsh, one of the Walshes of Bridge Street.
His father Willie Walsh who had the pub was married to that wondrous Hughes woman Delia.
(Her uncle Charles Hughes – a most pleasant man and a most pleasing man –
Was the first Chairman of Westport Urban District Council.)
Young Seamus and his wife Mary MacBride, the fair lady also from Bridge Street,
Grand-niece of the Major – the audacious, wandering Major –
(Her grandfather Hugh Coen opened his drapery in the course of *my* life-time)
Have reared their family, one son and four daughters, in the Old Rectory.
Seamus is a roofer. Self-employed, he has his own business
In Carna in Connemara. Why Carna?
Because he likes to speak Irish when and where he can
At home or at work without having to make a fuss
Just as he likes to play the piano impromptu, informally –
Victorian ballads or Moore's Melodies or Gilbert and Sullivan
Or hits from 'Cats' or 'Evita'.
He has five men working for him full-time, five part-time.
No man has worked harder for his wife and children
Than the same Seamus Walsh. His wife and children want for nothing.
The cynics of the town – of whom there are the same quota
As in my time – the town lawyers, the town know-alls –
Knowingly wink and nod when the chat is about Seamus:

'The New Ireland' they dub him and they guffaw
At the idea of the Old Rectory being amok with the Barbie Dolls,
Pop-Star Posters, Play Stations, Nike trainers of the Walsh family
And at the phenomenon of the head of the house
Being a Roman Catholic roofer and not a Church of Ireland clergyman.
When he is not putting a new roof on a house in Clifden
Or he is not driving one of his children to music and drama
Or to football or swimming or running and jumping
Or he is not taking out his wife to dinner in 'La Bella Vista'
Seamus Walsh may be found browsing his bedside books –
Joseph Cassidy, The Messenger, Ulysses.
He exudes the physicality of the wild, pilgrim spirit.
He exudes the spirituality of fierce, hard work.
And I, Canon James O. Hannay, alias George A. Birmingham,
Who was lazy but by no means the idlest of men,
Back in my old home, the Old Rectory in Westport –
Of the psalmists' pleasant places, pleasantest of many –
Have to say that I am mindful with envy
At its twenty-first century atmosphere of carefree sanctity.

John A. Murphy
The Singer and the Song

RUTH DUDLEY EDWARDS AND
ÚNA O'DONOGHUE

'He had outgrown Cork; he had to get out of Cork,' said John A. Murphy of Seán O'Faolain in an RTÉ documentary commemorating the writer's centenary. He referred also to the city's 'stifling provincialism' and quoted O'Faoláin's description of it as 'the smothering feather-bed'. Yet John A. himself stayed put in Cork, which – despite its, at times, strenuous efforts – could not stifle this free and provocative spirit. In time Cork became proud of what it viewed as its famous son's contrariness – not least because he is deeply, even aggressively, proud of his native place. John A. is only half-joking when he advises: 'Never ask people where they're from because if they're not from Cork they'll be ashamed and if they are you'll know it.'

Teacher, lecturer, historian, politician and singer – above all, singer – John A. has ever been driven by an intense, quizzical curiosity about life. John A.-watchers will know the folded-arms-and-intense-expression stance, which indicates he is listening intently but also pawing at the ground waiting to erupt from the starting stall or – if displeased – framing the barbed, sometimes truculent, response.

John Augustine Murphy, born in Macroom on 17 January 1927, was the product of an interesting mixed marriage. While Timothy Murphy was a carpenter from small-farmer, artisan and Fenian stock, who later became a publican, Nellie O'Shea was middle class and her father a genteel, moderately prosperous draper and Redmondite. But the daughter converted from Home Rule to Sinn Féin and the Gaelic League and shared her husband's intense nationalism. The Murphy family had little money, but Nellie's education had equipped her with the skills that made the family home rich not just in the sound of music, but in a wide musical culture, in which her husband was a willing and skilful participant: 'The piano, a wedding present from my mother's father, was the focus of our home, the shrine where we worshipped almost daily but where my mother alone officiated.'[1]

The three elder siblings did not benefit from their piano lessons with the chapel organist, so John A. was never offered the opportunity to learn – thus ensuring that his mother's shrine maintained its mystique. 'Waiting for my mother to come from the chapel or from some household chore to play the piano: . . . whirling around and around on the stool till I became dizzy . . ."stop that, child of grace, you'll be sick" . . . later on, lighting the butts of candles in their brass sockets . . . shadowy illumination on the music sheets . . . learning to turn the page at the right moment . . . snuggling into warm folds of sound . . . lifting childish treble to join her thin soprano . . .'[2] Small wonder that John A.'s manifold activities as scholar, teacher, writer, talker, politician, husband, father, grandfather, friend and carouser often seem to onlookers to be what he does between songs.

The family politics might be narrowly nationalist, but the musical taste was extraordinarily broad. Nellie Murphy played Strauss waltzes and led the family in singing songs by Brahms, Schubert, Gounod, Verdi, Stephen Foster, Gilbert and Sullivan, and Rogers and Hammerstein. They sang from the three volumes of *The World's Favourite Songs*, from the Edwardian music-hall repertoire with which she had grown up, and in time they learned contemporary pop songs from the sheet music brought home by young John A. And there were exotic additions to the canon from a 'Macrompian' pastor in Florida. John A. recounts how, many years later, he mystified American friends in St Louis as they watched the paddle steamers, by bursting into:

My bones are aching, my heart is breaking
No silver lining in the clouds I see
For years I've loved the dear old Mississippi
And look what Mississipi's done to me.

'Dead mother, never travelled at all, sharply remembered by great waters far away,' was what John A. remembered at that moment.[3] She is often remembered too, no doubt, when her son sings *My Home in Sweet Glanlea* – all nine long verses of it – the account of the narrator's innumerable imagined journeys to strange places, of which he has a geographically and historically slim grasp but which, when compared with Glanlea, always disappoint.

If Nellie 'had a catholic taste', said her son, 'it was above all an Irish catholic taste,'[4] so there was Irish dance music and *Songs of the Nation* (an anthology of Young Ireland ballads), *Songs of the Gael*, Moore's Melodies, ballads of the Wild Geese and, occasionally, of the Tan War and the Civil War. Nellie was fastidious, though, so 'The Boys of Kilmichael' was regarded as vulgar and her son was retrospectively proud that she 'greatly admired the noble Thomas Davis whose spirited but hopeless vision of Irish fraternity we often saluted – ironically, to the tune of Lillibulero'.[5] It culminates with:

English deceit can rule us no more,
Bigots and knaves are scattered like spray –
Deep was the oath the Orangemen swore,
'Orange and Green must carry the day.'

Macroom – where they spoke 'Hiberno-English', according to John A., – 'was a condescended-to *"baile gallda"* on the *"bothar na Gaeltachta"*, a despised stage on the pilgrimage west to the last dwindling language reservations'.[6] But though Father sang exclusively in English, Mother sang such Irish songs native to the area as 'An Capaillín Bán'. The young John A. learned those songs too, and his Irish-speaking cousins made the language seem fascinating and exotic.

As her son would be, Mother was both temperamental and a perfectionist. She would sometimes for quite long periods eschew the piano despite piteous wails from the children, most frequently because she thought it proper to mourn even people they hardly knew. Perhaps as a private tribute to her, John A. sometimes withdraws his favours. Those of us who have cleared the competition out of the way so that an impatient John A. could be given the platform have on the odd occasion been peeved when for no apparent reason he obdurately spurned all requests to perform.

Mother's perfectionism showed itself in the wince at a false key or a jangled chord, but also in her insistence that, in gratitude for having a good voice, one was required to work hard; her protesting son was forced to sing 'seconds' in intricate duets, which trained him to harmonize any song spontaneously. 'The cardinal sin in singing was to go off key. In the middle of a Christmas carol or a rousing ballad, my mother would sweep her hands off the keys, clap them to her ears and emit a horrified shriek: "Jesus, Mary and Joseph, someone is FLAT! Is it you, Thade?" "Blast it, woman," in that loud voice which belied my father's extraordinary gentleness, "I never went flat in my life."' John A. lived in terror of being so accused.

The household was political and religious as well as musical. Father took the *Irish Press,* he gave Fianna Fáil his half-crown on national collection Sunday and sometimes he would sing:

> De Valera lead you
> Soldier of the Legion of the Rearguard.

The children would gaze admiringly at the annual receipt from HQ with the franked de Valera signature, which 'was carefully folded and reverentially placed under the Sacred Heart lamp. Thus did we honour the twin and sanguine pieties of Faith and Fatherland. God was in his Irish Catholic heaven and de Valera would surely put things right one day with our part of the world.'[7] Never would Murphy Senior countenance any criticism of his political god: 'Dev was the fatherland personified.'[8]

John A. was eight when de Valera came to Macroom. 'I remember vividly the marching band and the horses, the blazing tar-barrels and, in the town square, the upturned sea of dark, hungry (some literally so), passionate faces beneath the Town Hall balcony.' After his speech, de Valera was taken to the house of John A.'s uncle by marriage Daniel Corkery (ex-guerrilla, a veteran of the First Dáil and at this time a Fianna Fáil TD) and John A. 'was ushered into the Presence. My mother led me upstairs into a sitting-room where the Long Fellow sat on an armchair by the fire. I think I did something like a double genuflection (as at an exposition of the Blessed Sacrament) as he murmured a greeting in Irish.'[9]

It was around this time that John A. began making speeches to anyone who would listen: the combination of showman and passionate student of politics that was to make him so formidable as a senator was already audible. As a teenager, during the Second World War, he was burdened by the common belief that Ireland was at risk,'which was a lot of boloney but that's the way it seemed then'.[10] When he cycled the twenty-four miles to Cork to see de Valera review an army march-past, 'I wanted to be the living element of that great and unifying consensus of Irish neutrality which is central to the history of the Irish state.'[11] An ambition to join the army was vetoed by his mother, who, like most of her class, thought soldiers were common.

Religion was also a potent element in his life. As an altar boy he loved the liturgy, the ritual, the gold plate and the vestments, and, like his parents, he found the dogma comforting; but like many another sensitive adolescent troubled by forbidden sexual desires, he was terrified by those preaching about hell-fire and retribution.

Overall, John A. was a bookish, serious and pious child, a star performer in the De La Salle Brothers' classroom and a dud on the playing-field. Yet his father had been on the Cork Gaelic football team that won the All Ireland in 1911 and John A. early on became the passionately partisan supporter he still is.'I once had a bet with John A. that Cork would not win the most elusive double of all – the All Ireland Final in football and hurling in the same year,' recalls Peadar MacManus.

> The bet was even money – this was very generous of John A. because the possibility of Cork winning the double was regarded as remote. What I had not realized was that John A. had a secret weapon. He brings his father's All-Ireland medal to every game in which Cork plays. At crucial moments in the game, John A. strokes the medal to invoke his father's spirit. Obviously, it does not always work. Unfortunately, his father's spirit was in top form that year because Cork won the double and I lost my bet. John A. said it was one of his sweetest victories.[12]

When it comes to Gaelic football, as with Cork, John A. Murphy has never revised his beliefs: when in 1993 plans for a £100 million redevelopment of Croke Park were announced, his comment was: 'Far from five-course lunches and hospitality suites the GAA was reared.'

At eighteen, John A. passed the civil service exam but also, to the delight of his parents, won one of the three county council university scholarships. While at University College Cork, he lived with other scholarship boys in the Honan Hostel, a cross-faculty, élitist and intellectually exciting community where he was largely protected from the snobbery so obvious in the wider student body.

Of the three famous professors with whom he came into contact, two were insular: the UCC president, Alfred O'Rahilly, was an authoritarian, fundamentalist Catholic and Daniel Corkery (no relation), the Professor of English, was a proponent of cultural insularity. But James Hogan, the Professor of History, who thought John A. the best student he ever had, introduced him to a wide and liberating cosmopolitan world of ideas. And while he was an industrious and respectable student, the exhibitionistic side of John A. was evident on the dance-floor where he and Cita McCarthy (whom he married in 1952 and with whom he had five children) conducted their courtship: he matured into a man who did not fear ridicule as he tangoed with a rose in his teeth.

When John A. took his First Class Honours in 1948 (with first place in History and Latin), he was tentatively moving beyond traditional constraints on his thinking. Fianna Fáil he now considered to be stale and inept and 'the de Valera *aisling* [the vision of a frugal, pastoral, Irish-speaking utopia] in the face of emigration, unemployment and grey poverty'[13] simply futile. His flirtation in 1948 with Sean MacBride and his republican/socialist Clann na Poblachta was brief, but he fed his developing liberal instincts with a subscription to the *New Statesman.* 'My instinctive – almost hereditary – dispositions coloured my views for a long time,' he wrote, 'being only slowly modified by my study of history and other influences.'[14]

At St Finbarr's diocesan seminary, Farranferris, John A. was the only layman among the staff of thirteen, teaching History, Latin and English and declaiming long passages of Shakespeare to his captive audience. He was increasingly more liberal than the priests, with whom he had a happy and convivial relationship, for they, like many others over the years, quickly succumbed to John A.'s charm and wit and the intoxicating vigour of his talk. He still, like them, saw the Church of Ireland as heretical, but he no longer accepted dogma uncritically when it conflicted with his shifting political views. At twenty-four, when the Catholic bishops condemned the Mother-and-Child scheme brought forward by Dr Noel Browne, whom John A. thought a hero, he argued his case and stood his ground against his clerical colleagues.

While at Farranferris, John A. wrote an MA thesis on Murrough O'Brien, the first Lord Inchiquin, a hate-figure for Irish Catholics and nationalists, which he turned into a series of articles for the *Journal of the Cork Historical and Archaeological Society*. Along with his research on Lord Mountcashel, whom he described as 'the prototype Wild Goose', this made it possible for James Hogan to recruit him as an assistant lecturer in the UCC History Department in 1960.

Those were not the days of narrow specialism. 'You taught everything,' he recollected. 'I taught European and Irish history. I remember teaching with great interest the Crusades, the Renaissance and the Reformation.' John A. was a riveting teacher whose students found him inspirational, multi-faceted, entertaining and kind: 'Knowledge, wisdom, ideas, the very joy of living', said Professor Seán Ó Coileáin of John A. as a teacher,'– these were things not to be hidden away but to be communicated, and there has scarcely ever been a better communicator.'

John A. would become Professor of Irish History in 1971, when he was only forty-four, and serve on the UCC governing body and the Senate of the National University of Ireland. He would lecture on his subject at home and abroad, he would edit the *Journal of the Cork Historical and Archaeological Society*, and he would write distinguished essays and books, but it was clear from a very early stage that he would not confine himself to an exclusively scholarly life. It was indeed his deep interest in politics that inexorably drew him as an historian towards modern history. His *Ireland in the Twentieth Century* (1975) was a wonderful little book, and in academic journals and collections of scholarly essays and back copies of *The Irish Times* and the *Sunday Independent* are innumerable lively, illuminating, iconoclastic, provocative and sometimes mischievous reflections on the national psyche of independent Ireland. His passion for modern history and his deep love of UCC would be married in *The College*, published in 1995 to mark its sesquicentennial.

The first big political test for John A. at UCC followed on the Congo crisis of 1960 and the murder of nine Irish soldiers serving with the UN forces in Katanga. 'Two conflicting worldviews emerged in the UCC debate,' he wrote years later. 'The conservative Irish Catholic mindset regarded the UN with considerable suspicion, seeing it as a secularising institution . . . and muttering darkly about the coercion of "Catholic" Katanga. On the other side, there was much enthusiasm for the idea of an independent Irish foreign policy favouring neither Cold War side and making a small, but notable, contribution . . . to the cause of international peace and understanding . . .'[15] New and untenured and at odds with the senior members of his department, John A. argued his side of the case at student debates and public meetings. Eoghan Harris was a UCC student then:

> Conor Cruise O'Brien and the Congo became a huge moral and political issue. At that time UCC was a small, intensely Catholic, intensely conservative university, whose political life was effectively controlled by Professor James Hogan, his powerful ally Senator Professor P.M. Quinlan and a student organization called Christus Rex. Hogan and Quinlan saw every international conflict as part of the mortal struggle against communism. But they brought a particular passion to their campaign against Conor Cruise O'Brien, both because of his relationship with Maire Mac an tSaoi (they were terrible puritans) and because they believed O'Brien to be a communist fellow-traveller who was supporting the communist Patrice Lumumba against the Catholic Moshe Tshombe and blocking the secession of Catholic Katanga. At that time you could lose your job or fail your exam by being branded a communist. So when Hogan and Christus Rex called a mass meeting, attendance by all the history faculty was well nigh compulsory. For

> Murphy not to attend was as good as giving his notice in terms of tenure. But he went further.
>
> With incredible courage he spoke at a tiny counter-meeting on the same night, organized by a courageous Capuchin called Father Vianni. Hogan was furious. What I remember of that night was the Christus Rex mob howling outside the Murphy–Vianni meeting, and within the room Murphy looking like a ghost. Apart from anything else he had great respect for Hogan, and it grieved him to have to go against him. But go against him he did, his jaw set, his voice firm, his mind in gear, his fragile face set in stone. Grace under pressure.

John A. survived, but the episode fuelled his religious doubts. As a young married man, he had found totally hypocritical the clerical line on family planning: 'You were supposed to bang away in the name of God …' *Humanae Vitae,* the 1968 unexpectedly hard-line papal encyclical, appalled him and he became increasingly anti-clerical.'I think I went on from there to see the shortcomings of the church and the divisive role of religion in Irish history and particularly then in the context of the northern troubles.'[16] As one of the few academics prepared to flout Church rules in the mid 1960s by participating in a Protestant service for a dead colleague, he saw as wrong and uncharitable those members of UCC who stood outside. 'There was certainly no Holy Spirit informing their actions.'

When John A. stopped practising, he did so openly,'though to be honest at the same time I didn't parade it from the housetops or put an announcement in the *Cork Examiner*'.[17] He looks back in some astonishment at the extraordinary dividing line in his life that transformed him in middle age from committed Catholic to a secular liberal,'very much aware of the evils of Church influence in Irish society, both historically and in the day's politics'.[18] In time he would become an atheist.

Escaping from religion was a liberation; so were visits abroad. He was already a popular guest lecturer in the United Kingdom, but from the early 1970s he was one of the first Irish-based historians to become closely involved with the vibrant American Conference for Irish Studies, which he attended regularly. As well as making many short trips, he was visiting professor at the Loyola University Chicago in 1974, at James Madison University in Virginia in 1979, at Boston College in 1984–5 and at Colby College, Maine, in 1987, and the deep and lasting friendships with fine historians like Larry McCaffrey, Emmet Larkin and Jim Donnelly helped lay the basis for important exchange programmes with UCC.

In America too John A. was frequently drawn into political controversy. 'When I went there first, there was a wall of Irish-American ignorance. Any real understanding of the complexity of Ireland was simply absent at that stage. I hope I helped to inform people in that regard.'[19] That he did succeed owed much to the intense empathy for ordinary people that John A. has never lost. 'What we might regard as a kind of inferior culture for Irish-Americans held them together in their bad years. Their songs and stories and their admittedly exaggerated visions of the old sod gave them great solidarity and cohesion. We have no right to sneer at them.'[20] In recent years John A. has taken to America his singing lectures – which illuminate our island story through the history and words of the songs.

It is a feature of John A. that wherever he goes, he may talk and sing, but his eyes and ears and mind are open. Politically, from the beginning of the Troubles, his lively intelligence was more and more directed at what we euphemistically call the national question. He was never anything other than a vehement critic of the Provisional IRA, but he did lead a protest in Cork in 1972 over Bloody Sunday and during the 1970s he found himself challenging much of the analysis and some of the actions of the Provos' great enemy in the Republic, Conor Cruise O'Brien. John A. disapproved, for instance, of Section 31 of O'Brien's 1975 Broadcasting Act, which banned Sinn Féin and other terrorist front-organizations from RTÉ – foolishly believing, as he later admitted ruefully, that they would come off second best against professional interviewers. He rejected the O'Brien view that to accept the Easter Rising as legitimate was to give aid and comfort to the Provisionals, the natural heirs of a small cabal of unelected revolutionaries. The John A. view 'was that the Easter Rising was the wellspring of the flow of events leading to the foundation of the state, which should not, therefore, relinquish custody of the 1916 dynamic and its ideals to the Provisionals'.[21]

In April 1977, to mark the publication of a new biography of Patrick Pearse[22], the warriors fought to a draw on television in a debate that excited much interest nationally. They continued to argue about Irish nationalism subsequently in *The Crane Bag*, where John A. accused O'Brien of failing' to realise that a sense of nationality (*pietas* towards the past, commitment to the present, hope for the future) is an integral and essential part of the common Irishman whose lifestyle, unlike that of Dr O'Brien, is of necessity bounded by domestic horizons.'[23] By now, they were both in Seanad Éireann, for in 1977 O'Brien lost his seat in the Dáil and was subsequently elected a senator by Trinity College graduates while John A. topped the poll of their NUI equivalents.

John A. had won with the help of an eager group of campaigners who loved and admired him personally, but his RTÉ debate with Conor had expanded his already large constituency to include anti-O'Brien nationalists. 'I recall the late Tomás Ó Fiaich, then President of Maynooth College and afterwards Cardinal Primate, promising me his first preference vote with the phrase "well, now, any man who can put Conor in his box . . .".'[24] Many of these would become disappointed as John A. moved reluctantly but inexorably toward the O'Brien position on 1916, while never following him into the Unionist camp. Robin Dudley Edwards, Professor of Irish History at University College Dublin, regretted John A.'s election, for while he greatly admired his political courage and agreed with his views, in his world Clio came first, and he mourned the books that might have otherwise been written.

John A.'s election to the Senate symbolized a gathering together of his passions and interests in a forum which he respected as a vital check on government, while being clear-minded about its need for reform. Surrounded mainly by placemen and retired and would-be TDs, John A. showed his qualities of commitment, diligence, honesty, fearlessness and exuberance. He quickly discovered how to make the best use of the system to maximize his contributions, using all the mechanisms of the Seanad – private member motions, raising matters on the order of business and initiating adjournment debates that demanded the presence of the relevant Minister.

There is scope for more than one Ph.D. thesis on the impact of John A.'s sparkling, trenchant and uncompromising speeches and contributions to that ocean of mediocrity in 1977–83 and 1987–92. Apart from the high politics of Church and state, the Irish language, education, Anglo-Irish relations, foreign policy and Northern Ireland, he took part in debates on all aspects of society and the economy (and also contributed to the legislative process). His political philosophy he summed up as: 'Disentangle, not destroy, the meshed threads of history – the tribe from the nation, language and culture from nationalism and physical force, the Roman Catholic church from the nationalist; an independent foreign policy and public control over national resources.'[25]

'Let us cherish our particular allegiances and traditions,' he told the Seanad in 1979, *à propos* what he believed to be a tribal Bill which made contraceptives available only on a doctor's prescription and to married couples. 'The nub of our tragedy in this island is that in the past we have persisted, and we still persist, in confusing the tribe with the nation, in confusing Irish with Catholic.'[26] The argument that 'Middle Ireland' was so conservative on contraceptives that it wished them unavailable to anyone else was 'inconsistent with the principles of civil and religious liberty' and should be countered by the government. 'It is a selective conditioning. "Middle Ireland" has not been conditioned to have tender consciences about all kinds of other issues, about social injustice, land speculation, sleazy mergers, the alienation of our natural resources, the glamorising in TV interviews of financial spivs.' The Health Minister, Charles Haughey, had been exhorting people to take responsibility for their own health in such matters as smoking and drinking and 'not to clog up the doctors' waiting rooms'. Now this same minister was 'providing that couples will clog up the doctors' waiting rooms entirely unnecessarily because in this matter they are not only not unhealthy but are bursting with health and vigour and have no business there at all'.

Haughey had described the Bill as 'an Irish solution to an Irish problem.' John A. commented,

> I could not agree more that this is a very good description of this Bill. It carries all the hallmarks of that kind of Irishness which is the most unprepossessing of our natural characteristics . . . I am talking about the

> tendency to say one thing and mean another, to pretend to be doing something while dodging the issue, the ostensible fulfilment of a promise to deal with a situation while, in fact, not facing up to the situation at all. It may well be threatening penalties which may never be enforced, turning the blind eye: 'Sure we all know they do not mean it. We know where we can get them but mind you I said nothing.'
>
> In this case 'Irishness' means bringing in a pathetic legislative measure which will make no difference to the fortunate citizens who know where to go and who have never had any family problems because they can always get the service they want. The Bill does nothing for those who are in genuine and desperate need. It is, indeed, an Irish solution to an Irish problem . . . [which] can fairly be translated as 'an Irish Catholic solution to an Irish Catholic problem'. . . It is a tragedy that in 1979, at this juncture of modern Irish history we should be offered a denominational Bill from a Minister who is particularly well aware that a secular State is an integral part of Irish republicanism.

Later he would attack the presence of the Irish army at religious ceremonies and bolster his argument with what Bishop Kinsella of Ossory said in 1835 on the subject to Alexis de Tocqueville[27] – as always, where possible, putting the issue in historical context.

To describe John A. as a thorn in the side of the Fianna Fáil government and its Senate majority is too simple: at times he more resembled a stake in its heart. When Haughey became Taoiseach, John A. spoke presciently of how this

> recent palace revolution . . . has pointed up more than ever the close alliance between top politicians and the world of very big business. As a historian, and, indeed, as the child of Fianna Fáil parents, I regret to make the observation that Fianna Fáil is, in fact, no more. The simple faith of the small man, with his humble subscription, who placed his shilling or his half-crown on the collection table back in the thirties and forties – my own people, in fact – has finally been betrayed. Within the last week, we have been told that austerity lies before us, that belt-tightening is the order of the day. Are these injunctions going to be taken seriously, coming from this Government and this Taoiseach?

A new idealism and a new patriotism was possible only 'if our political, social and economic system is totally transformed, only if the republic of virtue is established.' Members of the Oireachtas should have to declare their commercial and business interests and political parties the sources of their funds. 'However, all moves in the direction of what I would call the republic of virtue are not likely to make any greater progress in the next two years. At the same time, it is in all our interests to hope – it must be hope rather than confidence – that the new Taoiseach will serve the nation with the same dedication and single mindedness which up to now he has largely applied to the pursuit of political power and the accumulation of a considerable personal fortune.'[28]

The hypocrisy of the *'A-chara-mise-le-meas'* brigade who professed devotion to the language, but could neither speak nor understand it, was another favourite target. Ruthlessly, John A. used his mastery and fluency in Irish (in what he described as 'the kingly and mellifluous West Muskerry dialect') to confuse and provoke. But it was his unambiguous anti-IRA stance that invoked the greatest hostility, especially when he denounced support for the Hunger Strikers: 'the essence of the issue is that those who support the campaign for political status for the H-Block prisoners are supporting the grisly and murderous campaign of the Provisional IRA . . . a war against a million Irish men and women of a different tradition, a different allegiance, a different religion . . . a total contradiction of the true republican tradition.'[29] The H-Block committees' campaign, he told the Cork Rotary Club, was reminiscent of the fascists' rise to power, 'undermining the normal process of law, putting up black flags everywhere and ordering people to shut their doors.'[30]

There was hate mail that included bullets, mock bombs and excrement and a black eye when he objected to *An Phoblacht*, 'this terrorist rag', being sold in a pub. John A. laughed it all off. Harder to endure was another moment that pointed up his extraordinary moral courage. Eoghan Harris tells the story:

> At the Munster Final in 1981, after the death of Bobby Sands, Frank Murphy, a power on the Cork County Board, came over the loudspeaker system asking for two minutes' silence for two ESB workers from Newcestown who had been accidentally electrocuted that morning – and then suddenly slipped in 'and for the Hunger Strikers'. Enraged by this sly effort to hitch a H-Block lift on the backs of two brave ESB workers, John A. shouted loudly, 'What about all the Protestants that were murdered?' Some 80,000 people got to their feet, but Murphy did not move. He sat in the stand, sat out the silence and people who saw him saw the same thing I saw in UCC twenty years before – a fragile face set in stone. Grace under pressure, of the sort I wish to be spared.[31]

Northern Ireland affected some of his friendships, especially when he became an unapologetic partitionist. Peadar MacManus remembers,

> The North loomed over the Merriman Schools of the Seventies and Eighties, but was never adequately discussed . . . John A. was perceived to be more and more at variance with the Merriman mainstream view, but his right to be so at variance was strongly defended. In spite of the prevailing Voltairian spirit, John A. seemed to become convinced that he had become estranged from many of his Merriman friends. There was a wonderful argument between himself and Breandán Ó h-Eithir in Keane's pub in Lisdoonvarna. I remember an argument between John A. and Seán MacRéamoinn in Lahinch.
>
> Things came to a head when John A. read a paper on the North that suggested that Northern nationalists were different, that they had a different historical experience, that they were disruptive and destabilizing

> in the South, and that it would be better if the Republic accepted that its future would be a 26-county state. The audience was hostile. Nell McCafferty and Seamus Martin denounced the idea that they were any less Irish than the people of Macroom or less entitled to be Republican. Patricia Coyle made a particularly brilliant dissection of his arguments. They were all warmly applauded . . . John A. seemed quite taken aback by the reception of his paper, and I think relations were strained for quite a time after this.[32]

Out of this, in 1986, came the hilarious satire on revisionism, 'The Gentle Black and Tan', written by Seamus Martin and Breandán Ó h-Eithir. The targets are John A., Ruth Dudley Edwards and Conor Cruise O'Brien and (with a new verse added by the singer) it is still a favourite in John A.'s repertoire. The original ends:

> So farewell you blinkered nationalists
> A warning take from me,
> If you want to seem progressive
> Then revise your history.
> And pay heed to our three heroes
> Murphy, Edwards and Your Man
> Who clear the name and sing the fame
> Of the gentle Black and Tan

Many were not surprised that he lost his Senate seat in 1983, but he regained it four years later, when many of the voters recognized what was once articulated by Ciarán MacMahúna: 'you could be on the opposite side to him, but when you saw some of the company you were in, you changed sides.' John A. attacked bigotry and discrimination in the Republic, argued for extending extradition to cover political crimes, proposed sarcastically that novenas be made for the British to stay in Northern Ireland 'because we certainly could not handle the consequences of withdrawal'.[33] One of his closest allies in the Senate was David Norris, the Trinity senator who had forced a change in the law on homosexuality by taking the Irish government to the European court. One John A. speech against video censorship ended thus:

> I wonder what criterion will the censors apply to the different categories. They might follow the rather facetious rule which, I understand, was observed in Hollywood at one stage. In the films for general viewing, the hero gets the girl; over 15, the villain gets the girl; and over 18 everybody gets the girl.
>
> MR NORRIS: Over 21 the hero gets the villain.
>
> PROFESSOR MURPHY: I will not go into other variations, Senator Norris.[34]

There is much to record in John A.'s extraordinary odyssey, but it seems right to end with music. 'He was the best pub singer of Irish songs in Irish or English I have ever heard,' wrote Peadar MacManus, in what he called a 'bowdlerized memory of John A.'.

> He could and often did sing non-stop for three hours at a stretch. It was rare to have to call the pub to silence because John A. had the gift of being able to command attention from the most philistine rabble. Difficult songs like 'Na Conneries' or 'Sliabh na mBan', long ballads like the 'Cill na Martra Exile', rousing songs like 'Father O'Flynn', funny songs like the updated versions of the 'Shan Van Vocht' – they rolled off his tongue and he never fluffed a line. His memory was phenomenal, and his renditions were rarely challenged.

Like all great performers, John A. did not like to have his performances interrupted. The first time that Sean Ó Briain attended at a Merriman Winter School, he joined in one of John A.'s songs. He had an excellent light operatic voice, but John was a solo performer and was not having a duet. He stopped in the middle of the song, walked away, had a solitary pint, and then rejoined the company. After half an hour he then resumed his solo performance.

On the British–Irish conference circuit, to which he has brought so much controversy and fun, one of the great memories comes from a meeting of the British–Irish Association where Lord Armstrong, the ex-Secretary to the Cabinet, played the accompaniment for John A.'s rendition of 'Whack Fol The Diddle'.[35] Sample verse:

> Oh, Irishmen forget the past
> Whack fol the diddle fol the di dol day
> And think of the time that's coming fast
> Whack fol the diddle fol the di dol day
> When we will all be civilized
> Neat and clean and well advised
> Oh, won't Mother England be surprised?
> Whack fol the diddle fol the di dol day

The last word goes to the man himself: 'Impugn my scholarship, if you will, challenge my political motivations, spread scandal about my private life, even pollute my pint, but at your gravest peril accuse me of "going flat".'[36]

John A. Murphy

SCHOLARLY PUBLICATIONS, NEWSPAPER AND PERIODICAL CONTRIBUTIONS, SENATE SPEECHES AND OTHER ADDRESSES

A. Books

Stair na hEorpa: I (Baile Átha Cliath, 1955).
Stair na hEorpa: 2 (Baile Átha Cliath, 1958).
Justin MacCarthy, Lord Mountcashel (Cork, 1959; Antrim, 1999).
Ireland in the Twentieth Century (Dublin, 1975, 1989).
Co-ed. with J.P. Carroll, *De Valera and his Times* (Cork, 1983).
The College: A History of Queen's/University College Cork 1845–1995 (Cork, 1995).
Ed. *The French are in the Bay: The Expedition to Bantry Bay 1796* (Cork, 1997).
University College Cork in words and pictures (with Andrew Bradley) (Cork, 2005).

B. Articles

(Dublin is the place of publication unless otherwise stated.)

1957 'Séamus Ó Conghaile: A Thuairimí agus a Thionchar', *Comhar* (Lúnasa).
1959 'Smaointe ar an Stair', *Irisleabhar Mhá Nuad*.
1964 'The Expulsion of the Irish from Cork in 1644', *Journal of the Cork Historical and Archaeological Society*, 69.
1965 'The Support of the Catholic Clergy in Ireland, 1750–1850', in J.L. McCracken (ed.), *Historical Studies V*.
1965 'The Sack of Cashel, 1647', *Journal of the Cork Historical and Archaeological Society*, 70.
1967 'Inchiquin's Changes of Religion', *Journal of the Cork Historical and Archaeological Society*, 72.
1969 'Priests and People in Modern Irish History', *Christus Rex*, XXIII, (Oct.–Dec.).
1971 'The Politics of the Munster Protestants, 1641–1649', *Journal of the Cork Historical and Archaeological Society*, 76.

1975 'Eamon de Valera, the Politician', *Ireland Today* (Department of Foreign Affairs Bulletin: Sept. 1975).

1976 'The Groves of Soviet Academe', *UCC Record*, No. 51.

1976 'Identity Change in the Republic of Ireland', *Études Irlandaises*, No. 1.

1976 'Identity in the Republic of Ireland Now', in B.M. Touhill (ed.), *Varieties of Ireland: Varieties of Irish America* (University of Missouri-St. Louis).

1978 Introduction and Afterword, James Stephens, *The Insurrection in Dublin*, (Gerrards Cross).

1978 'Further Reflections on Nationalism', *The Crane Bag*, 2.

1979 'Discours sur l'élimination du colonialisme dans le monde', *Compte rendu de la LXVe conference interpalementaire* (Genève).

1980 'Seán Ó Ríordáin agus an Pholaitíocht, in Eoghan Ó hAnluain (ed.), *An Duine is Dual.*

1980 'The Friday Night Court', in Paul Durcan (ed.), *The Cork Review*, No. 4 (Westport: Conn.).

1980 'The Influence of America on Irish Nationalism' in D.N. Doyle and O.D. Edwards (eds), *America and Ireland, 1776–1976.*

1981 'Religious Majorities and Minorities, North and South, Then and Now', in *The Crane Bag Book of Irish Studies 1977–1981*.

1981 'The Mind of Republicanism', in D. Watt (ed.), *The Constitution of Northern Ireland: Problems and Prospects.*

1983 'Eamon de Valera: Informal Reflections', *The Recorder* (Journal of the American Irish Historical Society), Vol. 44.

1983 'The Achievements of Eamon de Valera', in P.J. Carroll and J.A. Murphy (eds), *De Valera and His Times* (Cork).

1986 'A Look at the Past', in J.McLoone (ed.), *The British–Irish Connection*.

1987 'Post War Society: the Ambience of a College', *The Irish Review*, No. 2 (Cork).

1988 'A Catholic College: UCC in the 1940s and 1950s', *The Irish Review*, No. 4 (Cork).

1988 'The Anglo-Irish Treaty and After: The Canadian Model and Context' in R. O'Driscoll and L. Reynolds (eds), *The Untold Story: The Irish in Canada* (Vol. II).

1989 'Religion and Irish Identity', in *Irishness in a Changing Society* (The Princess Grace Irish Society, New Jersey).

1991 'History and the Journal', *Journal of the Cork Historical and Archaeological Society*, 96.

1991 'Ireland: Identity and Relationships', in B. Crick (ed.), *National Identities: The Constitution of the United Kingdom* (London).

1993 'Cork: Anatomy and Essence', in P. O'Flanagan and C.G. Buttimer (eds), *Cork: History and Society* (Cork).

1993 'The Piano in Macroom', in S. Dunne (ed.), *The Cork Anthology* (Cork).

1995 'Cuimhne Dhá Laoch: Mac Curtain and MacSwiney', Exhibition Essay, Cork Public Museum.

1997 'A "Godless College"?, in P. Corkery and F. Long (eds), *Theology in the University: The Irish Context.*

1998 'The 1937 Constitution: Some Historical Reflections', in T. Murphy and P. Twomey (eds), *Ireland's Evolving Constitution 1937–1997* (Oxford).

1998 'Myself and "the Cruiser"', in R. English and J.M. Skelly (eds), *Ideas Matter: Essays in Honour of Conor Cruise O'Brien.*

1999 'Ireland 1798–1998', in M. Glazier (ed.), *The Encyclopaedia of the Irish in America* (Notre Dame).

2000 'Irish Neutrality in Historical Perspective', in B. Girvin and G. Roberts (eds), *Ireland and the Second World War: Politics, Society and Remembrance.*

2000 'Aloys Fleischmann, Colleague and Friend', in R. Fleischmann (ed.), *Aloys Fleischmann 1919–1992* (Cork).

2000 'Seán Ó'Faoláin and UCC', *The Irish Review*, No. 26 (Cork).

2000 'James Hogan: Mentor and Colleague', in D. Ó Corráin (ed.), *James Hogan, Revolutionary, Historian and Political Scientist.*

2003 'Republic of Ireland', in L. Ruckenstein and J. O'Malley (eds), *Everything Irish* (New York).

2004 'Cork', in J.S. Donnelly, Jnr (ed), *Encyclopaedia of Ireland*, vol. 1 (New York).

2005 'A University city' in J. Crowley et al. (eds), *An Atlas of Cork City* (Cork).

2005 (with Cliona Murphy), 'Burials and bigotry in early nineteenth century Ireland', in *Studia Hibernica* (forthcoming).

Entries Contributed to Royal Irish Academy Dictionary of Irish Biography on:

Daniel Corkery (1878–1964), writer, cultural philosopher and literary critic.

Daniel Corkery (1883–1961), revolutionist and politician.

Denis Rolleston Gwynn (1893–1971), journalist and historian.

Justin MacCarthy, Lord Mountcashel (*c.* 1643–1694), Jacobite leader and military commander.

Murrough O'Brien, Lord Inchiquin ('Murrough of the Burnings') (*c.* 616–1673), Parliamentary commander in Confederate War.

An tAthair Peadar Ó Laoghaire (1839–1920), pioneering writer in modern Irish.

Alfred O'Rahilly (1884–1969), scholar, university president, controversialist.

Timothy ('Thady') Quill (*c.* 1860–1932), subject of celebrated mock-heroic ballad.

Christy Ring (1920–1979), celebrated Cork hurler.

Bertram A.C. Windle (1858–1929), scholar, university president.

John B. Keane (1928–2002), playwright, writer and humourist.

C. Honorary Editor

Honorary Editor, *Journal of the Cork Historical and Archaeological Society, 1965–1979,* vols 70–84.

D. Radio lectures

*Thomas Davis Lecture Series (*unpublished)*

19 Feb. 1967. 'The Irish Party System, 1938–1951', published in K.B. Nowlan and T.D. Williams (eds), *Ireland in the War Years and After* (1969).

17 Jan. 1971. 'The "New" IRA, 1925–1962', published in T.D. Williams (ed.), *Secret Socieities in Ireland* (1973).

21 Jan.–13 May 1973: consulting editor, *Religion and Irish Society: Clergy and People in Irish history**, 17-lecture series.

18 Feb. 1973. 'The Priest in Penal Times and After'.

13 May 1973. 'The Perspective of History'.

9 Mar. 1975. 'O'Connell and the Gaelic World', published in K.B. Nowlan and M.R. O'Connell (eds), *Daniel O'Connell: Portrait of a Radical* (Belfast, 1984).

15 Jan. 1978. 'Put them out! Parties and Elections, 1948–1969', published in J.J. Lee (ed.), *Ireland 1945–70* (1979).

10 May 1981. 'The Church, Morality and the Law', published in D.M. Clarke (ed.), *Morality and the Law* (Cork, 1982).

31 Aug. 1983. 'The European Economic Community', published in L. de Paor (ed.), *Milestones in Irish History* (Cork, 1986).

13 Nov. 1983. 'Censorship and the Moral Community', published in B. Farrell (ed.), *Comunications and Community in Ireland* (1984).

21 Dec. 1986. 'New Beginnings, 1912–1925: An Irish Perspective', published in Georóid Ó Tuathaigh (ed.), *The Long Relationship* (unpublished).

5 Mar. 2001. 'The Listener's Perspective' (*Radio in Ireland 1926–2001**, ed. John Bowman).

Radio na Gaeltachta

4 Nov. 1982. 'An Eaglais agus an Stát in Éirinn: ré de Valera'.

1 Oct. 1984. 'Cumann Lúth Chleas Gael agus an Pholaitíocht'.

RTÉ, TV

9 Dec. 1974. 'Irish and Catholic' (*A Question of Identity* series).

E. Newspaper and other articles

'A Question of Identity: A Catholic View', *The Irish Times*, news feature, 9 January 1975.

'O'Connell in His Time and Since', *The Irish Times*, supplement, 6 August 1975.

'The Historical Perspective on the Early Years', *The Irish Times*, fifty years of Fianna Fáil, 19 May 1976.

'Taking the Constitutional Path: Breaking the IRA Link', *Irish Press*, supplement on Fianna Fáil 1926–1976, 26 May 1976.

'Keywords in Irish Historical Rhetoric', *Sunday Independent*, interview with Ciaran Carty, 13 February 1977.

'Violence and the Men of 1916', *Irish Press*, summary of RTÉ TV discussion with Conor Cruise O'Brien, 19 April 1977.

Foreword, Ted Nealon, *Guide to the 21st Dáil and Seanad* (1977).

'Irish Republican Army – IRA', *World Book Encyclopaedia* (1978).

'A Legacy Difficult to Decipher: An Analysis of the Pearse Cult', *Irish Press*, supplement, 10 November 1979.

Interview, Rosita Sweetman (ed.), *On Our Backs: Sexual Attitudes in a Changing Ireland* (1979).

'Eamon de Valera and Neutrality', *Irish Press*, supplement on de Valera, 14 October 1982.

'Tackling the Crisis' (governmental policy on broadcasting), *Irish Broadcasting Review*, No. 16, spring 1983.

'The Provos and Irish History', *Irish Independent*, 23 December 1983.

'Nationalism and the GAA', *The Irish Times*, centenary supplement, 1 September 1984.

Series of articles on the Anglo-Irish Agreement, *Cork Examiner*, 12–16 November 1985.

'The Meaning of the Home Rule Bill', *The Irish Times*, feature, 9–10 June 1986.

'A Pyrrhic Victory They May Live to Regret' (divorce referendum), *Irish Independent*, 28 June 1986.

'Recent Irish History', introduction to *Blue Guide Ireland*, 1987, 1992 and 1995 editions.

'The First Dáil', *Irish News*, 30 January 1989.

BBC2 TV, 'The Republic and the North', broadcast, 26 September 1990. Text, *Sunday Independent*, 7 October 1990.

'Michael Collins, Violence and the North', *Cork Examiner*, centenary supplement, 14 October 1990.

'Sé mo thuairim féin ...', *Feasta*, Bealtaine 1991.

'Past Presidents', *The UCC Graduate*, autumn 1995.

'Carrigdhoun', *Irish Ballads*, Special Issue, Ireland of the Welcomes, 1996.

'The Banks of My Own Lovely Lee', *Irish Ballads*, 1996.

Interview: 'Holding Forth', *Voices of Cork*, ed. Vincent Power, 1997.

'1798: Commemoration and Legacy', *The UCC Graduate*, summer 1998.

'How the Republic Remembers Its Fallen', *Belfast Telegraph*, 11 November 1998.

'Cork: The Millennium Overview', *Cork Corporation Millennium Year Book*, 1999.

'The Opening of Queen's College Cork', *The UCC Graduate,* 2000.

'Cork University Press in Context', *Cork University Press Seventy-fifth Anniversary Catalogue,* 2000.

Interview, *History Ireland,* Vol. 9, No. 2, Summer 2001.

'Building relationships: College and city', *The U.C.C. Graduate,* September 2004.

Obituaries

Florence O'Donoghue, *Journal of the Cork Historical and Archaeological Society,* 72 (1967).

Tom Barry, *The Irish Times,* 4 July 1980.

M.J. O'Kelly, *Journal of the Cork Historical and Archaeological Society,* 87 (1982).

Br. Bernadine Quigley, *The Irish Times,* 10 December 1990.

Séamus Pender, *Journal of the Cork Historical and Archaeological Society,* 96 (1991).

Aloys Fleischmann, *Sunday Independent,* 26 July 1992.

Noel Browne, *Sunday Independent,* 25 May 1997.

Jack Lynch, *Sunday Independent,* 24 October 1999.

F. *Sunday Independent* columns

'The Government, Sinn Féin and the Primate', 22 January 1984.

'Easter, 1916: The View from 1984', 22 April 1984.

'Magnificent, But Not History' (Neil Jordan's *Michael Collins*), 10 November 1986.

'Violence: What Can the Churches Do?', 14 August 1988.

'Myth Out, History In', 1 January 1989.

'Home Rule?' (critical assessment of Hume's view), 26 February 1989.

'The Irish-American Labyrinth', 19 March 1989.

'The GAA and the Nation: Emerging from Tribal Trenches', 16 July 1989.

'Not Guilt-edged, This Security' (defence of Second World War neutrality), fiftieth anniversary article, *Sunday Independent,* 3 September 1989.

'Injustice, Extradition and Common Sense', 25 March 1990.

'If the 1916 Rising Hadn't Happened . . .", 24 March 1991.

'The Hearts and Minds Separated by 75 Years', 31 March 1991.

'A Paper to Freedom' (Minister for Education Brennan's Green Paper), 5 July 1992.

'Facing the Bracingly Chilly Secular World' (the challenge facing the Roman Catholic Church in Ireland), 14 March 1993.

'The Regression to Rhetoric – Hume–Adams alignment', 2 May 1993.

'Significance of the Gaelic League' (centenary article), 1 August 1993.

'Peace, Pacification and Praise' (Dublin–London Joint Declaration), 19 December 1993.

'Big Fella Cult Misleads', August–September 1996.
'The French are in the Bay' (1796 expedition), 20 April 1997.
'A Vision beyond Nationalism' (bicentenary reflections on Daniel O'Connell), 18 May 1997.
'What Can We Do this Easter Morn But Shout Hallelujah?' (Belfast Agreement), 12 April 1998.
'An Unborn Nation in the Womb of Time' (the formation of Northern Ireland Executive), 5 December 1999.
'State Edges Away from Church' (army withdraws from Corpus Christi processions), 2 July 2000.
'The Significance of the Kilmichael Ambush', 26 November 2000.
'No Cardinal Error' (why Archbishop Connell is the right man for a Red Hat), 28 January 2001.
'A Fresh Look at P.H. Pearse', 8 April 2001.
'Was John Hume a Sinn Féin Patsy?', 23 September 2001.
'GAA leaves Tribalism Behind' (defeating Rule 21), 2 December 2001.
'Time to Reclaim the Tricolour from Sinn Féin', 10 June 2002.
'Proving that Paddy Could Govern Himself' (eightieth anniversary of Fine Gael's foundation), 27 April 2003.
'Republicans Rewriting History – Sinn Féin Revisionism', 7 September 2003.

G. Speeches in the Irish Senate

John A. Murphy was elected to Seanad Éireann (the Irish Senate) in the National University of Ireland constituency in 1977 and served from 1977 to 1983 and again from 1987 to 1992. While the range of his contribution is listed in the index to each volume (*Seanad Éireann, Parliamentary Debates,* Official Report, vols. 87 (1977) to 99 (1983) incl., and 116 (1987) to 133 (1992) incl., particular attention is drawn to the following:

Education

Adult Education: vol. 93, cols. 260–70, 318–22, 21 November 1979.
Adult Education: vol. 98, cols. 1075–8, 14 July 1982.
National Institute of Higher Education, Dublin, Bill: vol. 95, cols. 176–9, 19 November 1980, and cols. 254–60, 312–15, 323–5, 26 November 1980.
Thomond College of Education Bill: vol. 95, cols. 368–72, 389–91, 3 December 1980.
University of Limerick Bill: vol. 122, cols. 2205–17, 2287–91, 1 June 1989.
Mature Students: vol. 126, cols. 2134–40, 6 December 1990.
Marine Institute Bill: vol. 123, cols. 1932–4, 1935–40, 1955–8, 14 February 1990.
Green Paper on Education: vol. 134, cols. 529–35, 22 October 1992.

Constitutional review

'Constitutional Crusade': vol. 96, cols. 143–68, 9 October 1981.
Fiftieth Anniversary of Constitution: vol. 118, cols. 1120–31, 4 February 1988.
Review of Seanad Éireann: vol. 116, cols. 634–40, 3 June 1987.
Role of Seanad Éireann: vol. 130, cols. 261–74, 30 October 1991.
Tenth Amendment of Constitution Bill (Single European Act): vol. 116, cols. 122–30, 25 April 1987.

Northern Ireland, Anglo-Irish affair

Extradition Proceedings: vol. 98, cols. 1762–7, 7 July 1982.
Extradition Act, 1987: vol. 121, cols. 1111–22, 7 December 1988.
British White Paper on Northern Ireland: vol. 97, cols. 692–7, 718–22, 16 April 1982.
Call on government to clarify its Northern Ireland policy: vol. 118, cols. 799–810, 21 January 1988, and cols. 915–19, 28 January 1988.
Call on government to state reaction to proposed Northern Ireland integrated education reform: vol. 120, cols. 2550–54, 2559–60, 12 July 1988.
Northern Ireland and Anglo-Irish relations: vol. 121, cols. 947–51, 30 November 1988, and cols. 1231–45, 8 February 1989.
Call on government to repeal Articles 2 and 3: vol. 124, cols. 712–22, 14 March 1990, and cols. 955–60, 21 March 1990.
Call on government to promote process of political accommodation in Northern Ireland: vol. 133, cols. 1208–12, 1244–7, 1 July 1992.

Church, state and public morality

Family Planning Bill 1978: vol. 92, cols. 701–19, 4 July 1979, cols. 881 ff. (3rd stage, *passim*).
Separation of Church and State: vol. 119, cols. 809–14, 4 May 1988.
Army at Religious Ceremonies: vol. 132, cols. 2002–12, 3 June 1992.

Economy

White Paper on National Development: vol. 89, cols. 329–36, 24 May 1978, and cols. 365–78, 31 May 1978.
Role of Aer Lingus: vol. 95, cols. 1700–1703, 15 April 1981.
Buy Irish: vol. 95, cols. 532–6, 10 December 1980.
Buy Irish: vol. 118, cols. 644–5, 20 January 1988.
Recall of Seanad Éireann, State of Economy: vol. 99, cols. 13–22, 30 September 1982.

Foreign Policy

Call on government not to join military pact: vol. 96, cols. 1103–14, 1164–8, 2 December 1981.

Call on government to re-affirm positive neutrality role: vol. 122, cols. 638–48, 654–8, 15 March 1989, and cols. 880–84, 12 April 1989.

Role of Army in International Peacekeeping: vol. 122, cols. 1548–53, 10 May 1989.

Heritage, environment, communications

National Heritage Bill: vol. 98, cols. 564–9, 30 June 1982, and cols. 681–7, 1 July 1982.

Radio and Television Bill: vol. 120, cols. 825–44, 21 June 1988.

Environmental Protection Agency Bill: vol. 127, cols. 709–18, 23 January 1991, and vol. 128, 3rd stage cols. 820–1839, *passim* April–May 1991.

H. Significant unpublished lectures/addresses

(The texts of these lectures/addresses will be deposited in the Boole Library, UCC.)

'Violence in Modern Irish History.' NUI O'Donnell Lecture, UCC, 14 November 1973.

'The Survival of Non-Violent Sinn Féin, 1919–1921.' American Conference for Irish Studies, Stonehall College, Mass., 25 April 1975.

'Kerry and the Elizabethans.' Balliol College, Oxford, February 1976.

'William O'Brien, His Own Man.' North Cork Writers Festival, Doneraile, 9 October 1976.

'Irish Politics and Revisionism.' American Conference for Irish Studies, Denver Co., April 1977.

'Primary to Post-Primary: Bridging the Gap.' Mary Immaculate College of Education, Limerick, 13 May 1978.

'The Necessity of Detribalising Ireland.' Social Study Conference, 6 August 1978.

'The Professions and Irish Society.' Irish Pharmaceutical Congress, Tralee, 9 October 1978.

St Patrick's Day keynote address. Gaelic Arts Society, Pittsburgh, Pa., 17 March 1979.

'The "Independent" Politician in Modern Irish History.' American Conference of Irish Studies, Harrisonberg, Va., spring 1979.

'Whither Irish Foreign Policy?' Berkeley lecture, Cloyne, 6 October 1979.

'Church, State and Morality in Ireland.' 'A Sense of Ireland Conference', London, 5 March 1980.

'The H-Block Campaign and Public Opinion.' Address to Cork Rotary, 27 July 1981. (See *Irish Independent* report, 22 July 1981; *National Democrat*, September–October 1983).

'Ireland, Small Nation, Large World.' Northwestern University, Boston, Mass., 22 October 1981.

'Post-Independence Nationalism.' James Power memorial lecture, Waterford, 18 November 1981.

'Religion in Ireland, 1882–1904.' Centenary lecture, James Joyce Institute, Dublin, 19 January 1982.

'Ireland–US Relations.' St Patrick's Day guest speaker, Friendly Sons of StPatrick, Philadelphia, 17 March 1982.

Michael Collins commemoration address, Béal na Blá, 22 August 1982.

'De Valera, the Legacy.' Boston College, Irish Studies Series, October 1982.

'The Ireland of Joyce and de Valera.' Keynote address, conference on Joyce and his contemporaries. Hofstra University, NY, 21 October 1982.

'The Anglo-Irish Treaty and After: The Canadian Model.' Canadian Association for Irish Studies, Toronto, 3 March 1984.

'The GAA in Irish Life.' Irish Club of Belgium, Brussels, June 1984.

'The 1880s: A Politically Dramatic Decade.' Hopkins Conference, Dublin, July 1984.

'The Priest in Modern Irish History.' Merriman Summer School, Lahinch, 20 August 1984.

'What Price Irish Unity?' McGill University, Montreal, 24 January 1985.

'A View from the South.' Balch Institute for Irish Studies, Philadelphia, 23 March 1985.

'John Redmond: A Reassessment.' American Conference for Irish Studies, Tacoma University, Wash., 22 April 1985.

'Making Sense of Irish America.' Somerville and Ross Lecture, Skibbereen, 8 September 1985.

'Southern Attitudes to Irish Unification.' San José State University, Calif., 28 November 1985.

'John Redmond and Cork Politics.' Cork Historical and Archaeological Society, December 1985.

'Anglo-Irish Relations Now.' House of Lords study group, Westminster, 12 March 1986.

'A Nation in the Womb of Time.' Prize Day speech, Ashton School, Cork, 14 November 1986.

'From Home Rule to Hillsborough: A Century of Anglo-Irish Relations.' Boole Lecture, UCC, 12 December 1986.

'Independent Ireland and the US: Divergent Policy Trends.' Cushwa Centre, Notre Dame University, 2 March 1988.

'Ireland, US and Their Constitutions.' San José State University, 6 April 1988.

'Ireland Tomorrow: A Credo.' Listowel Writers Week, 4 June 1988.

'Historical Attitudes towards Emigration.' McGill Summer School, Glenties, 14 August 1988.

'Education and the Church.' National Parents Council – Primary, Annual Conference, 20 April 1990.

'National Identities and the UK Constitution.' Coleg Harlech conference, September 1990.

'Religious Ethos and the State.' Swift Lecture, St Patrick's Cathedral, Dublin, 14 October 1990.

'Parnellism after Parnell.' Parnell Summer School, 20 August 1991.

'Primary Education as Social Engineering.' INTO Conference, Dundalk, 19 March 1993.

'Rural Ireland: A Utopian Myth.' Merriman Summer School, Ballyvaughan, Co. Clare, 20 August 1994.

'Extra-Mural Relations: Town and Gown 1845–1995.' UCC 150th anniversary celebrations, Boole Public Lecture, UCC, 7 November 1995.

'Terrorism in Modern Irish History.' Gárda Siochána International Conference on Terrorism, Dublin, October 1998.

'William Carleton in Political and Social Context.' Ninth William Carleton Summer School, Clogher, 8 August 2000.

'The Political Song in Modern Irish History.' Boston College public lecture, 26 September 2002.

SECTION 2

Essays

One Commonwealth, Three Nations
The Concept of a Nation in English Republican Thought 1640–80

DESMOND M. CLARKE

When Algernon Sidney (1622–83) wrote, on the very first page of the *Discourses Concerning Government*, 'that Nations should be well informed of their rights', he articulated explicitly and prominently an intuition that had been developing in English republican thought for more than forty years.[1] This was a period of unprecedented revolutionary change in England, which coincided with the first significant state-building initiatives across the Channel in the United Provinces and in France. The execution of Charles I in 1649, the lengthy Protectorate during which Cromwell, with and without the support of parliament, ruled the associated kingdoms of Ireland, Scotland and England, and the restoration of the monarchy in 1660, provided ideal historical circumstances for a radical questioning of the origin, limits and scope of political authority. Students of political theory today are more familiar with Locke's *Two Treatises of Government* (1690), with its emphasis on representative government and the separation of powers, and with Hobbes's attempt prematurely to deconstruct that theory in the *Leviathan* (1651), than with original political theorists of the parliamentary cause. We are also more likely to think of Milton as the great English poet of paradise lost or regained, and of Cromwell as the most unwelcome guest who ever visited the island of Ireland, than to think of their respective literary and military adventures as inspired by a republican ideal. The reality, however, was both more complex and more interesting. Locke was heir to the conceptual results of those involved in forging a new ideology in direct response to the political, economic and military experience of the civil wars. Writers such as Cromwell, Milton, Harrington, Nedham and Sydney constructed a political theory that was designed to support and justify their revolutionary actions.

In doing so, these writers appealed above all else to the right of the people to defend their liberty against abuse. It would have been impossible to succeed in this task by creating a completely novel political theory. Any justification that was likely to succeed had to appeal to what people already accepted in some sense, to some ancient constitution or fundamental law that was beyond dispute.[2] Thus they borrowed heavily from familiar republican sources, especially Machiavelli, and they applied those insights to their unique political experiences.[3] In this project of construction and adaptation, the theorists of the English Republic also relied on a relatively new concept to help identify who the 'people' were and why they could act collectively in defence of their claimed rights. This novel conceptual resource was the concept of a nation.

The origin of the term 'nation', applied to a people who share a common culture, history and territory, is both obscure and ancient. As Hastings has shown, the term has been used in this sense at least as early as Bede's *Ecclesiastical History of the English People* (*c.* 730).[4] In the intervening centuries it has developed into one of the central theoretical terms in contemporary political theory. Not surprisingly, the centrality of the term is matched by a corresponding degree of confusion about its meaning. 'Nation' is one of those essentially contested concepts that is so frequently used that the disagreement about its meaning is camouflaged. Debates about its definition tend to divide along the same lines as proponents or critics who believe that national identity has had a positive or baneful effect on political developments in the modern period. Most modernist critics argue, following Ernest Gellner, that nationalism is an ideology cultivated retrospectively to support the reality of nation-states and that this insight helps make intelligible the emergence of new national identities, for example the construction of a British national identity in the eighteenth century.[5] Others, such as Anthony D. Smith, argue that there have existed distinctive cultural, linguistic communities long before the development of the modern state and that we should look to them for an understanding of national identity.[6] Any resolution of this debate requires a much more detailed history of the concept 'nation' than is currently available. We need to know how the concept was used or abused by those for whom it did some theoretical work, in history or political theory, and we cannot assume *a priori* that such a history, if written, will produce a coherent and uniform development of what is now generally recognized as a multi-layered concept. The history of the concept may reveal that we have merely inherited the conceptual confusion of its historical development without being sufficiently conscious of its inherent ambiguities. If so, those who appeal to national identity to support contemporary claims to political autonomy or otherwise must first establish the legitimacy and theoretical coherence of the concept that is expected to bear such a weighty justificatory burden.

This chapter is a contribution to one segment of that complex history. Here I examine the ways in which the concept of a nation was used by republican thinkers in England from about 1640 to 1680. I shall assume, as others have previously suggested, that English republican thought emerged in response to the political uncertainties of the Protectorate rather than as a theory that caused the downfall of Charles I.[7] The most urgent requirement of a new political theory was a demarcation of the respective powers of the king and parliament. But in addressing that question, writers such as Milton or Nedham could not avoid completely the related question about the legitimate territorial scope of English political power, however it might be exercised. Scotland and Ireland were distinct political and cultural realities, in some sense, and any plausible theory had to provide a justification for English rule in such inhospitable dominions.

There is a well-known methodological problem involved in looking for a concept in use by writers of an earlier period. One needs to have some working definition of the concept in mind before beginning the search; otherwise one would not be able to recognize it if it is found. On the other hand, one needs to avoid the danger of reading back into earlier texts concepts that are so alien to their context that one is guilty of blatant anachronism. We think of national identity today in terms of some or all of the following characteristics: a distinctive community of people, sharing a common public culture (especially a common language), extended in history, linked with a particular geographical territory and, especially, a consciousness among the people of their distinctiveness.[8] There is no reason to think that the king's subjects in France, for example, or the citizens of the United Provinces in the early seventeenth century satisfied all these conditions exactly. Presumably, an emerging political consciousness develops *pari passu* with its conceptual articulation. Thus, unless novel concepts are introduced suddenly by stipulation, one should expect to find words being used with varying degrees of ambiguity for lengthy historical periods before their central meaning becomes settled.

Hence if English republican theorists genuinely rely on the concept of a nation during the Civil War, it is not enough simply to find frequent uses of the term 'nation' in their writings. One needs to find that it carries the added value of a justification for the parliamentary cause, thereby implying that it operates as a concept in a political theory. The appeal to 'nations' should signal an awareness of the reality of distinct communities of people which are characterized by their culture, language, religion or similar traditions, and whose claim to exercise political authority over themselves is acknowledged by other similar communities. Before examining the explicitly written political tracts of Nedham, Milton, Harrington and Sydney, it may be helpful to look initially at the speeches and writings of one of the primary agents of political change, Oliver Cromwell.

The political realities of English rule in Scotland and Ireland are reflected in Cromwell's speeches throughout his political career. In the 'Protestation' to members of parliament, 3 May 1641, he talks about efforts 'to preserve the union and peace betwixt the Three Kingdoms of England, Scotland and Ireland'.[9] The language of distinct kingdoms was both familiar and apparently unproblematic, although the subsequent suppression of the English monarchy and the parliamentary limitations on regal power called for a new term to describe the people and/or the territory over which political power was exercised. Not surprisingly, talk about the English nation assumes a new role after 1649. The death warrant of Charles I charged all 'Officers and Souldiers and other the good people of this Nation of England' to assist in its implementation.[10] The English nation is uppermost in Cromwell's rhetoric after the Act proclaiming a Free State in 1649, but the term is also applied to Scotland and Ireland. Thus when Cromwell arrived in Dublin, on 14 August 1649, he commended those who supported the campaign against 'the barbarous and bloodthirsty Irish' with the objective of 'propagating the Gospel of Christ, the establishing of truth and peace and restoring that bleeding nation to its former happiness and tranquility . . .'.[11] On the Scottish campaign the following year, Cromwell wrote to Wesley (the Lieutenant-General of the Scottish army) complaining about the Scots' adoption of Charles II as king of England, Scotland and Ireland: 'under the pretence of the Covenant . . . a King should be taken in by you, to be imposed upon us; and this done to the satisfaction of God's people in both nations . . . as is alleged, together with the disowning of malignants, although he who is the head of them . . . be received.'[12] Thus England, Scotland and Ireland – but not Wales – are characterized in various contexts, over a number of years, as distinct nations.[13] Accordingly, when Cromwell addressed the first parliament of the Protectorate on 12 September 1654, he claimed to have been appointed 'by Act of Parliament General of all the forces in the three nations of England, Scotland and Ireland'.[14]

Although Cromwell recognizes three nations, he normally mentions only one commonwealth. The first documents signed by him after appointment as Protector all begin with: 'Oliver Lord Cromwell Protector of the Commonwealth of England, Scotland and Ireland'.[15] On this occasion he announces that 'His Highness in his care of the State, and Publick Justice thereof . . . is pleased . . . to make Lawes and Ordinances for the peace and welfare of these nations'.[16] However, even this standard locution is modified in cases where the Commonwealth becomes involved in international relations. A document ratifying a treaty with the Dutch (19 April 1654) begins, as usual, with 'Oliver Cromwell Protector of the Commonwealth of England, Scotland and Ireland', but this is subsequently described as a 'Proclamation . . . concerning a Cessation of all Acts of Hostility between the Commonwealth of *England*, and that of the United Provinces, and their respective people'.[17] A later Treaty with Portugal, on 10/20 July 1654, is concluded between 'the Republic of England and the Most Serene King of Portugal',[18] and a similar communication with Louis XIV, on 4 December 1655, refers to the 'friendship which has been sanctioned by God's blessing between this Republic [i.e. England] and France'.[19]

The implicit recognition of other nations is reflected in Cromwell's appeal to international law, or what he calls 'certain laws recorded in the code of nations', when he complains about the non-payment of restitution for English ships captured during the reign of Frederick I. 'It is useless to provide for the free exercise of commerce between nations by solemn compacts mutually agreed upon, when in default of payment merchants are deprived of their monies.'[20] Of course, there is no implication in the language of three nations that the nations in question are equal in political status. While England is a nation, a commonwealth, or a republic, Ireland is described only as a nation within a commonwealth, with the status of a 'dominion'.[21]

The lack of any previously accepted standard usage of the term 'nation' left it open to creative semantic manipulation. Cromwell needed a neutral term for what had been separate kingdoms before Scotland, Ireland and England were amalgamated into a single commonwealth-kingdom, and 'nation' was an appropriately flexible term for that purpose. But it was also something much more than a term with a relatively unsettled semantic history. One of the most dominant features of Cromwell's rhetoric throughout this period was an appeal to the good of the people and the moral necessity to adapt political structures to protect the *salus populi*. This was a central claim, for example, in the debate surrounding the Nineteen Propositions of 1642. According to Charles I, the benefits of a monarchy included 'the uniting of a nation, under one head to resist invasion from abroad and insurrection at home'.[22] But Cromwell's reply (7 February 1650) was: 'That it hath been found by experience, and this House doth declare, That the Office of a King in this Nation, and to have the power thereof in any single person, is unnecessary, burdensome, and dangerous to the liberty, safety, and publick interest of the People of this Nation; and therefore ought to be abolished.'[23] One might ask why the *salus populi* suddenly emerged in the 1640s as a dominant political value and why, in particular, it required the abolition of an hereditary monarchy. One hypothesis is the following.[24] The exercise of the veto by Charles I over the Militia Ordinance in 1642 focused the attention of the parliament more than ever before on the arbitrariness and unlimited scope of a royal veto. If the parliament was in any sense representative of the people, and if the king could override their decisions arbitrarily, then the people collectively were dependent merely on the will of one man. It was a core belief of republican theory that the freedom of individuals, and of a people collectively, was inconsistent with the arbitrary exercise of power by rulers.[25] Hence the emergence in republican theory of a link between the freedom of the people considered collectively as a nation and the slavery that would result from arbitrary rule by any one person, including the monarch.

The public interest of the people was also linked with another feature that is widely recognized today as characteristic of claims to national identity, namely, some kind of special election by God that is similar to the special covenant between the God of the Old Testament and the Jewish nation. For example, Cromwell set aside 23 May 1654 as a day of celebration for the treaty with the Dutch. In declaring the special holiday, he wrote: 'the dispensations of the Lord have been as if he had said, *England* thou art my first-born, my delight amongst the Nations.'[26] Not only England, but Cromwell too had a special mission from God. He often used the language of divine election in going into battle, in celebrating victory in battles,[27] and especially when abolishing the monarchy or even suspending parliament to protect the liberties and interests of the people. 'It had pleased God not only to reduce Ireland and give in Scotland, but so marvelously to appear for his people at Worcester, that those nations were reduced to a great degree of peace, and England to perfect quiet'; despite these successes, however, parliament refused to reform, in 'opposition to the people of God, and his spirit acting in them'. Thus it became 'most evident to the army . . . that this Parliament . . . would never answer those ends which God, his people, and the whole nation expected from them'; and 'it was judged necessary and agreed upon, that the supreme authority should be by the Parliament devolved upon known persons, men fearing God, and of approved integrity'.[28] God's special election of his chosen people and his protection of their interests could be achieved, according to Cromwell, only by entrusting political power to those whom God trusts.

Cromwell may have been too busy fighting battles against the king and invading neighbouring nations to clarify the concepts of a nation and a commonwealth, despite the frequency and prolixity of his speeches and written communications. He thus enlisted the support of political theorists, pamphleteers or others who were supportive of the parliamentary cause, to articulate a political philosophy that could justify his military crusade. As already mentioned, the ultimate principle to which the parliamentarians appealed was the *salus populi*, and one might therefore expect republican theorists to explain what they meant by 'the people' whose interests they claimed to defend, and how they came to have the rights that were claimed on their behalf by Cromwell.

John Milton and Marchamont Nedham were among the first to support the parliamentary cause in print, and both assumed the concept of a nation or people who, collectively, can make legitimate claims against tyranny, even if the alleged tyrant is the king. Milton published *The Tenure of Kings and Magistrates* in February 1649. This book is an extended analysis of the fundamental freedom of the people, of the source of political authority in the decisions of the people, and of the appropriate response of the people to the abuse of political power. Milton refers in the first sentence of *Tenure* to the nation. 'If men within themselves would be govern'd by reason, and not generally give up their understanding to a double tyrranie, of Custom from without, and blind affections within, they would discerne better, what it is to favour and uphold the Tyrant of a Nation.'[29] The first principle of Milton's political theory is: 'No man who knows ought, can be so stupid to deny that all men were born free . . . and were . . . born to command and not to obey.'[30] It follows that 'the power of Kings and Magistrates is nothing else, but what is only derivative, transferr'd and committed to them in trust from the People, to the Common good of them all, in whom the power yet remaines fundamentally, and cannot be tak'n from them, without a violation of their natural birthright'.[31] This fundamental or natural freedom constitutes the people collectively as what Milton calls 'a free Nation'. If they lack the power to decide on their own government, they would forfeit the 'root and source of all liberty, to dispose and oeconomize in the Land which God hath giv'n them, as maisters of family in their own house and free inheritance'.[32]

The background image is of free people to whom God has given a country and in whom he has entrusted the liberty to decide their own form of government. Milton argues that this is so fundamental that anyone 'of whatsoever Nation' who respects this is an Englishman, whereas if 'an Englishman, forgetting all laws, human, civil, and religious, offend against life and liberty, to him offended and to the law in his behalf, though born in the same womb, he is no better then a Turk, a Sarasin, a Heathen'.[33] The same themes are addressed in *Eikonoklastes* (1649). Here again, and in his *Observations upon the Articles of Peace* (1649), Milton assumes nationality as a given, although he argues that the liberty of the people in a commonwealth is more fundamental. Given the context in which he was writing, his primary objective was to defend the right of parliament to depose the king if he abused his authority to the detriment of the people. 'It were a folly beyond ridiculous to count ourselves a free Nation, if the King not in Parlament . . . might appropriate to himself the strength of a whole Nation as his proper goods.'[34] However, despite his references to the 'English nation'[35] and to the three nations of England, Scotland and Ireland,[36] Milton objected in his *Articles of Peace* to giving Irish people 'a law-giving power of their own . . . as absolute and supream in that Assembly [i.e. Kilkenny] as the People of *England* in their own land'. To do so would have amounted to 'alienating and acquitting the whole Province of Ireland from all true fealty and obedience to the Commonwealth of England'.[37]

Marchamont Nedham had been employed by the Commonwealth since 1650 as editor of the its quasi-official gazette, the *Mercurius Politicus*, and his pamphleteering skills were subsequently exploited to produce a republican tract in defence of the parliamentary cause, *A True State of the Case of the Commonwealth* (1654). The first sentence of his book refers to the enemies of God and his people, 'banding themselves against the Rights and Liberties of this Nation'.[38] In this relatively short pamphlet, Nedham argues that the recent political developments in England were due to the intervention of God on 'behalf of our Nation' and of 'his people',[39] and in the course of explaining God's intervention he mentions the 'nation' no less than fifty-five times. As already evident in Cromwell's writings, Nedham recognizes the distinct nationality of Ireland and Scotland, referring to the common 'defence of three such Nations, as *England, Scotland* and *Ireland*', and the 'advantage it will be to these three Nations, to have their whole strength and Force combined thus under one head'.[40] This is an unlikely and implausible justification for the enforced unification of the three nations and it invites further analysis about what exactly Nedham may have meant by a nation.

He offers the same defence of the parliamentary cause that had been proposed by Cromwell, namely, that the war with the king was not motivated by opposition to the king as king, and that it was not waged in support of one type of government rather than another.'Government under this or that Form, was not the moving Cause of the great"Controversie,"but those common ends of safety and Freedom, for which all sorts of Governments we instituted are appointed.'[41] The king was deposed, he claims, because he preferred 'the advancement of his own and his Posterities Will and Power, against the Publick Interest of the Nation'.[42] The ultimate appeal, then, was to the'the safety and Freedom of our Nation' (p. 8),'the common interest of this Nation' (pp 18, 25), and 'the true Interest of this Nation' (p. 32). Nedham argues that the'Civil Rights and Laws of the Nation' (p. 14) are best protected by'the Supreme Law-making Power . . . [of] the People in Parliament' (p. 11). More explicitly he asks, and answers immediately:'Who hath the power of altering old Laws, or making new? The people in Parlament; without them nothing of this nature can be done' (p. 28).

These questions about who exercises ultimate political power in a given country evidently presuppose agreement about its borders. Where does the nation's territory begin or end, and may it expand outwards by conquest or otherwise? Nedham assumes a distinction between native Englishmen and foreigners. He refers to 'our Fleets at Sea, which are as the walls and bulwarks of this Nation against Invasions of Foreiners'.[43] One might extend this assumption to an explicit claim that the natural boundaries of the nation are set by its geographical limits as an island, but this would not account for Scotland as a distinct nation. His argument against the claims of Charles II includes a reference to his being half French, and a supporter of an alien religious faith. 'If we reflect upon the Person of the Young Pretender, he is by bloud almost a stranger to this Nation, being by the Mother a *French-man* . . . His Religion (if any) is at best, you know, but a devotion to Prelacy (which was bequeathed to him in legacy) having forfeited his Oaths to the *Scottish* Nation, and all his other Pretences of Religion there, before ever he left the Country.'[44] If Charles II were to return and claim the throne of England, Nedham argues, one would be concerned about'the desperate Crew of forlorn Fugitives, Foreiners, and Papists, that he must bring along with him, which will like Locusts devour the whole Land before them . . . the Nation itself will be too little for him and his.'[45] There is little doubt that the English nation was implicitly defined, at least partly, by its commitment to some form of Protestantism, and in opposition to Papists. As Nedham reminds his readers:'Remember also what we of this Nation are to stand for, the preservation of our Religion, our Liberties, and all that is dear and precious among men.'[46] In keeping with this, the final sentence of the book summarizes the objectives of good government as the'Peace and Settlement to this distracted Nation . . . for the glory of the Most High God, the advancement of his Gospel, the protection of his People, and the benefit of Posterity'.[47]

When James Harrington took up the challenge of constructing a political theory to support Cromwell (to whom his book is dedicated), he wrote *The Commonwealth of Oceana* (1656). Harrington was conscious of the problems raised by Scotland and Ireland, to which he refers on the first page of *Oceana* as 'Marpesia and Panopea, now provinces of this commonwealth'.[48] He justifies the conquest of these two provinces in terms of (a) distributing land in Ireland that was underused, and (b) emancipating the people of Scotland from their feudal lords.[49] He also suggests that Ireland, as a nation, is 'the soft mother of a slothful and pusillanimous people, [and] is a neighbour island, anciently subjected by the arms of Oceana'.[50] The creativity of his definition of the boundaries of a commonwealth are illustrated when he compares the geography of Venice with that of the islands of Oceana: 'the sea giveth Law unto the growth of Venice, but the growth of Oceana giveth law unto the sea.'[51] Thus the natural geographical boundaries of Venice were linked with the political boundaries of the corresponding republic; but in the case of England, he claims, its jurisdiction was rightly extended beyond its natural boundaries. This rhetoric justifying the expansion of Oceana into neighbouring islands is developed with some semblance of reason in one of Harrington's aphorisms, where he claims that Wales is too small to survive as an independent political entity: 'If a country be very small and not able to subsist of itself, as Wales, it may be safely united and held; but the advantages that Wales hath . . . is not that which England is able to afford unto such a country as Scotland, without subjecting her neck unto the yoke.'[52]

But even this is unconvincing. For Harrington is aware of the implications of ruling by force, and of allowing what he calls 'foreigners' to take control of a given country. He refers to the Mamelukes, who did not allow any natives to share in government of the dominion they had conquered lest they gradually take control: 'national or independent empire, of what kind soever, is to be exercised by them that have the proper balance of dominion in the nation; wherefore provincial or dependent empire is not to be exercised by them that have the balance of dominion in the province, because that would bring the government from provincial and dependent to national and independent.'[53] In other words, if government were exercised in conquered dominions in the same manner as in the conquering country, it would lead to secession. He then applies the same question to England: 'if a prince or commonwealth may hold a territory that is foreign in this, it may be asked why he may not hold one that is native in like manner? To which I answer: because he can hold a foreign by a native territory, but not a native by a foreign.'[54] When that line of argument fails, Harrington reverts to the more standard Cromwellian rhetoric of an ancient commonwealth modelled on God's rule in Israel.[55]

Since 'government is no other than the soul of a nation or city',[56]

Harrington must assume that a nation is independent of any particular political structures that provide it with good government. There are some clues to what he means by a nation in references to 'the different nations, by whom it [Oceana] hath been successively subdued and governed'.[57] These include the Romans, Saxons, Danes and Normans. A nation is evidently a people, rather than a territory,[58] distinguished by what Harrington calls a 'national conscience'. Although we recognize today that the following argument is obviously fallacious, he argues: 'if the conviction of a man's private conscience produce his private religion, the conviction of the national conscience must produce a national religion.'[59] The national religion should be in the care of the 'council of religion' and its members should protect liberty of conscience so that no gathered congregation should be molested unless they are 'Jewish or idolatrous'.[60] Thus, for Harrington, there are references to the 'conscience of the nation', a specific 'genius of this nation', a 'militia of the nation', the 'interest of the nation' and a 'soul of the nation'.[61]

The culmination of this developing consciousness of the nation in English republican political thought is found in Algernon Sidney's *Discourses Concerning Government.* Sidney's work is a chapter-by-chapter critique of Robert Filmer's *Patriarcha,*[62] the same book which prompted Locke's *Two Treatises of Government*. Where Filmer's book is brief and implausibly traditional, Sidney's is extremely prolix and revolutionary. Sidney's *Discourses* also includes a detailed index with a full column of entries under 'Nations'.[63] Filmer had raised the question about the division of the world's population into natural units in two ways. Since he was defending the theory that all authority was originally given directly by God to Adam and then passed on in some way to successive generations, he needed to acknowledge the distribution of people into distinct nations. This resulted, in his biblical account, from the proliferation of linguistic groups after the tower of Babel.[64] The second way in which Filmer groups people into natural communities provides part of his argument against the danger of secession. He argues that if political authority had been granted originally to all the people of the world collectively, they would have had to meet and agree on the establishment of distinct commonwealths.[65] It is most unlikely, he argues, that this ever happened. However even if all political authority had implausibly been distributed in this way among all the people equally, there would be a more serious problem of not being able to prevent groups of people seceding from a commonwealth and establishing a new commonwealth. Filmer's theory was that Adam's authority must have been passed on, from one generation to another, to the heads of families and this presupposes some kind of natural division of the people of the world into distinct nations.

Sidney's *Discourses* is a detailed discussion and refutation of Filmer. He argues that, if the crown in England is hereditary, it must be so 'by the will of the people'.[66] Since kingdoms are established either by force or by the consent of the people, those who disagree with his general thesis must accept that 'force doth always create a right'.[67] I shall not review Sidney's arguments in favour of the fundamental thesis that political authority comes ultimately from the consent of the governed, but shall focus instead on the relation between that thesis and the concept of a nation or people.

Sidney's fundamental thesis is: 'to depend upon the will of a man is slavery.'[68] This principle applies both to individuals and to nations collectively.[69] The legitimate government of a people can derive only from their consent, and it cannot be based on conquest. 'No right can come by conquest, unless there were a right of making that conquest, which, by reason of the equality that our author [i.e. Filmer] confesses to have been among the heads of families, and as I have proved goes into infinity, can never be on the aggressor's side.'[70] A group of 'freemen, who think it for their convenience to join together, and to establish such laws and rules as they oblige themselves to observe' may create a commonwealth. This principle applies whether the number of men involved is large or small; 'ten men are as free as ten millions of men; and tho' it may be more prudent in some cases to join with the greater than the smaller number, because there is more strength, it is not so always.'[71] This allows for great variations in size between nations, because 'every people proceeds according to their own will'.[72] In contrast, the creation of absolute monarchies 'entirely extinguishes' man's natural liberty, even if the people were willing to accept them.[73] In cases where such absolute monarchs have insufficient power to destroy their own people, they 'have stirred up foreign nations against them', as is evident in the 'wars with Scotland in the years 1639, 1640, the slaughters of the protestants in Ireland in 1641'.[74]

In other words, the right of nations to establish a form of government that suits them and that is freely adopted by the people is the ultimate source of political authority:

> Nations, being naturally free, may meet, when and where they please; may dispose of the sovereignty, and may direct or limit the exercise of it, unless by their own act they have deprived themselves of that right: and there could never have been a lawful assembly of any people in the world, if they had not had that power in themselves.[75]

No individual can acquire authority over a nation, therefore, except by the consent of the people, and any other exercise of power is merely *de facto* rather than *de jure*.[76] Besides, if anyone were to ask 'how nations come to have the power of doing those things', they would evidently be asking the wrong question. For 'liberty being only an exemption from the dominion of another, the question ought not to be, how a nation can come to be free, but how a man comes to have dominion over it'.[77]

Although Sidney has not defined exactly what he means by a nation nor suggested how disputes about national identity might be resolved, his central thesis about the rights of freemen, and the invalidity of conquest as a method for establishing *de jure* political authority, implies a willingness to consider the claims of any plausible candidate for nationhood. He specifically refers to England, Scotland and Ireland as distinct nations.[78] More significantly, he argues that 'the revolt of a nation cannot be called a rebellion'. The reason is that individuals within a nation are required to observe the laws that are enacted by themselves, but a whole nation cannot be obliged to observe a law imposed by someone else: 'the whole body therefore of a nation cannot be tied to any other obedience than is consistent with the common good, according to their own judgment.'[79]

One might remain sceptical about the motivation of these authors in appealing to the concept of a nation as the ultimate subject of republican freedom, and one might worry about their exploitation of the concept to express political views that were as much in need of justification as the novelty of their arguments suggests. But it is impossible to avoid the conclusion that the fundamental principle that inspired republican thought in England, from 1640 to 1680, presupposes the concept of a people acting collectively to establish political structures that are adopted freely and are likely to protect their interests and their liberties. That principle presupposes the reality of a pre-political group of people who have enough in common to support the success of such endeavours. In making this assumption, these republican theorists were using not only the term 'nation', but the concept of a nation. They initially applied the concept of a nation primarily to England, as if it were a paradigm of a select people chosen by God to rule both themselves and their otherwise ungovernable neighbours.[80] But this was already enough to raise doubts about what makes any people a nation, especially if the concept is applied by revolutionary theorists for whom appeals to the divine right of kings were nugatory. As Sidney remarked, 'It is natural for nations to govern, or to chuse governors.'[81] Once the question is raised about justifying the exercise of political power over any people, then – assuming that 'might is right' is not an acceptable answer – the central problems of modern political theory emerge clearly and the inextricable links between history and politics become apparent.

Current political debates in Ireland appeal, implicitly or otherwise, to what are assumed as settled principles of democratic theory, including the principle that the ultimate source of political authority is the consent of 'the people'. Thus, for example, the principle of consent has been given a central place in the Good Friday Agreement.[82] One of the most pressing issues underlying that principle is the problem of demarcating the membership of a given people or, in other words, of deciding who must be consulted when determining their 'consent'. It is obvious that geography alone cannot answer that question. One must also take account of the culture, history and consciousness of the people involved. Once these factors are included, however, it becomes obvious that what is readily agreed as a principle becomes very much contested in its application.

I have argued here that the principle of consent derives, not originally from Locke's *Second Treatise*, but from those English republican theorists of the Civil War who first identified *nations* as the ultimate source of political authority. The principle was articulated in its modern form not in the settled practices of representative government, but in the ideological construction of English nationalism. It is therefore not surprising if the principle of consent continues to reflect the complexity and contentiousness of its historical roots. Irish nationalists have traditionally appealed to the integrity of the 'Irish nation' (and the consent of a majority of its members) as a basis for their claims to political control over Northern Ireland. Unionists make a parallel claim, which is supported equally by appeal to the concept of British nationality. It is an enlightening irony of history that contemporary champions of Irish nationality and of British nationality, in Northern Ireland, both describe their apparently exclusive identities by using the concepts invented, in the English civil wars, to justify the success of the parliamentary cause.[83]

Personalities and Politics
The Presidency of Munster and the Lords Lieutenant 1660–72

LIAM IRWIN

The establishment of provincial presidencies in Munster and Connacht was an important part of Tudor strategy to enhance royal authority over regions remote from, or too independent of, central government. In the conditions of mid-sixteenth-century Ireland, the placing of a crown-appointed official with strong administrative, judicial and military power in these provinces proved to be a key element in the eventual conquest of Ireland.[1] The continuation of the system as a normal feature of administration in the changed circumstances of the seventeenth century, however, created the potential for a serious clash of authority between the central and provincial governments. This issue eventually became a major problem in Munster during the Restoration period when the powerful, ambitious and duplicitous Roger Boyle, Earl of Orrery, was president.[2] It was particularly acute during the viceroyalty of James Butler, Duke of Ormond, up to 1669, but the fundamental problem was only resolved by the abolition of the entire presidency system in 1672.[3]

Lord Broghill, Orrery's title prior to 1660, had played a key role in the politics of the three kingdoms in the previous two decades. He had been instrumental in preserving the Protestant interest in Munster during the 1640s, both by his military expertise and by his ability to boost the morale of his besieged fellow settlers. Having transferred his loyalty to parliament in the later stages of civil war, he became a key supporter of, and advisor to, the Cromwellian regime. In 1655 he was appointed President of the Council in Scotland and two years later strongly supported the move to have Cromwell assume the kingship. However, as the Protectorate collapsed, he reverted to royalism and played an important role in gaining the support of Irish Protestants, especially the Cromwellian planters, for the restoration of the monarchy. As a result he had expectations that Charles II would reward him with the lord lieutenancy of Ireland. His appointment as one of the three lords justice for the interim government of Ireland, in October 1660, further encouraged this ambition.[4] However the life-long and unambiguous loyalty of Ormond to the royal cause and his support of the king in exile ensured that the position of the chief governor and king's representative in Ireland was given to him. Broghill's reward was the earldom of Orrery and the lesser, though still welcome, prize of the presidency of Munster, which he had been given in the autumn of 1660.[5]

The Munster presidency was not intended to supplant in any way the authority of the lord lieutenant over the province. He could instruct the president on all aspects of policy and could overrule any of his decisions. He had power to appoint all magistrates and the president had no official authority to propose or reject candidates for office. Even the appointment of the provincial council was in the hands of the lord lieutenant and both he and the members of the Irish council were entitled to a place on it when they were within the province. In practice, however, the presidency was not a subservient regional administration simply implementing without question orders from the central executive. The economic and strategic importance of the province and the position and authority of the lord president ensured considerable initiative and freedom of action. On occasion, roles could even be reversed and the presidency might exert pressure on the executive to initiate, modify or abandon policies. Orrery's important role in ensuring Irish Protestant support for the restoration of Charles II,[6] his crucial work on drafting the Act of Settlement[7] and his experience as a lord justice of Ireland prior to Ormond's appointment, together with his close relationship with the king and influential English ministers enabled him to use his office in a positive and powerful manner. If he chose to oppose a particular policy, the pressure he could exert, and the support he could draw upon, were considerable. The freedom of the lord lieutenant to introduce changes of policy affecting the province was thus circumscribed and while the president never, even indirectly, had a veto and measures were implemented despite his forcefully expressed opposition, the constant need to consider the reaction of the local administration usually worked to the benefit of the president. For the first two years of his presidency Orrery was, in addition, one of the lords justice with joint responsibility for the government of the country. This inevitably led him to blur the distinctions between both offices and made the transition to his subordinate role from 1662 onwards more difficult.

Ormond was appointed in November 1661[8] but did not come to Ireland until the following summer.[9] Nevertheless Orrery was left in no doubt that his freedom to make decisions had ended. The lords justice were given orders that no offices, lands, pardons or church licences were henceforth to be issued by them nor any commands in the army be filled: they were to confine themselves to the routine civil administration and defence of Ireland.[10] Secretary Nicholas sent strict instructions to the lord chancellor of Ireland that Ormond was to be consulted on all Irish affairs.[11] The news of Ormond's appointment coincided with an attack of gout for the president but as soon as he had recovered he sent assurances of his loyalty and affection. In particular he stressed the attitude which, as president, he would adopt; 'you shall on all occasions receive such cheerful and dutiful obedience, as shall convince you, I am not more pleased with that high trust on any account, than on my being thereby in a more significant condition to serve your grace'.[12] This anxiety to avoid any possible confusion about the powers which his office gave him is again shown in his next letter to Ormond. 'If anything of mine for the presidency of Munster . . . does appear inconsistent or repugnant to your grace's grant, I will cheerfully resign my patent with such alterations and restrictions as may best square with and confirm what your grace shall get inserted in your grant.'[13]

This initial fulsome assertion appears ironic when viewed against the lack of co-operation which came to characterize their relationship. Its significance, however, should not be underrated. Orrery was careful to disguise any disappointment he may have felt at not being appointed lord lieutenant. If he still harboured any hopes of obtaining the position in the future, the best approach would be to ensure that his role in Munster would demonstrate his political and administrative ability and underline his value for the English interest in Ireland.[14] To accomplish this he would need the support of the lord lieutenant. Ormond, for his part, respected the ability of the president and was keenly aware of the reliance which the king placed on him.[15] There was, therefore, a mutual willingness, strengthened by its basis of self-interest, to have an unambiguous, efficient and cordial working relationship.

Such a development never took place and the reality of their attitude to each other was in stark contrast to their original stated intentions. No single explanation can adequately or convincingly account for this but perhaps their contrasting personalities provide a key. The excitable and impatient temperament of Orrery did not suit the more taciturn and deliberate approach of Ormond. Orrery's conviction, which he did not always conceal, that he had a better understanding of the requirements, not only of his province, but of Ireland, annoyed Ormond and may at times have been a factor in his decision to ignore or reject the president's advice and exhortations. Ormond was well aware of the influence which Orrery had at court, including his apparent personal high standing with both the king and the Duke of York. To this mixture of respect, caution and perhaps jealousy, was added the lethal element of suspicion. Ormond was frequently warned that the president was engaged in a continual intrigue to secure his removal so that Orrery himself might obtain the lord lieutenancy. Within this general framework three phases in the relationship between the two men can be traced; an initial one of gradual mistrust punctuated by occasional outbursts and clashes, a brief period of seeming reconciliation and a final bitter deterioration culminating in Ormond's dismissal.[16]

The discovery by Orrery of the so-called 'fanatic' plot of May 1663 was the occasion of their first open clash. This conspiracy, between some discontented army officers and Cromwellian planters apprehensive about the level of decrees restoring land to Catholics by the Court of Claims, did not present a major threat. The president however took a particularly alarmist view and requested that all Non-conformist sympathizers should be seized as a precaution. Ormond, believing that there was little danger, not least since the plot had been betrayed, refused to take such action. This led Orrery to write directly to the king complaining that his concern for the security of the province was being undermined by the inactivity of the lord lieutenant. While making his criticism of Ormond's policy clear, he was careful to emphasize that he had not disobeyed it, remarking somewhat disingenuously, 'I cheerfully submitted to his view.'[17] The ill feeling between them which resulted from this action was intensified by the president's policy within the province. While obeying Ormond's directive against a general seizure of all suspects, he nevertheless proceeded to purge the garrisons of the major cities and generated such an air of panic that it effectively destroyed the lord lieutenant's strategy to trap any remaining plotters. This was the first occasion where the president demonstrated the way in which a regional administrator could frustrate policy without formally refusing to obey specific orders. It left a legacy of bitterness to which an insight is given in a letter, later in that year, from Ormond. Protestations of fidelity and obedience are only of value, he pointedly informed the president, if they are followed by 'deeds which confirm their sincerity'.[18] In addition to his own direct experiences, the information he received from other sources reinforced his doubts about the sincerity of Orrery's continued assurances of loyalty.[19]

The outbreak of the Dutch war in 1665 renewed the strategic importance of the province and raised new issues of policy and authority which were not clearly defined. The attitude to be adopted towards French ships which came into the Munster ports was one of the first problems on which the president sought clarification.[20] When prisoners were taken from a Dutch ship, captured in the Shannon estuary in February 1666, the question of their fate had to be referred to Ormond.[21] While such occurrences presented a constant opportunity for dangerous misunderstandings, they were usually settled amicably. The real problem arose from the security situation. Ormond, though he acknowledged the danger, refused to accede to what the president regarded as essential demands to meet that threat. The most basic requirements, which Orrery repeatedly requested, were the immediate payment and supply of the army, the raising of a militia and the arrest of the leaders of the Irish and the English Non-conformists in the province.[22] Ormond agreed with the demand for the army but pleaded an inability to grant it. The president's reaction is interesting; he apparently accepted the truth of this but felt that he should continue to press for action nevertheless. His function was to articulate the needs of Munster; how these were to be met and the problems they posed for the lord lieutenant were not his concerns The refusal of his other demands was clearly due to Ormond's disapproval of them and Orrery reacted angrily to what he saw as a rebuff. He considered the Dublin administration to be poorly informed about, and consequently unsympathetic to, Munster's needs. The value of a local governor was precisely to avoid such an occurrence and the rejection of his analysis and advice devalued and undermined his office. The question of arresting those whose loyalty might be suspect was simply an extension of the dispute between them on this point in 1663 and Ormond's rejection of it again could hardly have been unexpected by Orrery.

The proposal to form a militia, however, could not be dismissed by the lord lieutenant as unacceptable or impossible. It would not be a drain on the treasury nor require elaborate government involvement in recruitment, training or administration. Such a scheme to form a voluntary armed and trained band was certain to receive approval if it had Ormond's support. The lord lieutenant's reluctance to seek such authorization caused a further and more serious clash with the lord president. Ormond's hesitation was based on his doubt about the value of such a force. The only contribution it could make in the event of an invasion, he wrote to Arlington, would be to keep the 'numerous, necessitous and therefore discontented Irish from rising and destroying all behind us whilst we have an enemy before us'.[23] He regarded this as a minor consideration in the context of any French advance through the province. He differed fundamentally in this respect from Orrery, who saw the formation of the militia as a factor which would prevent a French invasion. Although the lord lieutenant finally instructed him to proceed with the organization of the force in June 1666 the ill feeling that the equivocation and delay had aroused was a further ingredient to the recipe of mistrust and suspicion that was slowly poisoning their relationship.

The reconstruction of the fort at Kinsale became a new issue of contention. This was a project which the president had been urging since the French threat arose. The authorization by Ormond in June 1666 to Sir Robert Byron to undertake the work under Orrery's direction appeared to remove one of his main complaints about the neglect of the province.[24] Initially this proved to be the case and probably contributed to the brief period of cordiality which followed. However, the failure to supply sufficient money for the work, which forced Orrery to pay for it from his own resources, caused a new rift.[25] In September 1667 Orrery complained that he had received a mere £500 on assignments, on which he had been unable to collect anything until August 1667, and still had received less than half of their value. Without his own money, and loans from the burgesses and inhabitants of Kinsale, the work could not have been continued.[26] The president linked these complaints with an attack on the management of financial affairs in Ireland. The inclusion of this criticism of Ormond's administration ensured that the serious rift between them was deepened considerably. A bitter exchange of letters signalled this new phase. If Orrery was aware that the assignments were the only means of payment available, Ormond wrote, then his complaint was either 'a very superfluous expression' or an insinuation that 'we had better means but wouldn't send them to you'.[27] In reply the president made no attempt to withdraw his basic complaint that, having been ordered to fortify Kinsale harbour, he had not been given the means to pay for it. He did, however, try to avoid further acrimony by accepting the less offensive interpretation of his action: 'I do not pretend to express myself well, but I am sure I never did intend to offend your grace or my lords of the council.'[28]

The president's propensity for discovering plots against the government, which he reported in alarmist fashion to Ormond with requests for immediate and severe counter-measures, was a further contributor to their poor working relationship. Orrery's scare-mongering, which was by any standards extreme, had a complex motivation. It arose partly from his naturally excitable and pessimistic personality, which led him to continually expect that rebellion was about to break out. His elaborate network of spies, designed to combat this threat, ironically fuelled his fears by producing unsubstantiated reports, either to obtain financial reward or justify their existence. He also hoped to obtain a greater share of supplies and equipment by conveying the impression that the province was under constant threat. In June 1666 Ormond changed his policy of exasperated disregard and sternly rebuked the president for his alarmist approach, particularly in regard to the canard of a French invasion and concomitant Irish rebellion. The depth of the lord lieutenant's anger is shown by his comment that the only explanation for Orrery's action seemed to be a desire to encourage such an eventuality.[29] This reprimand, apart from causing further resentment, was ineffectual. In his reply, five days later, Orrery made no reference to the rebuke but sent details of yet another plot adding the pointed comment, 'I thought it my duty to present your grace with this account.'[30]

It is difficult to see how Ormond could have done anything to bridge the gulf which inexorably widened between them. His actions indeed appear to have been extremely generous given the attitude and activities of the president. In May 1663, when Orrery was under suspicion at court, Ormond defended him. 'Lord Orrery's loyalty', he wrote to Secretary Bennett, 'does not depend on the mere receiving of favour.'[31] He never failed to acknowledge the positive benefits which the president's rule gave to Munster. His tour of inspection to the province in September 1666 was undertaken to please Orrery rather than to check on him. He did not find it necessary to go further than Kinsale, he reported to Arlington, 'such hath been the vigilance and extraordinary activity of my lord of Orrery in his province'.[32] He was not reluctant to use Orrery's expertise in particular areas or his useful English contacts where these could be of service.[33] He suggested that the president should independently inform influential men like Clarendon and Arlington of the bad condition of the army in the province in the hope that another voice added to his own requests for money might yield a positive outcome.[34] In April 1666 Ormond enclosed a letter from the president with a note for Arlington to show it to the king so that 'my lord Orrery's vigilance and prudence in his service may appear to him . . . and also that the king can see that what I say of the state of the country is confirmed by other of his principal officers'.[35] His care to avoid giving any offence to the president on matters of jurisdiction is underlined by his instructions to his son Lord Ossory, who was lord deputy in his absence in 1668, that Orrery had command of the army.[36] This authority came from Orrery's position of sergeant-major-general of the army in Ireland.[37]

The most notable attempt to create a better understanding between them occurred in September 1666 when Ormond visited the province. The opportunity to demonstrate to the lord lieutenant the range and quality of his work, particularly in defence, had long been coveted by the president. He embarked on a calculated campaign to impress his visitor not only by demonstrating how the province had thrived but also by elaborate ceremonial and entertainment as well. He greeted Ormond on the border of Tipperary and Limerick accompanied by his council and most of the nobility and gentry of the province. The six newly raised militia troops from Kerry, Clare and Limerick and two army troops were assembled for inspection. The lord lieutenant visited Limerick, Cork, Youghal and Kinsale and in each place the president presented a similar spectacle of his power and efficiency and ensured that all local officials provided suitable entertainment.[38] Superficially the visit was extremely successful and Orrery felt sufficiently satisfied to send a highly favourable account of it to Arlington.[39] This optimism seemed to be confirmed by a return invitation from Ormond for the president and his wife to stay with him and the duchess at Kilkenny castle, which was accepted in October. A plan to revive the Irish tobacco monopoly was discussed during this visit and was intended to set the seal on a new and better phase in the unhappy relationship between them.[40] In fact, apart from a short period of shallow friendliness untroubled by any contentious issue, their basic antagonism and mistrust continued, indeed deepened.

Ironically Thomas Morrice, Orrery's chaplain and earliest biographer, regarded this journey of Ormond to Munster as the cause of their deteriorating relationship. He suggested that the show of strength and spectacle that Orrery exhibited was resented by Ormond as too powerful for a subject and he regarded it less as a tribute than a threat from the president.[41] Morrice is a partisan and unreliable source. He errs on such a fundamental matter as the date of the suppression of the presidency[42] and his main concern is to show his subject in the most favourable light at all times. It is clear that the problems between both men had long predated this visit yet there may indeed be some substance to this suggestion. Orrery was almost certainly aiming to impress, not offend, the lord lieutenant. That Ormond could have regarded it as a form of intimidation is however a possibility, bearing in mind the general atmosphere of suspicion that existed. An intensification of the distrust between them, with a new dimension of bitterness on Ormond's part, is certainly evident from around this time, which makes Morrice's argument at least credible.

It is not easy to date precisely this qualitative change in Ormond's attitude but by the autumn of 1668 it was unmistakable. In his letters to his eldest son, the lord lieutenant abandons all his customary restraint and it is clear that by then he shared the opinion of his family and friends: 'I now take all fitting occasions to let the world know I look upon my lord of Orrery as no friend of mine.'[43] He was convinced that the president's purpose in seeking permission to go to England in March 1668[44] was to join in the intrigue then under way against him, and Ormond feared that Orrery's industry, ability and ambition would be only too effective because 'these times do too much resemble those wherein he was very active and learnt his politics'.[45] This was a clear reference to Orrery's involvement with the regime of Oliver Cromwell. He had confidence nevertheless that the intrigue would fail and took an uncharacteristic pleasure in denigrating the president, referring to his 'vanity, ostentation and itch to popularity'[46] as well as his malicious jealousy. On hearing that Orrery had suffered another attack of gout, he retorted, 'yet that is not his least infirmity'.[47]

The most insidious factor affecting their relationship was the persistent suspicion that Orrery coveted the lord lieutenant's position and was engaged in an intense and widespread intrigue to secure his recall. There were many in England who wished to have Ormond dismissed, particularly after the fall of Clarendon in September 1667, though the importance of such court intrigue in Ormond's eventual downfall has been questioned.[48] Orrery, while admitting that he came under frequent pressure to support such plots, always denied any involvement.[49] The willingness of Ormond to accept such assurances was usually weakened by his discovery of independent evidence which cast grave doubt on their sincerity.[50] The consequent distrust and suspicion made the improvement of relations virtually impossible.

The president's denials were based on the argument that he lacked any ambition to be lord lieutenant. The examples he offered in support of this claim however were so patently at variance with his actions that they destroyed his credibility. He claimed that he was inadequate both physically and mentally for such a demanding post; the particular financial and military problems were so great that he would not be equipped to deal with them; he had no interest in power for its own sake and had no need to seek it as he 'did never yet my own self beg anything for my friends or myself that your grace did deny me'.[51] Ormond remained unconvinced even when Orrery offered to resign the presidency and retire to England to prove his good faith.[52] It is difficult to see how the lord lieutenant could have accepted the argument that Orrery was uninterested in or inadequate for the major problems of the country while he was constantly offering unsolicited advice on those very questions.[53] His health, apart from periodic attacks of gout, was quite good, not interfering with his ability either to fulfil the duties of the presidency or play a significant role in English politics. Indeed he appears to have used his gout as a political expedient on occasion.[54] His argument that it would not have been in his interest to have a different lord lieutenant was only convincing if he did not hope to get the position himself, a view which few seriously entertained. The president was certainly consistent and unwavering in his denials. He repeatedly protested his innocence to the lord chancellor of Ireland, his cousin Archbishop Boyle, This, of course, may have been merely a clever ploy to offer independent proof to the lord lieutenant of his sincerity, knowing that there was close consultation between Boyle and Ormond. Orrery's admission to Conway in February 1669 that the Duke of Buckingham and himself were resolved to give Ormond 't'other heave'[55] has been interpreted as proof of his guilt.[56] This remark, however, was made after Ormond's dismissal and seems to refer to his continued embarrassing attendance at court. Orrery's apparent candour in admitting that he received offers to join in the intrigues must be seen in the light of his knowledge that Ormond was well aware of them and silence on the president's part could be interpreted as assent.[57] His reluctance to go to England in the winter of 1667/8, while possibly due, as he insisted, to his desire not to be used in such intrigues, can equally be seen as an astute move to convince Ormond of his innocence.[58] Given the president's love of intrigues, eagerness to retain his coveted position as a flattered and sought-after person at court and his obvious relish in exercising power, it is difficult to believe that he resisted the pressures on him. After his arrival in England in June 1668, when Ormond's position had become weaker, it does not appear that Orrery retained any loyalty to the lord lieutenant. Certainly by then Ormond, his wife and his close associates were convinced of Orrery's involvement.

The Duchess of Ormond, in particular, had always regarded his husband's ambivalent attitude to Orrery as a mistake and gave full vent to her feelings after the dismissal. The new lord lieutenant would not, she felt sure, make the same mistake but would recognize Orrery immediately for what he was, 'the most false and ungrateful man living'. The fact that the president did not succeed to her husband's office failed to convince her that he might have been innocent. She did, however, derive some comfort from the fact that he had not benefited from his treachery.[59] Orrery was aware that Ormond's family and friends felt this way. 'I do not doubt but fair Carrig's friends would make me as unfortunate as they would have me guilty.'[60]

After February 1669, with Ormond no longer lord lieutenant, contact between them ceased. Some attempts at reconciliation were made but proved abortive.[61] When Ormond was re-appointed in 1677, Orrery was no longer president and his brother, the Earl of Burlington, effected a reconciliation between them.[62] Ormond solicited his advice on the Irish revenue and on Bills for a new parliament while the resumption of work on the fort at Kinsale renewed their contact. Within a short time, however, Orrery was again sending long complaints about security policy and seized on the scare of the 'popish plot' to attack the lord lieutenant's approach. Inevitably

Ormond reacted sharply to this criticism and all the old animosity was rekindled. This illustrates, yet again, the personal basis of their failure to establish a satisfactory working relationship. Neither of them could alter their fundamentally different approaches to problems of government and the inevitable result was conflict.

In this period, as earlier, it is clear that the breakdown of their relationship was due to Orrery. His undue alarm at the slightest trouble, criticism of the lord lieutenant's actions even where he knew that they were all that was possible, and his tendency to report such criticisms directly to England were provocations he could have avoided if he had sincerely wished to work amicably with Ormond. The lord lieutenant would, it seems clear, have allowed him considerable freedom of action and been open to his advice had Orrery been more co-operative. Even with their existing poor relationship he had sought Orrery's help on issues where his expertise was of value. While the problems caused by Orrery's constant questioning of policy, especially in regard to the army, would have impaired their relations, its effects might not have been as far-reaching if there had been a fundamental level of trust between them. Ormond felt, justifiably, that he could never be sure where Orrery's loyalties lay or what his real motives were. As he confided to a friend 'there was always something of the councellor, of the friend, of the accuser and a great deal of the libeller' in him.[63] Given his experience of Orrery's duplicity, it is perhaps not surprising that his comment on reports of his imminent death in October 1679 was less than generous: 'we hear out of Munster that Orrery is past all . . . hope of recovery, but he has so often said to be so and yet recovered well enough to trouble all about him and the government to boot.'[64]

No change in the relations between the presidency and the central administration is immediately apparent after the dismissal of Ormond in 1669. Orrery was in London and his son, Lord Broghill, was vice president while Ormond's son, the Earl of Ossory, was lord deputy pending the arrival of Robartes, the new lord lieutenant. Neither Ossory nor Broghill, in caretaker positions and with the legacy of their fathers' enmity, was prepared to risk any confrontations at this point. In May 1669 a complaint was made about Broghill's torture of a prisoner.[65] The president was authorized, under the original 1570 Instructions[66] to use torture when examining defendants suspected of treason, murder or felony. This was in line with the powers of the presidency in Wales[67] though not in the North of England.[68] The charge against Broghill related to the torture of a French master of a ship, whose fingers had been severely burned. That Orrery himself used at least the threat of such tactics is clear from his own account of dealing with a Limerick merchant whom he suspected of being a spy for the French: 'I did to terrify him, menace him with the rack and ordered an officer to take him and to tie lighted matches to his fingers; but then, if he would confess nothing to be sure to take away the matches ere they touched his skin.'[69] Ossory as lord deputy was asked to investigate this charge but he refused, explaining that the known hostility between the families might 'render His Majesty's justice, which I have the honour to administer, liable to misconstruction'.[70]

A similar endeavour to avoid dissension characterized the brief period of Robartes' government. Orrery had to face impeachment proceedings before the House of Commons in November 1669[71] and had, therefore, little opportunity for involvement in the affairs of Munster. Robartes, for his part, found his stay in Ireland uncongenial and increasingly wished only to be recalled. As a result, no issues arose that could precipitate a dispute between the lord lieutenant and the presidency.[72]

During the administration of Berkeley, 1670–72, differences with the president again arose with all the fervour and ill feeling that such clashes had produced in Ormond's time. A new dimension was added by the failure of the lord lieutenant to act within the previously accepted framework of their respective authority. In September 1670 Orrery took exception to the wording used by Berkeley in the patents that he granted to the troops and companies of the army sent to the province. This implied that he had command over them. Orrery pointed out that the president had command of all the forces in the province and the consequent right to garrison the army as he thought fit and this authority seemed to be undermined by the terms of the patents. Berkeley assured him that this was not the intention and the incident was quickly resolved.[73] The lord lieutenant, however, found the necessity to do all business with the province through the president irksome. This was particularly true of a situation where speed of action was important and is typified by a case in September 1670 when three French Men of War came into Dingle. Having obtained Arlington's instructions, Berkeley was, as he noted tersely, 'bound by the style of this place' to inform the president, who would in turn instruct the sheriff. The fact that there was only a weekly inland post made the procedure even more cumbersome and his control consequently very inefficient.[74]

The main clash between them on policy related to Berkeley's benevolent approach towards Roman Catholics. In the context of the new English foreign policy, arising from the secret treaty of Dover, a pro-Catholic policy was in line with the king's plans. It is uncertain whether Orrery, despite his recent stay in London, fully appreciated this changed situation but he insisted that it posed an unacceptable threat to the security of Munster. Orrery was president of Munster and as such it was his duty to protect its interests, as he saw them. If they were neglected, particularly in the vital sphere of security, the ultimate consequences would be far more serious than any short-term problems that might arise from his refusal to accept such a policy.

The president's decision to embark on a vigorous anti-Catholic campaign in 1671 was such a flagrant repudiation of the lord lieutenant's authority that it permanently damaged their relations. An immediate indication of this was the refusal of Berkeley to grant Orrery's son, Henry Boyle, a lieutenancy in the president's own troop of horse. Orrery complained about this to the king, who reversed the decision. He also believed that Berkeley was planning to deprive him of his regiment but had been ordered not to do so by the king. The president's arrogant reference to the lord lieutenant's authority ('whatever he does that is fit, I obey: whatever that is not, I complain to my master who does me right and favour') illustrates his belief that he could act independently without any risk to his position.[75]

Berkeley must be held partly responsible for this; his weak and indecisive handling of problems relating to the province had, from early on, set the tone for such a development. Shortly after his arrival in Ireland he had instructed the vice-president to appoint three new militia officers in Limerick but he had refused. The reasons for this refusal, according to Orrery, were that the men were 'anabaptists or had married Irish papist wives or were people so beggarly or of such ill fame that the Protestants did judge themselves in danger while such were instructed in that important city'.[76] The lord lieutenant made a special journey to the province to assert his authority and, it was widely expected, discipline the vice president. However Orrery's support for his vice-president's action changed the situation. Berkeley was reluctant to face a conflict with the powerful lord president immediately on his return from a flattering reception in England and on an issue which was capable of much misrepresentation. The intensity of local Protestant feeling may also have been a factor in the decision of Berkeley to compromise. He took personal responsibility for the reliability of the officers and agreed that the matter was now closed. The episode was an embarrassment for the lord lieutenant and his annoyance was clearly demonstrated by his petulant refusal to accept an invitation to dine with Orrery before his hasty departure from the city.[77]

As well as this initial failure to assert his authority, Berkeley's transgression on areas that the president firmly insisted were his responsibility, usually followed by an apologetic retreat, further damaged his position. These problems appear to have arisen from Berkeley's lack of familiarity with established procedure rather than any attempt to extend his authority at the president's expense. Orrery's refusal to accommodate himself to a moderate, much less a favourable, policy towards Roman Catholics and his policy of ignoring the lord lieutenant's commands through direct appeals to England inevitably meant that a satisfactory working relationship between them became impossible, a situation which continued right up to the suppression of the presidency.

Throughout the entire period of the Restoration presidency, then, relations between the president and the lords lieutenant were, at best, unsatisfactory. Disputes, intrigues, jealousy and distrust far outweighed the periods of uneasy cordiality. It was largely Orrery's fault that his relations with men such as Ormond and Berkeley, as different both in character as in the policy they hoped to implement, should have been equally poor. However the relationship of the actual institution of the presidency and the central administration can be argued to have worked surprisingly well in the circumstances and there was no undue damage to the province as a result. The constant demands by the president for measures to safeguard the welfare and security of Munster, even where extreme or arguably unreasonable, resulted, on balance, in his obtaining more concessions than would have been conceded to a more conciliatory person. It is also important to note that neither Ormond nor Berkeley ever attempted to weaken the president by deliberately undermining his power within the province. For his part, Orrery, despite his powerful contacts at the English court and close relationship with the king, made no attempt to circumvent Ormond as chief governor by appealing for permission to pursue an independent line in Munster. He realized that Ormond's standing with the king was as great as his own and any attempt to undermine the lord lieutenant's position or authority would be unsuccessful. This is in sharp contrast to the situation with Berkeley where Orrery embarked on a provocatively independent line. While this was initially successful in relation to relatively minor matters, his refusal to follow the tolerant approach towards Catholics required in the diplomatic climate of the early 1670s led eventually not only to his dismissal but the abolition of his office. When the presidency was used to threaten the authority of central government on an issue of sufficient importance, a potential problem for most of the seventeenth century, then the termination of a system that had long outlived its original purpose became inevitable.

Daniel O'Connell and the Debate on Anti-Slavery, 1820–50[1]

MAURICE J. BRIC

In Ireland, the year 1829 is principally remembered as the year of Catholic Emancipation. It also marked the rising importance of a new type of popular politics that would address 'the ills of humanity in every direction'. Some of the relevant issues, such as Catholic Emancipation, parliamentary and agrarian reform, the Poor Laws, temperance, and the maintenance of the Established Church, had a particular resonance in Ireland. Others, such as the campaigns to abolish slavery, and to promote the status of women and Jews, did not touch Ireland in as direct or popular a way. However, they all attracted O'Connell's attention and offer an intriguing insight into the ways in which the wider world of reform influenced his political language and outlook. Their international ambit also enabled O'Connell to articulate a more universal rhetoric of liberty and equality that would not be confined to a particular place or issue.[2] As a result, O'Connell featured in all the major debates on contemporary reform on the two sides of both the Irish Sea and the Atlantic. In this paper, I want to focus on one of these debates: that on the abolition of slavery.

During the late eighteenth century, the campaign to abolish the slave trade made little impact on Ireland.[3] After 1800, however, the Act of Union brought all Irish issues, as well as the personalities who spoke for them, into a wider world in which moral as well as economic arguments were made in the British parliament, where William Wilberforce (1759–1833) led the anti-slavery interest during the first quarter-century. In June 1807, his motion to abolish the slave trade passed both houses. Three years earlier, it had been unsuccessful, although on that occasion it had received the support of thirty Irish MPs who, not having any 'local interests connected with the Slave Trade . . . were eager to assert their humanity'. However, other MPs were concerned that the increasingly 'moralistic language' of those who supported the anti-slavery movement might be used with equal eloquence and emotion to address 'the cause of the poor [and] downtrodden' of Ireland. Later on, O'Connell recognized that, for similar reasons, Catholic Emancipation would be well served by locating it within the broader reform movement.[4] An involvement in a variety of reform issues would also enable him to cultivate a less confessional image as well as give him access to a group of reforming MPs who, at least before 1830, would be otherwise outside his circle. O'Connell was also brought into contact with one of the most important popular movements in contemporary Britain, the Society for Mitigating and Gradually Abolishing the State of Slavery throughout the British Dominions (SMG), which, after 1823, led the popular movement to promote 'the total and immediate abolition of negro slavery'. In May 1830, the SMG was reconstituted as the Anti-Slavery Society (ASS).[5]

Among its activities, the SMG/ASS co-ordinated thousands of parliamentary petitions from all parts of Britain and Ireland. These petitions were significant, and not just because of the specific issues that they raised. The organizations and large gatherings that they involved and the complex networks that they invented were part of the machinery of a new political literature and a more populist politics.[6] For similar reasons, the petitions on Catholic Emancipation were important in contemporary Ireland and although a small number of anti-slavery petitions were filed from there during the 1820s, largely through Quaker networks, it was not until after 1829 that O'Connell became actively involved in the anti-slavery cause.[7] Shortly after his election, O'Connell sponsored a meeting in Dublin requesting parliament 'to name a day from which all Negro children thereafter born in British colonies should be free'. He also addressed anti-slavery societies in Cork, Dublin and London. There, he attacked slavery as 'a high crime against Heaven' and one on which he would 'enter into no compromise . . . in the name of humanity, and according to the law of the living God'. He also linked the anti-slavery and Catholic Emancipation movements as well as the circumstances of the Irish peasant with those of the unfree slave. Indeed, the mast-head of the American anti-slavery newspaper, *The Liberator*, might have been written for him from this time onwards: 'Our Country is the World – Our Countrymen are all mankind.'[8]

In the United States, the American Anti-Slavery Society (AASS) had been leading the campaign since December 1833 towards the 'immediate' and 'entire' abolition of slavery there. However, this proved to be an unwieldy organization which, by 1838, numbered some 1,350 individual societies across the country.[9] Thus, it was perhaps inevitable that differences would emerge between the two principal centres of anti-slavery activities, Boston and New York, and between their respective leaders, William Lloyd Garrison (1805–79) and Lewis Tappan (1788–1873). However, the issues that divided the AASS were tactical rather than geographical. Tappan wanted to steer clear of the emerging women's movement and other reform networks because, in his view, they would distract from a focus on slavery. However, for Garrison and his supporters, as C. Duncan Rice has observed,

> the antislavery campaign was only one front in a millennial war, where it was mere tactical common sense to integrate efforts with those on other fronts. In any case, it was not logically possible to handle slavery as a single issue, since it was only a symptom of a disorder that threatened every organ of society.

They also opposed force as an instrument of agitation while party politics were 'mostly . . . a cover for those who dare not, or will not, carry their Anti-Slavery into their Churches and religious bodies'. By extension, Garrison criticized the churches for not opposing slavery more vigorously, thus challenging the established churches that had traditionally led the discussion on moral issues. Thus, as his friend, the Revd Samuel May (1810–99) recalled,

> The truth is that the Calvinistic party in this country [the United States] have so long been accustomed to rule, direct and manage, as they pleased, all benevolent enterprises and all moral and religious associations, that they could not submit to join in a cause led by one, and in which Unitarians, Quakers, and Women were admitted to an equal participation.

In 1839, these differences finally split the AASS between Garrison and what was to become the American and Foreign Anti-Slavery Society (AFASS), led by Tappan and his supporters. Moreover, it was inevitable that, as the World Anti-Slavery Convention of 1840 approached, these differences would be discussed in Britain and Ireland as well as in America. As the Boston abolitionist Wendell Phillips (1811–84) suggested to George Thompson (1804–78), one of the most influential leaders of the anti-slavery movement in contemporary Britain, 'A *European* construction is decisive . . . *Your* appeals sink deep . . . Distance lends them something of the awful weight of the verdict of posterity.'[10]

Since 1824, the Irish anti-slavery movement had been most obviously organized by the Dublin Association for Endeavouring to Promote the Mitigation and Gradual Abolition of Slavery in the British Colonies. Five years later, Charles Orpen formed the Dublin [later, Hibernian] Negro's Friend Society (HNF). However, although in April 1830 2000 tickets were distributed for an abolition meeting in Dublin and there was a large attendance at a similar meeting in Cork, anti-slavery was a cause rather than an organized movement in Ireland and operated there within the wider networks of reform.[11] Moreover, as much as O'Connell supported the cause of anti-slavery and similar causes, the relevant organizations were not part of the Catholic world and, indeed, were seen by some as a threat to it. Orpen's father-in-law was Major Sirr (d.1841), a much-reviled figure among Catholics and, like Orpen, a board member of the HNF. The HNF also had a close relationship with the Hibernian Bible Society, which saw reform in terms of the 'New Reformation' that was anathema to Irish Catholicism. When the Agency Committee's influential lecturer, Charles Stuart (1783–1865), visited Ireland in the earlier years of that decade, he was sponsored by the HNF and spoke mainly in Protestant churches and meeting-halls as part of what his biographer has described as a 'personal quest for spiritual purity and salvation, and promoting the Bible'.[12] Thus, for all its objective and moral commitment to reform, the anti-slavery movement was perceived by some Irish reformers as having not only a Protestant, but also a powerful anti-Catholic strain, and, as such, it encouraged suspicions that such societies were ultimately more committed to a narrow proselytism than to broad reform.[13] Moreover, they promoted a kind of individualistic 'moral autonomy', as Rice has termed it, which challenged the public role of both the Catholic middle classes and the Catholic priests, whom O'Connell for his part regarded as the moral leaders of a new Ireland.[14] Although he admired Garrison's views on social and political development, he also saluted the Tappanites for promoting reform through church as well as political networks. Thus, his support of Garrisonian radicalism was not open-ended.

Despite the obvious presence of O'Connell after 1830, the Irish anti-slavery movement had always been driven by Quakers. Through their wide personal, religious and publication networks, Irish Quakers were well informed on slavery and abolitionism and between 1838 and 1842, the *Irish Friend*, edited in Belfast by William Bell, also highlighted the relevant issues in a community where the publication and exchange of pamphlets and addresses were part of an established culture.[15] Ireland's Quakers shared much of Garrison's radicalism as well as his commitment to non-resistance. However, despite Garrison's undoubted effect on the anti-slavery movement in Ireland, leaders such as Richard Davis Webb (1805–72) and Richard Allen (1803–86) were also influenced by people nearer home. Many Quaker women were involved in a number of reform causes and, aside from their moral authority within the home, and the influence of their writings and charitable work, they had their own anti-slavery societies.[16] Although these were often presented as 'auxiliaries' to their male-dominated counterparts, they were neither secondary nor supplementary to them. Through their international church connections, societies such as the Hibernian Ladies' Negro's Friend Society and the Dublin Ladies' Anti-Slavery Society, which were established in 1833 and 1837 respectively, also maintained their own networks of advice and information, some of which developed as a result of marriage and business contacts as well as through organizing boycotts of slave-grown sugar and contributing to the fund-raising bazaars that became a distinctive means of raising money in American anti-slavery circles. They also gave women a forum from which they might address their inferior political circumstances. As Clare Midgley has suggested,

> it becomes clear that women, despite their exclusion from positions of formal power in the national anti-slavery movement in Britain, were an integral part of that movement and played distinctive and at times leading roles in the successive stages of the anti-slavery campaign.

Whether as a cause or result of these connections, some of these Quaker women were very advanced in their ideas. For example, in Hannah Webb's reformed and renewed world,

> There would be no slaves, no kings, no beggars, no lawyers, no doctors, no soldiers, no palaces, no prisons, no creeds, no clergy, no sects, no war, no grinding labour, no luxurious idleness, no peculiar Sabbath or Temple, but every day and every place 'holiness unto the Lord', no restraints but mutual restraints, no constraining power but love.[17]

Although O'Connell could not draw on the far-flung networks of the Quakers, he was no less an internationalist and saw the anti-slavery movement as part of a wider advocacy 'of civil and religious liberty all over the globe, and wherever tyranny exists'. After he was elected to parliament, he lost little time in meeting the anti-slavery leaders in Britain, inside as well as outside the House. In May 1830, he addressed the general meeting of the ASS together with Wilberforce, Henry Brougham (1786–1868), the future lord chancellor and later lord chief justice, Thomas Denman (1779–1854), and MPs Stephen Lushington (1782–1873) and Thomas Fowell Buxton (1786–1845), all of whom were interested in reform issues. It was at this meeting that the ASS proposed that parliament should fix on a definitive date to abolish slavery in the West Indies. Some of the delegates were also dissatisfied with the conservative leadership of the ASS. As a result, the more radical Agency Committee evolved in 1831, including a sub-committee for Ireland, together with an active network of itinerant lecturers and agents and a more energetic system to put pressure on parliament and parliamentary candidates. However, although it is estimated that some 150 parliamentary candidates pledged support for the abolition of slavery in 1832, this particular campaign was relatively low-key in Ireland, not least because such individualized strategies suited emerging factional leaders like O'Connell. The more populist approach culminated in a convention held in London in April 1833, at which it was resolved to address the Prime Minister. The Emancipation Act which followed abolished the institution of slavery in the British colonies. However, it also set up a £20 million compensation fund for slave-owners who would be affected by the measure and, while this was offensive to many people, the proposal that there should be a seven-year period of 'apprenticeship' between slavery and freedom was even more so. Indeed, Allen and others believed that this would make the lot of the West Indian slave even worse and, as a result, they began to campaign for the *immediate* abolition of slavery. To this extent, while the Emancipation Act was seen as a response to popular opinion, many believed that the process which had brought them even a limited success could be used to address the Act's shortcomings as well.[18] The lesson was not lost on O'Connell.

O'Connell remained a powerful presence within the anti-slavery movement in Ireland. However, unlike the Allens and the Webbs, he remained aloof from the day-to-day organization of the Hibernian Anti-Slavery Society (HASS), which had been established in September 1837 to co-ordinate opinion and organize petitions on the subject. HASS also addressed the limits of the Emancipation Act of 1833 which, following a Caribbean visit during 1836/7, Joseph Sturge and Thomas Harvey suggested had made the lot of the West Indian slave worse rather than better. A large number of petitions followed to ensure that, as Allen saw it, 'our coloured brother should have free and independent power over his life and limbs'. Many of these were incorporated into motions which were tabled in February and March 1838 to bring apprenticeship to an immediate end. In May, a convention met in London to support these parliamentary initiatives and Allen and Webb were designated to lobby specific members of the two Houses on the issue, including the Prime Minister (Russell), the President of the Board of Trade (Labouchere) and the former Governor of Jamaica, the second Marquis of Sligo. On 22 May 1838, Sir Eardley Wilmot again proposed the motion. This time, it was carried by a majority of three but because it had been introduced unexpectedly, some feared that the government might try to reverse it. However, at a celebration to mark Wilmot's success, O'Connell declared that he would 'perish the Ministry who should dare to attempt such an unrighteous course'. As he offered his views, O'Connell knew that some 75,000 Irish women had already signed a supportive petition to Queen Victoria and that Lord Sligo had admitted that 'the facts' of labour and labourers in the West Indies were 'much worse' than had been presented.[19] The effect of Wilmot's motion was to abolish slavery, although, in the event, the West Indies' Assemblies themselves agreed to free their apprentices from 1 August 1838, thereby making the motion redundant. However, the removal of the West Indies as a focus for the activities of the anti-slavery movement was also to lead to a certain lack of clarity and consistency in pursuing the wider goal of 'universal abolition', which, after 1839, would be co-ordinated by the British and Foreign Anti-Slavery Society (BFASS). Indeed, it was O'Connell who, when replying to Sturge's invitation to celebrate the end of apprenticeship in Birmingham on 1 August 1838, had suggested this 'new departure in anti-slavery thought':

> Make one of your professed objects *to consider the propriety of forming a society to aid in the universal abolition of slavery* . . . enable us to begin the work with the vile and sanguinary slaveholders of Republican America. I want to be *directly* at them.

This phase of the anti-slavery movement was boosted by the World Anti-Slavery Convention which was held in London between 12 and 23 June 1840.[20]

The delegates came from United States and France as well as from Britain and Ireland. Seventeen came from Ireland, including four from Cork and three from Belfast. Also attending were scholars such as George Downes (*c.*1790–1846) and R.R. Madden (1798–1886), the political economist Robert

Ross Rowan Moore (1811–64), as well as the leading reformer James Haughton (1795–1873), the Belfast Presbyterian minister the Revd James Morgan (1799–1873), William Martin, the Quaker who had encouraged Father Mathew to establish the temperance movement, and Father Mathew (1790–1856) himself. However, the delegation was dominated by the Webb and Allen families.[21] O'Connell also attended, although, in a gesture which reflected the extent to which reformers on both sides of the Irish Sea interacted on these issues, he did so as a delegate of the Glasgow Emancipation Society (GES). In the words of James Webb, he was 'well received' as a figure of international as well as national status. As Garrison recalled,

> When O'Connell made his appearance, the applause was absolutely deafening. He made a speech of great power, and denounced American slaveholders in blistering language – at the same time paying the highest compliments to American abolitionists.[22]

Also present were women such as Maria Waring, Hannah Webb and Mary Edmundson (1818–1906) who were either married or otherwise related to men who had important roles in the anti-slavery movement in Ireland.[23] Benjamin Robert Haydon's famous painting of the event depicts such women 'as helpful and inspirational wives, mothers and daughters rather than as activists in their own right'. However, this was an inaccurate portrayal because these women took a self-confident and independent view of the proceedings and opposed 'those silly men [who] didn't choose to receive' the female delegates who had been sent to represent some of the anti-slavery societies in America. Not being delegates themselves, of course, these Irish women expressed their views from the observers' gallery and it was from here that a kind of 'alternative court' at the Convention developed. When Garrison, O'Connell, the black abolitionist Charles Lenox Remond (1810–73) and others also visited the gallery, it was clear that the split that had already taken place within the anti-slavery movement in the United States was now appearing on the other side of the Atlantic as well. As the leading American abolitionist and feminist Lucretia Mott (1793–1880) wrote in July 1840, the World Convention

> was no more than a conference of the British & Foreign A.S. Society, to be composed of such members as their 'Com. of Arrangement' should choose to select – that the name of 'the World's Convention' was merely a 'poetical licence' – alias – a rhetorical flourish – [which] . . . has seen meet to ordain and enact, that women should not compose part of their august body . . . a World's Convention' has yet to be held.[24]

The Convention had 'a strong effect' on the Irish. During their time in London, the delegates met established British mentors such as Thomas Clarkson (1760–1846), James Birney (1792–1857) and George Thompson, as well as Garrison, Mott, Elizabeth Cady Stanton (1815–1902) and other Americans who would become lasting influences on the reform movements of mid-nineteenth-century Ireland. The decision to exclude the female American delegates led to a long association with the more radical wing of American abolitionism. Moreover, as Garrison later recalled, it did 'more to bring up for the consideration of Europe the rights of women, than could have been established in any other manner'. What the more radical American delegates had done was to challenge Europeans to recognize that, in Waring's words, women were 'not dolls' but 'human beings' and although there were divided opinions on the subject, most of the Irish delegates agreed with her.[25]

Although many put O'Connell on the radical side of the convention, he initially opposed seating the female delegates because, as he explained to Mott, 'to admit women to an equal share and right of discussion' might provoke 'ridicule . . . if the Convention were to do what is so unusual in England'. On 'mature consideration', however, he suggested that it was an 'injustice' as well as 'impolitic' not to seat them, especially because 'the American ladies have persevered in our holy cause, amidst difficulties and dangers, with the zeal of confessors, and the firmness of martyrs'. O'Connell also recognized that in pursuing '*charitable* categories', women had 'the same duties, and should therefore enjoy the same rights with the man, in the performance of their duties'. Thus, while some welcomed O'Connell's apparent change of heart, he still remained somewhat ambivalent on the status of women in political as opposed to philanthropic movements. Other slices of Irish society were less circumspect on this point. Thus, for example, the Presbyterian minister the Revd James Morgan, a delegate to the London Convention from Belfast, opposed the way in which women's rights had surfaced as part of anti-slavery agitation and indeed, most churches, whatever their views on slavery, reflected the belief of W. Thompson's *Irish Statement Protesting against Slavery Imposed on Women* (London, 1825) that women in contemporary Ireland were subject to their men in matters of political and public concern. Some even questioned whether women should be signing petitions to parliament.[26]

The London Convention also witnessed what Alfred Webb termed a 'painful schism . . . in the Anti-Slavery party'. In a sense, this was no surprise because while the anti-slavery movement had a central objective, it was inherently diverse and not always understood in the same terms by its varied supporters. After 1840, these differences could no longer be easily contained, especially within the churches. Either in their internal arrangements or in their relationships with one another, churches were never united on how or why they wanted to promote reform. Within Quakerism, for example, the promotion of reform led to a split between those who were guided by a narrow reading of the Bible and those whose recognition of the 'inner light' highlighted individual conscience and, thus, a rejection of hierarchy. This was not just a theological difference because it also influenced why, in some cases, radicals such as Mott and Garrison were 'bitterly opposed' in London and why in Dublin, where Quakers were 'mostly

Hicksites', they were welcomed. Quakers (like other Protestants) also had an uneasy relationship with Catholics at a time when, in Webb's words, 'the present beau ideal of Irish liberty is – the ascendancy of the true [Catholic] Church – [and] the restoration of the Churches to the Catholics'. However, Webb believed that O'Connell's 'moral power' would prevent 'sectarian division' in Ireland. This was not an easy assignment because, as Webb remarked to Quincy, the popular 'notion' was 'simply that by making up a good strong show of physical force, the English will repeal the Union through fear – or else, they – that is Paddy – will take it by force'. Thus, although Webb and others acknowledged O'Connell's sincerity on 'the great questions of civil & religious liberty', they were wary that their involvement in the wider issues of reform might also be seen to indulge O'Connell's more immediate political commitments in Ireland.[27]

The tensions that existed within the Irish anti-slavery movement also surfaced during the visits of lecturers who travelled to Ireland after the London convention. Garrison's reputation remained high and the anti-slavery movement in Ireland acknowledged this when he arrived in July. Garrison stayed with the Webbs, where O'Connell called on him. When Remond visited Cork in November 1841, Jane Jennings wrote that 'no one could listen unmoved to his appeals on behalf of the suffering and oppressed' and that he provided the kind of inspiration which the anti-slavery movement had been waiting for and had 'so long witheld'. Other speakers visited Belfast, Waterford, Limerick 'and other chief towns, finishing the series with a large, enthusiastic gathering in Dublin, at which O'Connell made one of his most withering speeches on American slavery'. Despite such welcomes, the reality was that, in Ireland, reform was driven by different concerns than was the case in either Britain or America and while O'Connell espoused most of these concerns during the 1830s, they were secondary to Repeal. Moreover, although O'Connell's status as 'the Liberator' of Irish Catholics had made him the 'uncrowned king of Ireland', many of his supporters felt that his views on slavery distracted from their immediate causes in Britain and Ireland as well as compromised the support which they received from America.[28] O'Connell's '*contretemps*' with Andrew Stevenson, the American ambassador in London, may have brought an alleged 'conspiracy against the life of Daniel O'Connell' to the floor of the House of Representatives. However, it again highlighted the fact that the question of slavery had many constituencies and that while the language in which it was discussed was emotional and volatile, it was not always altruistic.[29]

O'Connell never hid his opinions on slavery. During the 1830s and 1840s, he attacked it as 'a hideous tyranny', 'to be put down, not to be compromised with; and to be assailed without cessation and without mercy'. From this, it was a short step to criticize the 'freemen of America' as 'hypocrites, tyrants, and unjust men . . . degraded and dishonoured', 'the star-spangled banner of republican America' as 'stained with the deep, foul blot of human blood', and the 'sacred honour' of the Declaration of Independence as a 'perjury' while Americans recognized 'property in any human being'. At a time of rising American nationalism, many Americans greatly resented such attacks on the very symbols of their republic which, in the words of George Washington, whom he also castigated as a slave-owner, would 'improve on the experience of mankind'. O'Connell also questioned Americans' commitment to democracy and republicanism. The former he saw as incompatible with their 'conduct towards their slaves'. Because of this, he suggested that they were 'traitors to the cause of human liberty, and foul detractors of the democratic principle'. The latter was implicit in what he termed a society with 'the worst of all aristocracies . . . an aristocracy which had been aptly denominated that of the human skin'. Such moralistic tones were not unusual among abolitionists. Neither was the call for the 'speedy, [and] immediate abolition' of slavery.[30] However, O'Connell was no ordinary abolitionist because his views would have a particular influence among Irish-Americans, not least because they raised the question as to 'who spoke for Ireland' in America. While this was a simple question, it had complicated answers, especially because in forging a new identity and 'ethnicity' in America, Irish-Americans were not prepared to be blindly guided by a leadership that they had left behind in Ireland. Neither were American abolitionists always comfortable with the colourful and strident ways in which some anti-slavery visitors from Britain spoke and behaved while in the United States, a point which some of the American delegates raised at the London convention. With the War of 1812 a very recent memory, many Americans still suspected that anti-slavery visitors were in reality, foreign 'agents' who were intent on 'overthrow[ing] the young republic by dividing it over slavery'. This was raised during Thompson's visit to America in 1834/5, for example, as was the point that for all the close and historic ties with Britain, the United States was mature and self-confident enough not to look to the old imperial country for 'encouragement and guidance'. Such sentiments were also reflected in a growing sense of nativism in contemporary America where abolitionists were 'cast as allies of foreign tyrants' who did not have the best interests of the United States at heart.[31]

Irish-Americans did not want to be caught up in these debates. Neither did they welcome anybody who questioned their loyalty to their new homeland and, however innocently, presented them as 'un-American'. Against this background, O'Connell's 'Address from the People of Ireland, to their Countrymen and Countrywomen in America' was controversial. This address had been drawn up during 1840 and was signed by some 60,000 people, headed by O'Connell and Father Mathew. In it, O'Connell repeated that while he had a 'feeling of admiration' for America, 'the foul blot' of slavery was 'the most tremendous invasion of the natural, inalienable rights of man'. O'Connell specifically asked Irish-Americans 'to unite with the abolitionists, as the only consistent advocates of liberty', to correct this. The implied criticism of Irish-American organizations was clear. Moreover, his statement that he would not 'recognize' any American 'as a fellow-man, except those who belong to anti-slavery societies', and that 'those who uphold slavery are not men as we are, [and] are not honest as we are', raised predictable comments and reflected O'Connell's misunderstanding of the role and function of such networks in an American, as opposed to an Irish, setting. This was also underlined by O'Connell's appeal to Irish-Americans 'never to cease your efforts until perfect liberty be granted to every one of her inhabitants, the black man as well as the white man . . . treat the coloured people as your equals'. Again, this was a difficult issue because it reflected a misunderstanding on the Irish side of the Atlantic that the concerns of Irish immigrants in America were not *sui generis*. Whatever O'Connell may have thought of the supposed 'inconsistencies' of American democracy, Irish-Americans did not like to be compared with 'free blacks' or to support abolitionism as an equivalent to their own history and circumstances. John O'Connell's observations that, in the free northern states, where most Irish immigrants had settled and had considerable political influence, 'free people of colour were subject to the greatest indignities in railway trains, churches and even in grave yards' also challenged the 'new associations' that the Irish established in America not to be 'forgetful of the older associations they had left at home'.[32]

However, the Irish diaspora was no longer that united and while John O'Connell informed Haughton in 1842 that 'there is no abatement of zeal on the part of the Repeal Association in the blessed cause of negro freedom', the reality was more vague. On 28 January 1842, O'Connell's address was presented in Fanueil Hall, Boston. Garrison chaired the meeting, which included 'a large number of the Irish inhabitants of Boston and vicinity' as well as members of the Massachusetts Anti-Slavery Society (MASS). Garrison had hoped that the address would build a bridge between his movement and O'Connell's exiled constituents and thus break up what he saw as a 'stupendous conspiracy' between Irish America and the Democratic party, especially in the South. For Garrison, the Democrats may have supported Repeal and sent 'donations' to Ireland but theirs was a 'pretended sympathy for Ireland' that extended no further than their interest in the Irish vote and the role which Irish-American organizations played in mobilizing it. As such, the address questioned the moral basis not just of the pro-slavery 'enterprise' but also of Irish-American politics.[33] However, in the cut and thrust of contemporary American politics, many Irish-Americans regarded the rhetorical flourishes of far-away politicians, such as O'Connell, and of presumptuous friends in America, like Garrison, as disruptive influences on their actual position and potential role in American life. For all its humanitarian rhetoric, therefore, the address had a significant political subtext and was an important milestone in defining new relationships within the Irish diaspora.

For their part, the (Boston) *Pilot* and (New York) *Argus* 'sneer[ed] at the

Address' and denied its 'authority'.[34] Individual Repeal associations in America also felt challenged by O'Connell's address and they told him so. In the meantime, Garrison and Remond presented the address in Albany on 21 April 1842 although by then, it was clear that O'Connell was adopting a more pragmatic approach to Irish America. He maintained his opposition to slavery but stated that 'the Irish Repealers would not interfere, either directly or indirectly, with American slavery' and that whatever course he took as an individual, he would, when speaking 'on behalf of the Irish people', maintain the 'strictest neutrality' on the subject of every American institution. While this might have quietened Irish-American organizations, it dismayed many anti-slavery activists, as did his estrangement from Garrison in late 1843. In May 1843, the Pennsylvania Anti-Slavery Society decided to address O'Connell and to make a moral connection between Repeal and abolitionism. In a response that he delivered before the Repeal Association on 9 May 1843, O'Connell again condemned slavery and declared that he did not 'care for the consequences' in saying 'shame upon every man in America, who is not an anti-slavery man; shame and disgrace upon him!' He realized the importance of this new intervention, suggesting also that it 'never came regularly before us until now. We had it introduced collaterally.' However, his statement that he was reflecting 'the sentiments of the Repeal Association' and that later that year, he spoke 'as the representative of the virtues of the people of Ireland' on the same issue, challenged Irish men and women 'over the broad Atlantic . . . [to] dare countenance the system of slavery that is supported there, [for otherwise] we will recognize you as Irishmen no longer'. These reflections were brought into the highest relief when in response to a letter from the Cincinnati Irish Repeal Association on 11 October 1843, O'Connell issued his most closely argued and unequivocal address on slavery and Irish-American attitudes to 'the most hideous crime that has ever stained humanity'.[35]

The address repeated familiar themes, stressing again that 'slavery was repugnant to the first principles of society'. It also castigated Irish-Americans in unusually strong terms, suggesting that

> the generous, the charitable, the humane, the noble emotions of the Irish heart have become extinct amongst you . . . that you should become the apologists and advocates of that execrable system which makes man the property of his fellow man [and] destroys the foundation of all moral and social virtues.

In this context, O'Connell recalled that in the House of Commons Lord Morpeth had once referred to the 'superior social morality of the poorer classes in Ireland over any other people', implying that Irish emigrants had not carried this moral code with them to America. As such, they were 'pseudo-Irishmen'. The implication that Irish-Americans were also not 'moral' caused great offence, as did O'Connell's suggestion that Irish-Americans were entrapped within a 'congregation of the wicked, who consider man a chattel and a property, and liberty an inconvenience'. O'Connell also referred to the controversial subject of racial equality, rejecting the notion 'that the negro is really inferior as a race' and that 'the two races cannot exist together on equal terms'. Such statements displayed a mixture of bravery and *naïveté* especially when he suggested, as a corollary, that in contemporary America, educational, social, economic and even political barriers that were influenced by 'caste, creed or colour' were, *ipso facto*, artificial, unnatural and 'insulting' to 'humanity'. The response among Irish Americans was predictable. In the Southern states, Repeal associations in Natchez and Charleston tried to distance themselves from O'Connell by distributing their funds among local charities. More generally, others in Irish America questioned O'Connell's presumption to speak for them, either directly or indirectly, and were offended by suggestions that in some way they had to *recover* the honour of 'the land of your birth'. As such, even when the address was discussed in tandem with the Pope's recent statement on slavery in Fanueil Hall in November 1843, the comment of John Tucker, vice-president of the Boston Repeal Association, is instructive: it 'was his duty to remind the audience that the Irish-Americans were ruled neither from Rome nor home'.[36] Such a sentiment may also explain why senior Catholic prelates such as Bishops Hughes (of New York) and England (of Charleston) also criticized O'Connell's address. O'Connell was Catholicism's greatest lay leader and a hero to millions of Irish-American communicants. Thus, like individual Irish-American leaders and organizations, American bishops knew that they too had to take every opportunity to counteract charges that they were being directed by influences outside the state. As such, American bishops, no less than their secular counterparts in the Irish-American community, were not willing to allow O'Connell to tell them 'the best way to disarm their malice'.[37]

By 1845, influential sections of Irish America had come to regard O'Connell's opinions on slavery as a mixture of mischief, arrogance and intrusion. Many also disagreed with his opposition to the incorporation of Texas and Oregon into the United States although here differences of opinion also reflected the growing split within the Repeal movement in Ireland. Some of O'Connell's younger supporters and, in particular, those who wrote for *The Nation*, suggested that these issues might lead to an Anglo-American war and that O'Connell should focus on the domestic implications of this possibility rather than, for example, whether or not the admission of Texas would increase slavery in the United States. However, O'Connell never saw his support for the anti-slavery movement as a *quid pro quo* for 'Irish causes'. This did not sit well with everybody, although, in any event, many Irish-Americans made it clear that they would maintain their own views on Irish affairs, whether or not these coincided with those whom they had left behind in Ireland. Against this background, O'Connell's interventions challenged the nature of the wider Irish community. They also marked an important chapter in the reinvention of an Irish diaspora that, at least in so far as the Atlantic world was concerned, was the sum of two halves, the New and Old Countries, each of which had its own concerns and interests, as well as leaders who did not always agree. Thus, when O'Connell died in 1847, the MASS suggested that 'no man's character was submitted to such opposite constructions' as his was. However, O'Connell's involvement in the anti-slavery movement sheds some small light on the paradoxes of a career that made him a radical and a conservative, a nationalist and an internationalist, and a champion of equality in a deferential society.[38]

The Beginning of the Irish Effort to Provide for the Roman Catholic Foreign Missions before the Famine

EMMET LARKIN

When the student population of the national seminary at Maynooth peaked at some four hundred and fifty in the early 1830s, the Irish Church was faced with a very significant and real challenge. Having maximized the number of secular clergy required by the Catholic community in Ireland, within the constraints imposed by its economic resources, the Irish Church was now presented with the serious problem of how to provide sufficient clergy for the rapidly increasing needs of the foreign missions. This apparently burgeoning demand for foreign missionaries was the result of two independent developments. The first was prompted by the Catholic revival, both at home and in France, after 1815. The second was the result of the vast exodus from Ireland that took place between 1780 and 1845, when it is estimated that some 1,750,000 people emigrated.[1]

The renewed French interest in foreign missions was given great impetus with the founding of the Association for the Propagation of the Faith in Lyons in 1822, which not only raised considerable sums of money in the Catholic communities throughout the world to support the missions, but also published *Annals* that graphically described its work and needs. In the twenty-two years following on the founding of the Association at Lyons, forty new bishoprics, or vicariates apostolic, were erected by the authority of the Holy See, and the Congregation of Propaganda in Rome became responsible for the administration of a vast missionary network 'in the five parts of the world'.[2] The chief problem for the authorities at Propaganda was not only to find the necessary vicars apostolic, but also to recruit the missionaries to staff this new and far-flung spiritual empire.

With the end of the Napoleonic Wars and the Treaty of Paris in 1814–15, the British had acquired by conquest a considerable number of strategic possessions from the French and the Dutch, and they naturally preferred that English-speaking British subjects be appointed as vicars apostolic and missionaries in the new colonies. By the early 1840s, therefore, because of the lack of available manpower among English Catholics, Irish vicars apostolic had been appointed to British Guiana, Trinidad, Cape Town, Mauritius,

Calcutta, Madras, Bombay and Guinea (Africa), and all were anxious to recruit Irish priests, seminarians and nuns for their missions. Even those vicars who were not Irish, such as those at Agra (India) and New Holland (Australia), for example, visited Ireland to recruit for their vicariates. Though Australia was initially governed by English Benedictines, the order simply did not have the manpower to staff the Australian Church, and in a short time it became essentially an Irish mission, governed by Irish-born bishops and priests. The new vicars naturally turned to Maynooth, and to a lesser extent Carlow College, to recruit their clergy.

Between 1835 and 1840, for example, the recently appointed coadjutor to the vicar apostolic of Trinidad, Richard P. Smith, who was Irish, made at least two visits to Ireland to recruit priests, and, by 1840, he had increased the number of priests in Trinidad, Tobago and Dominica from ten or twelve to between fifty and sixty.[3] In the early summer of 1837, William B. Ullathorne, an English Benedictine, and vicar general of the vicar apostolic of the Australian mission, visited Ireland and was very successful in persuading some dozen young priests, mainly from Maynooth, five ecclesiastical students from Kilkenny College, five Sisters of Charity from Dublin and several school teachers to return with him to Australia.[4]

On 3 March 1839, Myles Gaffney, the senior dean at Maynooth, reported to Paul Cullen, the rector of the Irish College in Rome, that in the previous twelve months Maynooth had sent out thirty priests to the foreign missions, including eight to Trinidad and four to Cape Town.[5] Some six months later, on 17 September, the venerable Archbishop of Dublin, Daniel Murray, informed Cullen that he had just received a most difficult commission from the Propaganda. He was asked, he explained, to find six priests for the East Indies, and three each for Bengal and Tibet, 'but our poor Country has been so drained of late by the Missionaries it has sent to Australia, Madras, Trinidad, and the Cape that my hopes are not very sanguine of being able to succeed'. The task would be made easier, Murray suggested, if the prospective recruits knew who they were to serve under and also if the vicars apostolic were Irish. Cullen apparently replied that Propaganda was still most anxious to recruit missionaries, and especially for India. When Murray wrote to Cullen again some three months later, he reported that he had failed to find any missionaries for India and that the forty priests who had gone to the various parts of the world in the last eighteen months had apparently drained the missionary spirit. He again advised Cullen that the best way to secure recruits was to appoint British (read Irish) vicars apostolic everywhere possible, then let them visit Ireland, and they would be able to secure the necessary priests and students.[6]

Two months later, on 2 February 1840, Dean Gaffney also wrote to Cullen again, commiserating about the failure to find anyone for the Indian mission and explaining that something more than the current *ad hoc* method of recruiting was necessary. 'I was sorry,' he began, 'we were not able to do something for the Mission of India. His Grace, Dr. Murray, sent me part of your letter relating to the subject.' 'I did all I could in the College,' he assured Cullen, 'but have been as yet unsuccessful. At present the Missionary Spirit seems to have fled from us for a time. I hope it will return again soon for the benefit of those who are bereft of all spiritual consolation.' 'I wrote to Waterford,' he then reported, 'thinking to derive some assistance from that quarter, as the subjects are more numerous than the wants of the diocese, but did not succeed.' 'We must', Gaffney maintained, 'get a seminary in Ireland for Foreign Missions. Nothing else will do.' 'I and other clergymen in the College,' he confessed, 'have been thinking of such an establishment for some time past. Had we such a Seminary in Ireland we would in a year get 100 candidates. The Bishops of Cloyne, Cashel, Ossory & Meath have not places for the one third of the students who propose themselves for the Ecclesiastical state.' 'It is to be lamented,' Gaffney concluded sadly, 'that we have not pecuniary means in this country where we have such excellent material for supplying all the Foreign Missions with Priests.'[7]

When he visited Ireland later that summer, Cullen informed his vice-rector at the Irish College, Tobias Kirby, that the situation with regard to securing missionaries had not improved over the previous six months. 'Cardinal Fransoni wrote to me some time ago,' Cullen explained on 15 August 1840 (referring to the prefect of Propaganda), 'to see if I could get some missionaries for the Indies. I have made inquiries of Dr. Murray, Dean Gaffney, and others, and it appears it is very difficult to get anyone at all at present.' 'The country was drained,' he pointed out, referring to the vicars apostolic of Trinidad and Bengal respectively, 'by Dr. Smith, Dr. Carew and others.' 'There are many students,' he assured Kirby, in summing up the whole case, 'who wd enter a college for such a mission but have not means to get through their studying. Some might join a Vicar Ap. if he were here and known in the country, but it is hard to expect they will set out to join a Superior whose name or country they do not know.' 'Mention these things if you please,' Cullen requested Kirby in conclusion, 'to the Cardinal – if there were a College for the Foreign Missions in Ireland, it wd be well supplied with students.'[8]

Indeed, for more than a year before Cullen wrote this letter to Kirby, and apparently unknown to him or the Irish and Roman authorities, a college for the Foreign Missions had been founded and was in operation in the parish of Youghal in the diocese of Cloyne and Ross. The college, St Mary's, had been founded by a young Cloyne priest, John Foley. How or when Cullen came to learn of the college is not known, but when Kirby visited Ireland in the summer of 1841 to raise funds for the Irish College, Cullen asked him to learn what he could about Foley and his enterprise. 'Do not forget,' he reminded Kirby on 25 September 1841, 'to make inquiries about Father Foley's establishment – and see whether any good can be done by it.'[9] By the time Kirby received this letter, he had already visited Youghal and St Mary's. 'I was at the Youghal College,' he reported to Cullen in a letter post-marked 20 September. 'It is a surprising business. No one knows how Mr Foley has done it. But the work is done.' 'A noble establishment,' Kirby further assured Cullen, 'is really in operation; there are about 35 promising young men already there in a state of ecclesiastical training for the foreign missions. The College is conducted by four zealous & exemplary priests, contracting volunteers for the good work.' 'Dr. Foran,' Kirby added, referring to the bishop of Waterford and Lismore, 'is a zealous supporter & contributor to it, and he authorized me to say in his name all that was good of it & and its zealous founder. The Rev. Mr Foley is a most Holy Priest.' 'All in his College,' Kirby then explained, 'are Missioners. I mean giving their labours freely for the good of the Missions – Priests, servants & workmen – together training, the latter in a particular manner.' 'Those he has,' Kirby observed, referring to the workmen, 'are admirable men. I asked him for a couple of them for our College & he offered them most freely, even their head who is a most singularly handy, useful & holy man.' 'I said then,' he finally informed Cullen, 'that on my return to Rome & consultation with you, we would most probably send for two or three. But think of the matter, *& poi Il Signore li dirigerà* [and then the Lord will dispose].'[10]

Shortly after consulting with Cullen on his return to Rome in late October 1841, Kirby wrote a short, undated memorandum for Cardinal Fransoni recommending Father Foley's establishment in Youghal, which apparently had been founded some two years before. Kirby explained that he had visited the college and there were between thirty-five and forty students in residence and four priests to train them. They paid only a little for their food, but the rest was free. Finally, Kirby requested Fransoni to recommend the college for a grant to the Association for the Propagation of the Faith at Lyons. In a note dated 24 November 1841 on the back of this memorandum, it was recommended that Foley be written to and granted a subsidy by the Propaganda of 300 Roman scudi, or about £60.[11] Fransoni then wrote to Foley on 3 December formally approving of his college, explaining that the subsidy would be forwarded to him by Cullen.[12] Kirby also wrote to Foley announcing the glad tidings, and he replied on 8 January 1842 that he was not well able to express 'with what transports of joy' he had received the letter announcing that his college was now 'under the mighty Power of Propaganda'. Students, he explained, were flocking to the college in great numbers and the house needed to be enlarged. He was already receiving requests from John Murdock and Andrew Carruthers, the vicars apostolic respectively of the Western (Glasgow) and the Eastern (Edinburgh) districts of Scotland, and the bishops of Ossory, Dublin and Waterford had given him permission to collect in their dioceses.[13]

Some two months later, on 22 March, Foley informed Kirby that he had three sensible workmen to send out to him – a tailor, a baker and a labourer. He had presently fifty students and more were expected after

Easter. There were only two things, he added, that were necessary for the complete success of the establishment: a grant from the Association in Lyons, and to know how he could have the young men who finished their course of studies in the college ordained. If he received the grant from Lyons, Foley assured Kirby that he would have a hundred young men in his establishment before three months were out. He then further assured Kirby in conclusion that the oath to go on the foreign mission was required of all his students when they began their study of theology.[14] On receiving this letter Kirby again wrote Fransoni on 8 April, assuring him that all was progressing well with Foley and his establishment, and though there was a regrettable shortage of economic means, there was no lack of candidates or local enthusiasm for the college. 'It is truly consoling,' Kirby explained to the cardinal, 'to see how a devoted people in the midst of so many privations demonstrate the most heroic generosity in promoting this and similar works of piety.' 'A farmer,' he observed, by way of example, 'has offered a house, cows, horses, and whatever he had for the use of the College, and another said he wished to offer a field for the same object.'[15] Kirby also apparently persuaded the authorities at Propaganda, without Cullen's knowledge, to permit Foley's ordinary, the Bishop of Cloyne and Ross, Bartholomew Crotty, to ordain his students on completing their studies for the priesthood.[16]

At the same time that Foley's missionary college in Youghal was thus making considerable progress, another young priest was also attempting to establish a missionary college in Dublin. John Hand, who was a native of the diocese of Meath, had been educated at Maynooth, and was ordained by Archbishop Murray in December 1835 for the diocese of Dublin. While at Maynooth, Hand had been much influenced by a zealous group of seminarians who, in the process of examining their vocations for the priesthood, had become concerned about being able to save their souls in the secular ministry once they were ordained. These young men began to develop another vision of their vocation. They hoped to form a community after their ordination in order to conduct parish missions, and in this they were much encouraged by the authorities at Maynooth and by Archbishop Murray. Their ideal community was the Congregation of the Mission, a French order, founded by St Vincent de Paul in the early seventeenth century, whose main work was conducting parish missions. After their ordination, these young men founded in August 1833 a community in Dublin in anticipation of eventually establishing a branch of the Congregation of the Mission, or Vincentians, in Ireland.

Two years later, in June 1835, on completing his studies at Maynooth, John Hand joined them at their recently acquired house and school at Castleknock on the outskirts of Dublin. He continued to live with them for more than three years, when the little community was finally charged by Archbishop Murray with the pastoral care of a portion of the Dublin parish of St Paul in Phibsborough. Hand and a senior member of the community,

Thomas McNamara, were then assigned to the little chapel of ease there, St Peter's, in September 1838. In that same month there occurred another signal event in Hand's life that was to have a profound influence on his future. On 18 September 1838, the Association for the Propagation of the Faith based at Lyons was established on a national basis in Ireland at a meeting in Dublin.[17] From that date, and as the small community at Castleknock moved closer to their vision of forming a branch of the Congregation of the Mission, Hand began to discern more and more clearly that his true vocation lay not with the home mission, but rather with the foreign. Over the next two years he became even more convinced that he had been called by God to found a missionary college in Ireland.

The idea for such a college had also been ripening in the minds of the Irish bishops for some time. In the autumn of 1832, the Irish-born Bishop of Charleston in the United States, John England, visited Ireland to recruit clergy for his mission, and had extended conversations with a number of the Irish bishops, who proved very favourable to his proposals of founding a missionary college in Ireland to supply the needs of the American mission.[18] As an interim measure, he made arrangements with the presidents of Maynooth and Carlow Colleges to select candidates who would continue their studies in Ireland for some years when they would then transfer to his seminary in Charleston; and if he found their learning sufficient and their conduct good, he would ordain them and provide them with a mission.[19] On his return home in 1833, England reported to his South Carolina Church Convention the arrangements he had made in Ireland.[20] Later in October of the same year, at the Second Provincial Council of Baltimore, England audaciously proposed that a central seminary be established in Ireland for the Church in the United States. Not surprisingly, the Americans refused to adopt the proposal. The Irish bishops, however, apparently continued to think in terms of an Irish college for the foreign missions. When William Ullathorne arrived in Ireland in June 1837 to recruit for the Australian mission, he found the Irish bishops he met at the Trustees' meeting at Maynooth still enthusiastic about establishing a missionary college in Ireland. 'At that time,' Ullathorne later recalled, 'the Irish prelates were seriously thinking of founding a College for educating priests for the British Colonies and foreign settlements, and the Primate, Archbishop Crotty, asked me to draw up an estimate of the probable number that would be required. This I did and gave it into his hands.'[21]

At their annual meeting in early February 1838, the Irish bishops received a formal request from the prefect of Propaganda, addressed to their Primate, the Archbishop of Armagh, to consider the state of religion in the colonies. The bishops then resolved that 'the prelates who are Trustees of Maynooth College, together with three prelates from each province do form a committee to carry into effect the intention of the Holy See respecting the mission to be established in the British Colonies'.[22] There is no evidence that the proposed committee, which would have included virtually the whole hierarchy, ever met or took any action in regard to Propaganda's mandate. The reason for the Irish bishops' curious non-compliance, however, was not far to seek. By 1838, the finances of Maynooth were already in serious disarray, and in the next several years, the situation became progressively worse as the accumulated debt rose even higher. Whatever the good intentions of the Irish bishops might have been about Propaganda's missionary plans for Ireland, they simply could not meet the additional financial burden such an effort would certainly entail, and hence their very prudent decision to rest on their oars.

In these very lean years for both the Irish Church and the economy, meanwhile, John Hand continued to pursue his dream of a missionary college for Ireland with a quiet perseverance. He carried on his apostolate to the poor at Phibsborough, while at the same time establishing a branch of the Lyons Association for the Propagation of the Faith to collect their pennies for the foreign missions.[23] He not only fired his enthusiasm by reading the *Annals* of the Association, which emphasized the need for heroic sacrifices, but like Father Foley later, he was deeply moved by the generosity and zeal of the people. In these years before the Famine, the average annual contribution in Ireland to the Association was between £6,000 and £7,000, of which the province of Dublin contributed more than half, an extraordinary sum given the hard economic times.[24] While Hand's own calculations with regard to raising funds for his college were always touched by an element of the unreal, his trials over the next two years proved to be very real indeed. His *confrère* at Phibsborough, Thomas McNamara, later summed up Hand's situation well. 'He was young,' McNamara observed, 'he had no position, possessed no influence of any kind, and was unknown outside the community. He was so humble and modest that he felt the greatest effort in revealing his design to anyone.'[25]

He did, however, eventually find a powerful protector and mentor in Archbishop Murray, whose support and confidence in him were the *sine qua non* of his success. Also, after considerable diffidence and delay, Hand wrote in the summer of 1840 to two French missionary societies requesting information about their constitutions and rules, and both societies responded at great length. Hand then drew up his plans for a missionary college, which he completed and sent to Archbishop Murray towards the end of the year. In brief, he undertook to raise between £16,000 and £17,000, given the sanction and co-operation of the bishops, by establishing, in all the towns in Ireland, centres for the Propagation of the Faith. As an even more unrealistic alternative, he proposed that each of the 4,000 priests (there were in fact only 2,400 priests in Ireland in 1840) should contribute £4 each a year for a total of £16,000. The bishops would form the governing board of the college and supervise its administration at their annual meeting in Dublin each year. The professors and students, in addition to sharing the classroom together, would also share their meals and recreation. A College Council would be formed to maintain good order and strict discipline. Other matters discussed in Hand's plans were the rules for students, the horarium, the dress code and the advantage of the college being located in the city rather than in the country.[26]

Just what Murray's reaction to this proposal was is not known, but on 30 December 1840, Hand seized the initiative by circularizing the bishops with a printed letter announcing his purpose of establishing a missionary college under their patronage, and asking them for an opportunity of explaining his plan at their upcoming general meeting in Dublin in early February in the new year.[27] His petition was granted and Hand submitted his proposals to the assembled prelates on 5 February. No contemporary account of the interview has survived, but some latter-day reminiscences shed some light on the encounter and its issue. When Hand was asked 'how he could reasonably hope to raise £6,000 a year for the support of his College', he replied, 'I offer you the charity of Irish Catholics as my security.'[28] The bishops, however, were unimpressed and they flatly rejected his proposal. Years later, the Bishop of Meath, John Cantwell, who was very partial to Hand, reported on the reaction of the bishops. 'From what I saw and heard around me on the benches,' he explained, 'I am convinced that every Bishop except Dr. Murray and myself had the strange notion that the balance of Father Hand's reason was disturbed . . . and that his judgement could not be trusted in the affair.'[29]

Shortly after this crushing rebuff by the bishops on 5 February, Hand, undaunted, set out for Paris and Rome in pursuit of his dream. As he explained to Archbishop Murray on 13 February, he had already consulted with Paul Cullen and Nicholas Wiseman, rectors respectively of the Irish and English Colleges in Rome, about his *modus operandi*. 'Their advice,' he reported, 'is that I should visit the principal colleges of France and Rome and spend sufficient time to acquire a practical knowledge of the different systems of conducting such an establishment.' They also suggested, Hand added, that he should 'take down in writing everything likely to prove useful at the new institution about to be got up here . . .'.[30]

Hand arrived in Paris on 23 February, and spent the greater part of the next five months at the *grand seminaire* of St Sulpice in the Place de St Sulpice, and at its novitiate and house of studies, La Solitude at Issy, just outside Paris, living and learning about the way of life of their unique religious community.[31] He also visited the other missionary societies in Paris, such as the Saint Esprit and the Missions Étrangères, and took copious notes on their constitutions and regulations. In August, Hand set out for Rome via Lyons and Marseilles. At Lyons he visited the Association for the Propagation of the Faith, where he was deeply disappointed when he was informed that it was not the policy of the Association to make grants to help found missionary colleges. After visiting the Sulpician and Marist houses in Lyons, Hand set out for Marseilles, where he spent some ten days with the Oblates of Mary Immaculate before sailing for Cività Vecchia and Rome in late October.

He arrived in Rome on 2 November, where he spent the next three months in a fruitless attempt to gain an interview with Cardinal Fransoni, the Prefect of Propaganda. This was a very surprising turn of events, especially since Hand was the bearer of a sterling letter of recommendation from Archbishop Murray to 'their Excellencies the Cardinals and Prelates and other Ministers' in Rome,[32] and particularly because Fransoni had during this same period fulsomely endorsed Foley's college at Youghal. The problem appeared to be that Hand had failed to win the confidence of Cullen, while Foley had done so. 'The Rev. Mr Hand is here in Rome,' Cullen informed Archbishop Murray on 23 November, 'examining the missionary institutes of the City, but he has not yet made up his mind about what he is to do, and I fear he is not energetic enough to overcome all the difficulties, which he must, before he can realise his aims.'[33]

During the next ten weeks, Hand continued to mark time in Rome until fortuitously he was invited on 5 February 1842 to the annual festival in honour of St Agatha of the Goths, who was the patroness of the Irish College. The presiding guest of honour was Charles, now Cardinal Acton, who had just been raised to the Sacred College some two weeks before. On being introduced to the Cardinal, Hand explained what had brought him to Rome. Acton expressed considerable interest and explained that he was due to meet Cardinal Fransoni the next day, Sunday, at the Vatican. He promised to do all in his power to promote Hand's cause with the cardinal prefect. Acton was as good as his word and secured Hand an interview with Fransoni on 7 February, with Kirby in attendance. The prefect approved the project on the spot and asked Hand for a petition that he might present at the next Congresso, or meeting, of the cardinals of Propaganda for their formal approval. The Rescript, which followed on the approval of the cardinals of Propaganda and the Pope, was dated 28 February, and was as handsome an endorsement by the Holy See of Hand's dream as he could have possibly desired. The material points made in the Rescript addressed to Hand were:

> In view, therefore, of the assurance given in your petition that sufficient funds are available for the foundation of a mission house in Dublin, and of the hope you offer that many ecclesiastics will devote themselves to the work of the missions, the Sacred Congregation not only approves of the plan you propose but also commends it in every way . . .
>
> Therefore, as the Sacred Congregation recently declared in favour of the house at Youghal in the diocese of Cloyne and Ross, so now it declares in favour of this proposed house in Dublin: namely it gladly takes this house under its patronage and will leave nothing undone to aid it and promote its welfare.
>
> Finally, as a token of the highest honour and to give incentive to the furtherance of this admirable work, it is my happy duty to inform you that our Holy Father Pope Gregory XVI whole-heartedly approves of the

> plan to found this house and bestows on it his apostolic blessing, so that the work may issue in an abundant and fruitful harvest.[34]

After receiving from Hand the news of his extraordinary achievement in Rome, Archbishop Murray, who had occasion to write Cullen on 19 March, could not resist a reference to their differences over the character of John Hand. 'I perceive the good Mr Hand,' Murray observed, 'has succeeded thus far to his heart's content.' 'He looked so quiet,' Murray reminded Cullen, 'that you thought he had no energy. You can hardly have a notion of the energy and perseverance of that man.' 'If his future success,' the archbishop added prophetically, 'be equal to his energy, it will be great indeed.'[35]

Several months later, Cullen visited Ireland again in the early summer of 1842, and he wrote Kirby a long letter about what he had heard about both Fathers Foley and Hand. 'You asked me about Mr Hand. Everyone in Dublin (the vicars general among the rest) thinks he will not succeed.' 'The Bishops,' Cullen observed, 'do not like Mr Hand, and will not encourage him. However, he is very persevering, and perhaps contrary, to the opinion of the world he may succeed.' 'F. Hand,' Cullen then explained, 'has disagreed with the [Dublin] committee for the Propagation of the Faith. They called him to account for having stated to the Propaganda that he had *amplas pecunia in prompta* [sufficient funds available] as the rescript says, to begin the work, whilst really he had nothing but vague promises. He however thinks that with the approbation of Propaganda he will weather out the storm, and be able to get on.' 'Thus you see,' Cullen added pessimistically, 'things are not looking well – perhaps however *infirma mundi eletit Deus* [God chooses the weak of this world] in this instance, *ut confundet fortia* [so that he may confuse the strong].'

Cullen was even more pessimistic about the Cork college. In the same letter he told Kirby, 'I fear Foley's establishment is not going on as well as you imagined. I saw a most excellent priest, who had been lately there, and who is anxious for the success of the enterprise – but still he gave me information that makes me fear that F. Foley is not over prudent.' 'He has established,' Cullen explained, entering his bill of particulars, 'a penitentiary for disgraced females within a few yards of his college – a most dangerous experiment – he has also received students of very dubious character from distant parts of Ireland, without ever asking for a testimonial of their conduct from Priest or Bishop. This will destroy the name of his college.' He had heard that one of Foley's professors, Forbes, was about to leave 'in which case he has no one remaining fit to teach anything to the students. As an appendix to all this, it is reported there is an execution out against him for £700 – if all these things be true, there can be little reason to hope.' 'I will shortly go to see him,' Cullen promised, 'and then I will be able to write more decisively.' 'In the meantime,' he complained to Kirby, 'I fear it was a very dangerous thing to give him faculties to promote students to orders.''Many persons promoted in that way,' he warned, 'will never leave Ireland, and perhaps may occasion much confusion in the country. The Bishops, at all events, will be very jealous, for neither Dr. Foran nor Dr. Crotty was ever consulted on these matters.''It wd. be better,' he advised Kirby, 'not to be in too great a hurry about giving privileges and faculties in such cases. If things turn out badly, you will get a great blowing up. I was questioned several times about the privilege of ordaining lately granted, but as I knew nothing about it, everyone says it was you obtained it.''Don't say anything on these matters, however,' he finally cautioned Kirby, referring to Propaganda, 'until I shall have been in Waterford and Youghal when I will write to you again.' 'I fear,' he then concluded sadly, 'the foreign colleges will not be very successful.'[36]

Cullen was unable to visit Youghal for another ten weeks, and when he finally wrote to Kirby on 15 October, he was still not very sanguine. 'I called on F. Foley,' he reported. 'He has about 70 students in his house – his house is too small for so many and I fear there can be no discipline in it. He expects to have 100 in a short time.''I begged of him,' Cullen explained, 'not to increase his numbers – but if possible to reduce them to 30 or 40, and to educate them well.''Mr Forbes,' he pointed out, 'has left him. He has now a young Frenchman teaching theology, and I think he is badly provided altogether with professors. I fear the thing cannot go on well, unless a few good men join him.''If they write from Rome,' Cullen advised, 'it wd. be well to exhort him not to attempt so much to increase his numbers, and to promote discipline and instruction – it wd. be well also if he wd. consult the Bishops about the subjects he receives. They are all jealous of the way he acts.''I told all this to F. Foley himself,' Cullen noted in conclusion, 'and he sd. he wd. attend to my advice.''If you write,' he finally urged, 'give the poor man the same advice.'[37]

Kirby apparently did not write to offer Foley his advice for some three months, but when he did in late January 1843, he asked him to reply by return of post. The urgency of Kirby's letter was undoubtedly the result of newspaper reports by Frederick Lucas in the Catholic journal, *The Tablet*, that some of the young girls at Foley's refuge had not only become *ecstatica*, but *stigmata*, and that Foley, as their confessor, believed their cases to be genuine. 'Mr Lucas, the proprietor of the Tablet,' the parish priest of St Patrick's in Waterford city, John Sheehan, reported to Cullen on 24 January, 'is here working up subscribers'. 'There is a rumour,' he explained, 'of stigmata in Cork – but some Priests from Cork attended by Mr Lucas of the Tablet have visited the persons and they have declared their unqualified conviction that the credulity of the Confessor & Chaplain have been most shamefully imposed upon.'[38] Complicating matters even further, Foley had also written Cardinal Fransoni on 7 February, reporting the cases of the stigmata.[39]

'I have had,' Foley confessed to Kirby in his long reply on 12 February, 'sad & sore trials these last three months.'

> I had four or five students almost finished & had lost a good deal by them, two of them were from another College & highly recommended. But I afterwards got sad complaints of their conduct. Let who will ordain them, & let their friends accuse me. I dismissed them. I had 2 or 4 more preparing for Rt. Revd. Dr. Borghi, Bishop of Hindoostan. When they heard of the African [correctly – Indian] climate, they shuffled and did all they cd to get other Missions unknown to me. I did not like this underhand work no more than I liked the spirit they manifested to spread bad principles among the students of having [being able] to choose whatever Missions they like, so that when I had two Missions to offer them on the part of Propaganda to which they were to make a vow, they wd. not hear of a vow at all. When there was a ferment in the College I dismissed these lads also.

'I come now,' Foley finally reported, 'to the poor afflicted girls of that asylum which you yourself saw & which you so friendly visited,' adding, 'you are undoubtedly after reading flaming articles in the Tablet & & of them.' 'I have written,' he explained, 'to the good & illustrious Cardinal abt. them.'

> It is known that I have done so and nothing has struck terror into the hearts of the Protestants and bad Catholics and into the hearts of those who wish all this affair to be villainy & imposition than my having given publicity of the matter to Rome. At this moment the Protestants here are in great fury. Protestant & Catholic papers, particularly the Waterford Chronicle & and the Tablet, have raged against us.

'If they said,' Foley maintained, 'this was all the work of the Devil I wd. not feel much for it.' 'But their great argument,' he complained, 'is that these girls have needles or knives, or pins or something to open these wounds. It is true that the five wounds are open, but the most incredulous are confounded when they see no inflammation abt. the Stigmas.' 'Doctors,' he further assured Kirby, 'are equally astounded at this.'

> Yesterday Friday 10th inst. I had a doctor at mass. He sat near one of the girls. At the moment of the elevation [of the Host] her hands were raised upwards. As is usual with her at that hour, the back of the hand, that was just under the doctor's eye, bled from the Stigma . . . Then during the day she bled from these Stigmas two or three times.

'Whenever she goes to communion,' Foley finally insisted, 'her Stigmas bleed. Could the Devil do this.'[40]

Some six weeks later, on 1 April, Foley wrote to both Kirby and Fransoni again, going over much the same ground about the stigmata.[41] In his letter to Kirby, he further explained that his bishop, Bartholomew Crotty, had banished his poor females to the neighbouring diocese of Waterford, where Foley hoped 'they will have a more pious Clergy to protect them than where they were'.[42] Three weeks later, on 20 April, one of the curates in the parish of Youghal, Richard Smiddy, made an interesting entry in his diary, concerning the local uproar caused by the affair of the stigmata. 'There has been much said and written,' Smiddy observed, 'about certain females who were thought to be the subjects of miraculous appearances at the Rev. Mr Foley's castle.' 'From the commencement,' Smiddy maintained, 'I suspected that something wrong was going on, and now after the investigation instituted by the Bishop, there remains in my mind no doubt about as to its being a wicked imposition, got up by some villains in that place, for some purpose or other of their own.' 'It was perhaps unfortunate,' he added, 'that the thing was not exposed sooner, and suppressed, but it was not in our power to do so, as from the moment we manifested incredulity, we were not allowed an opportunity of examining the matter to our satisfaction, and could not, of course, therefore, denounce the proceedings.' 'The parsons,' Smiddy noted finally, 'who could not let such an opportunity pass, published a "Protest" against the "miracle" and, as usual, they took occasion to calumniate the Catholic Religion in general.'[43]

After receiving Foley's letter of 1 April, Kirby was requested by Cullen, when writing to Michael O'Sullivan, a very able and prominent Cork priest, to ask what was happening in Youghal. 'In answering to Dr. C's query about Foley's establishment,' O'Sullivan replied on 15 May, 'I regret to state that it has declined considerably, though not in my opinion from the affair of the Ecstatica, but from the want of professors'. 'These females,' he observed, 'have been removed to another part of the country, but still their strange appearances continue to manifest themselves.'[44] Over the next four and a half months, the college in Youghal continued to decline, and the reasons were not hard to find.

'I have abt. thirty boys,' Foley explained to Kirby on 2 October, 'still in the College. I can't at present take in more for want of means.' 'All the clergy will soon I hope join me,' he reported, 'but it is hard to find a friend among them when I have the Bishops against me, Dr. Crotty [of Cloyne] & Dr. Foran [of Waterford].' 'These girls,' he pointed out, 'are still in Dr. Foran's diocese. This good Bishop refused me faculties to hear the Confessions of the poor girls, who are now six months without confession, mass or communion.' 'Rev. Mr Sheehan himself,' he added, referring to the parish priest of Youghal, 'now confesses we are cruelly treated. He was one of the investigators and one of the best to oppose the rest.' 'One of the witnesses,' he further confided, 'who watched over the girls at the investigation told me lately that she wd. swear she saw the blood issuing clearly from the Stigmas, which circumstance she concealed not thro' malice, but by being bothered and puzzled by the questions the Examiners put to her. It is an undoubted fact that the Examiners, Bishops, and all have grossly handled this matter.' 'All here are believing now,' Foley insisted in conclusion, 'and are unmercifully condemning the Priests and Bishops who condemned these poor innocent victims who are now more wonderful than ever.' That same day, Foley wrote to Fransoni asking him to secure the Pope's protection for his two stigmata.[45] Fransoni, who obviously intended to ask Foley's bishop for more information, wrote mistakenly instead to the bishop of Galway on 21 October, who replied on 6 November that he knew nothing about the reputed ecstatics in his diocese.[46] This was to prove to be the last mention in the Propaganda correspondence of Foley or his college in Youghal.

In the meantime, Kirby had written to Foley again, explaining that he would prefer that the lay brothers Foley proposed to send to Rome should come by land through France rather than by sea. In his reply, Foley turned again to what obviously had become an obsession. 'Now I am certain,' he insisted, in what was to be his last letter to Kirby, on 2 November 1843, 'that the College will flourish when it is once proved that these poor, afflicted & banished girls are innocent and are let return home to their asylum.' 'Dr. Crotty,' he reported of his bishop, 'I am exceedingly sorry to say it – has lost common sense and common judgement on this subject.' 'Dr. Foran,' he then added more bitterly, 'is as bad if not worse than Dr. Crotty. Neither of these Prelates wd. come & see these girls themselves but remain prejudiced by the lying and calumnious reports of *Baron* [editor of the *Waterford Chronicle*] & *Lucas*.' 'I have no hopes,' Foley then concluded sadly and pathetically, 'but from the Propaganda where I expect justice will be done for me.'[47] Foley was obliged to endure his earthly purgatory for nearly five months more before he was released by death on 29 March 1844. The cause of his death is unknown, but, perhaps, it was not far from being of a bewildered and broken heart.

When Cullen had written to Kirby from Ireland in late July 1842 about the prospects of both Foley's and Hand's colleges, it will be recalled, he had pointed out that Hand was still only in the position of being able to promise an establishment. In September 1842, however, Hand finally founded his college by taking a lease of thirty-one years on a small estate of some thirty acres at an annual rent of £226 16s. It contained a very fine Georgian mansion, Drumcondra House, then just outside the Dublin city limits on the north side. Because the property had once been part of the pre-Reformation priory of All Saints, Archbishop Murray suggested that the ancient designation of All Hallows would be an appropriate name for the new college. Over the next several weeks Hand, with two colleagues and one student, took possession of the property. One of those colleagues, Bartholomew Woodlock, later wrote to his old Roman friend, Tobias Kirby, on 14 June 1843, when All Hallows had been established for more than a year and a half, giving him a long account of the beginnings of the community. 'At last we may say,' Woodlock began, 'it was opened on last All Saints' Day 12 months; three of us said Mass here on that day in the drawing room; we had no chapel; we had but one student; the house too, which is a very fine one, had been let go very much to ruin, and was in a very dilapidated state.' 'Our funds,' he explained, 'were also very small. Mr Hand had collected but a very few hundred pounds, and many predicted that before 6 months the College would be at an end.'

'Thanks be to God,' he piously added, 'who protected us, and to His B.

Mother who assisted us by her all-powerful intercession, it was not so.''We are here after almost 2 years,' he reported, 'without any penny of debt; with almost £2,000 in the bank, and with what is far better than all this, a body of students between 40 and 50, who thank God, are giving us great satisfaction.'

> We ourselves are six in number, supported, as you [are] aware, by the College, and living in Community, but receiving no salary; and we shall probably be nine or ten before the end of the year. Nearly all our students are destined for some particular mission, (of course, we receive none but such [as] intend to go on some foreign mission,) and we already opened communication, and are partially paid for students by Bishops in the 5 parts of the world. Six students went from this with Dr. O'Cliffe [coadjutor to the vicar apostolic of Calcutta], 4 of whom had been with us for some time; and Dr. Murray has kindly promised to come out at the beginning of next month to ordain 3 others for the Western District of Scotland.

'With regard to the management of the Students,' Woodlock pointed out, 'we have adopted in a great measure the plan of St. Sulpice in Paris; dining with them and mixing with them as much as possible even in the hours of recreation, and thank God, with a most happy result as at the same time, that they treat us with the greatest respect, they also treat us with the greatest freedom, and (as far as is compatible with our relative situations), almost as some of themselves.'[48]

Though Woodlock's account of the beginnings of All Hallows was generally accurate, it did mask some of the early difficulties concerning the nature and growth of the student body. The figures for matriculation, attrition and annual class size for 1842–50 are revealing.

TABLE XI[49]

YEAR	1842 2 months	1843	1844	1845	1846	1847	1848	1849	1850	TOTALS
MAT.	11	39	30	32	38	33	30	30	35	278
ATT.	7	6	9	15	17	12	9	17	11	103
M-A	4	33	21	17	22	21	21	13	23	175
% A	64	15	30	47	44	36	36	57	32	37
C-S	4	38	54	66	70	75	[77]	80	92	N.A.

Matriculation figures were relatively constant, averaging thirty-three students a year after the first year, but this is a far cry from that abundant supply of vocations predicted by those who had been enthusiastic about the founding of missionary colleges. Indeed, the high attrition rate of 37 per cent for 1842–50 also belied that prediction. The improvement, moreover, in class size from 38 to 92 between 1843 and 1850 represents a kind of statistical illusion because, theoretically, there could not have been any ordinations before the students had completed their required five-year course of study in 1847–8, and the increase in class size, therefore, was a function of those students who had survived the attrition rate between 1842 and 1847, but had not completed their course of studies. The figure of 92 for the class size in 1850, therefore, would have been even greater, had not many of the students, who matriculated between 1842 and 1847 come from other colleges, including at least sixteen of Father Foley's former students from Youghal and eight from various other colleges, where a number had already completed either their philosophy or some of their theology. Indeed, by the end of 1845, twenty-one students had been ordained and were serving abroad.[50]

One of the early disappointments suffered by Hand was a patent lack of expected demand for Irish missionaries. In the summer of 1842, before All Hallows opened, Hand had written to the bishops and vicars apostolic of America and the British colonies soliciting their adoption of his prospective students for their missions.[51] The overall response was negative, and many did not reply at all. A significant number of American bishops, surprisingly, pleaded poverty as their excuse, and only the bishops of Vincennes in Indiana and Hartford in Connecticut responded positively. The response from the British colonies was more encouraging. In reporting to Propaganda in September 1843, Hand explained he had thirty-eight students, and twenty-nine were assigned to foreign missions – five for the United States and twenty-four for Britain and the colonies, including seven for Madras, six for the Western District of Scotland, three each for British Guiana and Trinidad, two each for Calcutta and Sydney, and one for Agra.[52] Two years later, in 1845, fifty-five of the sixty-six students had been assigned to foreign missions – ten to the United States and forty-five to Britain and the colonies, with fifteen for India, eleven for Scotland, five for Trinidad, three each for Australia, Canada, British Guiana and Mauritius, and one each for England and Wales.[53] These figures, however, revealed another cleavage, besides that between the United States, on the one side, and Britain and her colonies on the other, and that was the distinction between the white and the non-white missions, soon to become much more significant in the history of the Irish foreign missions. In the figures cited above, for example, of the 55 assignments made in All Hallows in 1845 for the foreign missions, 29, or 53 per cent, were to white missions and 26, or 47 per cent, to non-white missions. Between 1866 and 1872, on the other hand, of the 266 All Hallows priests ordained for the foreign missions, 252 were for white missions, or 95 per cent, and only 14 for non-white missions. In a word, the world of Irish foreign missions in the nineteenth century was not only to be a post-Famine phenomenon, but it was to be a largely white, English-speaking one as well.[54]

Why did the 1840s prove so unpropitious a time for the Irish foreign missions when all the signs in terms of both the supply and the demand had been apparently so auspicious? The short answer, as is all too often the case in augury, was that the seers misread the signs, and the reality was lost in the appearances. The fact was that, during the decade of the 1840s and into the early 1850s, the demand for Irish missionaries was not yet a real one. That demand did not become real until the Famine and its aftermath resulted in the great diaspora of the Irish people to the whole of the English-speaking world. Moreover, the demand for Irish missionaries in the non-white and non-English-speaking world, either before or after the Famine, never really became significant until the early twentieth century, when the African missions and the Maynooth mission to China were launched.

Nova Scotia, Ireland and the British Empire in the Writings of Charlotte Elizabeth Tonna, 1829–46

CLÍONA MURPHY

Nova Scotia has been described as 'the oldest, most mature, and most susceptible of the British North American colonies to cultural influences from the mother country'.[1] This could also be applied to England's nearest colonial neighbour, Ireland. This paper focuses on the writer Charlotte Elizabeth Tonna (1790–1846), who visited both places and whose strong opinions on cultural influences, particularly where religion was concerned, were conveyed to her English reading public over the course of her two-decade writing career.[2] A series of articles on her visits (Nova Scotia, 1815–18, Ireland, 1819–24 and 1837), called 'By-Gone Days', appeared between January 1836 and June 1839 in *The Christian Lady's Magazine,* which she edited (1834–44). Ireland was also the focus of poems, religious tracts, and the travel reminiscences, *Letters from Ireland* (1838).[3] It also features in her autobiography, *Personal Recollections* (1841), and four novels.[4] Her writing skills equipped her to describe what she had observed and her religion, extreme Anglican evangelicalism, provided her with an interpretative framework.

Tonna was a prolific writer[5] and has received most attention in connection with her publications on the impact of industrialism; *Helen Fleetwood* (1841), *The Perils of the Nation* (1843) and *The Wrongs of Woman* (1843).[6] Although she has since been overshadowed by writers like Charles Dickens, Mrs Gaskill and Benjamin Disraeli, her writing was considered as significant in influencing factory legislation.[7] Her religious publications were popular in Britain and the United States,[8] going into many editions throughout the century, and have also been the focus of scholarly attention.[9] However, her reflections on the periods spent in Nova Scotia and Ireland, and her thoughts on their condition after she left, have been largely neglected.[10]

Historians of Ireland may have passed her over because her work has been lost in the plethora of travel writings by other English Protestants.[11] They have ignored the somewhat misleadingly named *The Christian*

Lady's Magazine, unaware that it is replete with information on Irish life, politics, economics and religion.[12] The virulent anti-Catholicism of *The Protestant Magazine* (which she also edited, 1841–6), can also obscure its historical content. The same could be said of Tonna's Irish novels with their Protestant, evangelical, imperial perspective and long theological ramblings. Nevertheless, they are rich in their portrayals of Ireland and support the claim, which has been made with regard to her industrial fiction, that she used novels as a 'structural device to heighten the reader's sympathetic understanding of the subject'.[13] Feminist historians may have been put off by her lack of enthusiasm for the 'cause' and her religious conservatism. Despite its name, *The Wrongs of Woman* is not a feminist work but rather a celebration of domesticity.[14] One imagines she should have been of greater interest to historians of the Orange Order since she regularly came to its defence and wrote poems in its honour, but this has not been the case.[15]

Histories of Nova Scotia, too, appear to have missed the value of her selective descriptions of its people and terrain, and her published work has merited only the odd footnote and a few mentions in specialist articles.[16] According to one writer, 'Few bibliographers of *Canadiana* seem to have recognized that she was once a resident of Nova Scotia.'[17] Perhaps, this was because her visit was brief, a little more than two years, and the sources are relatively obscure. Moreover, Nova Scotian historians are also faced with an abundance of travel tomes.[18]

Despite this neglect, Tonna's writings deserve some attention as the reflections of an educated, if somewhat bigoted, woman on two very different parts of the British Empire, both of which she regarded as colonies, though on distinct historical paths. Her world-view projects an image of the native peoples, the settler classes, and their place within the Empire that is common to both, especially in contexts where the Catholic Church is seen as the enemy.[19]

Her first husband, Captain George Phelan, of the 7th battalion of the 60th Rifle Corps, was the catalyst for Tonna's travels. She married him while he was on leave in London. When he was posted to Nova Scotia in 1815, she followed shortly, as she did when he went to Ireland, in 1819, to 'prosecute a law suit' concerning family land near Kilkenny.[20] While he was thus the initial reason for her going abroad, he seems to have had little influence on her, or even time with her, when she arrived and certainly not much impact on the memories she took away or on the opinions she formed. For most of the period in Nova Scotia, Captain Phelan was in the garrisons in Annapolis and Windsor while she stayed with friends. And, in Ireland, the couple appear to have been living apart as he 'was in Dublin for months together prosecuting his law-suit'.[21] When it concluded and he was posted to 'America', she remained in Ireland with her mother.[22]

She provides little detail about this marriage, which may have been doomed from the start since she resented taking on the Irish name 'Phelan'.[23] Some sources suggest that Phelan beat her.[24] In 1830, she wrote to the author of *Sketches of the Native Irish*, Christopher Anderson, 'I declare to you, that I now view the cruelties which imbittered [*sic*] my life, even from the altar, at the hands of a real native Irishman and his family, as part of the retributive justice of the Lord, – vengeance for the wrongs that my fathers did to his fathers and their country . . .'[25] As well as confusion in the sources concerning the circumstances of her marriage, there are conflicting opinions about when she left Ireland but it seems clear from her writings, and from observations of her contemporaries, that she left for England in 1824 and did not return to Ireland again until 1837.[26]

The time spent in Nova Scotia is detailed in the 'By-Gone Days' series, over several months in 1838 and 1839, and is discussed, briefly, in *Personal Recollections*.[27] An earlier insight appeared in letters written to and from Tonna, in a pamphlet published in Halifax in 1820. Later in life, she ordered her letters to be destroyed and may have been unaware that these (and those to Anderson) survived and were published. The pamphlet was written by the philanthropist Walter Bromley, a campaigner who wrote on behalf of the native people of eastern British North America.[28] The letters he included date from spring 1818. They show a vulnerable young wife, rather than the strident author, and record her immediate impressions in contrast to her later, structured interpretations written with the aim of providing moral lessons.

Writing twenty years later in *The Christian Lady's Magazine*, she describes her five-week trip across the Atlantic and her stays in Annapolis and Halifax.[29] Halifax Harbour is noted as 'a port of the very first importance to England'.[30] The extensive forests, colourful humming birds and fireflies are written about with great wonder. Her endeavours to cope with 'the violent transition of the seasons' are portrayed with a certain amount of humour.[31] More importantly, she also discusses her encounters with the English settlers and the native peoples, the Mi'kmaq, whom she (and others until recently) called 'Micmac'. She also referred to them as 'Indians' or 'Aborigines'. In the background are the Acadians, as well as French, Poles and Germans now in the British army (after being captured in Spain at the end of the Napoleonic Wars). She alludes to the 'Free Negroes' who lived in huts in the woods, many of whom had fled slavery in the United States.[32] This contact may have been formative in her later interest in Abolitionism.[33]

Tonna mixed with the top echelons of English colonial society in Halifax, including the Lieutenant-Governor, Lord Dalhousie. Looking back from 1839, she remembered his 'paternal kindness of two years incessant continuance'.[34] She was also friends with the Anglican Bishops Charles Inglis and Robert Stanser.[35] Of Stanser, she wrote to Bromley, in 1818, that 'My acquaintance extends but little beyond the family of the good Bishop', a curious statement considering how she remembered the Lieutenant-Governor years later.[36]

In Ireland, too, she managed to mix with the upper classes, listing Lord Mountsandford (who, like Lord Dalhousie, 'entered with a father's interest into all that concerned me'[37]), Lord Carrick, Lord Roden, Lord Mandeville, Lord Carbery, Lord Farnham and Lord Lorton among her acquaintances. A frequent visitor to Kilkenny Castle, she even had the key to let herself in by the side gate.[38]

According to her second husband, Lewis Hippolyte Tonna (twenty-two years younger; they married in 1841), Ireland was where she experienced her 'religious awakening'.[39] This meant, in effect, that she joined a minority group within the Anglican Church who believed in 'Vital Christianity' and who felt impelled to reach those outside the church.[40] After her separation from Phelan in the early 1820s (he died in 1837), she began to write for the Religious Tract and Book Society of Ireland, publishing religious pamphlets and moral stories for children, which went into many editions, with titles such as *The Hen and Her Chickens* (1827), *The Bird's Nest* (1827), *The Fortune Teller* (1829), *The Glow Worm* (1831) and *Good and Bad Luck* (1834).[41] She later moved on to more ambitious works. In particular, her experience of being in a house that was attacked by the Rockites in Knocktopher, Co. Kilkenny, resulted in the novel *The Rockite* (1829), which tells the story of Maurice Delany who eventually (like most of her protagonists) repents and converts.[42]

Her Irish publications reflect the mood of the 'Second Reformation' which endeavoured to convert the peasants of Ireland to the 'true church' and take up where the first Reformation failed.[43] She knew, through personal encounters or correspondence, most of the prominent evangelicals in the country before the Famine, including Archbishop Trench of Tuam, 'so lovely a character',[44] Henry Monck Mason, the secretary of the Irish Society, the Revd Charles Gayer on the Dingle Peninsula, the Revd Nangle in Achill,[45] the Revd Mortimer O'Sullivan,[46] and the Irish-speaking ministers the Revds Tomás Moriarity, John Gregg[47] and Charles Seymour.[48]

When she first came to Ireland she was determined 'not to like it – in plain terms, to hate the country, and to despise the people . . .'. However, this sentiment was short-lived: 'I left the country, as an exile leaves his home: I pined and drooped and still my heart yearns towards its beloved shores.'[49] When she returned in 1837, much to her delight by steam instead of sail, she toured several counties, beginning in Wexford and going through Dublin, Westmeath, Down, Armagh, Derry and Donegal. This trip resulted in *Letters from Ireland* (1838).

Catholic Emancipation was the defining event for Tonna who believed many 'perverse' government Acts grew out of it, including the introduction of national schools, the restrictions on tithes and the funding of Maynooth. For Tonna, Daniel O'Connell was 'this great apostle of evil'[50] and his name is prominent throughout her work, from mentions of the 1828 Clare election in footnotes in *The Rockite* to references in articles in *The Protestant Magazine* and *The Christian Lady's Magazine.* Indeed, she was vilifying him in the latter publication right up to her death in 1846. She followed his speeches in parliament with great intensity and one of them inspired her poem 'The Grave-Yard of Derry'.[51] When he turned up at the same anti-slavery meeting in London in 1840, she left in horror.[52] The Catholic archbishop 'the turbulent' John MacHale[53] ranked along with O'Connell in her disdain, as did 'the notorious' Bishop Doyle[54] and she was suspicious, too, of Father Mathew and his temperance movement.[55]

Tonna was opinionated and exuded a superior attitude towards her compatriots who did not have her travel experience and geographic knowledge. She complained of 'the ignorance that confounds the United States with the British provinces: all is *America*; that it is a very distant, barbarous country, the only civilized part of which is a flourishing republic' and claimed that 'beyond being able to point out on the map its situation, and to testify that it belongs to Great Britain, I find people in general alike ignorant and indifferent in all that concerns it . . .'.[56] She quotes a 'native of Nova Scotia' who asserted that the 'loyal, the thoroughly British provinces of Nova Scotia and New Brunswick, seem to be alike uncared for and unknown'.[57]

She had similar frustrations about the ignorance of English people concerning their neighbouring island; 'The ignorance prevailing with regard to Ireland, even among the most educated classes of society . . . is disgraceful and its betrayal in conversation . . . would be ludicrous were it not so lamentable.'[58] In a serialized, fictionalized autobiography of 'Terance O'Grady' in *The Protestant Magazine,* the protagonist wished 'the good Christian people of England had a better understanding as to the real case of their Irish neighbours'.[59] Tonna saw herself as providing that understanding as she hoped 'to remove an unfounded apprehension, or unjust suspicion, as to this lovely country and its interesting inhabitants'.[60]

However, she admitted that while she wandered around the grounds of Kilkenny Castle, in the early 1820s, she 'mused on days of Ireland's bygone greatness, though not then well read in her peculiar history . . .'.[61] But, by the time she published *Letters from Ireland* in 1838, she claimed to have 'a long and intimate acquaintance' with Sir Richard Musgrave's *Memoirs of the Different Rebellions in Ireland* (1801), which was formative in her belief concerning the culpability of Catholic priests in 1798.[62] Thomas Leland's History *of Ireland* (1775) and Sylvester O' Halloran's *A General History of Ireland* (1778) were also included in her reading.[63] Above all, there was Christopher Anderson's *Historical Sketches of the Native Irish and their Descendants* (1828), which she stated in 1836 'for six years has been our favourite guide'.[64] This is not surprising, as Anderson's outlook very much reflects Tonna's evangelical perspective. His book was also the source of statistics on the Irish language for evangelical groups who sought to convert Catholic peasants through that medium and his figures seem to provide the basis for Tonna's campaign for a chair of Irish at Trinity.[65] In their correspondence he wrote that he knew of her, had read some of her pamphlets and expressed the hope that' . . . if the Lord spare us, perhaps we shall be better acquainted before we meet on the streets of the heavenly Jerusalem'.[66]

In October 1839, Tonna began publishing a series of articles entitled 'Letters to A Friend', in *The Christian Lady's Magazine,* written by 'S.M.', whose aim was to 'search into Irish history'.[67] Among book reviews she included *Real Scenes in Irish Life* (April 1839), *Inquiries of an Irish Peasant Concerning Religion* (November, 1838) and Henrietta Chatterton's *Rambles in the South of Ireland* (July 1839). Tonna commended Henry D. Inglis's *Ireland in 1834*[68] and showed her familiarity with the travel literature by claiming that two-thirds of Baptist Wriothesley Noel's *Notes of a Short Tour through the Midland Counties of Ireland* (1837) was plagiarized from Inglis.[69]

Besides reading histories and travel works about Ireland, she also examined and published parts of 'Blue Books' and various parliamentary reports. This was in keeping with the research methodology she had already practised with regards to her industrial writings.[70] In 1836, she published a 'Selection of Parochial Examinations Relative to the Destitute Classes in Ireland' in *The Christian Lady's Magazine*.[71] Two years later she quoted extracts from the House of Lords 1,490-page investigation into Irish education with the purpose 'of treating our readers who may not have access to the books in question'.[72]

Researching Nova Scotia had proved to be more difficult. In a letter to Bromley in February 1818, she referred to the fact that she had read his 'excellent little treatise' on the Mi'kmaq.[73] He enclosed another unnamed pamphlet in his next letter, which was most welcome, as she later recalled, because reading material in Nova Scotia was scarce.[74] It was problematic, too, when she was living in England trying to research the history of the colony. However, she did discover that 'the early history of Nova Scotia possesses some remarkable features, highly illustrative of the wily devices of the Jesuits, who fought hard for supreme domination of the infant colony'.[75] Tonna acknowledged her debt to the first written history of the province, Thomas Haliburton's *Historical and Statistical Account of Nova Scotia* (1829), which she describes as the 'production of a patriot, a gentleman, and a man of sound sense'.[76] She may also have read Crosskill's *A Comprehensive Outline of the Geography and History of Nova Scotia,* published in 1838. While Crosskill does not mention her, he mentions her friend Lord Dalhousie, and his information on the Mi'kmaq is similar to what she published a year later in *The Christian Lady's Magazine.*[77]

There clearly was more literature available to her on Ireland and she had lived there twice as long as in Nova Scotia: not surprisingly it received a greater share of her attention. She admitted that, 'our readers . . . are in the habit of complaining (as we have been told by third parties) that Ireland occupies too prominent a place in this magazine'.[78] In January 1838 she characterized their complaints in the following manner, '"What! More of Ireland and the Irish?" Dear friend, yes. You do not know enough of them yet, not even if you be cradled in the very bosom of the Green Isle.'[79]

Tonna felt compelled to write both as an evangelical Anglican and as an enthusiast for the British Empire. Hindus in India, transportation to Australia, the slave trade and the overstretched resources of the British navy were all topics that concerned her. Nova Scotia and Ireland were seen by her as dependencies requiring nurturing and interference by the 'mother country'. The native peoples had to be saved from their own barbarism and from the ambitions of the Roman Catholic Church.

However, she also referred to Ireland as the 'sister country' or 'sister island', indicating the confusion many English had about their relationship with Ireland.[80] The fact that she addressed herself to the 'English reader' reinforced the idea that the indigenous peoples were the 'Other'.[81] An air of imperial responsibility permeates her work: 'Among our vast colonial possessions I know of none advancing such manifold claims of our sympathy, as the British settlements in North America.'[82] She also spoke of the 'Debt of our Duty' toward Ireland and wrote in 1835 that 'Ireland calls for no small proportion of our sympathy'.[83] This sense of 'duty', evangelical and imperial, influenced her perceptions of both the native peoples and the colonial settlers.

The indigenous people Tonna met in Nova Scotia, the Mi'kmaq, are described three years later in terms reminiscent of Chateaubriand's version of the 'noble savage' in *René* (1801), but with reservations. Strong visual images are conjured up when she writes of 'the swarthy Indian, shooting his light elegant canoe along the surface of the stream, or bartering his simple merchandize of fish, moose venison, or sugar drawn from the sweet maple'; or 'the squaw, his spouse, with her bright-eyed papousie suspended at her back, in its coffin-shaped habitation of birch-bark'.[84] A passage describes the Mi'kmaq, dressed in deep blue, emerging out of the thick forest, trekking across the white snow, wearing snow-shoes and carrying moose meat.[85] The accuracy of her portrayals had been endorsed by Bromley; 'her letters are replete with pious and benevolent sentiments, and the picture she has drawn of our Indians, is too correct to be doubted by anyone'.[86]

According to Paulette Chiasson, by the late 1820s 'the largely favourable descriptions of the Micmac and his ability to survive the rigours of the North American climate were being supplanted by extensive criticism of the Micmac lifestyle'.[87] Tonna's largely positive depiction had a religious basis. While she had great admiration for the English settlers in Nova Scotia, she admitted that 'the only fault I had to find with them was their indifference towards the poor relics of the Indian race still dwelling in the woods . . . ' and added that 'The Indians are wholly despised; scarcely looked on as the same race, by the generality of the colonies'. She observed that Lord Dalhousie, 'scarcely could succeed in stirring up a momentary interest for the dispersed Aborigines . . . what between lukewarmness on one side, and suspicion on the other, he found himself completely baffled'.[88] A conclusion she came to in Nova Scotia, reinforced in the years that followed, was that the indigenous people were 'the offspring of Israel's scattered tribes'.[89] She wrote to Bromley, 'many unequivocally Jewish customs . . . prevail among them, even to this day, with their striking resemblance of countenance to the ancient people of God . . .'.[90] The 'Jewish–Indian theory' was one which surfaced at various times over the centuries and was used by different groups to suit their agendas.[91] For Tonna, it was a way of claiming the Mi'kmaq back into the fold and away from the Catholic missionary competitors; 'the poor aborigines of Nova Scotia occasion me a most bitter pang, when I reflect on the fact of their being all at this moment under the bondage of the worst enemy to Israel and her king – Popery'.[92] In 1839, she strongly recommended that the evangelical effort that had been tried in Ireland be put into effect in Nova Scotia, 'that individuals brought to receive the light of the gospel' be 'sent back to their native brethren with the message of peace . . . rendered acceptable by being breathed in their own accents'.[93]

Tonna claimed to be familiar with the social mores of the Mi'kmaq. She was annoyed when she learnt from a friend, in 1839, 'that some lady . . . had been writing a book wherein she adduces my dear old friends the Squaws of British America, as a triumphant elucidation of the [feminist] "system"'. She had not seen the book, nor did she intend 'wasting any time upon it . . . but the idea of a despotic Squaw in a Wigwam was to me so exceedingly new, so absurdly opposed to all that I ever witnessed or heard of among the Indian race . . .'. She concluded that 'the squaws . . . bright eyes would dilate with wonder, not unmixed with ridicule, could they hear themselves cited as specimens of female aggrandizement over the male sex . . .'.[94] She felt confident in making such assertions because she 'enjoyed a high place in the affections and confidence of those interesting people'. This 'affection' was the result of her taking care of an injured Mi'kmaq for a few weeks after he had been 'wounded by a party of our soldiers, and left to perish in the woods'.[95]

Such apparent familiarity with the indigenous people is also evident in her writings on the Irish peasants. However, for Tonna, the native Irish were the furthest thing possible from the 'noble savage' and were living in pitiable conditions, residing in holes in the ground and in smoke-filled huts made out of turf. She describes one such dwelling in *The Rockite* as

> low, long, and very narrow: a rude partition of sticks and sods of turf screened off a portion of it, a coating of mud, laid in patches, at once strengthened the walls and concealed their substance. Large stones

> appeared to occupy the place of tables; while seats were provided by loose bundles of bog-wood, and little heaps of turf. The latter, indeed, seemed to answer all domestic purposes; for crumpled very small, and mixed with dead leaves, it formed the only substitute for beds throughout the dwelling; of which in all probability, it served both for foundation and superstructure. Nothing resembling a fire-place was to be seen, nor a single utensil for cooking. A large broken pitcher stood in one corner, and near it what seemed to be the remains of a milk pail.[96]

The misery of such living conditions is also conveyed in a passage in *Personal Recollections*:

> Our property consisted of a large number of poor cabins, with their adjoining land, forming a complete street on the outskirts of town, which was greatly in arrear [*sic*] to the head landlords, and a periodical 'distress' took place. On these occasions a keeper was set over the property; some legal papers were served, and the household goods, consisting of iron kettles, wooden stools, broken tables, a ragged blanket or two, and a little store of potatoes, the sole support of the wretched inhabitants, were brought out, piled in a long row down the street, and 'canted,' that is, put up to sale, for the payment of, perhaps, one or two per cent of the arrears. This horrified me beyond measure . . .[97]

However, just as the Mi'kmaq are portrayed as rather charming in their canoes or plodding through the snow, so, too, the Irish peasants could be picturesque. In her *Recollections*, she describes how

> On that great festival of the peasantry, St. John's Eve, Mr C. resolved on giving his tenants and neighbours a treat that should also enlighten me on one of their most singular relics of paganism. It is the custom at sunset on that evening to kindle numerous immense fires throughout the country, built like our bonfires, to a great height, the pile being composed of turf, bog-wood, and some such other combustibles as they can gather. The turf yields a steady, substantial body of fire, the bog-wood a most brilliant flame: and the effect of these great beacons blazing on every hill, sending up volumes of smoke from every point of the horizon, is very remarkable. Ours was a magnificent one, being provided by the landlord as a compliment to his people, and was built on the lawn, as close beside the house as safety would admit . . . The fire being kindled, a blaze shot up, and for a while they stood contemplating it, with faces strangely disfigured by the peculiar light first emitted when bogwood is thrown on: after a short pause the ground was cleared in front of an old blind piper, the very *beau-ideal* of energy, drollery, and shrewdness, who seated on a low chair, with a well plenished jug within his reach screwed his pipes to the liveliest tunes, and the endless jig began . . . An Irish jig is interminable, so long as the party holds together; for when one of the dancers is fatigued, a fresh individual is ready to step into the vacated place quick as thought; so that the other does not pause, until in like manner obliged to give place to a successor. They continue footing it, and setting to one another,

> occasionally moving in a figure and changing places, with extraordinary rapidity, spirit and grace. Few indeed among even the lowest of the most impoverished class have grown into youth without obtaining some lessons in this accomplishment from the travelling dancing masters of their district . . .[98]

But such festivities were in contrast to the daily drudgery of the peasants' lives. When she attempted to explain their miserable living conditions, she blamed not the land system, but Daniel O'Connell and the money he squeezed out of the peasants through the Catholic Association and the Repeal movement. The Catholic clergy, too, bore the blame, with their excessive fees and promotion of superstition; 'popery holds our poor sister in an iron chain'.[99] Moreover, the priests' power was enhanced by a subservient parliament. In 1839, she concluded that

> Having yielded political power to the clamour of their flock, we immediately conceded to the priests whatever they pleased to demand, or to accept, at our hands. The government grant was withdrawn from scriptural schools, and all money, all the patronage conferred on a system of education, of which the certain issue, if not the intentional drift, is to deliver the whole rising generation into the hands of the Papacy.[100]

While the native Nova Scotians were, according to Tonna, part of the lost tribes of Israel, the native Irish had lost their way more recently. In her version of history, their ancestors had belonged to the true church which had been corrupted by continental Catholicism and had not undergone the purification of the Reformation. She was echoed in such books as Monck Mason's *History of the Origins and Progress of Irish Society* (1844) and MacWalter's *The Irish Reformation Movement* (1851).[101] The solution to this clerical grip on the peasantry was a concerted evangelical effort and she was involved in supporting evangelical Anglican societies, such as the Irish Society, which sought to convert peasants, particularly through the Irish language. This crusade took on a personal aspect when she adopted a deaf mute boy called, wonderfully, Jack Britt, and took him to England with her in 1824.[102] She frequently used his road to conversion and his 'concern' for the Catholic Irish back home to urge readers to support missionary efforts in Ireland. Her time with Jack Britt extended over a greater period (he died in 1831) than with the injured Mi'kmaq – but there was the same sense of patronage of the disadvantaged native.

The scale of Irish immigration into England meant that, in a sense, Tonna never left Ireland. While she was living in London in the 1830s, she worked closely with the Irish Society and was active in setting up a church and schools in St Giles in London. She raised significant amounts of money through *The Christian Lady's Magazine* to support the project and brought Irish-speaking preachers to the capital.[103] She frowned upon missionaries who preferred to go to more exotic locations when there was a need closer to home; 'few are the missionaries who will step fifty yards out of their daily path to exalt the light of the gospel among the dark abodes of wretched St. Giles'.[104] She told a missionary who had studied to go to India 'that language [Irish] was not a whit less attainable than Hindostanee'. Besides imposing her evangelical views on the London Irish, she also expressed concern for the spiritual welfare of migrant Irish workers who laboured in the hop fields in Kent. In 1837, she raised money to send an 'Irish teacher' to them. 'We summoned our trusty Irish teacher, and providing the necessary sum for his journey of some thirty-five miles, requested him to go and try what he could do among those lost sheep of the fold of Erin.'[105]

There is a scene in *The Deserter* (1836) where Irish-speaking harvest workers are gathered together in a barn in the English countryside to listen to the Bible being read to them in their native language. O'Brien, the protagonist, found that 'his heart [was] penetrated by the persuasive sound of a language inexpressibly dear to it'. In the evening he spoke to the other men in the lodging house about the meeting. While some denounced it as an attempt to turn them from their religion, 'Still it was Irish, and proved a sufficient inducement to overcome the scruples of many . . .' All agreed to tell their countrymen on neighbouring farms about 'the opportunity afforded of hearing a very fine book in their own tongue'. O'Brien was asked by the steward who hired him,

> 'Speak truly and honestly, do you think that they would not pay equal attention to that man, if he was reading an English Bible?'
>
> 'I think not, sir. It is not the book that takes their minds, so much as the language.'
>
> 'Why so?'
>
> 'Partly because they understand it so much better; and partly, because they love it a great deal more.'[106]

This fictional representation of the proselytizing hopes of Tonna (and the Irish Society) is somewhat undermined by an actual teacher's report to her that one of his readings in Irish was interrupted when 'some bad one came up with a club, and said he would run it down my throat if I did not cut away. What brought such a turn-coat as I was to delude them, or strive to draw them from the religion of their forefathers?'[107]

When Tonna was writing about her experiences abroad, she lived in an England that she believed was being undermined from within, and this coloured her writing on Ireland and Nova Scotia. While she supported certain causes lead by evangelical Anglicans like Michael Sadler and Lord Ashley (reforming the factory system)[108] and William Wilberforce (abolition of slavery), she was opposed to many other movements. As well as being appalled by a parliament which granted Catholic Emancipation, she was disappointed with an increasingly liberal Anglican Church (which she often contemplated leaving).[109] She was contemptuous of the Chartists, and their

Irish leader Feargus O'Connor, and of the Utopian Socialists and Robert Owen.[110] Her anti trades-union stance is apparent in her novel *Combination* (1832), which depicts the unfortunate circumstances that befall the Reily family who emigrated from Ireland to the city of 'M.' and joined a 'combination' or trades union.

In 1831, she wrote to a Miss Ould, 'These are days of great and increasing gloom, and I fear the cloud will burst both over us in England and over our beloved green isle also.'[111] Her pessimism is still apparent in 1834, when she writes, 'But, alas for England! A spirit of blindness has fallen upon her and under its influence she pursues a course of inevitable self-destruction.'[112] This opinion was reinforced as the decade continued. She opposed what she saw as concessions to Catholics in the Canadas after the rebellions of 1837–8[113] and in 1840 she pointed to the 'awful proof of what misgovernment is doing in Ireland by its wicked connivance with popery'.[114]

This gloom (a word she frequently used) led her to idealize the English settlers and their descendants in the colonies. She reversed the usual colonists' ideal of 'home'. For her, the 'Englishness' and loyalty of the settler classes were all the more admirable because the people at 'home' were not living up to the ideal. She wrote, 'No place could be more thoroughly English in feelings, habits and principles than Nova Scotia.'[115] Part of the reason for their 'Englishness', she believed, was that settlers there were not contaminated by liberal ideas coming from 'our frivolous continental neighbours . . . they preserve the old English character far better than it is now preserved in the mother country'.[116] Indeed, 'Nova Scotia is, I firmly believe, the most generally and devotedly loyal of all our colonies: the attachment of its people to the mother-country is beautiful; and their partisanship in all questions between us and the United States most zealous.'[117] In 1839, she wrote of a young Nova Scotian friend who had recently arrived in England using the expression 'since I came home', and she regretted that England did not better appreciate 'such loyal, gallant hearts'.[118]

The 'Englishness' of these settlers is also remarked upon in other contemporary travel accounts: 'The general society of Halifax . . . appeared to be more like that of an English seaport town, than any we had met with since leaving home.'[119] However, the impression of Englishness that Tonna and others associated with Halifax was a reflection of the company they kept. Had the Acadians, Scottish, Irish and Blacks been part of their social *milieu*, perhaps their conclusions on the general outlook of Nova Scotians would have been different.

Tonna's admiration for 'English' settlers in Nova Scotia paled beside her view of their counterparts across the Atlantic, 'a body of men having been found unalterably true to the church and to the throne, not only above suspicion, but relied on as the very sinews of English dominion in Ireland'. Anglo-Irish Protestants and Protestant converts were, in her mind, in a far worse plight than the comfortable Anglicans in Halifax. They were in a state of crisis. She wrote, 'Among ourselves Protestantism is menaced: in Ireland, Protestants'.[120] When funding was reduced for Anglican clergymen as a result of government Acts in 1833 and 1838, she perceived it as 'the attempt literally to STARVE [her capitals] the Protestant clergy at their posts' and she conducted a fundraising effort in *The Christian Lady's Magazine* to help these men and their families.[121] The Protestant clergymen and Anglo-Irish landlords with whom she was acquainted were praised for their benevolence, despite the obstacles posed by secret societies and Catholic authority figures. Tonna concedes that absenteeism was indeed a problem, but mainly because it gave more power to the priests. She wrote that after the Union when many of 'Ireland's Protestant Aristocracy' moved from their 'tall spacious houses in Sackville Street' and went to London, their land

> was left in the hands of agents, who at best could have no such feeling of personal interest in it and its poor tenants as would belong to the proprietor: and the people, roused from a state of passive idleness to one of active mischief, were wholly abandoned to the operations of the popish priesthood . . .[122]

She could, on occasion, sound more radical, declaring in 1830, for example, that she 'must confess that although reckoned a desperate Orangewoman, I am kindled into something like rebellion when I view the series of oppressions by which the lords of the soil have been goaded. I would almost compare them [Irish peasants] to American Indians, kept in barbarism for reasons best known to the colonists. I can truly affirm that the most obstinate enemies to the Irish aborigines are among those who revel in the fat of the land.'[123]

However, in a series of articles called 'Politics', four years later, which supposedly was a monthly report of conversations her 'uncle' had with others about contemporary issues, she again outlines the ideal role of the landlord in religious terms.

> Next, let every landholder who really feels the importance of the crisis, exert himself, both by example and by precept, to draw others into the same patriotic combination, and steadily remain at his post, overlooking his own tenantry, putting down the spirit of insubordination, as far as his power extends, encouraging works of public utility, that may employ the hands of the redundant priesthood. To this, as a matter of infinite moment, must be added the establishment of scriptural schools, where the best antidote is provided for that poison, which the infant peasantry inhale with the very breezes that freshen their land. And, by way of finale, let us have an Irish professorship in Trinity College.[124]

While she recognized that there were problems with some landlords and made such recommendations for their improvement, her support of the loyal Protestants in the Orange Order underscores the point that she regarded true loyalty and patriotism as lying outside the imperial centre. In *Derry: A Tale of Revolution* she established a glorious past for the Protestants of the city. According to her, the Orange Order was 'the strongest earthly prop of the British throne in their country', and 'the expression [the Orangeman] really means something good, loyal, and thoroughly Protestant'.[125] Her admiration is conveyed in her poems 'The Orangeman's Submission', 'Maiden City', 'No Surrender' and 'The Grave-Yard of Derry'.[126] This admiration did not go unrecognized. When she visited Derry in 1837, she was made an honorary member of the Apprentice Boys.[127]

While she mainly wrote about these locations separately, there are numerous parallels between Tonna's depictions of Nova Scotia and Ireland. The demography of both was simplified into that of native peoples, the settler or English class, and troublesome priests. In both she envisaged saving the native peoples, not just in terms of rescuing their souls for eternity but, more specifically, saving them from the Catholic Church in the present. She recommended that the policy already in place in Ireland – converting the natives through their own language – also be put in place in Nova Scotia. However, there was a certain contradiction between her view of England as having the responsibility of spiritually protecting the native peoples, and her concern about a parliament that was becoming more lenient with regard to Catholic entitlements.

Despite their simplifications and biases, her writings are of some historical value and should not be dismissed because she was a bigot. Whether she was describing the Mi'kmaq, the Halifax gentry, O'Connell's latest antics in parliament or the bravery of the Orangemen, she brought those worlds to her readers and made it part of their *Zeitgeist*. Although she occasionally read *The Tablet*[128] and other Catholic publications, she remained, like her Catholic opponents, intellectually within a separate public sphere and she helped shape and reinforce its beliefs. Her writings not only reflected certain moments in history, but they also endeavoured to reshape the past and direct the future in a way that made sense to her public, which shared her conservative, imperialistic and evangelical views.

Young Ireland in Cork, 1840–49

MAURA CRONIN

'There is no such party as that styled Young Ireland,' snapped Daniel O'Connell in July 1845 in the course of a heated exchange with Thomas Davis.[1] In this he was at once both correct and mistaken. Young Ireland was never separate from O'Connellism until 1847, and yet it was much more than a ginger group within a larger movement. It was a way of thinking, of reacting (sometimes unreasonably) against the ideas of the past, and of challenging political realities with political ideals.

What was true of Young Ireland island-wide was particularly evident in the experience of that group in Cork city, where the tensions of the 1840s can be variously interpreted in terms of social class, political ideology, family rivalry and unashamed scrambling for the perks of office. This was a new era in Irish urban politics. In Cork, as elsewhere, the successive reforming measures of Catholic Emancipation (1829), parliamentary reform (1832) and municipal reform (1840) had driven Protestant society into a position of permanent political minority, replacing it with a (largely) Catholic élite characterized by all the self-confidence of the *arriviste*.[2] But such self-confidence did not go unchallenged, either by those sub-groups that had failed to make it into office under the new dispensation, or by those within the élite whose age, educational background and ideological bent made them question their own recent heritage.

Young Ireland in Cork originated within this latter group – the sons (and, to a lesser extent, daughters) of the successful élite that had helped to displace political Protestantism in the city over the previous two decades. They belonged to the lower levels of mercantile society and the higher ranks of retailing. Denny Lane, for instance, was the son of a distiller, Charles Denham Murphy belonged to the prominent brewing family; Michael Joseph Barry was a merchant's son; the Varian brothers, Isaac and Ralph, were manufacturers; and Felix Mullan was proprietor of a hardware establishment. Their potential mobility out of the world of business into the professions, via medical and legal training, was as important as their family and social *milieu*. Though Lane was destined for the family business, he moved beyond the Cork commercial scene through his education in Trinity College and the King's Inns. Like Michael Joseph Barry, he was called to the Bar and though neither subsequently practised law, their Dublin experiences both in the Repeal Association and, more particularly, in the immediate coterie of Thomas Davis and the Trinity Historical Society, introduced them to a world of ideas foreign to the Cork mercantile world from which they came.[3] Both Lane and Barry were part of the circle from which the *Nation* newspaper emerged in 1842, and when they returned to Cork at indeterminate times between 1839 and 1843, they brought back with them the *Nation*'s philosophy.[4]

Their impact on the Cork political scene was initially minimal and for at least three years after the foundation of the *Nation* there was little or no public awareness of the existence of a body called Young Ireland, whose activities were largely confined to poetry writing, and then under cover of pseudonyms.[5] However, they remained in constant correspondence with the Dublin circle, Lane corresponding with Davis, and Michael Joseph Barry with Smith O'Brien, on affairs in the southern city. From this correspondence it was clear that the Cork Young Irelanders were *au fait* with the issues threatening to alienate Davis's group from the mainstream Repeal Association, but also that these issues had little impact on the political scene in Cork. Although Barry criticized the financial affairs of the Repeal Association in October 1844, and Denny Lane clashed with O'Connell at a private dinner over the integrity of Young Ireland, such incidents had little or no public impact.[6] Similarly, there was very little local controversy about the Colleges Bill, for although there were differences of opinion among O'Connellites on the question of religious teaching in the proposed colleges, the exchanges were remarkably good humoured.[7] Even the Repeal issue, despite the great popular excitement in 1843, did not become a vital part of Cork politics until 1845 when, for the first time, a distinction was drawn in the local press between 'Repealers' and 'liberals' (i.e. O'Connellites in favour of reform but not of Repeal), and the question of accepting only pledged Repealers for public office became a serious proposition.[8] It was only when there was a convergence of sectional tensions, some local, some national, that the Cork Young Irelanders found themselves forming a clearly defined group. One tension was the increasingly bitter controversy between O'Connell and his younger followers concerning the moral justification of the use of force – a controversy culminating in the drafting of the divisive 'Peace Resolutions' in July 1846. By itself, this largely theoretical issue would hardly have greatly influenced the course of Cork local politics. The other – and far more important – tension, which decisively split O'Connellism in Cork and brought the Young Ireland group into the open, centred not on abstract principles but on complex rivalries within the O'Connellite political élite in the city.

From the early 1830s, the control of Cork city politics, as in other Irish urban centres, had been fought for by three main groups. Firstly, there were the Tories, progressively undermined by political reform. In the second group were those supporters of O'Connell who sought an acceleration of the reform process, but who wished to maintain the Union, while the third group was comprised of those O'Connellites who sought both increased reform and the repeal of the Union. Though the latter two groups were linked by their loyalty to O'Connell and together regarded the Tories with undisguised animosity, they also regarded one another with considerable suspicion. This was the case since Repeal, first mooted in the early 1830s, met two contrasting responses from the more prosperous merchants on the one hand and the artisan and retailer element on the other.[9] The latter combination, reflecting contemporary British working-class radicalism, equated Repeal with reform, self-help and political rectitude and pushed for the dissolution of the Union on every possible occasion.[10] The mercantile element, on the other hand, consisted of those liberal merchants who, in the 1820s, had withdrawn from the Tory-dominated Committee of Merchants in order the form their own politico-economic body, the Chamber of Commerce. A mixed denominational group which included Catholics, Protestants and Dissenters, the Chamber of Commerce was characterized by O'Connellite religious tolerance and political pragmatism. They put economic advancement before any abstract patriotism, and were more than ready to waive Repeal if the commercial interests of Cork demanded it.[11] Between these two groupings there was constant wrangling, and the tensions became even more aggravated after the election in 1841 of a new town council under the provisions of municipal reform. O'Connellites (both reformer and Repealer) flooded the council, carrying seven of the eight city wards and leaving the Tories in a minority of seven seats in a total of sixty-four.[12]

The O'Connellite victory was not, however, as complete as it at first appeared, for the internal divisions hitherto hidden from the public now came squarely into the open on the prominent stage of the new town council. The new councillors belonged mainly to the merchant, manufacturing and professional classes – a predictable result in a system opening local government only to citizens possessed of £1,000 per annum above debt. But it excluded from office a large number of politically aspiring individuals from among those retailers, master craftsmen and unionized journeymen who had long regarded the Chamber of Commerce with suspicion and had, since the mid-1830s, organized themselves in the Cork People's Hall.[13] This vocal group had doggedly (though unsuccessfully) pressurized public representatives into declaring for Repeal and pushing it in the political arena, and their sense of exclusion following municipal reform was compounded by the new town council's lukewarm attitude on a number of issues prioritized by the People's Hall – the abolition of Ministers' Money, the establishment of an Irish Manufacture Mart for the city, and – above all – the issue of Repeal of the Union.[14]

However, for the city's O'Connellite élite, the uncertain benefits of

Repeal had, as in the two previous decades, to be weighed against the more tangible advantages of reform within the context of the Union. Like O'Connell himself, they were pragmatists – though perhaps in an economic rather than a political sense – and by the 1840s many of them were convinced that the benefits of O'Connell's 'Whig Alliance' in general, and of the upward mobility provided by municipal reform, in particular, was far preferable to the uncertainties of political agitation for the elusive Repeal. As one die-hard Repealer (himself a merchant and a veteran of the Emancipation agitation of the 1820s) summed it up in a letter to O'Connell:

> There is great indisposition on the part of the people who may be called the middle classes to join in agitation for the Repeal. This is chiefly grounded on the conviction that its attainment is impracticable . . . We have no lawyer now amongst us who will speak a word on the subject . . . There are offices for public prosecution, clerkships of the peace and of the Crown to be occasionally given away, and a repealer solicitor . . . will be as far from fitting one of them as Yorick's head was from fitting a mitre . . . It is true that these observations do not apply to the humble classes of the people. They have never tasted nor do they expect to taste the fruits of public employ, and they will be as ready to hurrah for Repeal as ever . . . If you were here and called a meeting, a house large enough to contain your apparent adherents could not be procured. When you would have gone away, away also would go the steam of Repeal.[15]

It was in this atmosphere of disgruntlement with the urban élite's political caution on the Repeal issue that there emerged into the open the Young Ireland group centred on the two 'young repeal barristers', Denny Lane and Michael Joseph Barry. They did not emerge alone, but as one of two new forces in Cork urban politics, the other and larger being the newly enfranchized burgess body, drawn from the city's retailers – pawnbrokers, tobacconists, vintners and grocers. In 1841 these had formed the Cork Burgess Association, ostensibly to help the town council revise the burgess lists, but really to remove control of the council from the Chamber of Commerce merchants and transfer it to the ratepayers.[16] These two groups joined ranks with the People's Hall to attack the reformed town council and the Chamber of Commerce on a number of Repeal-related issues, ranging from the financing of the city's Repeal Reading Room to the debate over federalism, and finally centering on the demand for a Repeal pledge from candidates for public office.[17] The pledge issue, something of a hardy annual in Cork politics since the 1830s, caused a furore among the city's public men. Most objected vehemently to the pledge as excessive electoral control. Others agreed with the pledge in the case of parliamentary representatives, but were less certain of its desirability on local boards where the main issues were commercial rather than political. Members of parliament, particularly the chameleon-like Dan Callaghan, who represented the city since the early 1830s, managed to avoid the pledge, but popular pressure was less easily avoided in municipal government and in early 1843 a number of town councillors had been pushed (some willingly, some not) to take it.[18]

It was this pledge rather than the 'peace resolutions' which proved the flash-point in Cork politics, driving a final wedge between the mainstream O'Connellites and Young Ireland and their supporters. The issue came to a head in the summer of 1846 following the appointment of new members to the Cork Harbour Commission. Most of this body's thirty-four members were nominated by the town council. Under Tory control before municipal reform, the Harbour Commission passed into the hands of the O'Connellites, but it seems that neither before nor after 1840, had it been considered a political body and, at least in theory, no man suitable for office had ever been excluded on political grounds.[19] As the demand for a Repeal pledge for public representatives grew, however, this 'non-political' appointment system came under attack and when, in June 1846, a majority of the town council, elected four non-Repealers to the Harbour Commission, the issue came to a head.[20] Those who supported the controversial vote, many of them pledged Repealers themselves, defended their vote on the grounds that no Repealers were available to fill the vacant places on the Harbour Board, and that, as a matter of principle, politics and commerce should be separate – a stance that infuriated the Repealer groups centred on the People's Hall. The ensuing show-down between the council on the one hand and the People's Hall and its allies on the other was politically significant for a number of reasons. Firstly, it brought to a head the long-standing tensions between the city's new élite and the frustrated O'Connellite out-groups. Secondly, it brought into focus the dilemma facing Cork's mercantile O'Connellites who, not for the first time, had to choose between elusive political principles and complex economic realities. Thomas Lyons, a veteran Repealer and one of those attacked following the Harbour Board debacle, put clearly his fears regarding the stand taken by the People's Hall:

> These few demagogues in the course they are pursuing would destroy the trade and commerce of the city, and our municipal institutions . . . Being at length convinced . . . that by aiding these mad people in their projects, I would ultimately bring ruin on our trade, our only stay in Cork, I felt bound to give way to reason and join the more prudent and well-thinking . . . Surely the trade of Cork need not be sacrificed to the glorious cause of Repeal . . . If unfortunately the people go on in their present course, the Conservatives will rule Cork again and then adieu forever to Liberalism and Repeal in the Capital of the South, and we must be their slaves.[21]

The controversy also brought home to the city's veteran O'Connellite reformers that the changes which they had set in motion in the 1820s with the Emancipation campaign had led to popular demands impossible to satisfy. When Richard Dowden, one of the most respected Repealers in the city's élite, and a co-voter with Lyons on the Harbour Board issue, lamented that he and his generation had 'not educated the people sufficiently to hear the truth', he was expressing the dismay of the moderate Liberal overwhelmed by the potentially destructive power of 'the people'.[22] Finally, the divisions consequent on the Harbour Board vote foreshadowed the final confrontation between Old and Young Ireland since most of those who attacked the council on this occasion sided with the seceders from Conciliation Hall some weeks later.[23]

The division between Young Ireland and O'Connellism in Cork was, therefore, a product of both national and local circumstances. As Thomas Lyons expressed it in his summing up of the Harbour Board controversy, it was a matter of pragmatism *versus* unattainable ends, of economic prosperity *versus* the will o' the wisp of Repeal. It was also, though undoubtedly shaped by conflicting attitudes to the controversial 'Peace Resolutions', a manifestation of the local struggle, between a *parvenu* élite in the Chamber of Commerce and reformed town council and the upwardly aspiring retailer element, their progress blocked by an impenetrable glass ceiling in the form of property qualifications, family monopoly and patronage networks.

On the Young Ireland side, the controversy was also the expression of impatience with the perceived political caution of the older generation. While the gap between the People's Hall and the Chamber of Commerce was no simple generational one, those who supported Young Ireland were all aged from their mid-teens to early thirties, too young to understand the political climate that had shaped the attitudes of those individuals now referred to as Old Irelanders.[24] They had no first-hand experience of the emergence of the Chamber of Commerce as the bastion of Cork O'Connellism, and the struggle that it had sustained in quest of municipal and parliamentary reform. The gap between Old and Young Ireland in Cork was indeed a generation gap. The younger men, though generally unwilling to hurt O'Connell while he lived, and revering his memory when he died, felt that while their eyes might 'rest with fondness on the glories of the past, they must not allow its bright radiance to throw a false colouring over the actions of the present'.[25]

But the impatient young men were to be overtaken by others more impatient than themselves – some from within their own ranks, others from a somewhat lower social *milieu* and a more militant mentality. Hints of this were already clear when, in January 1847, the new Irish Confederation was formed. Cork was well represented on the new body's committee, most of those involved having long been connected with the pledged Repealer and Young Ireland element in Cork city.[26] In Cork, the Confederation had its own meeting room in the South Main Street, but its activities never reached the newspaper columns, and the general inactivity of its members was reflected in the scanty references to Cork in the Irish Confederation minute book.[27] The famine raging in the city partly explained this inactivity,[28] but the stagnation was also due to internal divisions within the Confederates' own ranks, the settlement of which demanded a pragmatism that, when manifested by the town council and Chamber of Commerce only months previously, had been denounced as treachery. As Michael Joseph Barry explained to Smith O'Brien, in the bitter atmosphere following the split between Old and Young Ireland, only a softly-softly approach would succeed in 'acquir[ing] the confidence and support of the people'. He was right, as proven by the uproar at the public meeting eventually held to launch the Confederate Desmond Club in the city, when the organizers were shouted down as the 'murderers of O'Connell'.[29] Moreover, Barry and the leadership of the new body found themselves – another irony – under attack also from their own more extreme followers, 'enthusiasts, [who] lack the calm reflective character to give weight to their opinions' but who would pull the movement in a more extreme direction over the following eighteen months.[30]

One source of internal discord was the Desmond Club's main thrust as a cultural and educational rather than an active political body. Building on foundations established by the short-lived Cork Historical Society of the previous year, it promulgated the teachings and philosophy of the late Thomas Davis through lectures on Irish history, culture and the revival of native manufacture, classes in drawing and the Irish language, and the facilities of a reading room where members could pursue self-education through the medium of a large selection of Irish, British and American newspapers and periodicals.[31] The club's initial membership was quite small, but it was drawn from those radical and disgruntled groups who had formed the backbone of the People's Hall since its foundation in the late 1830s and supported the Burgess Association since 1841 – artisans, grocers, minor merchants, pawnbrokers and vintners, and many others whose non-inclusion in contemporary trade directories indicates a relatively humble socio-economic background.[32] Though they willingly subscribed to the cultural programme of the Desmond Club, they were, along with the 'enthusiasts' in the leadership, looking for something stronger, and it was in response to this pressure and to the excitement generated by events on the continent that in early 1848 the Cork Confederates became more assertive.

In January, the formerly moderate Repealer *Southern Reporter* was taken over by Michael Joseph Barry and Charles Denham Murphy. Although Barry confided to Smith O'Brien that an initially cautious approach was needed lest the former readers of the paper be alienated, the first few weeks of the takeover coincided with the outbreak of the February Revolution in Paris, and the *Reporter* was transformed within a short time into a vociferous exponent of revolution *à la française*.[33] At almost the same time the Desmond Club's lecture programme became appreciably more revolutionary, ditching topics like the 'Ancient Civilization of Ireland' in favour of the life of Wolfe Tone, the villainy of Pitt, the rebellion of 1798, and contemporary political movements in Europe.[34]

This was the point at which Cork Young Irelanders-turned-Confederates made their choice between caution and culture on the one hand and militancy on the other. Carried along by the force of his own rhetoric, Barry confided to Smith O'Brien:

> I had little faith in parliament at any time – none now. I consider it to be a complete delusion to expect that from the justice or reason of an English government anything is to be had, and have no faith in any policy which does not tend to work upon their fears.[35]

Other younger members like the nineteen-year-old Joseph Brennan were even more excitable. Fond of slogans like '*aristocrats à la lanterne!*', he scandalized even the Desmond Club by proclaiming, when the Mayor refused to call a public meeting to congratulate the French nation, that Ireland had 'a surplus of landlords and fat aldermen' and that 'blood was a commodity of which there would soon be a very lavish expenditure'.[36]

From February to July 1848, excitement in Cork city continued to grow, partly due to the escalation of events in France, partly to national events like the arrest and prosecution of Thomas Francis Meagher, John Mitchel and William Smith O'Brien, and partly to local reactions to these events. The cheers for O'Connell and Old Ireland were a thing of the past, and the famine-exhausted city crowds, if they shouted at all, did so for the French Republic and John Mitchel.[37] By early April, the reported subversion of soldiers and the repetition of the hitherto inconceivable words 'To Hell with the Queen!' caused serious concern.[38] Mitchel's imprisonment a few weeks later led to disquieting scenes where mobs of men, women and boys marched through the city's streets until after midnight, and a sense of expectancy seeped through the urban crowd:

> Vast numbers of idle and evil-disposed persons assemble in [Patrick Street] in front of the warehouses daily, and remain until a late hour of the evening, who are all in a state of disaffection to the present government, and who assemble for the sole purpose of discussing politics; the general subjects of discussion being the grievances which they consider this country is enduring under (as they term it) the Saxon Yoke, the right they consider that Irishmen have to sever the Union . . . and the probabilities of a successful attempt for the purpose with expressions of great hostility to the present government, and their desire to change it for a democracy.[39]

At the same time, rifle clubs were formed, the open manufacture of pikes increased, the sale of firearms rocketed, and city Confederate leaders set about establishing a network of clubs throughout city and county.[40] To frightened onlookers, particularly among the Protestant conservative community, it seemed that a rebellion was about to erupt – an impression fuelled by the number of club titles associated with 1798 – Wolfe Tone, William Orr, Lord Edward, Sheares, Arthur O'Connor, Oliver Bond – and by the staging in July of a huge pro-Smith O'Brien demonstration in the city park to which the club members marched in formation, dressed in their working clothes as a tribute to the revolutionary artisans of Paris.[41]

But the apparently monolithic popular movement which loyal and law-abiding citizens feared was seriously divided. For months, the local Confederate leadership had watched with some trepidation the radicalization of their movement. They now found themselves in the same dilemma experienced by the O'Connellite élite two years earlier – unable to control a popular movement which they had themselves unwittingly unleashed. The new clubs, radiating out from the recently established Cork Citizens' Club in the city, represented the desperate attempts of a rhetorically revolutionary but actually very nervous leadership to control the spiralling popular excitement. This comes across in the proposed structure of the club network – a veritable model of order, central control and decorum – the latter summed up by the (hardly revolutionary) prohibition of smoking 'or any other objectionable practice'.[42]

Among the cautious leaders, Michael Joseph Barry stood out, though perhaps less because of the degree of his caution than because the contrast between his public rhetoric and his private fears was preserved for historical scrutiny in the local press and his regular correspondence with Smith O'Brien. For all his flamboyant editorials, he was a bourgeois revolutionary, cautious at heart, and despite his bombastic editorials in the *Southern Reporter,* replete with references to 'duty', 'people's will', 'fair fight', 'despotism' and 'liberty', he was no militant.[43] As early as February 1848 he expressed regret that the militant and 'mischievously foolish' John Mitchel was fast becoming the darling of the crowds and of the Cork Confederates, claiming to 'see evidence of a more levelling and ultra-democratic spirit amongst them than I like'.[44] A month later, in the middle of a eulogy of the French people, he paused to warn that 'a revolution is like Saturn, it sometimes devours its own children. Patriots, like Frankenstein, by breathing life into an inanimate mass, raise it up, it may be, to be a power which hunts themselves to death.'[45]

Other leading lights in the Confederation agonized less than Barry about the discrepancies between revolutionary idealism and reality. We know little of what Denny Lane thought, as most of his political correspondence had been with Davis (dead for almost three years at this stage) and he did not communicate with Smith O'Brien as Barry did. He did, however, take a leading part in organizing the Mitchel Defence Fund, and was instrumental in inviting Thomas Francis Meagher and Smith O'Brien to Cork, making a rousing speech at the ensuing public meetings.[46] Others like Isaac Varian, John Walter Bourke and John O'Brien did not commit their thoughts to paper, but continued to organize clubs in and outside the city, and it was during such a drive at Crossbarry in July, when they made use of 'scandalous and seditious words', that the authorities seized their opportunity to nip potential disturbance in the bud. The Crossbarry trio was arrested on 18 July, two days later Cork was proclaimed, and extra police were drafted into the city.[47]

The immediate reaction of the city's Confederate leaders to the proclamation showed more than anything how illusory had been the fears of revolution. Some resigned immediately, and the rank-and-file who had been primed for 'a blow in defense of their country' were now advised to 'be tranquil . . . and attempt no violence. If your officers are arrested, elect new ones in their stead, and await for the advice of those you trust and know.'[48] Though political excitement continued, the leadership and followers had already parted ways. Warnings of caution were ignored as club members prepared to defy the proclamation and begin the rebellion, but the excitement lasted for only one night. Seditious songs were sung and the proclamation placards smeared with mud, and as the police searched for arms, they were followed by crowds of women who cursed them loudly, wishing that 'the black sickness will whip away all those bloody infernal peelers', and called on the menfolk to 'pull the bloody peelers to pieces'.[49] But the leaders had left the scene. Denny Lane, Michael Joseph Barry, Ralph and Isaac Varian, Charles Denham Murphy and Felix Mullan had been lodged in gaol; others of less importance were said to be emigrating to America; and the disaffected in the city were soon quietened by a show of force by the fleet.[50] The release of the local Confederate leaders four months later caused little stir. Felix Mullan & Company, who had openly displayed and advertized firearms all through 1848 had, since August, confined their advertizing to the realm of spoons, forks, drawing-room grates and kitchen ranges, and by September the People's Hall, that nucleus of Cork repeal fervour and Young Ireland nationalism, had been taken over by a dealer in old clothes.[51]

Young Ireland in Cork gave its last kick in 1849, when the *Southern Reporter* clashed with the Catholic bishop Dr Delaney over a proposed collection in aid of Pius IX, then in exile. The *Reporter*, while expressing sympathy and admiration for the pontiff, maintained that Ireland would not be justified in sending money abroad while her people were starving at home. Young Ireland came worst out of the dispute, Delaney having denounced them as the Church's 'inveterate and bitter opponents [who], professing Young Ireland principles . . . perhaps think themselves bound to sympathise with all the revolutions of all times and all countries'.[52] By now, however, the term 'Young Irelander' was an anachronism. Many of those so termed joined in the loyal scramble to welcome the Queen when she visited Cork in July 1849. But as the town council prepared an address to Her Majesty, and prominent citizens jostled to offer their residences for the entertainment of the royal visitors, a few faint squeaks of protest broke through the loyal clamour. There were some signs behind the scenes that the remnants of the Confederate Clubs planned to break any windows illuminated for the royal visit.[53] On the town council, Edward Brady, one of the most vocal Irish Confederates in Cork in 1847 and 1848, demanded unsuccessfully that the council's address to the Queen include a reference to Repeal and the release of the state prisoners, while James Dwyer made cynical suggestions that Her Majesty should be entertained in the dining hall of the Cork Union Workhouse.[54]

Parliamentary and municipal politics resumed their accustomed even tenor. In the city by-election of 1849, the Tories and erstwhile O'Connellites put forward only one candidate each and consequently divided the representation between them, while the town council returned to dominant issues of civic patriotism and commercial enterprise, without the unwelcome disruption caused by Repeal.[55] The young men whose ideas had disrupted city politics from 1845 onwards were not even heard of. Those who had been imprisoned for their seditious activities emerged from prison as highly respectable citizens and either returned to their family businesses or left the city for successful careers elsewhere. The decade-long Young Ireland interlude was over.

So what, if any, was the long-term legacy of Young Ireland generally, and of the Cork Young Irelanders in particular? Their journalism and their literary work, mostly poetry, were characteristic of that 'ideological stockpile' of romantic nationalism, militancy and religious devotion which became the hallmarks of this formative period.[56] It is difficult to assess the popular influence of these writings in their own time. There is no doubt that they made a considerable impression on the immediate readership of the *Nation,* many of whom emulated such sentiments in their own poetic attempts and sometimes moved on from poetry to a more active political consciousness. In the Cork context, one such emulator was the young Ellen Mary Downing ('Mary' of the *Nation*), who briefly emerged from her sheltered bourgeois girlhood as the daughter of the Fever Hospital's resident medical officer to write rousing pieces like 'Forget Our Wrongs?' and 'The Logic of a Blow' and to engage in a brief courtship with the young Joseph Brennan.[57] Among the broader public, and further down the social scale, the Young Ireland poets' influence is less tangible. Some of their poems certainly met a response among the public, sold as broadsides soon after their appearance in the newspaper, but Young Ireland's high-minded patriotism and exalted religious tolerance proved no match among the ballad-singing public for the sectarian sentiments and millenarian hopes which characterized the most successful broadside compositions.[58]

The influence of Young Ireland's romantic nationalism was really most powerful after the demise of the movement itself. This influence stretched on for well over a century, carried forward by a series of song-books like the *Spirit of the Nation* (including such numbers as Michael Joseph Barry's 'Step Together' and 'The Green Flag' and Lane's 'Kate of Araglen'). Early in the following century, Father Walsh's *Songs of the Gael* re-popularized these numbers, while in the 1940s T.F. O'Sullivan published extracts not only from Lane and Barry but also from Isaac Varian and 'Mary'.[59] Preserved and expanded upon by (partisan but valuable) personal memoirs like those of

Gavan Duffy and Michael Doheny,[60] the songs' potent ideological mixture of cultural self-respect, militancy and heroic failure was also perpetuated by generational transmission in those families involved in the heady events of 1848 and 1849.[61] It also passed into formal education to underpin the history and literature textbooks published by the Christian Brothers from the 1850s onwards.[62] It permeated academic historical writing in the 1940s when scholarship and centenary commemorations fused in a number of works by Denis Gwynn, T.F. O'Sullivan and others.[63] Even as late as the 1960s, it shaped the primary school history textbooks published in independent Ireland, the tedium of date-saturated chapters being relieved by stirring political verses from Davis, Ingram or 'Speranza'.[64] Ironically, however, the most long-lived Young Ireland song, at least in the Cork context, was only subliminally political. This was Denny Lane's 'Irish Maiden's Lament' (better known as 'Carrigdhoun'), which still continues to figure in the song repertoire of the older generation in the city. Why did it maintain its appeal? It did so precisely because it omitted *passé* political references, and because its pervasive nostalgia for a real place and for lost love allowed it to transcend time.

Outside the realm of song-writing and romantic nationalism, the legacy of Young Ireland in Cork was one of re-awakened political realism. This realism was clear at opposite ends of the political spectrum – among those who continued to support revolution and among those who deliberately turned their backs on it. The first group was to be found among the Confederate rank-and-file disappointed by the fiasco of 1848. From then onwards they put their faith in a more militant and less bourgeois-dominated movement, Fenianism, and it was significant that some of the most tenacious city Fenians in the 1860s were men who had cut their political teeth in the Irish Confederation.[65] The second group, the leaders, mostly returned to their natural *milieu* of the family firm, the town council and the Chamber of Commerce. Some, like Denny Lane and Joseph Ronayne, could never shake off their experience of political excitement and cultural revival in the 1840s and either involved themselves in the politics of Home Rule or in the continued literary promulgation of Young Ireland ideas on cultural identity, industrial revival and religious tolerance.[66] Others completely abandoned the ideas of the Forties. Michael Joseph Barry was one such: on his release from prison, he returned to journalism to support thereafter a policy of reform within the context of the Union, and briefly took the position of a Divisional Police Magistrate in Dublin in the 1870s.[67]

Contemporary judgements on the Cork Young Irelanders varied from contempt to adulation. In 1848 the *Cork Constitution* condemned them as 'fellows who have been deluding the populace into conspiracy and crime' while disappointed followers used the term 'renegade gaol martyrs'.[68] In the 1850s, those condemned were now praised for their 'calm and temperate spirit', while their obituaries in later decades, culminating in that of Lane in 1895, were veritable panegyrics laden with reference to their fairness, generosity and purity of purpose.[69] The truth was, of course, that Cork's Young Irelanders were neither renegades nor heroes. They were products of their immediate family and economic background, some prosperous retailers in their own right, others the sons of Cork businessmen, residing in the salubrious area of Blackrock, or Wellington Road, educated in diocesan seminaries, Trinity College or the King's Inns and (had the exciting events of the 1840s not interposed) destined for a successful career in law or in the middling or upper ranks of local business. Their wish for the regeneration of national self-respect and their genuine belief in the moral justification of physical force stopped short at the actual use of such force, and when they were overtaken by the horrors of the Famine and the snowballing excitement of 1848 they did not know what to do. In the event, though the more enthusiastic in their ranks and among their followers disagreed, they did the best thing – nothing. If, like their friend Smith O'Brien, they had allowed a rebellion to go off at half-cock, they might have gained a place in the nationalist pantheon, but they might also have brought havoc on their city's trade and people. In the end, whatever their rhetoric, they proved themselves true sons of the Cork mercantile élite – cautious, pragmatic and with an understandable mistrust in the forces of uncontrolled democracy.

Anticipating Memory
Landlordism, Agrarianism and Deference in Late-Nineteenth-Century Ireland

LAURENCE M. GEARY

> It was a hateful and heart-breaking sight to see manly looking men, young and old, doffing their hats and caps and cringing in abject manner to any person connected with an estate, and before magistrates and others associated with the administration of pro-landlord laws.[1]
>
> Michael Davitt

> *Resolved:* That we, the members of the Rossmore Branch of the Land League, hereby solemnly bind ourselves not to take off our hats to any man in future, except the priest.[2]
>
> P.A. Canon Sheehan

With characteristic ebullience, J.J. Lee has argued that the land war between 1879 and 1882 was a significant factor in emancipating the Irish rural population from 'the shackles of mental serfdom'. The tenants' involvement in land agitation shattered their inherited sense of deference towards their landlords, and forelock-tugging and cap-doffing to one-time social superiors were consigned to the past.[3] This erosion of traditional respect reflected the social and political transformation that was under way in Ireland in the last quarter of the nineteenth century.

Lee's thesis has drawn critical fire, cynics suggesting that hat-lifting is a non-quantifiable activity, a type of social engagement that did not come within the ambit of police record-keeping.[4] Those who lived through the period and experienced the land war at first hand were less dismissive of the symbolism involved. Michael Davitt, whose writings appear to have prompted Lee's observation, regarded the agrarian agitation that commenced in 1879 as crucial to the demise of social servitude, to the overthrow of feudalism in Ireland. Such an analysis is hardly surprising, given Davitt's temperament and peasant origins. What is surprising is that broadly similar sentiments were expressed by contemporary writers like George Moore and Anthony Trollope, individuals who came from an entirely different social background to Davitt and, in Trollope's case, who differed fundamentally from him in politics.[5]

Trollope's loathing for the revolution that was unleashed in Ireland in the late 1870s was captured in his unfinished novel, *The Landleaguers* (1883), which he began after completing a research trip to Ireland in June 1882. Some of the action in the novel revolves around the hunting field and, in particular, popular attempts to interfere with the sport. Fox-hunting was one of Trollope's great passions in life, one he shared with the Irish gentry.[6] As John Pentland Mahaffy – sportsman and Trinity College historian, among other accomplishments – put it in 1882: 'Many gentlemen are so devoted to this sport, that they regard the summer as merely a disagreeable interruption to hunting.'[7] During the land war, this activity, which was as much a way of life as a sport, was targeted. According to the inimitable William O'Brien, 'the landlords, for whom fox-hunting was all that the arena was for Nero, found their passages across the farmers' land forbidden by crowds of peasants, and were forced to turn home disconsolate with their hounds'.[8] Stopping the hunt was another manifestation of a changing social order, a protest against landlordism and those who facilitated, supported or sympathized with the system in any way.[9] Trollope claimed that in the early 1880s the Irish peasantry had united in a secret conspiracy 'to disturb the amusements of their betters', 'to put down the amusement of the gentry'. According to Trollope, hunting 'existed solely on respect', and, he added, 'anything that requires respect may be said to be over'.[10]

George Moore captured this change in social attitude far more subtly than the outraged Trollope, albeit at a later remove. In *Ave*, the first volume of his remarkable autobiography, *Hail and Farewell*, Moore contrasts the Mayo peasantry of his youth, in the decade after the Great Famine with their children and grandchildren at the turn of the twentieth century. Moore, who was born in 1852 at Moore Hall, the seat of the family's 12,000-acre Mayo estate, recalls attending Mass at their local parish church at Carnacun. On Sundays and holy days, the tenants assembled from their various villages, men and women walking on different sides of the road, 'the married women in dark blue cloaks, the girls hiding their faces behind their shawls, carrying their boots in their hands, which they would put on in the chapel-yard'. The elderly men were dressed in traditional swallow-tail coats, knee-breeches and worsted stockings, the young men in corduroy trousers and frieze coats. As the Moore family passed in their carriage, 'the women curtseyed in their red petticoats; the young men lifted their round bowler-hats; but the old men stood by, their tall hats in their hands'. Moore remembered that the family were 'received like royalty' when they entered the gates of the chapel and ascended the wooden stairs that led to the gallery, where the most privileged people of the parish congregated for worship. The situation was very different when Moore returned to Carnacun chapel some fifty years later; a social transformation had taken place, one that led him to conclude that the landlords' popularity, and all that the class represented, had disappeared with the laws that favoured them.[11]

This was William O'Brien's theme when he delivered a public lecture, entitled 'The Lost Opportunities of the Irish Gentry', at the Leinster Hall, Dublin, on 8 September 1887, in aid of the Sacred Heart Home, Drumcondra, a recently established Dublin Catholic charity. O'Brien's trial at Mitchelstown, Co. Cork on the following day, on a charge of inciting to resist eviction, gave spice to the occasion. One influential nationalist newspaper reminded its readers that while O'Brien was delivering his lecture and being fêted in Dublin's Leinster Hall, 'the government were preparing a plank bed and a suit of shame for him in Cork jail'.[12] A month earlier, O'Brien and the popular local leader John Mandeville had urged tenants on the heavily mortgaged Kingston estate at Mitchelstown to resist any attempts by the sheriff and bailiffs to eject them from their holdings. Large-scale agrarian evictions were pending on the property as a result of the tenants' adherence to the agitation known as the Plan of Campaign that occurred between 1886 and 1891. O'Brien informed the Kingston tenants on two separate occasions that they would be 'justified before God and man in resisting this outrage and defending [their] homes against these assassins'. He urged his listeners to set the estate in a blaze about its owner's ears should she proceed with evictions, and Mandeville encouraged a similar resistance.[13] In doing so, both were guilty of violating the recently enacted Criminal Law and Procedure (Ireland) Act 1887,[14] more commonly known as the 'Crimes Act', and were summoned to appear before the magistrates at Mitchelstown on 9 September.

The timing of O'Brien's charity lecture – he had agreed to it months earlier – and his trial at Mitchelstown was entirely coincidental; his chosen subject matter is unlikely to have been. O'Brien's theme was an important one in the contemporary agrarian and political context, but the trappings of the charity occasion were perhaps as significant and symbolic as the content of the lecture. An enthusiastic reporter with the *Freeman's Journal* described the scene when the proceedings commenced at 8 p.m.:

> The audience were all standing; hats were waved, handkerchiefs fluttered, while cheer succeeded cheer with such sustained vigour that it would be a sharp ear that could detect the intervals. The members of the audience did not take their places until the bands in the balconies at either side of the platform ceased playing 'God save Ireland'.

The *Freeman's Journal* observed editorially on the following morning that the whole occasion captured 'the heart of the Irish mystery', and commented on the 'currents of meaning' that ran through the proceedings. Among these currents were the presence of the Catholic Archbishop of Dublin, Dr W.J. Walsh, who chaired the proceedings, the Lord Mayor of Dublin in the second chair, three British MPs offering 'sympathy and lusty help' – Mr Labouchere, 'the enemy of all wrong'; Mr Thomas Ellis, 'the Parnell of Wales'; and Mr Brunner, 'the victor of Northwich' – at least eleven Irish nationalist MPs, as well as aldermen, town commissioners and Poor

Law guardians, parish priests and curates, barristers and solicitors, physicians and surgeons. Walsh's archepiscopal colleague at Cashel, O'Brien's impetuous and fiery friend Dr T.W. Croke, was unavoidably absent in London, but sent a telegram of support in which he described O'Brien as a 'pure-minded patriot', and prayed that he would emerge from prison 'as sound in health as he is brave in heart and unflinching'. Croke concluded with the inevitable rallying cry, 'God save Ireland'.[15]

The presence of such individuals on the platform and in the body of what was described as 'a vast assemblage of Dublin citizens' gave sanction and substance to the policies and activities of O'Brien and his fellow political activists. It was also a public manifestation of the clerical–nationalist alliance, and a reflection of the revolutionary changes that were underway in Ireland. The *Freeman's Journal* described O'Brien variously as 'the avowed, erect, and manly foe of the landlord classes', and 'the most uncompromising leader of the democracy against the landocracy'. The editor suggested that the delivery of a public lecture by O'Brien on the failings and diminishing stature of the Ascendancy, in the presence of the leading Irish churchman of the day, and with his tacit approval, was vivid confirmation that the Irish revolution was both real and fundamentally different to the 'democractic upheaval on the continent', which, he said, was essentially hostile to religion and religious influences. In contrast, the editor concluded, 'the beneficial agitation in Ireland' was 'arm-in-arm every step with the church of the people and with their prelates'.[16]

In his youth, O'Brien recalled in his lecture, the gentry were respected almost to the point of adoration. He and his companions in Mallow regarded the clubhouse in the town as 'a kind of seventh heaven', inhabited by beings of quite another order from mere people who worked for a living. These exotic individuals appeared to him to possess a God-given right to lord it over the people and to look down on them. 'It seemed part of the order and arrangement of the universe,' he said. However, the current decade of agrarian agitation and political activisim had punctured what appeared to have been providentially ordained, had 'moderated these gentlemen's estimate of their own importance', and brought them to what O'Brien called their present 'days of humiliation and helplessness'.[17]

O'Brien claimed that the Irish gentry had spurned various opportunities in the past to shape the country's destiny, had rejected a role that would have won them the people's affection, trust and support and placed them in the political vanguard. Their failure as a class meant that the initiative had swung from them to 'the democracy of Ireland', a democracy that sprung from and was inspired by the Irish national education system and by American political and social ideas and ideals, influences that were imbibed by post-Famine emigrants and relayed to their families, friends and neighbours in Ireland. In a conciliatory gesture, one that anticipated his later views on settling the land question, O'Brien stated that there was still time for the Ascendancy to harmonize their interests with those of their fellow Irishmen and to work for their country's future: 'The hour is never too late for Irish forgiveness – even for the class whose hands I am sorry to say are to this hour red with evictions, and whose voices are still hoarse with clamour for coercion.'[18]

The agrarian militancy and eviction backlash that convulsed Ireland from the late 1870s onwards was inconceivable a few years earlier. According to James S. Donnelly, Jr., the violent land war that erupted could only have been foreseen by 'a great leap of the imagination'.[19] Following the massive dislocation and mortality of the Great Famine, the country experienced a period of relative prosperity. From the mid 1850s to the late 1870s, productivity and price increases far outstripped the rise in agricultural rents. In these generally buoyant years, the majority of Irish landlords adopted a relatively benign attitude towards their tenants, a stance that was prompted less by altruism than by economic pragmatism. Many landlords were dependent on their tenants' goodwill if they were to discharge their own financial obligations and secure their estates. This necessity ensured that, in the quarter of a century after the Great Famine, harmonious relations generally prevailed between the owners and the tillers of the soil.

There were two interlinking strands to this relationship, the social and the business or contractual. The nature of the relationship was determined by ownership or occupancy, by the receipt or payment of rent. Relations between landlords and tenants in Ireland before the land war were not based on equity or equality, but on patrimony and social deference. This was clearly seen on significant family occasions, such as a marriage, the birth of an heir, a coming-of-age, recovery from illness. When Sir Arthur Guinness, who was regarded as an improving landlord, returned to Ashford House, Cong, at the beginning of January 1877, having spent three months in France convalescing from a major illness, the occasion was extravagantly celebrated by tenants on different parts of his 33,000-acre Mayo estate. The usual marks of such loyalty demonstrations were present, including welcoming committees, laudatory speeches and congratulatory addresses, illuminations, triumphal arches, torchlight processions, fireworks, bonfires, bands and music, and commemorative verse, the standard of which may be judged from the opening lines of 'On the Welcome Return of Sir Arthur Guinness, Bart., MP, to Cong, after his Happy Recovery from Severe Illness'

> Hang up a welcome banner
> On every tower and tree,
> The good Sir Arthur's coming
> From pain and danger free.

In response to one deputation of tenants, Guinness acknowledged 'the people's free, open and heartfelt expression of loyalty and attachment to him, a feeling he fully reciprocated and prized far more than their luminous display of fireworks and illuminations, and hoped the cordial feeling of unity between himself and his tenantry then existing would never be less'. He concluded that 'it was only through mutual attachment and confidence between landlord and tenant that Ireland could ever be prosperous and happy'.[20]

There was nothing exceptional about this particular episode. It was simply a manifestation of the traditional respect accorded by tenants to their landlords. Terence Dooley provides similar, if less extravagant, examples of coming-of-age and marriage festivities on the Clonbrock and Crofton estates in Co. Galway, and on others in Leinster.[21] The succession of 67-year-old James King to the earldom of Kingston on his brother's death in January 1867 offers a Co. Cork example of pre-land-war social lubrication. In July of the following year, James and his much younger wife, Anna, returned to reside in Mitchelstown Castle and 10,000 people assembled to welcome them to the town. According to the *Cork Examiner*, the demonstration was an immense and enthusiastic one, and nothing like it had ever been witnessed in Mitchelstown before. 'High festival was held in the streets – where large parties, abundantly supplied with porter, danced merrily around the bonfires – till another day had fairly dawned.' Kingston was presented with an address of welcome, which commended him for providing his tenants with long leases at existing rents, for his generosity to the poor during the previous winter and for his treatment of the labourers. The *Cork Examiner* concluded that Kingston richly deserved the people's 'uncounterfeited' welcome because he had shown 'a disposition to deal kindly by them', and had displayed an awareness of the duties as well as the rights of property.[22]

Davitt believed that manifestations of traditional respect, similar to those cited above, arose from defenceless tenants' fear of their landlords and of eviction. The 'cringing' of tenants before their landlords, their 'unmanly subserviency' was 'a moral malady, born of feudalism and fear'. According to Davitt, 'generations of suffering and tyranny had inflicted this slavishness of manner upon a Celtic peasantry'.[23] It is difficult to say whether the servility that Davitt complained of was genuine or formulaic, but the speed with which tenant obsequiousness was discarded after the commencement of the land war suggests that it was little more than a ritualistic veneer.

The harmoniousness that existed between landlords and tenants in post-Famine Ireland was shattered in the late 1870s by the onset of economic depression. The failure of landlords and their agents to grant voluntary rent reductions and their insistence on the payment of customary rents revolutionized popular attitudes and gave rise to the demand that the land of Ireland be reclaimed from the present usurping landlords and restored to its rightful owners, the Irish people. The land of Ireland for the people of Ireland, a term that required neither definition nor explanation, became both clarion call and homogeneous banner.

The revolution in attitude to landlords and to the Ascendancy class generally that occurred in a few short years can be gauged from the public pronouncements of Catholic priests and nationalist politicians who were involved in land agitation in the 1880s. Their message was simple: landlords were alien, base and parasitic. One Co. Limerick parish priest pronounced bluntly in 1888, 'I don't care who the landlord is, no matter what sort he is. If he was an angel from heaven he is a bad man provided he is a landlord.'[24] Nationalists condemned landlordism as iniquitous, an anachronism that retarded economic progress and stood between Ireland and self-government.[25]

It was a considerable achievement to mobilize and motivate the Irish rural population and to weld them into a cohesive, tightly organized and generally peaceful mass movement. How was this achieved? Perhaps the most important element was the weekly mass meetings, at which tenant and national rights were advocated. These assemblies of tenants and townspeople were addressed by nationalist members of parliament, visiting radical and liberal sympathizers, local leaders, many of whom were either serving or former members of the Fenian brotherhood, and the more radical and outspoken of the Catholic clergy. In a neat and ironic reversal of the respect that was traditionally accorded to landlords, those who were now intent on collapsing the edifice of landlordism were frequently serenaded to the place of assembly by bands playing patriotic airs, and the procession was invariably escorted by horsemen, sometimes several hundred strong, who were usually bedecked in green sashes and ribbons. When John Dillon and William O'Brien arrived in Portumna, Co. Galway, to advocate the Plan of Campaign in late 1886, for instance, the horses were taken out of the shafts and the young men of the town drew the car through the streets, while the local brass band played, 'See the Conquering Hero Comes'.[26] These nationwide public meetings were popular displays of nationalist fervour. They promoted solidarity among tenants and fostered anti-landlord sentiment. Exhortatory speeches were delivered and the complexities, as well as the politics and tactics, of the land agitation were explained.

In her bitter analysis of the land war, Anna Parnell attributed the popularity of mass meetings, or 'demonstrations' as they were often termed, to 'the terrible dullness of Irish country life'. Rural life in England was dull enough, she said, but it was 'a giddy round of excitement compared to the corresponding life in Ireland'.[27] Undoubtedly, there was a strong social element involved in these gatherings. It was not unknown for a football to be produced, for instance, or for the assembly to be provisioned gratuitously with bread and beer. Irrespective of the motives of those attending, the police acknowledged the impact of these gatherings. One account from the west of Ireland in 1887 claimed that the language used at public meetings was very strong and full of hostility to the authorities, and that the audience became greatly excited at the repeated denunciations of the government, the police, landlords and bailiffs.[28]

Accounts of these meetings were published and avidly read in the national and provincial press. In 1879 there were 120 provincial newspapers in print, and 132 five years later.[29] Their influence is captured in the following complaint against the nationalist *Kerry Sentinel*, a paper that was owned and operated by the Harrington brothers, Timothy and Edward. A parish priest from the neighbourhood of Tralee blamed all the 'mischief' in the county on the *Sentinel*; he informed the chief secretary that 'articles teeming with the most reckless abuse of landlords and agents, with the most pernicious advice and inflammatory utterances, appear in almost every number of that wretched journal . . . our simple-minded people are brought to a state nearly bordering on insanity'.[30] From the perspective of agrarian agitation, the most important paper was *United Ireland*, a weekly that was launched by Parnell and edited by William O'Brien, a journalist of wit, style and flair, and, at the time, possibly the most popular politician in the country. Detailed reports of the previous week's public meetings were accompanied by stinging editorials denouncing landlord rapacity and government cupidity, all of which helped to generate publicity, spread ideas and raise the political temperature.

The message that was sent out again and again at public meetings, and disseminated to a wider audience in the nationalist press was that unity and organization were essential if the tenants were to achieve their aims. Land-grabbing, that is the taking of farms from which others had been evicted, was regarded as the ultimate evil, and land-grabbers were rigorously boycotted. Such transgressors against the unwritten agrarian code were denounced by Davitt as 'the buttress of the rack-renting evil and the worst foe of the struggling tenant'.[31] They were castigated in vicious ballads, and shunned as if they were lepers of old, to use Parnell's phrase.

Boycotting, or social ostracism, was the most effective and widely used weapon in the tenants' armoury. It was employed against 'grabbers', landowners and their agents, process servers, solicitors, or anyone who supported the institution of landlordism in any way. Boycotting depended for its effectiveness on the complete disruption of the business and social life of its victims and proved to be a devastating weapon.

Boycotting was rigorously enforced on the Kingston estate at Mitchelstown. There were three exceptionally bitter rent strikes on this property during the 1880s, prompted largely by the family's financial difficulties. Traditionally, the Kingstons were paternalistic and improving landlords who had ceded to their tenants the 3Fs – fair rent, free sale and fixity of tenure – long before these demands were enshrined in the Land Act of 1881. However, the 25,000-acre Kingston estate was hopelessly encumbered. In the mid 1870s, following the death of her husband, Lady Kingston consolidated the various charges on the property into a single mortgage which she obtained from the Church of Ireland. The mortgage was for a staggering £236,000 and the annual cost of servicing this enormous debt consumed most of the income from the estate, leaving the owner with the barest of margins on which to live. Her refusal to meet her tenants' repeated demands for rent reductions in the 1880s, essentially because she was unable to do so, provoked some of the bitterest conflicts of the entire land war.

Numerous boycotting notices, each surpassing the former in invective, were posted throughout the Mitchelstown district during the course of the agitation on her estate. The language was biblically powerful and raw:

> Woe to the man or men on the Kingston estate who will betray their fellow tenants as their treachery will be as Cain's brand on their children and it were better that they were never born. The children of those who sold their country in former times now curse the bones of their vile ancestors in dishonoured graves and which of you will leave a similar legacy to your children.
> Woe to such a traitor!!!
> Boycott! Boycott!! Boycott!!!

Twenty years earlier 10,000 tenants and townspeople had openly welcomed Lady Kingston and her husband on their arrival in Mitchelstown. Now she was castigated by these self-same tenants as a 'usurper', a 'disgrace to her sex' and a 'hard-hearted' grass-widow'. Standish O'Grady, Lady Kingston's Catholic solicitor, attracted particular odium. He was variously described as 'that bloated attorney, O'Grady', 'Judas Iscariot O'Grady' and as 'Bullóg "Maria" O'Grady'. The police report translated Bullóg as a big, soft kind of fungus, and the innuendo in the reference to Maria, O'Grady's housekeeper, was obvious to all. Boycotting greatly affected O'Grady's legal practice. Clients who employed him were boycotted. His friends ignored him and he was asked by the parish priest not to attend the Catholic church in the town until the excitement had subsided. One of the estate bailiffs died during the course of the rent strike. The local undertaker refused to supply a coffin and eventually one had to be made at Mitchelstown Castle. The funeral was boycotted and the police were obliged to afford protection to the cortège. The children of a known land-grabber were asked to leave their classrooms and, when they refused, several hundred of their fellow pupils left the school and paraded around the town, preceded by bands and banners. The police escorted the boycotted children to their home to ensure their safety.[32]

Boycotting was often coupled with open intimidation. Many tenants were terrorized into supporting rent strikes. Although the two phases of the land war in the 1880s were based primarily on moral force, with the tenants' leaders constantly urging peaceful methods, there was an underlying current of violence. Land-grabbers, together with those who refused to join anti-rent combinations or those who paid their rent secretly, in fact all poltroons and backsliders, as they were termed, were often physically threatened or assaulted, or had their crops and property burned, or their animals maimed. Fear may have been a base motive for supporting the land war but it was a powerful one.

The ultimate landlord weapon against defaulting tenants was to evict them from their homes and farms, and evictions became one of the great nationalist rallying points. They were given wide and often indignant coverage in the nationalist and liberal press, generating sympathy for the tenants and publicity for the agrarian and political cause. Many landlords, like the infamous Marquis of Clanricarde, or 'Clan-Rack-Rent' as he was depicted, and Colonel O'Callaghan of Bodyke, Co. Clare, were notoriously exacting and uncompromising. In May 1886 hundreds of people gathered in Woodford to protest against evictions on a number of south Galway properties, including the Canricarde estate. The assemblage formed into a funeral procession and marched through the main street of the town. Some of the protestors carried a coffin that bore inscriptions denouncing Orangeism, freemasonry and landlordism. The symbolism was rendered even more explicit when the protestors burned the coffin, to the great delight of the enthusiastic crowd.[33] Unlike Clanricarde and O'Callaghan, James E. Byrne of Coolroe, Co. Wexford, was not regarded as a harsh or exacting landlord. Yet, he said, for months after evictions had been carried out on his estate in August 1888, the mildest salutation he received from his tenants was 'may you awake in hell in the morning'.[34]

Incitement and resistance to evictions landed many local and national politicians, as well as priests and tenants, in jail. The trappings of arrest and imprisonment helped to maintain the political excitement. So, too, did a plethora of comic, ridiculous, romantic and tragic incidents, including the treatment meted out to political prisoners, among them John Dillon and William O'Brien, whose health was a matter of public concern; the death of John Mandeville shortly after his release from gaol; the so-called Mitchelstown massacre, when three unarmed civilians were short dead while attending a public meeting on 9 September 1887, the day of O'Brien and Mandeville's prosecution; attempts by nationalist politicians to evade arrest; the courtroom and prison antics of O'Brien, Tim Healy, Tim Harrington and others. These and similar acts of defiance attracted publicity, politicized the nationalist population, and contributed to unravelling deferential ties.

The only effective way that Irish landlords could counter tenant cohesiveness and organization was by adopting similar strategies, but they failed to do so in any effective or meaningful way. There were a few landlord organizations in existence, such as the Property Defence Association, the Cork Defence Union and the County of Cork Landowners' Association, but they were apathetically supported. Arthur Hugh Smith Barry, MP, the wealthy owner of Fota Island in Co. Cork and most of the town of Tipperary, flayed the prevailing apathy of landowners and the Unionist population generally. He stated that the purpose of agrarian agitation in the late 1880s was to destroy landlordism as a social and political force. He believed that the only way to combat such an agitation was by mutual cooperation among the propertied classes. Unless they banded together, he argued, they would be defeated, and would lose their homes, their properties and their liberty.[35]

At the government's instigation, Smith Barry became the leader of a landlord syndicate that purchased the Ponsonby estate in east Cork in order to prevent its financially troubled and beleaguered owner from capitulating to the Plan of Campaign. Smith Barry was the only member of the syndicate whose identity was revealed, and he was vilified by his nationalist opponents. One unlikely consequence of this transaction was its impact on the workings of the board of guardians of Cork Poor Law union.

The local boards of guardians had long constituted the paternalistic fiefdom of landowners and the Ascendancy generally. In the 1880s Poor Law boards were specifically targeted by nationalists in the struggle against landlordism, and the decade witnessed a shift in the political balance on these boards, a transfer of power from landlords and their agents, who were mostly Unionist or Conservative in their politics, to tenant farmers, shopkeepers, publicans and others who supported the nationalist cause.[36] Nationalist guardians frequently used the weekly board meetings as a forum for airing contemporary political grievances, contrary to the regulations of the Local Government Board which forbade the introduction and discussion of matters unconnected with Poor Law affairs until the routine business of the union had first been disposed of, and only then with the consent of a majority of the guardians present.

Lord Salisbury's determination to impose twenty years of resolute rule on Ireland, and the activities of his nephew, Arthur Balfour, as Irish chief secretary led to frequent and bitter nationalist protests. At a meeting of the Cork board of guardians in March 1888, Dr Charles Tanner, the firebrand nationalist MP for Mid-Cork, asserted that the government's 'infamous conduct' obliged nationalists to use 'public board rooms' and other platforms to denounce their actions and policies.[37] Nationalists objected particularly to the arrest and imprisonment of their political representatives,[38] and to evictions, which, in addition to their inhumanity, contributed to pauperism and increased the rate-payers' burden.[39]

The formation of the landlord syndicate to purchase the Ponsonby estate had clear implications for the tenants' security of tenure, and, at a subsequent meeting of the Cork board of guardians, Tanner launched a vicious personal attack on Smith Barry, a fellow member of the board. Tanner's 'language incarnadined the air', to borrow a phrase from Susanne R. Day's satirical novel, *The Amazing Philanthropists*.[40] In the course of a long and frequently interrupted tirade, Tanner impugned Smith Barry's paternity and questioned his personal integrity. Several outraged Unionist guardians attempted to intervene on Smith Barry's behalf, but the intrepid doctor responded to them all in similar fashion. He called the chairman 'an ignorant bigot', another guardian an old fool, while a third was dismissed as a liar, a cur, a coward and a silly, ignorant old bosthoon. In a later exchange, Tanner told guardian Pratt that he was an ignoramus and that his proper platform was the circus, to which Pratt retorted that it was the only suitable arena for a dirty yahoo like Tanner.[41]

The Unionist press seized on these exchanges as a foretaste of what could be expected from a Home Rule parliament,'a choice specimen of the kind of thing we may expect if the Irish ever get their parliament in Dublin', opined one pillar of the English conservative press.[42] *The Times* suggested that the affair was'an interesting "object lesson" in the study of home rule', with its contempt for business-like procedure, its intolerance, and the vulgarity and indecency of the language employed by Tanner, who was cast as'one of the ornaments of the Nationalist party'.[43]

Such a response was entirely predictable. The Cork board of guardians did present an unedifying spectacle on 16 January 1890, but what it served to underline more than anything else was the transformation that had taken place in the Irish political landscape in a remarkably short time. The social and political ascendancy of the gentry had been fatally undermined by a decade of agrarian agitation, and cap-doffing and forelock-tugging, the traditional deference displayed by the plain people of Ireland to the quality, were being superseded by a new spirit of independence.'The day of aristocratic privilege was gone,' O'Brien informed his Leinster Hall audience on 8 September 1887,'and the power of the people, and the welfare of the people, must henceforth be more important elements in the government of mankind than coronets or Norman blood.'[44]

The social pre-eminence and prestige of the Ascendancy in Ireland, and its political influence and power, were based on the ownership and possession of land. However, the gradual erosion of the legal rights of ownership, coupled with an increasingly democratic and modernizing Irish society undermined the role and status of the gentry in the last quarter of the nineteenth century. The incisive breach in centuries-old class supremacy was made with the passing of the 1881 Land Act, a revolutionary measure, which, through its recognition of dual or co-ownership of the soil by landlords and tenants, made the demise of hereditary landlordism and the social deposition of landlords inevitable.

If the land war was the first act in the drama, the First World War served as the dénouement, if not quite the final curtain. The closing scenes were brilliantly captured in *Bowen's Court*, Elizabeth Bowen's homage to family and class that was at once both eulogy and elegy. The setting, appropriately enough, was Mitchelstown Castle, a splendid folly that was symbolic of its class, an 1820s financial extravagance that was to leave its owners exposed to tenant demands for rent reductions, and all their repercussions, more than half a century later. The occasion was the traditional Mitchelstown Castle garden party. The date was 5 August 1914, the day after England's fateful declaration of war on Germany.

Elizabeth, her father and a friend travelled 'in the large pony trap' from their family home, Bowen's Court, to Mitchelstown, some seven or eight miles away, where the Anglo-Irish from north-east Cork, and from counties Limerick, Waterford and Tipperary, had assembled.'For miles round, each isolated big house had disgorged its talker, this first day of the war. The tension of months, of years – outlying tension of Europe, inner tension of Ireland – broke in a spate of words.' In lyrical and elegiac mood, Bowen described the setting for this final gathering of 'the unmartialled loyalists of the south' – the storm clouds, literally and metaphorically, that blew down from the Galtee mountains on the exposed and isolated castle, the party that presaged the passing of a generation, a people and a way of life. In a valedictory paragraph, Bowen wrote:

> It was an afternoon when the simplest person begins to anticipate memory – this Mitchelstown garden party, it was agreed, would remain in everyone's memory as historic. It was also a more final scene than we knew. Ten years hence, it was all to seem like a dream – and the Castle itself would be a few bleached stumps on the plateau . . . Many of those guests, those vehement talkers, would be scattered, houseless, sonless, or themselves dead.[45]

Whence Parnell?[1]

OWEN DUDLEY EDWARDS

> What, without asking, hither hurried *whence*?
> And, without asking, *whither* hurried hence?
> Another and another Cup to drown
> The Memory of this Impertinence?
>
> *The Rubáiyát of Omar Khayyám*

Has Irish scholarship advanced so little in the professional lifetime of John A. Murphy that I can find no more modern question for examination in his honour than to enquire into the origin of Charles Stewart Parnell? Parnell, God knows, had his day in several courts – from the botched prosecution by W.E. Forster for illegal conspiracy in December 1880 through the Parnell Commission of 1888–9 to the undefended *O'Shea v O'Shea & Parnell* (1890) – and in such pleadings as contemporaries and historians would make concerning him in the posthumous court of public opinion, tangentially history. And have we nothing better to do with our time (rather than snag turnips, as adjured by Myles na gCopaleen), but to return to the pursuit of history by the study of Great Men, of all discredited proto-Fascist endeavours? Yet, there is still much to learn about Parnell, and in trying to understand two crucial influences on him – his American grandfather and his Catholic political 'godfather', Bishop Nulty of Meath – this paper seeks to throw new light on his unexpected emergence as a force in Irish public life. But was Parnell an Irish hero?

One can imagine the long, slow, faintly schoolboy grin with which F.S.L. Lyons must have set out his epigraphs for the first chapter of his magisterial *Charles Stewart Parnell*:[2]

> An Englishman of the strongest type, moulded for an Irish purpose.
>
> (Michael Davitt)

> . . . above all, Mr Parnell was an Irishman, Irish bred, Irish born, 'racy of the soil', knowing its history, devoted to its interest.
>
> (*Drogheda Argus*, 24 April 1875, celebrating Parnell's election to parliament)

> I have always held that both in appearance and to a large extent in character Parnell was much more American than either English or Irish.
> (T.P. O'Connor)

Davitt must have sounded much more English than Parnell did: the slightly chilling thought is that the Englishmen 'of the strongest type' whom he encountered in formative years would have been factory foremen and prison warders. While never Parnell's subordinate, he was for a time a prisoner of his moderate land policy.

Lyons obviously selected the *Drogheda Argus* from a host of other dubious Hibernicist publications, probably from the urgency of its plea, which slightly hinted at its suppressed unease, all the more because Parnell played down his historical knowledge, sometimes for fun (a much more important motive with him than historians have always realized).

T.P. O'Connor had one more formidable credential than the others: his wife was an American.

Irish contemporaries and historians have made much of Parnell's family, none more effectively than Roy Foster in his *Charles Stewart Parnell: The Man and His Family*, a rich Wicklow landscape with well-cut figures.[3] Foster's analogy to *Mansfield Park*, at one point, is happy in itself but also in its symbolism – Foster's work is as good as it is from his apprenticeship to Jane Austen. The instinctive male chauvinism of most historians discounts or distorts the importance of maternal origin, however involuntarily, and the alien antecedents of one parent are usually dismissed in accounts of a life in the country of the other. Yet Winston Churchill was shaped by his American mother and the world whence she came, much more than by the father and his ducal siblings who slighted the ebullient, extroverted, egregious youth.

In what is still probably the most widely sold (if the most questionable) of all his biographies, that by St John Ervine, the focus on Parnell's American mother (Delia Tudor Stewart) was distorted by fashionable racial theory and crude sexism. Parnell's father, Admiral Charles Stewart, war hero of 1812–14, prompted the usual homage to heredity from Ervine (whose shortcomings as biographer should not blind us to his quality as playwright and novelist):

> The swiftness of judgment and grasp of detail which were notable in Parnell, exciting the admiration and wonder of his contemporaries, were clearly inherited from 'Old Ironsides', and perhaps also his susceptibility to the love of women. One sees in the eyes of Parnell's mother a strong, lustful look, and we may believe that Parnell's highly sexual nature was derived by him from the distaff side.[4]

She did not die until 1898 (aged eighty-two) but though she concluded her largely American life in Avondale there is no reason to suppose that the then fourteen-year-old Ervine had strayed from his native Belfast to see her strong, lustful look for himself, and while she was certainly the mother of twelve children, in the absence of any question regarding their paternity one can hardly reduce her husband to a condition of asexual torpor.

Appreciation of this *farce malgré lui* may have encouraged more sober historians to devalue the American heritage, particularly when celebrated by Ervine in such lines as 'his [Stewart's] blood unmistakenly flowed through the veins of one of his grandchildren', and '[Parnell] had an uncanny gift, derived, no doubt, from his grandfather, "Old Ironsides" Stewart, of concentrating his thoughts on the essential matter and disregarding all else'. After what Bertie Wooster would call pure mashed potatoes such as this, it is hardly surprising that posterity left Old Ironsides at the scrap-merchant, more particularly when coupled with Ervine's thesis that Parnell's 'singular antipathy to the race from which he had sprung' [i.e. the English, not the Americans or the Irish] arose because his mother 'had deliberately misshaped her son's mind; and had reared him and his brothers and sisters in a rage which could not end otherwise than in the ruin of those whom it racked'.[5] Future historians well knew that Delia Tudor Stewart Parnell, like most mid-Victorian parents in landed society, probably did not rear her children at all, beyond passing vagaries: servants did that. Grandparents often had more to do with rearing than parents. The historian cannot judge whether a grandparent, never seen by a child, transmitted hereditary forms describable as blood with whatever physiological adjuncts. But the historian may infer what the child is likely to have heard of the grandparent whose name it bears. We may dismiss Ervine's nonsense without question in this context. The story of Charles Stewart was not one likely to induce Anglophobia: far from it. Irish Anglophobia arises from defeat. That particular Charles Stewart was never defeated. He never encountered the British without defeating *them*. Parnell thus grew up in a tradition far removed from those of ordinary Irish nationalists, whether Catholic, Protestant or otherwise: a tradition of victory.

It would be reaffirmed during his three visits to America, notably in his tour of January–March 1880, but he first learned it as a boy in Avondale, most dramatically through his grandmother, estranged from the war hero, and reported by John Howard Parnell as intimate above all with her grandson Charles. John testifies to their closeness when she stayed with the family in summer 1860, and that Charles, who always went up to say goodbye to her before leaving the house, was the last person to see her alive. What the old lady would naturally have talked about was her romantic courtship when Captain Charles Stewart came back from the sea during the war of 1812. After their wedding, on 25 November 1813, he returned to his war as reported by their daughter.

> 'What shall I bring you on my return?' he asked his young bride. 'Bring me a British frigate' was the reply. 'I'll bring you two.' Soon after this he kept his word by capturing the two vessels.[6]

Stewart's capture of the two British ships in the one engagement is a matter of fact. The promise may simply be a confection grown to adorn the feat, but what concerns us is that the story was told in the family, particularly to the hero's namesake. That Parnell would seek to capture two British parties for Home Rule in 1885–6 is not coincidence. As his American relatives would have said, he had been taught to think big. The Admiral died in 1869, two years before Charles's first visit to the country defended by his grandfather against the United Kingdom.[7]

Any knowledge of this American journey of 1871–2 that we have comes from John Howard Parnell, whose memoir and character have been eloquently rehabilitated by Roy Foster. Some of John's earlier recollections were reworked for his *Charles Stewart Parnell* (1916). This one was used by Barry O'Brien:

> One day we called to see a State Governor. When we came away, Charlie surprised me by saying, 'You see that fellow despises us because we are Irish. But the Irish can make themselves felt everywhere if they are self-reliant and stick to each other. Just think of that fellow. Where has he come from? and yet he despises the Irish.'... The idea that the Irish were despised was always in Charlie's mind. But you would never know it if some particular thing did not happen to stir him up at the moment ...[8]

The Governor of Alabama from 1870 to 1872 was Robert Burns Lindsay, a Dumfries Scot who emigrated to the USA in 1844 at the age of twenty, and began his Alabama life as a schoolteacher in 1849. This explains Parnell's point about his origin. In British–Irish social terms Lindsay was nobody compared to the Parnells of Avondale, not to speak of their English cousins, the Barons Congleton. His Alabama rise had been rapid, eventually becoming, as Governor, the chosen standard-bearer for the white Southern ex-Confederates, campaigning for what they termed 'Home Rule', or soon would. Why he so offended the lord of Avondale, whose brother was a considerable Alabama peach-grower, is unknown. John Howard Parnell alludes to Charles Parnell's interest in coal-mine investments at this point. There may have been an attempt by the Parnells to seek state government support for some project which would have won them profit, and Lindsay, of frugal traditions, hard-won advancement and election on anti-corruption issues, would be cold to such ideas.

Parnell told the Special Commission in 1889 that he did not 'mix with the Irish people in America' on his first visit. In fact, he exhibited a classic instance of what the Copernicus of Irish-American historiography, Thomas N. Brown, would later see as the mainspring of Irish-American nationalism: need for status improvement by means of an Irish identity which if not politicized and glamorized could drag the individual immigrant down. Parnell drew positive lessons from American Reconstruction by asking questions and becoming embroiled in arguments about it. John Howard Parnell records introducing him to 'Mr Matt Hill, uncle of the celebrated Senator Hill of Georgia, and they had many lively discussions together over the war. Charley's sympathies had hitherto been entirely for the North, but Mr Hill, who was a Southerner, succeeded in modifying his views.' Senator Benjamin Harvey Hill (1823–82) was at that point still a senator by courtesy, having served in the Confederate Senate but not as yet the United States upper chamber, which he reached in 1877 via the US House of Representatives from 1873 to 1877. Uncle Matt was thus presumably not much younger than the century, which gave Parnell insights into Confederate and post-Confederate politics in a deep historical context.

It pleased Parnell's mischievous sense of humour to portray himself as indifferent to history, but, in fact, he reasoned from history most effectively and turned Froudian controversies neatly to his purposes. But in 1871 his historical interests seem to have been chiefly American. If he knew nothing else, he knew about his grandfather. The evidence is that he knew a great deal else. William O'Brien recalled him on American history at Kilmainham and elsewhere, and it is unlikely that this awareness would have been accumulated after his American sojourn of six or eight months. More, O'Brien makes it clear that he argued Irish history in an American perspective:

> 'Ireland', he said, 'is too small a country for a rebellion. There is not enough room to run away.' There is, perhaps, a spice of his own pungent humour in the remark; but he argued it out as one of the deep truths of Irish public policy. 'Washington', he said, 'saved America by running away. If he had been fighting in Ireland, he would have been brought to a surrender in six weeks . . .'

The judgement may be the best six-word summary of Washington's achievement in the war of American independence. Whether it is or not, it rests on knowledge, not bluff. O'Brien added later:

> There was no subject on which Parnell better loved to chat than America and the American Revolution. He would delight to trace Washington through his constant retreats and devices for avoiding battle, holding that to his willingness to decamp and play an inglorious waiting-game it was due that the insurrection was not promptly suppressed by the troops. 'Washington would be a highly unpopular leader in Ireland,' he would say with a smile. For the United States of our day, bursting with youthful energy and rude strength, he had the admiration of one who was half American by blood and five-sixths in sympathy . . . 'The United States are the only people that could smash England. They may even be the means of freeing Ireland without the smashing.'[9]

He wore his American identity as an inheritance, and to T.P. O'Connor – and to others – he proclaimed it:

> . . . though intensely Irish, I have always thought . . . that in physique and in character, Mr Parnell was, above all things, American. That slight frame, inspired by inflexible resolution and dauntless courage, was the type of the strange and picturesque, and daring race which combines

> such extraordinary strength and enterprise of character with a physique more delicate in form and appearance than that of any other nationality in the Arian world. The pallid complexion was also the typical complexion of America, and, finally, the death-like grip of the will was suggestive of the iron resolution which is one of America's marked national characteristics.[10]

Lindsay viewed Parnell as a Scotsman looking at an Irishman, and a poor Scot looking at a rich Irishman, probably trying to be richer. Other Americans seemed to converse with Parnell not as though he was an American but as though there were no barrier in nationality such as divided them from other Europeans. Melville Stone, co-proprietor of the Chicago *Daily News*, was in Ireland in 1878. In counterpart to Parnell, his mother was Irish:

> I went down to County Wicklow for a lawn party at a gentleman's demesne. I was presented to a young woman named Lady Mary. What her real name was, or who she was, I have never known. It was quite enough to be presented to Lady Mary. We fell to talking. 'You are from She-*kay*-go?' she asked in a truly English drawl. 'Yes,' I replied. And then one may imagine my consternation when she continued with: 'And is that anywhere near where the dear young prince was killed?' meaning South Africa, where the Prince Imperial of France had lost his life a month earlier.
>
> A few weeks later, while coaching from Cork to the lakes of Killarney, we halted at a wayside shrine between Mallow and Glengariff. The usual group of barefooted beggars attacked us. 'Where are ye from?' asked a ragged old woman. 'From Chicago', I answered. 'And how's it gettin' along since yer fire?' she returned. It was not that she knew her geography so well, but, in common with so many other Irish peasants, she had relatives in our city from whom she had heard and in whom she was interested.
>
> I met Charles Stewart Parnell and told him of the Lady Mary episode. I shall never forget the quizzical, cynical look he gave me, nor how he fell to talking of conditions in Ireland. There was nothing of the emotional Irishman about him. Rather he was the cool, practical, analytical American type. 'I am not surprised,' said he. 'I have no doubt the young woman could have told you with whom the Queen drove out yesterday afternoon. These people live in the atmosphere of the British Court. They know nothing else.'[11]

Stone's crisp narrative in his *Fifty Years a Journalist* befits the future manager and maker of the Associated Press: already thinking in terms of global coverage and cosmopolitan sophistication, he saw in Parnell a fellow-rebel against archaic rule. He evidently saw a counterpart in more respects than an alien maternity. Both of them in fact reflected an impatient American rejection of United States isolation and British complacency. Stone's witness brings out a particular bond between Parnell and many Irish Catholics after his return in 1874: he knew the country where their relatives were, where their hopes so often lay, where the means from which to pay the rent might be found. The 'American letter', its financial enclosure ultimately destined for the landlord, was perhaps the first point on which he made good crowd contact – encouraging heckles and prompting obvious responses – in his first speech on his North American tour in January 1880.

Stone also illustrates another point. Parnell seems to have had a natural affinity for journalists, and this may also be an American inheritence. His closest friend, James J. O'Kelly, MP, was a crack American journalist. His most devoted admirers among the future anti-Parnellites were Justin McCarthy and William O'Brien. T.P. O'Connor's obsession with Parnell was so professional that, within ten days of Parnell's death, O'Connor's brief but full-scale biography had been published: it established much longer-lasting biographical contours for future historians than their curt dismissals of it have acknowledged, just as his earlier *The Parnell Movement* established so many factual bases for them. Parnell's greatest biographer Richard Barry O'Brien (as F.S.L. Lyons in the full flush of his own biography's success asserted) was a journalist who owed the genius of his book to the art of the interview. His best memoir from an English hand was that of a journalist, Alfred Robbins of the Birmingham *Daily Post*. His most recent major biographer is a journalist, Robert Kee. His lead associates other than John Dillon were at one time or another in their lives primarily journalists, and Dillon's prominence was initially due to his father's being co-founder of the most successful weekly newspaper of the 1840s in the United Kingdom, the *Nation*. And, of course, his name was forged by a leading Irish journalist, Richard Pigott, while his vindication from that accusation nearly ruined the most famous journal in the world, the London *Times*. And in the view of his follower Oscar Wilde he was ultimately destroyed by the journalists:

> The harm is done by the serious, thoughtful, earnest journalists who solemnly, as they are doing at present, will drag before the eyes of the public some incident in the private life of a great statesman, of a man who is a leader of political thought as he is a creator of political force, and invite the public to discuss the incident, to exercise authority in the matter, to give their views, and not merely to give their views, but to carry them into action, to dictate to the man upon all other points, to dictate to his party, to dictate to his country, in fact, to make themselves ridiculous, offensive, and harmful.

Wilde (reviewing a novel by Froude) had already contextualized Parnell's American identity:

> An entirely new factor has appeared in the social development of the country, and this factor is the Irish-American, and his influence. To mature its powers, to concentrate its action, to learn the secret of its own strength and of England's weakness, the Celtic intellect has had to cross the Atlantic. At home it had but learned the pathetic weakness nationality possesses. What captivity was to the Jews, exile has been to the Irish:

> America and American influence have educated them. Their first practical leader is an Irish-American.[12]

Was Parnell's infectious liking for journalists the product of his first American months? John Howard Parnell seems to have won him an important link in Patrick Moran of the *Atlanta Constitution*, the most influential newspaper of the ex-Confederate South: Moran later chaired the Georgia meeting for Parnell's later tour (the interruption of which after forty days by the UK general election of 1880 meant that John had to substitute for his brother). Henry Watterson of the Louisville *Courier-Journal*, its counterpart in the upper South, evangelized Kentucky for Parnell in 1880, hosting him with relish. Before 1871 there is no sign of any journalistic associations. After his return, he found his first major political ally in journalism. Alexander Martin Sullivan of the *Nation* was impressed by what he saw:

> a rather pale-faced and thoughtful but handsome and well-built young gentleman; quiet, undemonstrative, and refined. In personal appearance, in manners, voice, and accent, he is English, with a tinge of the American. A stranger would judge him to be a cultivated American who had resided a great deal in England, or a cultivated Englishman who had resided a good deal in America.[13]

What Parnell did for Sullivan was to symbolize a perspective come of age. The politics of Irish Catholicism had always found identity in overseas credentials, whether from Rome, Spain or most recently France: O'Connell and Stephens in their utterly different ways had gained their most dramatic political momentum from France, Paul Cullen from Rome. Parnell appeared in a generation that found its best hopes in the United States, where he himself had learned the Protestant/Catholic divide brought little or no immunity in an anti-Irish climate. The necessity was common cause to win respect. Ironically, if Parnell had been as conscious of his grandfather's religious and ethnic origin as he was of his life and achievements, he might have been less ready for a common destiny with his fellow-Irish Catholics. Irish-American Protestant Episcopalians made little impact as an ethnic group: they merged too easily with the American Protestant population, or with the Irish-American population, depending on whether their Irish or their Protestant end was foremost. The Scots-descended Ulster Protestants in America did assert their divergence from the Irish-American Catholics, especially as Irish-American nationalism gathered visibility, strength and political clout. But by that stage Parnell was ready to use his grandfather as a symbol of future 32-county unity, given his own place as his grandfather's chief political heir.

Once Parnell had accepted the principle of a common Irish search for respect, melding with an American yearning for international status, he developed the political approach which would prove so effective in evangelizing American public opinion to pass moral judgement on the Irish land system and, by corollary, on British control of Ireland. His self-education in working with Catholics was a necessary part of this, and despite one or two calumnies charging him with sectarianism (which seem to have originated with Protestant rivals), the indications are that most of his few friends were Catholics. But where did he first acquire intellectual communion with Irish Catholics?

The Meath by-election that brought Parnell into the House of Commons in 1875 in place of the dead John Martin naturally has pride of place in his biographies, and has received valuable discussion from a variety of eminent scholars. Yet what may have been its most seminal moment in the making of his politics seems to have gone uncharted. It has been rather like a complex jigsaw, with admirable work on individual pieces. Richard Barry O'Brien when writing his life of Parnell was, as Chairman of the Irish Literary Society in London, very much under the authoritative eye of Sir Charles Gavan Duffy, its Hon. President. Now in his early eighties, Duffy still combined an almost totalitarian ruthlessness in forcing his own version of history on posterity with a strange readiness to diminish his own role in the events described. He was particularly anxious to have the story of the Meath election retold on his terms. Gavan Duffy was not yet sixty in 1875 and, while a veteran of Australian politics as well as Young Ireland, was not yet ready to write himself out of future Irish public life. He had his local votaries in this election, headed by Father Peter O'Reilly who cabled him to Brindisi, where he had arrived from Australia:

> John Martin dead, telegraph will you stand for Meath. At a conference in Kells on Monday twenty-four priests present, much enthusiasm the bishop not disapproving. Come home, success certain.

In his *My Life in Two Hemispheres* published in 1898, the same year as Barry O'Brien's book, Gavan Duffy said he replied that he did not want a seat in parliament, and was prevented from campaigning by medical treatment for his voice, but that if elected, 'I would feel it my duty to stand.'[14] If nothing else, it showed he had lost little skill in either political adroitness or moral uplift.

The London *Times* on 3 April 1875 had covered Martin's (Presbyterian) funeral near Newry on 2 April, the mourners including only eight MPs but also 'Charles Stuart Parnell'. Martin had been his most enthusiastic sponsor at the preceding Dublin by-election. *The Times* noted an election meeting in Navan on the same night, 2 April, and that it had set a further meeting for Tuesday 6 April, and that Gavan Duffy was believed a likely candidate, as was the local solicitor Hinds, but that 'Mr C. Stuart Parnell has addressed the constituency, declaring himself as an advocate of denominational education and Home Rule' (i.e. in an election address). By Monday 5 April *The Times* thought it 'doubtful whether [Parnell] will be adopted by those who assume to advise the electors', an elephantine veiling of allusion to the Catholic clergy. *The Times* Dublin correspondent thought 'those' might disapprove of his having issued the address before seeking their permission so to do, and noted, among other possible candidates, Gavan Duffy.[15]

In 1910 Frank Hugh O'Donnell would claim that the Home Rule party leader, Isaac Butt, had offered him the Meath nomination in 1875, and that he refused. O'Donnell would sacrifice any truth on the altar of his own self-importance but when (briefly) taking himself off the stage he could be shrewd enough, as his next comments showed. (Allowance must be made for the anti-clerical bias at the time of writing: he oscillated wildly between extreme clericalism and anti-clericalism.)

> There can be no doubt that a powerful section of the Catholic clergy, not content with abstention from Home Rule – which was perfectly legitimate in members of their sacred profession vowed to unworldly aims – were casting about for means to revive the previous state of Irish politics, when the bishops had practically succeeded to that disposal of Government patronage which was enjoyed by O'Connell. To restore the prestige of O'Connellism, and to fight Home Rule with Repeal, formed an obvious sort of strategy. A large body of the most influential clergy in the diocese of Meath conceived the idea of raising Sir Charles Gavan Duffy as a rival to Isaac Butt. Gavan Duffy had been, like Mitchell [*sic*] and Martin, a Young Irelander, but had found more favourable jurors for lighter charges. After some years in the London Parliament, he had retired to Australia, risen to a front rank as a colonial statesman, and received knighthood. Gavan Duffy was too blunt for his clerical patrons. He declared his hostility to Home Rule in no mincing phrase. The country was not prepared for an open breach with the policy which it had just sanctioned at the Conference and at the polls. Gavan Duffy was informed that his case was hopeless. The field was open for the follower of Butt, the young Charles Stewart Parnell.[16]

In his 1898 memoirs Gavan Duffy had seen himself as victim rather than hero in the episode. His initial reply to Fathers Peter O'Reilly and Michael Tormey of Kingscourt had excused himself from campaigning, made no political commitments and invited the nomination as a blank cheque: he would not court Meath, it had to court him. Had he been able to pursue this in the silence he had sought, he evidently intended it to give him the nomination, after which he could not only oppose Butt's leadership, but even his party, inviting its MPs (one assumes) to regroup behind Gavan Duffy. He had supplicated nothing, and should he win nomination and election, he could remain his own man. He was winkled out of his shell by an unscrupulous fraud, and came clean against his own intentions. A telegram arrived after Gavan Duffy's reply to O'Reilly:

> John Martin dead. Parnell candidate of Home Rule League would probably retire if you join League and stand. Wire reply. William Dillon, 15 Nassau Street, Dublin.

Gavan Duffy was thus lured into admitting he would not join the Home Rule League. He replied to William Dillon by telegram:

> Thanks. I do not seek a constituency, but I am a Repealer, as I have been all my life, and if Meath elect me I will do my best in concert with the Irish members to serve the Irish cause. Should the constituency be dissatisfied with me at any time, I will resign. But if it be made a condition that I shall join the League and adopt its novel formula instead of the principles held by me in common with O'Connell, O'Brien, Davis, Dillon, Dr. [i.e. Bishop Edward] Maginn, Meagher, and all the Nationalists of my time – that I cannot do. Gavan Duffy.[17]

On this showing his divergence lay in support for an independent Irish parliament under the same monarch as opposed to a legislature subordinate to the Westminster parliament. A letter he wrote concurrently to William Dillon, in early April 1874 complained about the adverse effects of Westminster on Irish patriots' health (including Dillon's late father) and then observed:

> Considering that the Repeal Association in the era of its greatest power and authority found it necessary to recognize that opinion cannot be always cast in the same mould by opening its doors to Federalists, it is doubtful policy, I think, for Federalists to shut their doors on those Repealers who prefer the principles and policy of 1844 to those of 1874.[18]

This seemed fair and soft enough, but its subtext was that O'Connell had invited support from the Federalist Sharman Crawford who then complained that O'Connell had leaped into his boat and swamped it; Gavan Duffy might have sounded to a shrewd observer as though he intended to imitate O'Connell's effect in his own leap for a Home Rule boat.

Posterity has assumed Isaac Butt had gone through a conversion experience either as editor of the *Dublin University Magazine* in the 1840s or as counsel for the Fenian prisoners in the 1860s whereby he reached Home Rule; but Gavan Duffy, out of touch no doubt but perhaps more in tune with realities than subsequent historians, saw Butt as the enemy of Repeal in past and present. Therefore if Gavan Duffy had been nominated and elected in Meath, he would have set up his own stall and battled with Butt for the hearts and minds of the more nationalist-minded of his followers. O'Donnell was right in assuming Cardinal Cullen looked favourably on such an outcome in preference to the present electoral strengths of the Home Rule League under its predominantly Protestant leadership, and in concluding that his former abrasive relationship with Gavan Duffy would have cooled with age into nostalgic good feeling. To Cullen, that Duffy was a Catholic and Butt was not, made all the difference. He had mistaken his man: he might have forgiven Duffy, but Duffy was far from having forgiven him for the quarrels of the 1850s. That is not to say that the Meath clergy were Cullen's men, be they Bishop, parish priest or curate.

Both Barry O'Brien and Gavan Duffy denounced the William Dillon telegram as a forgery in 1898, and thereby left a pretty little problem for posterity. 'It was never signed by William Dillon', wrote Barry O'Brien, 'nor in any way authorised by him.' Who, then, drew Gavan Duffy into the open, and left him vulnerable to the rumour that he would destroy – or annex – the Home Rule League? His problem was that the rumour was true as to his intent, and his success as candidate and captor were both decidedly likely:

> The perplexing incident was that a son of John Dillon's should have used my telegram for such a purpose, and it was a great satisfaction to me to receive a letter from him informing me that his name was signed to the telegram without his knowledge or authority, and during his absence from Dublin . . .
>
> Mr William Dillon, on my strong insistence, at length named the person who had taken this liberty with his name, but after more than twenty years I am unwilling to complete the painful exposure. The offender is still busy in Irish politics, and poses, I perceive, as a man of honour and distinction, and perhaps he has learned to amend his ways; at any rate his father was a good Irishman of constant and unobtrusive patriotism, and for his father's sake I forgive him.[19]

Both Duffy and Barry O'Brien have left clues, and perhaps they intended the forger's identity to be plain: 1) It was not William Dillon, John Blake Dillon's eldest son, but it was someone whose identity he learned easily enough. 2) It was someone who had such ready access to the offices to William Dillon's solicitor cousin, Valentine B. Dillon, of 15 Nassau Street, that he could obtain and remove telegrams to William Dillon at that address. 3) It was someone prominent and respectable in Irish politics in 1898. 4) It was someone whose father, now dead, elicited strong emotive loyalties from Sir Charles Gavan Duffy, and that father had been invariably associated with Irish patriotism but had not been much in the public eye. It was, therefore, John Dillon. Nobody else fulfils all four criteria.

But why should John Dillon not sign the treacherous telegrams in his own name? Would not one son of John Blake Dillon have as natural a call on the confidence of Gavan Duffy as another? This answer may lie in John's relationship with John Mitchel. Both brothers had been active in 1873 in raising a £2,000 subscription to relieve the now poverty-stricken Mitchel who wrote to John (who presumably had won his attention as the more vehement nationalist), and when Mitchel had visited Ireland in summer 1874 he refused to stay with Home Rulers who invited him, including A.M. Sullivan and his brother-in-law John Martin. A Tipperary by-election led to Mitchel's uncontested election, the Disraeli government's subsequent declaration of his unfitness to stand as an undischarged felon and voiding of the election, and the dying Mitchel's return to Ireland to fight the next contest, in which John Dillon had to read his address in his only public appearance. Mitchel was re-elected. His victory was set aside by government in favour of the Tory who had won less than a quarter of his vote. Mitchel then died, with John Dillon the only non-family member at his deathbed. At Mitchel's funeral John Martin collapsed, to die a few days later in the Newry home of Mitchel's brother, where Mitchel had died. Probably John Dillon went to that funeral also, and if he did, he would have met the *protégé* of the Sullivans now expected to be a candidate for Martin's seat, C.S. Parnell, who had subscribed to Mitchel's re-election campaign. A.M. Sullivan was not present at Martin's funeral, as he was speaking in Bristol: T.D. Sullivan, his brother and current editor of the *Nation*, was. In the atmosphere of recrimination following the voiding of the dying Mitchel's victory to seat a wholly unrepresentative Tory, John Dillon was hardly in a mood to welcome home the alternative nationalist choice to Parnell, Sir Charles Gavan Duffy, full of his years and honours (specifically his Knighthood Commander of St Michael and St George), over the dead bodies of the revered Mitchel and the beloved Martin. The bogus telegram thus combined sublime Machiavellian patriotism with a Literary and Historical Society prank (Dillon had been its auditor the previous year). In its latter epiphany it puts John Dillon much more in tune with successive generations of that Society than they may have imagined of him.[20]

It was characteristic of John Dillon to force the pace beyond any authorization; it was characteristic of Parnell to take advantage of an unexpected bonus he might not have authorized. The telegram from Gavan Duffy rejecting the Home Rule League was put about by John Dillon, possibly also by Parnell, probably by the Sullivans and other supporters, and either that, or Gavan Duffy's detailed letter expanding his statement to William Dillon, came to the latter's attention on his return to Dublin in the midst of the Meath election. The episode left Gavan Duffy with resentment against Parnell, afterwards to find fruit in his account, and possibly in his conduct, of the Carnarvon episode of 1885. It may also have left Parnell with a strong sense of the zeal and ruthlessness of John Dillon, and explain why he never seems to have quite trusted him.[21]

But while Gavan Duffy in retrospect assumed the day had been lost for him when his excessively frank telegram to John Dillon's brother had been given widespread publicity, we have no reason to concur. We may posit John Dillon's return to Dublin from John Martin's funeral on the same day, 2 April 1875, with immediate despatch of telegrams, sent in the high heat engendered by political talk after the funeral. But meanwhile Parnell had made a different journey from the funeral. His route was arduous, from Newry to Navan, and the last twenty miles of it evidently took place on 3 April – 'on an outside car', recalled the man he went to see. He travelled from Presbyterian pastor to Roman Catholic Bishop, but Thomas Nulty might very well have agreed with the sentiments with which John Martin's minister had spoken of the dead MP as 'no hireling agitator, no heartless trader on the sorrows and sympathies of the people'. The Revd John Elliot's address set an appropriate agenda for the Bishop of Meath in enquiring of candidates in quest of John Martin's place. He was, of course, also concerned to ensure due deference to his own office and person, which may account for the London *Times* correspondent's awareness that Parnell's issuance of an address before meeting the Bishop invited possible reproach. F.S.L. Lyons assumed the election address's "soundness" on denominational education helped a good deal' – Parnell having declared himself its advocate – but Nulty would have seen that, by the time he gave Parnell a fairly frosty welcome. Lyons had assumed probable priorities for most Catholic bishops, but such did not bind Nulty of Meath, as Cullen had sourly noted while trying to prevent his episcopal appointment ten years earlier, by having assurances conveyed to the Vatican that there was madness in the family. (Cullen subsequently complained that the priests appointed to investigate the charges had insanity in *their* families.[22])

Parnell began by giving Nulty a letter from the parish priest of his own parish, Rathdrum, Co. Wicklow, the Revd Richard Galvin, a vigorous supporter of his. This was gratifying, all the more because Galvin had been Nulty's 'class-fellow'. Galvin may also have had something to say of his namesake, a priest in Alabama, who had known John and Charles Parnell when the latter was nursing the former after the railroad incident. Nulty's account of the meeting, given in 1888, continued:

> Before presenting himself as a candidate for the representation of the county of Meath, he came to solicit my approval and support. Mr Parnell was then but little known to the world. Except the information contained in [Galvin's] letter . . . I had no knowledge whatsoever of him. And yet, in a single interview of hardly two hours' duration, he revealed such extraordinary powers of intellect – such a ready and abundant command of fresh original resource that I, without the slightest fear of rashness or precipitation, committed myself to him with the fullest trust and confidence. I have never seen any solid grounds for withdrawing, or even modifying, the conviction with which I then trusted in him; not have I ever done so for a single moment. As I was thus the first Irish bishop who had absolutely committed himself to Mr Parnell, so I should naturally be the very last to abandon him.[23]

(When the time came to abandon him, Nulty was the most violent anti-Parnellite bishop of all; heartbreak had much to do with the violence.) Our other witness is Parnell himself, as recalled by his brother John:

> The election was practically the result of an animated interview which he had with the Bishop, after which the support of the clergy was assured. The Bishop at first was prejudiced against him, as Charley afterwards told me, but my brother's arguments were so convincing, and his personal charm of manner so great, that he succeeded in winning the Bishop's support, and that made his election certain.[24]

What persuaded Nulty? Cardinal Cullen was also in Meath at the time, convalescing from an illness, and with no improved opinion of the bishop as he morosely reported to his friend Monsignor Tobias Kirby in the Vatican on 13 April:

> Mr Mitchel and Mr Martin, both Protestants, great Young Irelanders, have lately died . . . They have had an election in Meath just now. The priests have the election in their hands, and it would be quite easy to return a Catholic, but the priests are so strange that they cannot make up their minds to select a Catholic however good. At the last election and the previous one, they selected Martin a Presbyterian or Unitarian and rejected Lord Fingall's brother a most devoted Catholic.

Oddly enough, another son of Lord Fingall had been passed over when Nulty was made a bishop, as Cullen may have half-remembered.

> At present, they are supporting a young Protestant, because he promises everything they wish though he will do nothing.[25]

Emmet Larkin must have enjoyed unearthing that prophecy. Nulty would have been mindful of Cullen's point, however little he liked its source: he did not share Cullen's yearning for a Catholic errand-boy, but a do-nothing MP had to be prevented, and a charming country squire or landed nobleman was suspicious in himself. John Martin had beaten the Hon. George Plunkett, a Tory, in 1871, with few priests in Fingall's son's favour, and subject to much local hostility when they were. Parnell would have combined the worst of both worlds, being both squire and Protestant. But Nulty was animated by sentiments stronger than clerical pragmatism. His diocese largely consisted of rich grazing land in Meath, Westmeath and Offaly but it had had its ugly evictions, and Nulty had encountered one as a raw curate in his late twenties near Mount Nugent, Co. Cavan, in the height of the Great Famine, remembering in graphic detail how:

> Seven hundred human beings were driven from their home in one day and set adrift on the world, to gratify the caprice of *one* who, before God and man, probably deserved less consideration than the last and least of them . . . The horrid scenes I then witnessed I must remember all my life long.[26]

It is easy to speculate about what Nulty said to Parnell on Saturday 3 April 1875. He would certainly have commented on Parnell being a landlord and asked him his views on the land question. Parnell would have given the reply he consistently gave to such questions from persons in authority, whether he knew anything about the subject or not: he would have said he knew little and asked what were Nulty's views. And Nulty would have told him.

Parnell's election address contained the same demand for the extension of Ulster Tenant Right to the rest of Ireland, as that issued by him in his unsuccessful attempt for parliament in the Dublin by-election of 1874. But after his meeting with Nulty his speeches changed from pallid pleas for Home Rule to forceful denunciations of land injustice. Gavan Duffy had pioneered Tenant Right as a parliamentary issue for Irish MPs in the early 1850s. What Nulty faced was a choice between the pioneer, now an international statesman intent on receiving a nomination and hence election as a political blank cheque for his leadership ambitions, or a young unknown ready to learn. The nationalist nomination meeting was further postponed, which suggests that Nulty was giving Parnell time to canvass and show how well he had learnt. Successive announcements for meetings on the 6th and then the 9th April were made, and the 12th was made the day for the Home Rule choice of candidate only when the High Sheriff had announced the 14th for closure of nominations and the 17th for the elections. *The Times* correspondent was still reporting the likelihood of Gavan Duffy's nomination on the 12th. Andrew Kettle recalled the Navan nationalist meeting of that day.[27] He did not comment on the place – Navan informally ranked as the Roman Catholic ecclesiastical capital of Co. Meath, being the Bishop's parish and thus his place of Meath county business, the ecclesiastical capital of the diocese of Meath being the Bishop's Palace in Mullingar. If Nulty was actually in Navan on 12 April, he stayed out of sight, as bishops did when not front and centre stage. Dillon had ensured the Home Rule League would support Parnell, more from fear of Duffy, one suspects, than from personal regard, since Parnell's Dublin by-election candidacy in March 1874 had been lack-lustre and initially inarticulate.[28] It was now vital that the Navan meeting settle on a nationalist candidate, since the Tory hopeful, a local landlord, J.L. Naper of Loughcrew, entered the lists that day, and, on existing figures, a straight split of the nationalist vote would give him the victory. The absentee celebrity of Duffy and the inexperienced visibility of Parnell could well cancel one another out. Kettle, an old Tenant League man living in nearby north Co. Dublin, and future father of Tom Kettle, knew some Tenant Right old faithful in Meath:

> Father Peter O'Reilly of Kingscourt, and his curate, Dr. Michael Tormey, were great Duffyites, and the latter came to Navan to propose Gavan Duffy, but, to quote his own words which he repeated years afterwards to some of the men who got up the steam in Navan: 'When I came near the town I heard people shouting for Parnell, and when I came into the town I could near nothing but Parnell, and when I reached the meeting place the people were wild about Parnell, so as I was expected to make some move in the matter I thought the best thing I could do was to say nothing about Duffy, so I proposed Parnell instead.'[29]

Roman Catholic clergy in the Ireland of 1875 well knew the danger of lying about matters known to the public, and Kettle's authentication of his own story, by citation of Tormey's repetition of it to Navan activists present at the meeting of 12 April 1875, merits respect. The strength of Irish clerical control would have made the laity all the readier to point accusing if surreptitious fingers at a transgressor priest. And Tormey portrayed himself in no glorious light. But what he meant by 'people' was as constructively vague as what the authors of the United States Constitution meant by 'people'. The London *Times* acidly described the 'county meeting' as one 'at which the Roman Catholic clergy were largely represented' and might have added that it was held in the study hall of St Finan's Seminary. It would have been the shouting and the wildness of other priests which would have had most impact on Tormey, more particularly if some of them told him that the Bishop was now behind Parnell. More, Tormey was making a leap in the dark in switching his allegiance to the untried Parnell from the Tenant Right leader of his youth: priests do not particularly seek to be led by episcopal light, but on the land question Tormey would have reason to respect Nulty. So he made his leap, and must have astounded those many who expected his speech to be a nomination for Gavan Duffy. Parnell had probably arranged to be proposed or seconded by a local curate, the Revd Hugh Behan, who would subsequently be his legal nominator and who gave an additional speech for him. Father Hugh Behan was the Administrator in Navan parish and was thus to be interpreted as speaking for its nominal parish priest, Nulty himself. He certainly did not offend Nulty by so doing; Nulty promoted him to a parish of his own later in the year. Tormey used his own situation to demand nationalist unity, rounding on the wretched local Protestant solicitor J.T. Hinds, whose recent credentials as a Home Ruler Tormey tore to flitters by exhuming his earlier opposition to the disestablishment of the Church of Ireland when he had last stood as a parliamentary candidate, in 1868. (Hinds got 88 then, and would get 138 in 1875, to Parnell's 1,771 and Naper's 912.)

Once nominated, Parnell gave a speech firmly grounded on the land question, so much so that his closest historian for these years, Roy Foster, found 'his profession of adherence to the Home Rule principle, which followed, . . . almost perfunctory'. The argument against the land question as an election issue was that the Irish tenant farmer (considered as a conceptual monolith) was prosperous in 1875, and that Gladstone's Land Act of 1870 had solved his problems. Nulty's memories would have put that in a different perspective. Parnell said:

> I am not going to praise Mr Gladstone's Act, for it has been proved to be miserably inadequate and has in some respects done harm for the tenants, having converted some good landlords into bad ones, and because it has not given the slightest protection to the tenantry over three-quarters of Ireland. I, however, as a landlord, maintain that the tenant has property in the land as well as the landlord and that we should hold fast to that principle and endeavour to pass a bill which will define what the interest of the tenant is and which will protect that interest. Without fixity of tenure and fair rents the tenants will never be happy, nor will the country be prosperous. Therefore I am sure you will believe me that I will, in and out of Parliament, support fixity of tenure and fair rents.[30]

Nulty had given him the fuel with which to set the heather on fire.

Foster suggests a possible problem with this interpretation: 'Parnell was then, as later in his career, more than careful about alienating the religious guardians of local opinion' (basing his campaign on the Bishop's prime concern certainly accords with that thesis),' . . . although, he told Davitt long afterwards, there was clerical disapproval of some of his references and he was informed "the priests of Meath know nothing about John Stuart Mill"'. Davitt is a perilous source on whose unsupported word to adopt someone else's alleged utterances, although his unreliability was not fully established until T.W. Moody produced his masterly *Davitt and Irish Revolution* some years after his pupil Roy Foster's *Parnell.* To his deep regret, Moody had to conclude that Davitt sometimes lied about past events in defiance of truth and in absence of any ascertainable motive.[31] Davitt in 1904 reproduced supposedly *verbatim* a reminiscence of the 1875 Meath fight, given him (he said) by Parnell in 1879:

> I went strong on John Stuart Mill upon the ownership of land and political economy in my speeches, but I noticed somehow that the priests who gave me great assistance did not seem to like this authority. One day a friend told me he had dined the previous evening with a number of clergymen, and that my speeches were the topic of conversation, and were not too highly praised. 'This young man', remarked one of the clergymen, referring to me, 'comes down to Meath and talks a great deal of John Stuart Mill, but I'd like to tell him that the priests of Meath know nothing of John Stuart Mill.'[32]

However, in February 1881 Nulty wrote 'to the Clergy and laity of the Diocese of Meath' in a Letter (presumably appointed for reading at Sunday Mass in all the Catholic churches, and probably a Lenten Pastoral):

> The late Mr Mill, the deepest thinker of his day, and the ablest economist that ever lived, demonstrated to evidence, a quarter of a century ago, the rottenness and injustice of the Irish laws of land tenure. He showed they stood condemned by every principle of justice and of reason; that they robbed the people of a whole nation, not only of their property, but of every motive and incentive for industry, thrift, and exertion to better and improve their condition. But Mill's powerful and eloquent exposure of this gigantic wrong has ever since attracted but comparatively little attention.[33]

Davitt in 1904 explained that Parnell was not in 1879 a hearty supporter of peasant proprietorship, which he would afterwards advocate in preference to Davitt's ideas of land nationalism: 'He frequently, in our conversations, expressed himself in favour of a solution of the question in the form of a state tenantry, under, of course, a Home-Rule or other national administration.' This may merely be face-saving: but any such conversations may also connect Parnell to Nulty, who in 1881–2 was being quoted by American reformers such as James Redpath and Henry George as an enemy of private property in land.[34]

Indeed, Nulty's comparative radicalism on the land question was of long standing. He had broken from Cullen's National Association in the mid 1860s because of its failure to make an issue of land. He had set up a Tenant Rights Society in Navan, addressing it on 'the *one* – the *great* – *the sole question of Ireland . . . the land question*'. He had advised in 1865 that the Irish in parliament should form an independent opposition, just as Parnell would say he believed must be done, and just as Gavan Duffy would complain Butt refused to do. His critique of Gladstone's Land Act of 1870 was what formed the basis of Parnell's in that speech at the nomination meeting at St Finian's on 12 April. But what, other than his ability to invite and absorb knowledge to his purposes, made Parnell for Nulty was what Thomas Flanagan would term the 'shape into which we . . . poured our hopes'. It was nice to have this young Protestant Wicklow squire with a historical name deferring intelligently to him. But Nulty had grown grey in the ten years of scrutiny of candidates, exceptionally receptive though he might be to lay choices. What had Parnell to offer? After Lord Robert Montagu (convert to Home Rule and to Roman Catholicism to win election for Westmeath in 1874, and subsequent apostate from both), converts were unwanted, save on purely spiritual grounds. Squires were two a penny – tenants' pennies. The Parnells had famous names, but Ireland had no shortage of such. But the grandson of a war hero of 1812 was another matter. There was a good deal of the eager boy left in Nulty. And Parnell had lived in America, the Mecca of so many in Nulty's flock and the source of so many subscriptions to his church collections. Galvin's priest cousin in America was a natural link of conversation. The freshness and originality of which Nulty subsequently spoke meant that he heard something exciting from Parnell that others would not have had. Nulty would have known 'returned Yanks', but few of them from post-Confederate Alabama. Nulty would have known heroes' grandsons, but fewer of them from victory in the American navy. Parnell's boyishness was appropriate in absorbing Nulty. But Nulty's was needed to adopt Parnell. More, he was exhilarated by a cosmopolitan pupil, to have come so far whether physically or ancestrally, and sit at his feet. The Irish episcopate of the nineteenth century greatly respected study: as Nulty's colleague in Galway John MacEvilly put it to seminarians: 'Do you see that Crass? Do you see that Crass on my billy? Do you know what put that Crass there? Shtiddy!' But they got little opportunity for tutorials on any detailed level, and Nulty on land was an authoritative teacher. At last he had found his student.[35]

Nulty's pivotal role in the education and election of Parnell made more impression on the Vatican than on subsequent historians. Archbishop Ignazio Persico, Papal Legate, informed his superiors in 1887 that Nulty 'is one of the most ardent Nationalists and the first to have brought about the election of Parnell as an MP'. But Persico seemed to realize that Nulty himself transcended this achievement, and perhaps may have sensed that Nulty was well to the left of Parnell:

> He has published various pastorals and pamphlets which have made a bad impression because of his extreme opinions on the lease/tenure of property in relation to the agrarian question and also for his antagonism towards the property owners. He is obstinate in his opinions, imprudent in his speech and public discourses and resolute in his opposition to the government.

John A. Murphy, bringing his customary firm-footed sardonic realism to bear on modern scholarship (which needs as much of that commodity as it can get, apportions 'some truth' to the 'view that the "devotional revolution", so-called, was a substitute Irish identity for a lost linguistic and cultural distinctiveness'. Whatever the depth of devotion (whose measurement is beyond human assessment), Persico grudgingly accepted its extent, since the diocese of Meath was

> sufficiently endowed with priests, churches and public establishments; there being 156 priests and 15 regular priests . . . 144 churches including parochial and rural buildings. There are schools in each parish looked after by the good Brothers and religious [nuns] and there is also a college.[36]

But as the prince of this army (and few military officers could match Persico's patronizing snobbery about non-priests in holy orders), Nulty bridged devotion and new as well as old Irish identity, looking forward to a new social order as well as venerating the struggles of his tenant-farmer parents.

Nulty aged as the 1880s advanced, with declining health and worsening eyesight. His rage when Parnell's sexual relations with Katharine O'Shea became known (with the undefended calumny that he betrayed her husband) made him the most extreme of all the Irish hierarchy. In part Nulty's greater vehemence derived from his left-wing status, as Davitt's did. In rhetoric at least, they went beyond Parnell's land solution, and they restrained themselves to be loyal to their triumphant general, and now all that self-restraint seemed nothing but the means to enable Parnell to indulge himself. Parnell in Meath is a Faustian tragedy. He owed his seat to the bishop, and he also owed him the sophistication with which he would return to the land question when (as Nulty had expected) its time arrived. And the priests who had established Parnell's power turned in 1890–91 and tore him like the spirits destroying an apprentice who falls foul of his master, the sorcerer. Parnell had enabled the priests to enter their kingdom, as the real power in Irish social life in place of the out-manoeuvred landlords. But to discover that their victory had involved furthering his fornication for ten years with a married Englishwoman was insupportable, for the humiliated Nulty above all. The genial 56-year-old in his prime who established Parnell as a parliamentarian in 1875 had collapsed into a miserable, vindictive, disillusioned, blind old man screaming from the altar that people should arm themselves in the election of 1892 with sticks against

Parnellite violence. The result was to reduce Meath politics to the faction-fights of Carleton's stories, recording the Ireland of a century earlier. Nulty's great calls for social justice had withered down to confirmation sermons such as that of May 1893:

> Parnellism is the greatest moral curse that ever appeared in this country. The last seven centuries have seen nothing to compare with it. It is a deliberate and wilful attack against the authority of the clergy, against the priests and against the bishops of the country.[37]

The architect was denouncing his proudest edifice.

> O my grief, I've lost him surely. I've lost the only Playboy of the Western World.

Daniel Corkery's *The Hidden Ireland* and the Politics of the Gaelic World

TOM DUNNE

The Hidden Ireland was second-hand in its scholarship and hastily assembled, largely from old articles and lecture notes, on buses and trains and in hotel rooms by an itinerant teacher of Irish; yet it has remained in print since it was first published in 1924, and can be seen now as a foundational text of the new Irish state. Indeed, its colourful partisanship and infectious enthusiasm for the Gaelic poetry of eighteenth-century Munster can still infuriate or engage. Its underlying philosophy has always been controversial, dismissed immediately by Corkery's young *protégé*, Sean O'Faolain, for its praise of 'the decadent drivel of the eighteenth century', which did 'more to retard Irish education than three centuries of foreign rule'.[1] Fifty years later, in 1978, at a seminar on Corkery at University College Cork, where he had been Professor of English from 1931 to 1947 (he died in 1964), I heard one former student, John A. Murphy, accuse Corkery of 'racist, narrow, exclusionist' views, while another defended him with equal vehemence. This defence, by Seán Ó Tuama, appeared in a special Corkery issue of *Scríobh* in the following year, which also included trenchant negative critiques by Declan Kiberd and Breandán Ó Buachalla, and a more sympathetic essay by Gearóid Ó Tuathaigh.[2]

A decade earlier, Louis Cullen had demonstrated how Corkery had misread the poetry as a record of unrelieved poverty, creating 'a dangerous confusion in which the living conditions and housing of the poorest are combined with the outlook and aspirations of the relatively prosperous'.[3] Historians since then have tended to ignore not only *The Hidden Ireland*, but also the value of eighteenth-century Gaelic poetry, despite Cullen's acknowledgement in a postscript to a reissue of his critique that 'it is doubtful if any more remarkable evidence exists in Europe of the intellectual, social and political recesses of an important and influential layer of society – essentially a middling group – in the rural world'.[4]

It was not until 1993 that a full-length study of Corkery appeared, Patrick Maume's superb first book, *'Life That is Exile': Daniel Corkery and the Search for Irish Ireland*. A much reduced version of an heroically long and erudite Master's thesis, which I supervised, this was one of the finest pieces of work by a postgraduate of the Irish History Department under John A. Murphy's headship.[5] Critical but also balanced in its judgements, Maume's work contained many new insights. In its analysis of *The Hidden Ireland* it also picked up on a comment by Francis McManus on Corkery's even more controversial book *Synge and Anglo-Irish Literature* (1931) that it 'was a continuation of the war of independence, and, indeed, an extension of the civil war. For his view was exclusivist, anti-colonial, fundamentally Gaelic and historically Catholic.'[6] In Maume's book, and in more detail in his thesis, *The Hidden Ireland* is analysed partly in terms of Corkery's continued commitment to the idealism of the Republican side in the Civil War, and his disdain for the compromises of politics. This struck a chord with me because, in the course of my own work on the poetry of this period, I had been conscious of the way that Corkery consistently depoliticized the Gaelic tradition. And so it seemed fitting that in a festschrift for John A. Murphy I should explore this theme in the light of Patrick Maume's insights, and mainly by looking at the sources available to Corkery and the use he made of them.

Daniel Corkery (1878–1964) became a nationalist in his early twenties, under the influence of the Gaelic League, which provided the main basis of his cultural philosophy for the rest of his long life.[7] He had grown up saturated in English culture, in a bookish, artisan family, carpenters in Cork city for generations. While his brothers became trade-union activists and socialists, this shy boy, with his stammer and lame leg, was drawn more to the medievalism associated with the Arts and Crafts movement in England, and the writings of John Ruskin and William Morris. Paradoxically, his later strident Irish nationalism was always tinged by this form of English Romanticism, particularly its elevation of the particularism and populism of medieval art over the universalism and élitism of the Renaissance. This formed an important subtext of *The Hidden Ireland*, and was set out at length in the introduction, which connected the medievalism, as he saw it, of eighteenth-century Gaelic poetry with 'a great struggle going on in modern literature between the dying spirit of the Renaissance and the rediscovered spirit of nationality'. The Renaissance was 'artificial . . . rootless', and 'one of its evil effects was to whiten all the native cultures of Europe to a common value'. Modern Romanticism was concerned mainly to reverse this, so 'that every Romantic movement is a national effort to discover for present needs forms other than the classical forms'. Luckily, 'the Renaissance hardly reached the Gaeldom', so that 'the medieval Irish Munster of the eighteenth century', far from being an anachronism, 'brings the mind right into the stream of modern literature'.[8]

Corkery became a teacher in poor, inner-city schools and his early writing targeted Cork bourgeois philistinism. His discovery of the Irish language, initially in the back lanes of the city, then in the small remaining Irish-speaking districts in west Cork and Kerry, and in the eighteenth-century literary tradition still remembered there, offered a very different and Irish antidote to all that he disliked in modern urban life; and he began to articulate the basis of his 'hidden Ireland' thesis in the early 1900s, particularly in articles for D.P. Moran's ultra-nationalist paper, *The Leader*.[9] While increasingly active in the Gaelic League and in the Cork National Theatre Society, he was slow to get involved politically. Indeed, his first play, *The Embers* (1909), was 'a Moranite satire on Irish politics, constitutional and physical force'.[10] When the little theatre, An Dún, became a Volunteer drill hall, Corkery immersed himself in writing his final novel, *The Threshold of Quiet* (published in 1917), and, while increasingly critical of the Parliamentary Party and Home Rule, he didn't commit himself to Sinn Féin until after the 1916 Rising, which he celebrated in his 1918 play, *Resurrection*. By now, Corkery felt alienated from more than 'that unnative Cork'[11] and had begun to reject the very idea of an Irish writer writing in the English language, despite his own considerable gifts and growing reputation (a landmark collection of short stories, *A Munster Twilight*, had appeared in 1916).

He acquired a basic competence in Irish, without ever becoming fully at home in the language, and found in the west Cork Gaeltacht (Irish speaking area) a lost Eden, where 'every field had a name . . . every hamlet had its song . . . before people learned to think imperially'.[12] In a 1911 lecture, he declared that 'the literature produced in Ireland, written in the English tongue' was 'scarcely worth talking about . . . because the Irish were not expressing themselves fully, as the Englishman was looking over his shoulder'.[13] This anticipated (by more than fifty years) Albert Memmi's classic formulation that 'the role of the colonised writer is too difficult to sustain', particularly when writing in the language of the colonial power. But, as Memmi was also to point out, choosing to write instead in the native, marginalized language would mean losing most of one's audience and influence.[14] Corkery continued to argue the Gaelic League ideal mainly through English, and even to publish short stories in that language, though his creative writing lost its impetus. Putting his energies into the movement to restore Irish and to connect with its ancient literary tradition, he was conscious of the dilemma of the revivalist in a colonial context, later articulated graphically and bleakly by Memmi the Tunisian:

> He is restored to a not very glorious history, pierced through with frightful holes, to a moribund culture which he had planned to abandon, to frozen traditions, to a rusted tongue.[15]

The Hidden Ireland is more optimistic and can be read as a sustained, and sometimes superb, attempt to make the tradition live, to reveal its glorious past and connect it seamlessly to the present, bridging the fissures made by colonialism and making English Ireland an irrelevance. Paradoxically, it succeeded best when it employed the literary skills that Corkery had honed in his English fictions. In this, and other respects, *The Hidden Ireland* has strong claims to be regarded as an early classic of post-colonial literature –

even in its systematic exclusion of the complex, often pragmatic political responses of the Gaelic world to conquest and colonization.

Corkery had, from the beginning, presented his idea of a 'hidden Ireland' as the antithesis of the world of conventional politics. He first used the term in a 1915 lecture, and the same year he argued in *The Leader* that the policies of constitutional nationalists and their 'pinchback institutions' (aided by 'our bat-eyed historians and their muck-raking learning') tended to 'reduce the whole nation to the level of a colony'. In the same newspaper, the following year, he dismissed that whole tradition, back to Grattan, as unimportant, compared with 'the hitherto hidden Ireland of which the Irish language spoke so intimately'.[16] He refused a nomination as a Sinn Féin candidate in the 1918 general election, but celebrated the heroism of the War of Independence in a 1920 collection of short stories, *The Hounds of Banba*. He defended the hunger strike to the death of his old friend Terence McSwiney, and this remained for him a potent symbol of uncompromising idealism. Predictably, he rejected the compromises involved in the Treaty, and for the first (and last) time took an active political role as a Republican propagandist, writing especially for the short-lived *Poblacht na hÉireann*, in 'these dismal days of constitution-making'.[17] But he remained primarily a teacher and writer, and his ultimate and enduring response to the Treaty was the assertion of a pure and uncompromised cultural tradition, uncontaminated by politics, which he located physically in the romantic, remote regions of Cork and Kerry, where he had learned Irish, and which were also strongly Republican in the Civil War.

The politics of Gaelic poetry had been problematic for those anxious to promote its importance or to make it available in translation, from the time of Joseph Cooper Walker and Charlotte Brooke at the end of the eighteenth century. They clothed the poetry in the language of contemporary Romanticism, especially as developed in McPherson's *Ossian*, and also, as Leerssen observes, imposed 'patriot sentiment and rhetoric on Ireland's Gaelic past'.[18] Their focus on heroic pre-colonial texts was part of the antiquarian tradition that asserted Ireland's claim to a sophisticated ancient culture.[19] Walker's stress on 'the genius of the Irish language for musical modulation' rather than on content, and Brooke's claim that 'the Irish language . . . is peculiarly suited to . . . plaintive and sentimental poetry' were to determine reception well into the twentieth century.[20] The foregrounding of the near-contemporary and still controversial Jacobite verse by Catholic enthusiasts, beginning with James Hardiman's *Irish Minstrelsy* (1831),[21] has been seen as a breakthrough. But Leerssen's claim, that by his publication of 'the anti-English *aislingí* [Jacobite vision poems] of penal times . . . the Hidden Ireland was finally allowed to reach the ears of the Irish public at large, and in its own voice', needs qualification.[22] Few could read the originals, and the translations supplied occluded their anti-settler, anti-Protestant sentiments, and reduced them to a sentimentalized patriotism that was a pastiche of Moore. Thus, for example, the last verse of 'Súil Cabhrach Éireann' ('The Expected of Ireland') with its traditional thirst for revenge on the English colonists, imagining them '*gan chóiste, gan chronóig, gan fhíon, gan mhairt-fheoil* [without coach, shelter, wine or beef]', ends with the prayer that this prophecy be fulfilled. But the translation reduces it to, 'When the pageant display and the banquet decay/O swift be the bolt Erin's vengeance to wreck.' Also, in introducing his 'Jacobite Relics', Hardiman insisted that while they contributed to the 'terrible conflagration' of 1798, they were now but 'curious literary fragments', sung for the beauty of their airs, and not for their political sentiments.[23] Edward Walsh went further in introducing his collected *Reliques of Irish Jacobite Poetry*, first published in penny weekly parts in 1844, claiming that the political content of these songs had *never* been significant. 'They were dear to the people from being in their native tongue, rather than from their political sentiments. They sang them to their beautiful native airs without troubling themselves much about the Pretender.'[24]

This was a constant theme of Corkery's, but he also reflected other views of the poetry developed by nineteenth-century cultural nationalists. Anxious to promote a new, inclusive concept of Irishnness, Thomas Davis disliked these Gaelic songs as 'very defective' and 'too despairing', 'their religion bitter and sectarian, their politics Jacobite and concealed by extravagant and tiresome allegory'. By contrast, in 'Scotch songs', 'love, mirth, patriotism are not the ornaments but the inspiration . . . They are full of personal narrative.'[25] Douglas Hyde, reflecting the Celticist stereotyping of Matthew Arnold, believed that 'the most noticeable feature' of 'the songs and folklore of our peasantry' was 'the entire absence of that narrative orderly faculty which so greatly distinguishes the poetry of the Teutonic nations. The Celtic poetic genius is essentially a lyrical one.'[26] This was also Corkery's view, and it limited his understanding of the Gaelic poetic tradition. In particular, his stress on the *aisling* as 'lyrical poetry at its most lyrical' allowed him to disregard its content. The people, he claimed, 'gave them welcome rather for the art that was in them than for the tidings'.[27] This reiterated core argument in *The Hidden Ireland* is an important key to its presentation of the poetry, especially in the central linked chapters on the *aisling* and its most important practitioners, Aogán Ó Rathaille and Eoghan Rua Ó Súilleabháin. The repeated assertion of the lack of any meaningful political content in poetry that he knew to be saturated in it reflects a profound unease with the reality of the tradition that he sought to promote. The royalism, sectarianism and general conservatism of Irish Jacobitism was anathema to this die-hard Republican, as was the pragmatic politics of the Gaelic world in its attempted accommodations with the expanding English state, reflected in fascinating ways in the earlier Bardic poetry. [28]

Corkery made modest claims for *The Hidden Ireland* and acknowledged his indebtedness to the literary scholars who had produced editions and translations of the texts that form the basis of his analysis. He also paid tribute to historians, especially to Lecky's 'noble work', and was content, he wrote, to play the 'part of *vulgarisateur*'.[29] The criticism that he wrote bad social history may be valid, but his crude sketch of unremitting poverty and persecution was intended only as a dramatic backdrop, highlighting his main concern, to celebrate the survival of a great literary tradition through its darkest age. The real question about *The Hidden Ireland* is whether it succeeds as literary and cultural history, and especially whether it establishes a meaningful connection between the élite tradition that ended with Ó Rathaille and the popular culture of the Irish-speaking peasantry that endured to his own day. This had preoccupied revivalists since Hardiman, and Corkery's basic argument – that the peasantry developed an instinctive understanding and trusteeship of the aristocratic tradition, under the leadership of peasant poets who spoke for them – was not new. Hardiman, for example, had claimed that the guardianship not just of the language, but of the literary tradition passed from 'the castle of the chieftain' to 'the cottage of the poor where they have been preserved with a sort of religious veneration'.[30] John O'Daly described the Jacobite songs as 'the natural poetry of the peasant's heart', while Edward Walsh wrote of the appeal of 'the poet's mastery' to 'the imaginative peasant'.[31] For Hyde, 'the Ireland of today is the descendant of the Ireland of the seventh century', and 'the continuation of Erin's national life centred on the mass of the people'.[32] But the main influence was, undoubtedly, Father Patrick Dinneen, lexicographer and editor, who in writing of his – and Corkery's – peasant-poet hero, Eoghan Rua Ó Súilleabháin, articulated what became the key proposition of *The Hidden Ireland*,

> Though an alien tyranny despised and crushed them, [the Irish] people were to Eoghan the true children of the Gael . . . the inheritors of 3,000 years of glorious tradition.[33]

Likewise, the poets of Croom, in Limerick, were for Dinneen, 'of the common people', and their verses tell 'the history of the inner life of the people'.[34]

What is most original and arresting in Corkery's version of this tradition is the evocative phrase, 'the hidden Ireland', whose power, Maume believes, 'springs from its double meaning, implying both continuity and loss'.[35] But it also promises a revelation, access to the *real* Ireland, invisible not only to the Anglo-Irish world of the eighteenth century and its historians, but also to Corkery's Anglicized contemporaries (and to us, their successors). But, Corkery's 'hidden Ireland' is a disappointingly narrow place. Having begun promisingly with the inclusive statement that it was 'in a sense coterminous with Ireland itself' (including even the still bilingual cities), within a few pages 'Gaelic Ireland, self-contained and vital' had 'become purely a peasant nation', then confined further to the poorest peasants, those on 'sterile tracts that were not worth tilling', and further still to those in 'the south-west corner of Munster', and more specifically to the area around Sliabh Luachra, on the Cork–Kerry border, 'the Attica of Ireland'.[36] This reflected, in part, Corkery's own limited experience (he several times cites encounters he had in the Cork and Kerry Gaeltachts), but it was dictated even more by his view of the Gaelic literary tradition, the main focus of his book. This tradition was moribund in Leinster, he believed, while in Connaught and south Ulster, 'the break with the past is noticeable'. But, in his favoured part of Munster, 'that great literary tradition' had its finest eighteenth-century exemplars in Aogán Ó Rathaille and Eoghan Rua Ó Súilleabháin, and, crucially, their verse was still to be heard 'on the lips of fishermen and ditchers'.[37] This also gave the area a contemporary resonance and he called it several times, 'the Irish-Ireland of that period in its fullest and richest'.[38] This focus also reflected the long-running argument in the Gaelic League between the majority, who sought to base the revival of the language on a new synthetic standardized version, rooted mainly in Connaught Irish, and the advocates of Munster Irish (like Dinneen), who argued that its greater continuity with the Gaelic literary tradition made it the only true basis for revival.[39]

In Corkery's core definition of his 'hidden Ireland'

> Irish-Ireland had become in the eighteenth century a peasant nation, harried and poverty stricken, with the cottiers smoky cabin for stronghold.[40]

However, these peasants 'were not a mob', but 'the residuary legatees of a civilisation that was more than a thousand years old. And this they knew'.[41] Vital to this was the fact that, ultimately, 'the Gaelic poets of the time were peasants', and while connected to 'that great literary tradition that for a thousand years had been moulding the Gaelic conception of life and letters', they still 'shared their people's life and, indeed, their thoughts'.[42]

This idealization of the peasant had parallels in the literary revival in English, as well as in other Gaelic League writings, especially those of Hyde and Pearse. However, it bore little relationship to the poetry, which Corkery claimed as his main source. In general, the sources underpinning *The Hidden Ireland* were very limited; his bibliography, had he published one, would have been a modest affair. His dismal view of social conditions in eighteenth-century Ireland, for example, was supported mainly by quotations from accounts of nineteenth-century poverty. His descriptions of the cabins of the poor came from Maria Edgeworth's novel *The Absentee* (1812), Michael Doheny's *The Felon's Track* (1848), W.R. Le Fanu's *Seventy Years of Irish Life* (1893) and his own observations in 'Ventry in 1915'.[43] A major authority cited throughout was the romantic historian Alice Stopford Green, more noted for a reductionist nationalism, than for scholarship. However, he had excellent sources for his analysis of the poetry, the core of the work. Indeed what inspired *The Hidden Ireland,* and made it possible, was the publication of scholarly editions of some bardic poems, and of key eighteenth-century Munster poets over the previous two decades. Osborne Bergin's editions, with commentary, of a range of Bardic poems had appeared mainly in *Studies*, 1915–26,[44] while Eleanor Knott's superb edition of *The Bardic Poems of Tadhg Dall Ó hUiginn* came out in two volumes, in 1920 and 1922. Father Patrick Dinneen's editions of the poems of Aogán Ó Rathaille (with Tadhg Ó Donnchadha, 1911), of Eoghan Ruadh Súilleabháin (1901), Seán Clárach Mac Domhnaill (1902), and of *Filí na Máig* (The Maigue Poets, 1906) were Corkery's main sources, together with Risteárd Ó Foghludha's edition of Brian Merriman's *Cúirt an Mheán Oíche* (The Midnight Court) in 1912. Most of these were published with English translations, as part of the Gaelic League effort to teach Irish, or had introductions to the poetry in English. Despite his own competence in the language, Corkery was reliant to a remarkable degree on these translations and introductions and was less comfortable working from originals. This is clear, for example, in his case-study of 'the Whitechurch Court of Poetry', which made little use of the editions of Diarmaid Mac Sheáin Bhuidhe Mac Cárthaigh and Seán na Ráithíneach by his friend Tadhg Ó Donnchadha.[45] These lacked translations or introductions in English.

But while Corkery relied generally on introductions and translations, he tended to disregard the contextualizing commentary of the scholarly editors, and in particular their demonstrations of the pragmatic politics of the Gaelic élites and how this was reflected in the poetry that they commissioned. Eleanor Knott, for example, showed how Tadhg Dall's poetry reflected the attempts of his patrons to reach accommodation with the expanding Tudor state, accepting English titles, becoming Crown officials or members of parliament, making strategic alliances with the colonial power. She emphasized the basic insincerity of the praise poetry that dominated the bardic output, pointing, for example, to 'the political cynicism' of Ó hUiginn's poem for MacWilliam Burke, with its famous opening line, '*Fearann cloidhimh críoch Bhanbha* [Ireland is but swordland]' and its endorsement of *Realpolitik*. But Knott acknowledged that 'modern taste' prefers the occasional 'reflective or contemplative pieces', in which the poet 'speaks with sincere emotion or with literary feeling' or 'those short, occasional pieces in praise of a woman or his companions'.[46] Such are the *only* poems featured by Corkery in his chapter on 'The Bardic Schools', which ignored political poems for patrons. In part this reflected his dominant view of the poet as romantic hero, but the avoidance of the politics of Bardic poetry was also deliberate, and established the pattern for the later chapters on the eighteenth century. Corkery declared that bardic verse should be sifted for 'the work of those who were poets as well as men of letters', as part of the process of developing a sense of 'a national literature'. But this depended even more on establishing the continuity of 'the tradition' which was his main concern, and led him, 'in choosing, then, some specimens of Bardic poetry' to focus on poetic treatments of 'the Schools themselves' as 'helping on our study'.[47] The only other evidence he can cite for such 'schools' – 'the University system of our nation', dedicated to the training of the aristocracy as well as poets – was the early-eighteenth-century account in English in the 'Memoirs of the Marquis of Clanrickarde', cited by Bergin. Corkery also echoed Bergin's weak argument concerning the lack of contemporary Gaelic sources for these 'schools', that 'to the poets, it was of course too familiar to need description'.[48] Corkery's long quote from this account featured the trainee court poet composing in 'a snug low hut', in darkness, prefiguring the 'dark world' of the peasant poets of the eighteenth century.[49]

A similar concern coloured his presentation of the 'courts of poetry' which in his account succeeded 'the Bardic schools'. These, too, had a crucial public role, 'a school for the humanities in general', educating 'the common people' and meeting mainly in taverns, yet the attraction of the case-study he chose, that of the Blarney/Whitechurch school, is that it is 'hidden in that far off clump of trees' from 'this Cromwellian-Williamite city of Cork', while his memorable evocation of the last meeting of the last court was set 'in some hidden spot'.[50] Yet he also wanted them to represent 'the visible blossoming of the ancient literary tradition', preserving it during 'the dark winter that overtook the nation'.[51] Corkery's core argument of cultural continuity hinged on the view that these 'courts', 'kept the flame alive', acting as a bridge between 'a dying aristocratic past' and 'the rougher accent, the self-trust of the democratic future'.[52] Again he had to admit to a lack of evidence (although, 'acquaintance with the nature of the Bardic schools, out of the death of which the courts grew, enables us in some measure to supply this want') other than 'the many passing references we find in the verses of the poets that frequented them'.[53] Yet he made little use of such material, presenting for the most part a succession of poets rather than a 'court' or an ongoing dialogue. He was thus enabled, yet again, to present poetry without politics, though acknowledging that the verses recited at these gatherings 'were nearly always written on current events, as was the Gaelic fashion' but insisting immediately that 'it was not the theme that was discussed so much as the art of the poet'.[54] This emphasis may partly account for his choice of the Blarney/Whitechurch 'court' as his case-study, rather than the better known example at Croom, Co. Limerick, which is covered instead in brief accounts of some of its participants in the weak final chapter of *The Hidden Ireland*.

His use of the editions of two of the Blarney/Whitechurch poets by Tadhg Ó Donnchadha further illustrated Corkery's obsession with depoliticizing the poetry. He ignored what Ó Donnchadha called Diarmaid Mac Sheáin Bhuidhe Mac Carthaigh's '*furfhógra polaitidheachta* [political proclamation]', the intensely Jacobite 'Caithréim Thaidhg agus Dhiarmada' ('The Triumph of Tadhg and Diarmaid'), and focused instead on his gentle poem on the loss of an old grey mare ('An Fhalartha Ghorm').[55] The lack of any edition of Mac Cárthaigh's successor, Liam Mac Cairteáin, an even more avid Jacobite, allowed Corkery to move on quickly to the last of this group, Seán Ó Murchadha, and his unassuming poetry of ordinary life. Corkery was happy, however, to quote his 'fierce lines' of satire on the killing of an unpopular baliff; the politics of agrarian violence, unlike that of Jacobitism, did not challenge the world-view he wished to present as that of the Gaelic literary tradition.[56] By contrast the Croom 'court' featured aspects of popular culture that were anathema to Corkery, such as drunkenness, sectarianism and bilingualism, and was best known for the political verse of Seán Clárach Mac Domhnall, who, in Corkery's view, 'unfortunately thought Jacobitism almost the only theme worth singing'.[57]

Corkery was aware that most eighteenth-century poets were of a like mind, but his instinctive recoil from the Jacobite message made it impossible for him to understand that it – and not some dubious continuity in 'institutional expression' from 'schools' to 'courts'[58] – provided a vital key to understanding the transmission of the Gaelic literary tradition from its pre-colonial élite forms to the popular culture of the Gaelic-speaking poor. Contemporary nationalists, including Dinneen, shared his inability to understand this, or even to take Jacobitism sufficiently seriously, and this was also true of his critics, from O'Faolain to Louis Cullen.[59] Only in recent years, with Breandán Ó Buachalla's monumental work on the *aisling* tradition, and Éamonn Ó Ciardha's connection of the poetry to its full range of political contexts, has Jacobitism emerged, in Ó Ciardha's words, as 'the main political culture on the island for the greater part of the [eighteenth] century'.[60]

The reasons why this reality has been so unpalatable to nationalists are clear in Ó Buachalla's analysis, which emphasizes Jacobitism's aristocratic, royalist and essentially 'British' ideology, seeking a restoration of the old élites and the old religion under the auspices of the Stuarts. The continuity with the *Realpolitik* of bardic poetry is obvious, but the Stuart cause ultimately became more symbolic than a matter of practical politics and this was particularly evident in the *aisling* poetry that mainly articulated and continued it. The formalism of this élite tradition proved not only enduring but enabling, capable, as Ó Buachalla shows in great detail, of conveying 'a powerful millennial message of individual and communal liberation'. And because this message could ultimately be adapted to articulate the sense of alienation and oppression felt by the Gaelic-speaking rural poor, it proved also to be 'potentially and eventually a radical rhetoric'.[61] This, it now seems clear, was a major factor in the endurance of the *aisling* as the dominant Gaelic literary form from its brilliant origination by the last of the great aristocratic professional poets, Aogán Ó Rathaille, through to the popular song tradition of the pre-Famine poor.[62] Corkery was correct in seeing the literary tradition as the key to cultural continuity, but wrong, even perverse, in insisting on confining its role to form, divorced from content. Ó Ciardha's odd claim that Corkery 'took up his pen in [Jacobitism's] cause', could not be further from the truth.[63] Instead, his clear distaste for it, understandable in the light of his rejection of the royalist and 'British' dimensions of the Treaty, comes through time and again.

But Corkery was too good and too engaged a scholar to be simply an ideologue. Indeed, the appeal and value of *The Hidden Ireland* lie partly in the tensions between his political bias and his anxiety to be true to the poetry he loved. In particular, his tortuous, contradictory analysis of the *aisling* (Chapter Five) repeatedly asserted, then rejected, the contemporary significance of the Jacobite message, resolving the dilemma by emphasizing technical brilliance or the 'music' of the form as its main appeal. It began by describing the *aisling* as the 'intimate expression of the hidden life of the people among whom it flourished' – or, a recurring image, 'In the glowing *Aisling* we find unwitting expression of the darkness that lay upon their life [*sic*].'[64] More specifically, he acknowledged that Aogán Ó Rathaille 'bound up the *Aisling* type of poem with the Jacobite cause. The *Aisling* proper is Jacobite poetry.' But he immediately veered away from considering what this might mean to declaiming that 'the true nature of the *Aisling*' lay in its dazzling technique. These poems 'do not move us, they dazzle us', and are memorable 'solely for their music'; compared to Scottish Jacobite poems, they were 'cold with distance'. Yet, whatever about the Stuart cause, 'Ireland is in all the *Aisling* poems, and the only lines in them that strike fire from us are those of her sorrows – her princes dead, her strongholds broken, her lands in the possession of churls'. However this insight is immediately buried in the claim that this was primarily 'poets poetry . . . lyrical poetry at its most lyrical. It is decoration'. True, 'they were the popular songs of the period', but the 'illiterates . . . learned in literature' who memorized them 'gave them welcome rather for the art that was in them than for the tidings'. Compounding the strained nature of this argument, he added (and later repeated), 'They were academic in their type of mind these peasants.'[65]

Commenting on the appeal of four highly ornamented lines by Eoghan Rua Ó Súilleabháin for his peasant audience, he found it in 'the subtle, irresistible witchcraft of their music', only to then note how 'the lines fall, as is ever happening in these poems, into the bitterness of earnestness as soon as the one root sorrow of all the tribe is reached – the Gael in bondage, his land in the grip of the alien' – but concluded by seeking refuge in the argument that weakened with each reiteration, 'It was to the decoration of this theme, to the vowel music, to the handling of the language that they gave all their thought'.[66] This remarkable pattern, repeated in the concluding section of the chapter, reflected profound unease with the argument being made and an inability to engage with a Gaelic mindset so at odds with that of contemporary nationalism. This, the dominant subtext, is suddenly glimpsed at the end of the chapter in the odd, seemingly inadvertent description of the United Irishmen as 'the Volunteers'.[67]

This pattern, of acknowledging the political core of the poetry, only to shy away from its implications for the real culture of 'the hidden Ireland', continued in the confused chapter on Aogán Ó Rathaille, 'the Dante of Munster', who 'gave intensified and rarified utterance to what was in the hearts of his people', although, as Corkery acknowledged, his poetry was 'frankly aristocratic . . . for the swarming poor . . . Ó Rathaille had no heart'. Instead, he articulated élite responses to the final phase of the colonial wars and confiscations, which Corkery believed made 'nearly all the Irish poetry of the sixteenth, seventeenth and eighteenth centuries . . . one impassioned outcry against England'.[68] This emphasis differs significantly from that of his only source, the Dinneen and Ó Donnchadha edition of Ó Rathaille's verse, which described him as 'above all others the poet of the ancient Irish nobility, who despises upstarts', and the recorder of 'the sorrow and suffering' of 'the Catholic Celt'. Corkery echoed this in describing the politics of Ó Rathaille's great patron, Sir Nicholas Browne, as that of 'Gaelic Catholic Ireland'.[69] But, while Dinneen and Ó Donnchadha described Browne as fighting for 'the cause of enlightened freedom and true toleration', Corkery claimed that 'his side of Ireland, the Gaelic side, would urge the whole of Ireland towards separation'.[70] It was difficult – indeed impossible – to illustrate this in the work of a poet who, for example, longed for the coming of the Stuart, '*In ainm an ríogh dhíograis bheas againn go luath / I gceannas na dtrí ríoghachta 's dá gcosnamh go buan* [In the name of the beloved king we will soon have, ruling over the three kingdoms and defending them forever]'.[71] So, once more, Corkery took refuge in the primacy of form, in this case the comparison with music. Ó Rathaille's elegies were like 'certain movements in Beethoven's symphonies', his lyrics like 'a Mozart sonata, compact of brilliancy, spontaneity and poise'.[72]

While he noted that the themes of the lyrics (which include the *aisling* poems) were 'but two; the first Ireland and it broken, . . . the second, himself, broken too', he evaded any need to explore this by declaring, 'in a lyric, the question of theme must ever be of small moment, the method of treatment being so nearly everything. A lyric is happy insomuch as it sings.' He dealt instead with the ways in which 'sometimes these two themes become one' by evoking the image of the poet as tragic hero.[73] This was based on Dinneen and Ó Donnchadha's literal reading of some of the late poems to prove that, in Corkery's words, Ó Rathaille 'becomes poorer and poorer and dies in poverty', and comes to identify 'his own personal torment' with 'the massed sorrows of his race'. Corkery's main focus, as ever, is on the poet, 'the man himself – utterly tragic . . . who was writing the elegy of the Gaelic race'. Having begun with the description of Ó Rathaille as 'the poet who . . . bound up the *aisling* type of poem with the Jacobite cause', Corkery proved incapable of exploring this theme, and instead ended by assimilating the poetry to the language of the romantic nationalism of his own day.[74]

So did many other revivalist editors and commentators, to such an extent that it became increasingly difficult to understand the Gaelic literary tradition in its own terms. Dinneen, in introducing his edition of the poems of Eoghan Ruadh Ó Súilleabháin, declared, 'The characteristic vehemence of the Irish Celt – his enthusiasm, his warmth of nature, his tenderness of heart – have in his songs found their highest expression.'[75] This text was the biggest single influence on *The Hidden Ireland,* whose hero and exemplar was Eoghan Ruadh Ó Súilleabháin. Corkery followed Dinneen closely in detailing the poet's life, and in his emphasis on his being, above all, 'a lyric poet of the first class'.[76] However, he conspicuously failed to emulate Dinneen's analysis of his best known work, the *aisling* poems. For Dineen they were 'a powerful means of instructing and delighting the popular mind', which, 'while bringing into prominence the present condition of the country, served to keep alive the leading traditions of the past'. Dineen dismissed 'the Stuart' as 'a mere poetic dream . . . of no real political importance', but recognized that 'the promised redemption [of the *aisling*] was duly believed' by 'the peasant', who was also 'enchanted by their music'. Corkery dismissed the 'nineteen *Aisling* (vision) poems' in a paragraph, remarking only on their 'most beautiful lyric qualities'.[77]

Once again, the focus was on the poet, not the poetry. Eoghan Ruadh Ó Súilleabháin, the 'wastrel with a loud laugh', 'a playboy, a Mercutio, albeit a rustic one', his memory still alive in Munster, represented the poet as folk hero, the epitome of his people. But he was emphatically 'not a folk poet; he was a literary man, singing for a literary audience'.[78] This was crucial to Corkery's central argument that the high literary tradition was transmitted through such peasant poets. The indulgent picture presented of the irresponsible rake, 'his wit, his daring, his way with the lasses', makes an interesting contrast with its sober, high Victorian author. Certainly he seemed bewitched by Ó Súilleabháin's colourful life as '*spailpín*' (itinerant labourer) or occasionally as teacher, until forced by 'bad behaviour' (Corkery's euphemism for sexual misconduct) to move on.[79] This led Corkery to include, rather surprisingly given its implications for his argument, Dinneen's account of his hero's time in the British navy, including the full text of Ó Súilleabháin's ballad in English, 'Rodney's Glory', celebrating a famous British victory, in which he took part.[80]

At several points in the text of *The Hidden Ireland* the crucial fact that the poets operated increasingly in a bilingual world surfaced briefly, only to be put aside, in the determination to present the ideal of 'Gaelic Ireland, self-contained and vital'.[81] This was achieved by making it 'purely a peasant nation', and yet it is clear from the beginning, when he is quoted apologizing in English for his transcription of an Ó Rathaille poem, that Eoghan Ruadh Ó Súilleabháin, the archetypal peasant poet, was fully bilingual. Not only that, but he recognized the demand for education in English among the poor, as is evident from his amusing advertisement for a proposed new school, which he asked the priest 'to publish from the altar'. Corkery also gives this in full in English, with the naive comment that while 'written both in Irish and English . . . it is strange that only the English version has come down to us in its entirity'.[82] He never confronted the implications of this bilingualism for his 'Hidden Ireland' thesis, or for the outlook and cultural formation of the poets; but his account of Ó Súilleabháin's period in the navy reflected an unease. He argued that the ballad 'Rodney's Glory' was 'written in a language which never crossed the poet's lips whenever he spoke what was in his own heart or in the heart of his race'. He depicted the poet as isolated among 'his illiterate English shipmates', 'the alien rabble of the lower decks', although the ballad depicted the gun crews as Irish, and the story accompanying it featured a bilingual Irish officer making the poet known to Admiral Rodney. Even more striking was the British patriotism of the ballad, linking it to the tradition of Bardic and Jacobite pragmatism, and describing the victory as won by 'both Rodney's guns and Paddy's sons', who 'fought like Irish heroes'. The ballad ended:

Success to our Irish officers,
Seamen bold and jolly tars,
Who like darling sons of Mars
Take delight in the fight
And vindicate bold England's right
And die for Erin's glory.

Corkery's attempt to balance this by quoting a verse from an *aisling*, in which the poet protests his distress, as a descendant of the ancient kings of Cashel, 'helping him (the English Monarch) that I do not wish to help', only added to the sense of confusion.[83]

After this odd presentation of its representative poet, Corkery's 'hidden Ireland' argument was, effectively, abandoned, and the book ended with an uneasy, largely negative account of the Clare poet Brian Merriman, some short accounts of 'Minor Poets', which were not integrated into the argument, and a brief conclusion that compared the 'traditional mould' of Irish poetry with that of ancient Greek sculpture, but signally failed to mention the thesis so powerfully articulated in the opening chapters. The circumstances of the book's composition may help to account for this trailing off into inconsequence, but it can also be argued that the complex, real world of Eoghan Ruadh Ó Súilleabháin, which he was honest enough to reveal, effectively undermined Corkery's ideal. He might have ended the book there – certainly it was the last chapter to engage his sympathies – but for the need to deal with another threat, the very different poetry of Brian Merriman, or, more accurately, 'the rhapsodies that Merriman's *Cúirt an Mhean Oíche* [the Midnight Court] has excited'.[84] His particular target was Piaras Béaslaí's essay introducing the 1912 edition of the poem by Risteárd Ó Foghludha, which proclaimed Merriman the first Gaelic modernist and realist, in contrast to the 'exaggerated, artificial, fantastic' tradition, 'medieval and reactionary', in which Eoghan Ruadh Ó Súilleabháin was 'the typical Gaelic poet'.[85] So exercised was Corkery by this attack that he ended his account of Ó Súilleabháin with an attempt to show that one particular poem of his had 'a sense of reality . . . a certain hardness of vision', 'the 'modern' note' as strong as anything in Merriman.[86] This was at odds with the emphasis up to then on his lyricism and further weakened Corkery's portrayal.

Corkery's difficulty with Merriman emphasized further the narrow geographical limits of his 'hidden Ireland', which, he now had to argue, did not even extend across the river Shannon to Co. Clare. This was not simply because of what he saw as the greater 'hardness and . . . bleakness' of Clare, which 'knew only one language, that in which bargains were made at the fair', but more particularly because 'the great literary tradition' hadn't survived there. It lacked 'a living court of poetry' and was part, instead of 'the splendid "school" of folk poetry that then flourished all over Connaught. *The Midnight Court* was 'great', but not 'unique'; it lacked 'the refinement that comes of a living literary tradition', and its theme was 'as old as the hills'.[87] His whole exposition of this long narrative poem centred on his argument with Béaslaí, whose view that Merriman should be seen as a moralist, for example, brought out what Ó Tuama called Corkery's '*meon Victeoiriach* [Victorian mentality]'.[88]

But there was also a political subtext to their disagreement. Béaslaí had impeccable nationalist credentials, having been a member of the IRB and a participant in the 1916 Rising, but he took the Treaty side in the Civil War, becoming its director of propaganda – a role directly opposed to Corkery's for a while. His championship of Merriman's realism prefigured some of the arguments used in the Treaty debates against the idealism and dogmatism of Republican diehards – the argument, for example, that Merriman's 'sanity' and 'entire absence of the sense of the spiritual . . . kept him from the extremes to which the poetic nature is prone to run'; that in pleading for 'healthy nature, the joy of life', he was opposed to 'the vice of mind'; or that the eighteenth-century poets found refuge from their difficulties in 'prophetic visions' and that 'in revolt against their environment, their hopes were based on a restoration of the past'.[89] Corkery's sneer at the language of Claremen as 'that in which bargains were made at the fair' may have a wider meaning in this context, as may his bleak conclusion that Merriman's tragedy sprang 'from some central weakness in himself'.[90] A little fanciful? No doubt, but Corkery's literary understanding and his politics cannot be separated easily; both were profoundly romantic and idealistic and recoiled from the compromises of pragmatism. The irony was that, while he was on the losing side in the Civil War, his romantic version of Gaelic poetry was to be dominant for more than fifty years, and became an iconic text of the Free State he had so despised.

To the New World and Back with Pipes, Fiddle and Flute
The Transmission of Irish Traditional Music

TOMÁS Ó CANAINN

I should like to look at the subject of cultural transmission and exchange in the context of Irish traditional music, with particular reference to America. It is an enormous canvas that no one person could possibly paint. Even when I do not use the terms transmission or exchange, I trust you will interpret the rather personal story I have to tell in such terms. I have had a lifetime involvement, in one way or another, with traditional music and even though I have never regarded myself as being in any way qualified – whatever that means – I have had the temerity to play, sing and lecture in universities and even to write a few books on the subject!

I cannot claim to have any really comprehensive view of the American situation, though I have played and lectured there and conducted a survey of *uilleann* pipe playing in various centres right across the States, including New York, Boston, Washington, Chicago, Detroit, Salt Lake City and San Francisco. I also like to think that my experience of living and playing Irish music in Liverpool for half a dozen years has given me an empathy with first-, second- and third-generation Irish musicians in the emigrant situation. Many of their attitudes are not unlike those of their brethren in America. I was a founder member of the well-known Liverpool Ceili Band that competed at the Fleadhanna Cheoil against the New York, Birmingham and London *ceilí* bands and made friendships with their members. As well as that, I played with the musical group Na Filí in America and England, over a period of ten years. Such things may or may not be relevant to understanding cultural transmission and exchange. I think they are, but even if they are not, they may help to explain the perspective of this particular Derryman.

I shall eventually focus on three Irish musicians of the late nineteenth and early twentieth centuries, whose influence on both the American and Irish scene was enormous. On my way to that final goal, however, let me mention two very humble musicians of the same period – relations of my own – who, if they were still living, would be astounded at being even mentioned in this august company. They were my grandfather Francey

Murphy, who played the fiddle, and his cousin Strone John Murphy, who would *ceilí* in my mother's home in Carnanban, some twenty miles from Derry. For me, one song they sang recaptures the simple spirit of their time and place. I see them as typical of the emigrants who left Ireland in those times, though in fact neither of them did. The itchy feet in our family were mostly on my father's side and a number of my uncles from Drumsurn went to America and stayed there. My father was one of those who went off to sea – an old Drumsurn tradition – and spent some years in America. However, back to this particular song, 'The Verdant Braes of Screen', which I still keep alive in our weekly musical session, where, as it happens, John A. Murphy is a shining star in our Tuesday evening Glanmire firmament.

I have no intention of going back 500 years to a certain Genoese sea-captain called Columbus, who was a good servant of Spain. Nor do I wish to tell you about all the Connemara traditional singers he picked up in Galway when he called in there to load up with turf on his way over! But let me try and set the scene for the nineteenth- and twentieth-century invasions of the New World by the Irish. Those involved would hardly have seen themselves as cultural emissaries, but they were, of course, by any definition of the word cultural. It is well documented that there was even dancing and playing of Irish music on some of the emigrant ships. Between 1856 and 1921 over four million Irish emigrated, not all of them, of course, going to America. Even in 1776 there were a quarter of a million Ulster men and women in the thirteen colonies, and by 1815 this had grown to 350,000, most of whom were Presbyterians. They were first called Scots-Irish or even Scots, to differentiate them from the mainly Catholic Irish, who began to come in great numbers at the beginning of the nineteenth century.

Estyn Evans sees the Presbyterian influence as being mainly in housing and land-use, influencing, as it were, the very shape of the landscape. The later Irish crowded into the cities and founded sub-cultures there, built bridges and railways, dug canals and retained, I think, more of their own culture in the new setting than did the Scots, whose traditions were, to a large extent, absorbed into the American scene, though their ballads, in many cases, retained their identity, much as they did at home in Ireland. These Scots first settled in New England, later moving south through the glens and mountains of Appalachia, to Virginia and Carolina. Cecil Sharpe, the English collector who travelled in the Appalachians in the early twentieth century, found more Scots-lrish than English ballads there. The later Irish were identified with the building of the railways from the middle of the nineteenth century onwards. There is a large corpus of labouring songs from this activity.

Many of the American ballads can be shown to have been adapted from their Irish counterparts, even in certain instances retaining a bowdlerized version of a Gaelic chorus, as in 'Siul a Ghrá', or 'Siul a Ruin' (cf. Alan Lomax), or 'Oh my Poor Drimeendoun', which sparked off Huddie Ledbetter's (Leadbelly) 'Oh, Oh, Which is Sweeter than Down'. This became the basis for 'Kisses Sweeter than Wine', sung by The Weavers. There is little doubt that the Irish street ballads, either sung by immigrants or imported as broadsheets, had a considerable influence on the American ballad scene, as had the seventeenth-century come-all-ye, undoubtedly an Irish invention. Some of the Irish songs became, in the opinion of the collector Phillips Barry, logging songs and shanties. He based his findings on collections he had made in East Maine. It is not surprising that the Irish influenced the songs of labour, as they were very active in the unions and much of their later political influence stemmed from this. A couple of good examples of this involvement spring to mind: Mary Harris from Cork, known as Mother Jones, a union organizer for the coal and steel workers from 1890 to 1919, and Lenora O'Reilly, who organized the New York garment workers.

It is interesting that the Irish emigrants tended to follow their neighbours to particular areas. I know from my own experience in the Kerry Gaeltacht that they went from that region to Springfield, Massachussetts, and one always had the impression that the old people in particular were more familiar with Springfield than with Belfast, or, dare I say it, Derry. I played in Springfield some ten years ago in an Irish club that expected its performers to be fairly up-beat. I felt that I should sing a song in Irish and chose a Kerry one, '*An Goirtín Eornan*'. I was surprised and delighted when an old man sang out along with me in every verse. He really made my evening and at the interval he assured me in perfect Kerry Irish that the feeling was mutual. He had been over there for more than forty years. I was encouraged to sing some more Gaelic songs in the second half of my programme that evening, until the euphoria was dispelled by a real Irish lady, who asked me in a strong American accent why I didn't know any Irish songs. I was forced to close that particular cultural transmission channel forthwith!

Many of the Irish street ballads were better known in America than here and their recent Irish popularity derives in some cases from their popularity in America. One cannot assume, of course, that because a song has an Irish reference in its title that it originated in this country. In fact, the Irish-American ballad has seen so many exchanges that it is well nigh impossible to make a worthwhile judgement on the source of many of the songs. Another genre, the sentimental stage-Irish songs, may be regarded as a product of Tin Pan Alley, produced by such as Jean Schwarz and William Jerome. However, I think it would be wrong to include in this category the compositions of Johnny Paterson, 'the Rambler from Clare.' Paterson, whose parents hailed from the North, did a kind of circus clown act in both Ireland and America, and was the composer of popular songs like 'The Stone outside Dan Murphy's Door' and 'The Garden Where the Praties Grow'. He doesn't exactly enter our story, but I feel obliged to add that the most prolific song composer of the period, Stephen Foster, was a descendant of Derry people.

The so-called nigger minstrels originally sang songs that were more than a little anti-Irish, but this gradually changed as the Irish infiltrated their ranks. The long list of Irish nigger minstrels of those days included names like Dan Emmet, writer of 'Dixie', Dan Bryant, George Christy, Matt Campbell, John Collins and the Irish-American writer Edward Harrigan, who, with the actor Tony Hart, later became involved in drama, as did one of the musicians we deal with later – though to speak of piper Patsy Touhey's forays into comedy as 'drama' is perhaps stretching things a bit.

But Touhey, among others, was also supported by the adherents of the Gaelic Revival movement and saw that movement as having considerable importance. That vast numbers of the Irish immigrants in America in the seventeenth and eighteenth centuries spoke Irish is well documented and is not surprising. It is also true, of course, that they soon realized the advantage that their knowledge of English gave them over other settlers from Europe. This led many of them to unlearn their Irish and brush up on their faulty English as quickly as they possibly could. But there were others of a different mind. The Catholic community of Beaver Island in Lake Michigan, for example, raised a storm in 1865 to have their non-Irish speaking priest removed from the island, since he could not minister to them in their preferred language. He was eventually replaced by Father Peadar Ó Gallchóir, an Irish-speaker from Tyrone, who remained on the island until 1889, ministering to his flock, whose parents had come from Arranmore in Donegal, bringing with them their baggage of language, music and traditions. Even today there are people on the island who have some understanding of the Irish language.

There is a wealth of documentation of spoken Irish in America in the eighteenth century. One knows of Matias Séamus MacConmidhe, born in Galway in 1776, a native speaker, who emigrated to America in 1784 and is known for his dictionary of the Spanish language: he deserves to be better known for his English–Irish dictionary, on which he spent the last thirty years of his life. It was unfinished when he died in 1842 and is now in the possession of the American Catholic Historical Society. The Cork poet Pádraig Piarais Cundun, composer of the song 'Tórramh an Bhairille', lived in Utica, New York, for the last thirty years of his life, sending home letters and poems in Irish to his friends in Ballymacoda.

But the real Irish-language revival in America came in the second half of the nineteenth century, at first with occasional articles in Irish in newspapers such as the *Irish American* and *Irish World*. One of the earliest writers of such articles was Michael J. Logan. The first organization formed to promote the language was the Philo-Celtic Society of Boston in 1873, followed by the New York Society for the Preservation of the Irish Language. Michael J. Logan, whom we have already mentioned, was the founder of *An Gaodhal* in 1881, a magazine in Irish produced at first with the Brooklyn Philo-Celtic Society, but later by Logan himself. In 1887 the Philo-Celtic Society of Boston published Irish for the first time, in their publication *The Irish Echo*. In 1880 Irish-speaking schools are reported in central Boston, South Boston, Boston Highlands, Quincy, etc. and in Newark, New Jersey in 1890, followed by Providence, Rhode Island in 1894. In 1895 a chair of Celtic was established in the Catholic University of Washington and in the following year Irish language courses were first provided in Harvard. This is not, of course, an exhaustive list.

The Gaelic League was established in New York in 1898 in an attempt to bring together a number of Gaelic societies from various American cities. One might see the visit to the USA by its President, Dughlas de h-Ide, in 1905 and his meeting with the American President as a belated acknowledgement of the position of the Irish language in the country, but, in fact, the movement had peaked before this and was on a gradual decline, though this would not have been obvious to those involved. The heady days of the late-nineteenth-century Irish revival were gone for ever.

Into this brave new world came three Irish musicians who were to influence and be influenced by the American scene we have described. They were flute-player Francis O'Neill, born in Tralibane in west Cork in 1849, piper Patsy Touhey, born near Loughrea, Co. Galway, in 1865, and fiddler Michael Coleman from Killavil in Sligo, born in 1891.

All three were instrumental in enhancing something they had brought with them from Ireland and sending it back home, repackaged and revitalized; O'Neill, with his collections of Irish music that achieved almost biblical status among traditional musicians; Patsy Touhey, with many hundreds of individually recorded Edison cylinders of his piping, which he sold at a dollar each or at ten dollars a dozen; and Michael Coleman, whose later commercial recordings influenced and continue to influence generations of Irish traditional fiddlers.

Francis O'Neill ran away to sea at sixteen years of age to become a cabin-boy, was ship-wrecked and later became a seaman on the Great Lakes and a schoolteacher, before working on the railroad in Chicago. In 1873 he joined the Chicago police, rising through the ranks to the position of superintendent in 1901. It is generally believed that O'Neill could arrange a job on the force for any Irishman who could play traditional music – that qualification was always more important than the applicant's height, weight or fitness. Writing in his book *Irish Folk Music* of his early years in Chicago, O'Neill says: 'Within the city limits, a territory comprising about two hundred square miles, exiles from all of Ireland's thirty-two counties can be found . . . every new arrival having musical taste or talent is welcomed and introduced to the Craft, to the mutual advantage of all concerned, and there is as much rejoicing on the discovery of a new expert as there is among astronomers on the announcement of a new asteroid or comet.'

O'Neill was transferred from the business area to Deering Street police station, situated in a very Irish area and reports that while desk-sergeant there he often took part in an impromptu concert, playing the flute while Patrolman Michael Keating forced a broomhandle rigidly against the maple floor at a certain angle to give a passable imitation of a kettle drum, all this to the applause of the other policemen.

A very famous piper, Bernard Delaney, settled in Chicago and became the centre of attraction for O'Neill and his friends. Within a few months, however, Power's Irish play, *The Ivy Leaf*, came to Chicago. The company's piper, Eddie Joyce, took ill and was sent to hospital. Delaney substituted for him and the drama company took him with them on tour at a very good fee, leaving a gap in the Chicago piping galaxy. O'Neill went to New York, where *The Ivy Leaf* was on tour, and brought Delaney back to a job as a Chicago policeman. Delaney subsequently became an important source for O'Neill's collections and was, in fact, one of the advisory committee set up to vet the tunes before final publication and establish the best versions. The other members were John McFadden, Edward Cronin, John Ennis and Sergeant Early. Sergeant James O'Neill was the musical scribe. Unfortunately, the committee met only once and couldn't make progress, everyone preferring his own version: the job was then left to the two O'Neills.

The result was the publication in 1903 of *O'Neill's Music of Ireland*, edited and financed by Francis O'Neill. It contained a total of 1850 tunes – songs and airs, as well as dance-music. More than half of the tunes were contributed by the musicians of the Chicago Irish Music Club. Francis O'Neill was the source of most of these, with Sergeant James O'Neill in second place. Four years later the dance-music was published separately in *The Dance Music of Ireland*, with 1001 tunes. This became what traditional musicians for the next sixty years called The Book, the bible of Irish traditional music and the standard reference.

One of the most impressive-looking pipers in a picture of the Chicago Irish Music Club, included in *Music of Ireland*, was John K. Beatty. His flowing locks, regal appearance and his enormous set of Taylor pipes made him seem the epitome of the traditional Irish piper. In fact, O'Neill tells us that Beatty was most certainly not a good piper, though he was a good lilter of tunes: somehow, his fingers couldn't perform on the chanter what his voice had no difficulty with. Not so long ago I met again the American piper who now owns this famous Taylor set: Joe Shannon, an excellent piper and a man who played for O'Neill himself at the Chicago World Fair of 1934, receiving a signed copy of O'Neill's book from the author. It was good to be present in Cork when Joe Shannon played music at the high speed of Touhey and his fellows on Beatty's famous pipes.

It seems that O'Neill's own favourite tune in his first collection was 'Tralibane Bridge'. He agreed with I.S. Dunning, a violinist and a former city engineer of Aurora, Illinois, who, in reviewing the first O'Neill collection, wrote: . . . the melody that captivated my fancy and that of my family above all others in the collection is *Tralibane Bridge*.' Tralibane was in O'Neill's home territory, near Bantry, and it was there that the clergy stopped the local dancing and music at the crossroads in his youth, something for which the Captain always expressed regret. Another of the many airs contributed by O'Neill was 'Catherine Tyrell', one of two versions of 'Caitlin Triall' in his first collection.

O'Neill notes that his *Music of Ireland* was well received by the reviewers, with one exception – a clergyman from Cork, who he does not name, but whom I assume to be Father Gaynor. This priest warned his audience in a public lecture of the great danger to Irish music from the efforts of those who had not the advantage of being born in the real traditional atmosphere, like himself. O'Neill comments: 'Why, bless his simple soul! What could have led him to imagine that Watergrass Hill had a monopoly of the traditional atmosphere of County Cork, not to mention the rest of Ireland?'

On a much later visit to Munster and Leinster, O'Neill commented that, returning after an absence of forty years, he saw nothing to indicate an Irish musical regeneration. He complained that he had not encountered a single piper or fiddler at five fairs he had attended, and only one ballad-singer. After hearing prize-winners at various competitions, he remarked: 'the conclusion is irresistible that the judges were certainly men of very liberal and generous impulses!' He was present at the Dublin and Cork Feiseanna. 'Their very best performers on any instrument at either Feis', he says, 'are easily outclassed in Chicago.' It is interesting that O'Neill visited the Munster Feis in Cork in 1906 and had great praise for the dancers he saw there, claiming that he had never seen their like, either in Ireland or America. But he was anything but complimentary about the musicians.

An important musician in O'Neill's story, but also a central figure in his own right was the piper Patsy Touhey. He was born in 1865, the son of a professional piper, James Touhey, who was himself the son of another Touhey piper, Michael. Patsy's father was patronized by Lord Dunsandle, whose forebears had patronized Carolan in the eighteenth century. Patsy was taken to America when he was three and on the death of James Touhey, when Patsy was only ten, his piping tuition was continued by Bartley Murphy, who had himself been taught by Patsy's father. At the age of twenty-one, Touhey went touring with Cohan's Irish Hibernia, as one of two pipers, the other being John Egan. Jerry Cohan, who ran the show, giving six performances a day, six days a week, with a Sunday rehearsal, was the father of George M. Cohan of 'Yankee Doodle Dandy' fame.

Touhey played a set of Taylor pipes, made by the Drogheda brothers Billy and Charley, who had started a pipe-making business in Philadelphia, making instruments of a more strident sound than the quieter pipes of earlier times. These were clearly much more suited to the American music-hall stage. They were in concert pitch, having a D chanter, with a wider conical bore and the very flat-looking regulator keys that are to be seen in all the pictures of American pipers of those days. Touhey could make them fairly hum, as few others could, with intricate chanter work and regulator playing that was effortless. I touched a little bit of history in Cork recently when I handled those famous Touhey pipes, now returned to

Ireland, owned and well played by Sean McKiernan, to whom they were presented. To come so near to Touhey in 1992 was a very special moment for me.

Touhey was a sensation when he played at the World's Fair in Chicago in 1893. One could hardly imagine a better illustration of the cultural change in Irish music effected by the American experience than that afforded by a comparison of the two pipers at the Fair – Turlough McSweeney, the Donegal Piper, playing an old instrument, while the younger Touhey sparked out high-speed ornamented reels on a brash new Taylor set. Touhey also played in 1903 at the Louisiana Purchase Exposition held in St Louis. He was quite involved with the Gaelic League, and played at their concerts and Feiseanna in the early years of this century. He is quoted in *The Irish World* of 1901 as saying: 'of course, the Gaelic movement here is supporting the pipes, as well as Irish music generally, and it seems only a beginning. In fact, I think the future of the pipes, as well as of the music and language, depends largely on the Gaelic movement.'

He was involved in Francis O'Neill's work in Chicago for Irish music and had this to say of it: 'the only organized effort I had observed to cultivate and popularise Irish pipe music in America was in Chicago. Frank O'Neill, now chief of police in that city, was the principal promoter of this movement and other leaders in it were Sergeants James Cahill and James Early and Mr John Ennis, all good players and enthusiasts.' O'Neill, who often differentiated between a musician's music and his personal qualities, had nothing but praise for Touhey, on all counts. The Loughrea piper was always keen to pass on new tunes, something that was not common among some of the American musicians. He was generous and friendly to newly arrived Irish musicians, helping them to settle in the new country and introducing them to other musicians.

Writing of Delaney the piper, Francis O'Neill said: 'Barney Delaney as a player of dance-music is simply indescribable. As an honourable man, or one having a germ of gratitude or appreciation of picking him off the street or tavern and making him what he is, he is intolerable.' Speaking of Touhey, on the other hand, he said: 'A stranger to jealousy, his comments are never sarcastic or unkind, neither does he betray any tendency to monopolise attention in company, when other musicians are present. In fact, Touhey is a notable exception in many ways, and if he possesses any less admirable qualities, they have escaped the notice of the writer, who has enjoyed his acquaintance over a score of years.'

At the end of the last century Touhey was involved in the vaudeville circuit, touring with Power's Ivy Leaf Company, performing music and acting in their plays. In the early years of this century he was well known for his part in the Burke and Touhey comedy partnership, giving three shows a day. As well as acting, he played the pipes as part of their double-act. It is known that the Irish tenor John McCormack objected to the stage-Irishness of Touhey's act at the New Orleans Fair in 1911.

In the context of this article, Touhey's greatest contribution to Irish music was in the corpus of recorded music on Edison cylinders that he sold through his mail-order firm at a dollar each, or a dozen for ten dollars. These he recorded individually in a tiny sound-proofed cubicle and sent out all over America and Ireland from an address in Bristow Street, New York. He advertised a list of 150 Irish airs, jigs, reels and hornpipes. In 1907, Dr Henebry from Waterford, who had been sent some of the cylinders, wrote: 'The Homeric ballads and the new Brooklyn Bridge are great, but Patsy Touhey's rendering of the 'Shaskeen Reel' is a far bigger human achievement. Why, there is no Irish musician alive now at all in his class. If things were as they ought to be, he should be installed as professor of music in a national university in Dublin. And that is what I think of Patsy Touhey and his pipering.' Commercial recording, which resulted from the invention of the gramophone, or 'Victrola', as it was first called, arrived a little late for Touhey, though he did make a few disc recordings for Victor Records, the first of which was released in 1920, the reel he played there being 'Drowsy Maggie'.

If Touhey's recording career was coming to an end at this time, another Irishman was replacing him – the 30-year-old wizard of the fiddle Michael Coleman. Born in Killavil, Co. Sligo, in 1891, the youngest in the family of James Coleman, a noted flute-player, Michael was interested from his earliest years in both fiddle-playing and step-dancing, both of which were highly regarded in the area. There were great fiddle-players all around him – Kipeen Scanlon, the Cawley brothers, Michael Gorman, Philip O'Beirne, Mattie Killoran, John O'Dowd and Richard Brennan, to name just a few. As well as fiddlers, Sligo in those days was well known for its pipers, and Coleman's earlier playing is said to have been considerably influenced by them. Coleman's older brother Jim, an excellent piper, was acknowledged by Michael to be a better player than himself. Of course, Sligo fiddlers James Morrison and Paddy Killoran were to rival (some would even say equal or surpass!) Coleman's fame.

Michael Coleman emigrated first to England and then to America in 1914. He married Marie Fanning in New York in 1917 and they had one child. Coleman played his music in bars, saloons and theatres, but it was through his recording career of the Twenties and Thirties that he exerted most influence on Irish music, both in America and in Ireland, where his recordings were hugely popular. Possibly his most famous early recording was of 'The Boys of the Lough', made for Vocalion in 1922. It became available in Ireland on a Beltona copy of the original, but was credited on the label to Dennis Molloy. It became, and still is, one of Coleman's most influential recordings, changing the whole character and ethos of what had been considered until then a simple tune, of no great depth. One recorded item is, for me, the most typically Coleman tune, perhaps the most copied of them all: it certainly was, in my youth. That tune is 'Bonnie Kate', followed here by 'Jennie's Chickens', in a Decca recording from 1934, with guitar accompaniment by Michael 'Whitey' Andrews.

Coleman soon earned what was in those days big money – a couple of hundred dollars for a few hours' work – but he would have earned more, and in the process given himself a guarantee of a comfortable retirement, if he had joined the big bands as a star, rather than touring alone, which he preferred. He fell on hard times after the Wall Street collapse, but his fortunes recovered somewhat when the recording companies restarted their Irish-music activities. He tried to set up fiddle classes, as a way of making money, but was not very successful, partly because he was not a good teacher and partly because his students often could not find him when they came for a lesson. By the 1940s he had become quite erratic and his drink problem made him less dependable, so that he got fewer and fewer engagements and was a poor man when he died on 4 January 1945 in the Knickerbocker Hospital, Manhattan.

The lives of these three musicians were their cultural message, and they left behind them transmitters that have not ceased to function. O'Neill's nine books revitalized the practice of Irish traditional music and became the new standard for musicians. Touhey's hundreds of fragile cylinders carried his musical messages until they could be re-recorded in our own day, to provide an inspiring model for a new generation of younger pipers. Coleman's dozens of 78 rpm discs so changed fiddle-playing, particularly in the middle years of the twentieth century, that many felt they didn't really know a tune until they had heard Coleman playing it.

That there are negative aspects to all of this, particularly the tendency of many musicians to attach too much importance to the authority of a manuscript or a recording of Irish music. This happens less nowadays, at least in the case of O'Neill or Coleman, but is just beginning to be a problem that pipers will have to solve for themselves – learning from the genius of Touhey, without allowing themselves to become clones of the great piper. That such problems arise is in itself a testimony to the greatness of the musicians involved. The present healthy state of Irish traditional music owes much to the three men I salute here.

The Revival of Knock Shrine

JAMES S. DONNELLY, Jr.

Historians concerned with popular religion in modern Ireland will probably never reach fully agreed answers as to why a notable Marian apparition occurred in the little village of Knock in Co. Mayo in August 1879. The explanations considered at different times have included hoax, optical illusion, collective hallucination, social trauma and plain miracle. More significant than this issue of cause, however, is the matter of consequences. From this striking religious event involving perhaps fifteen or twenty people as the original seers, Knock quickly achieved national and indeed international fame as 'the Irish Lourdes', with tens of thousands of pilgrims and hundreds of allegedly miraculous cures.[1] Of course, the religious environment that had made possible a Lourdes, a Marpingen or a Knock was one in which the cult of the Virgin Mary was firmly establishing itself in many less dramatic forms: new confraternities, sodalities, statues, images of many different kinds, prayers and liturgies, relics and religious stories. David Blackbourn has persuasively argued in his fascinating study of Marpingen that the nineteenth century in Catholic areas of western Europe witnessed 'a marked revival of emotionally laden forms of piety reminiscent of the Counter-Reformation' – a revival in which the cult of Mary was especially pronounced from about 1850 onwards.[2] Irish Catholics were at least as much affected by this strong Marian current as their co-religionists elsewhere in western Europe during the second half of the nineteenth century.

Knock's fame as 'the Irish Lourdes', however, was remarkably short lived. From the mid-1880s until the late 1920s the shrine failed to attract many pilgrims from outside the local area. Even the crowds that still gathered on 14 and 15 August for the feast of the Assumption and the vigil on the previous night had become much smaller than during those first few years after the initial 1879 apparition. The bitter and unedifying conflicts swirling around 'the Nun of Kenmare' (Margaret Anne Cusack) in the early 1880s had cast a certain pall over Knock and detracted from its aura of sanctity. Its greatest promoter, Archdeacon Bartholomew Cavanagh, died in December 1897, and his two immediate successors as parish priest displayed attitudes towards its once-famous shrine that ranged from sceptical to uninterested.[3] But what above all robbed the early Knock of staying power as an international Marian shrine of the first rank was the absence of official ecclesiastical approval, and most critically the approval of a succession of archbishops of Tuam. Neither John MacHale nor John MacEvilly nor John Healy had been willing to extend any positive endorsement to the apparitions and visions or to the cures that allegedly occurred at Knock, even though two Episcopal commissions which had examined the evidence had found no fault with the credibility of the original witnesses. None of these archbishops visited the shrine in an official capacity or attended pilgrimage ceremonies there, and few, if any, Irish bishops or heads of religious orders (male or female) apparently did so either. As a result, after the earliest years organized pilgrimages under the sponsorship of a diocese, religious order or other Catholic group practically ceased. When finally in August 1929 about a thousand members of St Michan's Conference of the St Vincent de Paul Society in Dublin came to Knock by a special train, they were hailed as 'the first organized pilgrimage in the fifty years since the apparitions'.[4] In general, the low-level traffic of the intervening decades consisted of individual pilgrims or family groups drawn mostly from surrounding districts.

But all of this was gradually to be transformed under the impact of a set of interrelated events and forces. Within a dozen years of the inaugural St Vincent de Paul Society pilgrimage in 1929, Knock had once again become a major international Marian shrine, and, in the eyes of its own promoters at least, the most important such shrine in all of Ireland. Soon after the close of the pilgrimage season in October 1940 it was estimated that 'up to a quarter-million pilgrims' had visited Knock shrine since the spring of that year – the largest number for a single season or year in its history to date.[5] Behind this transformation there stood, first of all, the tremendous upsurge in Marian enthusiasm in Ireland and the rest of Catholic Europe during the 1930s. Of special significance in the development of Knock was the phenomenal growth of the cult of Lourdes in Ireland in this decade, for the promoters of Knock took Lourdes as their model of what shape a major Marian shrine should take and how its status should be advanced. So strong did the Marian passion become in the Ireland of the 1930s that it is difficult to believe that the general religious environment for the lusty growth of a shrine like Knock could have been more favourable.[6]

But there were also essential changes in personnel and attitude in the Tuam archdiocese and Knock parish without which the great revival of the shrine would not have occurred. Crucial contributions were made by Archbishop Thomas Gilmartin, the parish priests Father John Tuffy and Canon John Grealy, and the husband and wife team of Liam and Judith Coyne. As befitted his background as a liturgical scholar and academic administrator, Gilmartin was an unusually cautious man and did not easily or quickly part company from his predecessors in his stance towards Knock. When first pressed in 1926 to lend some quite modest support to Knock shrine, he displayed considerable reluctance. In March of that year Father Tuffy, who had been parish priest of Knock since 1919, asked Gilmartin 'to sanction a formula of devotions for a pilgrimage which has existed in the diocese for fifty years, and which for its magnitude and duration is the largest and best known in Ireland'.[7] Faced with Tuffy's request, Gilmartin solicited advice from at least two ecclesiastical experts at Maynooth but unfortunately received contradictory opinions. One believed that Gilmartin was competent to permit the use of the formula of devotions proposed by Tuffy if in the archbishop's judgement 'there is a good, though not necessarily conclusive evidence for the apparition which is the basis of the devotions'.[8] But the second Maynooth expert was distinctly less encouraging. He told the archbishop that to give his sanction to the proposed formula of prayers 'would imply a recognition of the genuine, supernatural character of the events of [1879]' – a result that in his judgement was not warranted by the evidence.[9]

It was to be more than three years before Gilmartin finally took the crucial step of publicly associating himself with Knock shrine, and even then he re-echoed many of the views conveyed to him by the second Maynooth expert in 1926. Addressing the historic group of Knock pilgrims from St Michan's Conference of the St Vincent de Paul Society on the feast of the Assumption in 1929, Gilmartin cautioned his listeners that his unprecedented presence 'was not to be taken as giving any official sanction' to the 'alleged apparitions' of fifty years earlier, for the commission appointed by Archbishop MacHale in 1879 'came to no definite conclusion'. Churchmen, he observed, 'were taught to be suspicious about alleged visions or apparitions', an attitude justified by the fact that 'there had been several cases of fraud in connection with supposed supernatural phenomena'. Nevertheless, Gilmartin embraced Knock as a strong Marianist: 'It was from the angle of devotion to the Mother of God that he wished to be associated with the zealous and enlightened pastor of Knock in bidding the pilgrims a hearty welcome. Devotion to the Blessed Virgin was independent of all shrines, no matter how highly privileged they may be.'[10] (According to an authoritative source, Archbishop Gilmartin was finally prompted to embrace the shrine while reading his breviary one day in the grounds of the cathedral at Tuam. He is said to have told others that he had heard a voice crying, 'Go to Knock, go to Knock.' Having asked his chauffeur to take him directly there, he nearly had a serious car accident on the way and apparently attributed his narrow escape to divine or Marian intervention.[11])

This fiftieth-anniversary event in 1929 may fairly be considered a turning point on account of Gilmartin's positive intervention alone. His commitment was to be permanent, and his role an expanding one. But almost everything remained to be done before Knock could really become a major and well-appointed Marian shrine. Father Tuffy was forced to admit in the midst of its fiftieth anniversary that Knock 'was not well organized to receive pilgrims', though he expressed the hope that he and 'other friends of Knock' would be able to provide better facilities in the future.[12] Among the most serious physical problems were the small size of the 'apparition' Church of the Assumption; the absence of protection for pilgrims in inclement weather; the lack of special accommodation for invalids and the sick; and the fairly primitive conditions with respect to lodging, food, restrooms, parking and first aid. On the religious or spiritual side, Knock did not have as yet (apart from Gilmartin's guarded support) any of the marks of official recognition usually attached to an important Marian shrine.

Progress toward overcoming these formidable problems was at first quite slow. Local leadership was temporarily disrupted by the death of Father Tuffy in 1931. His replacement as parish priest, Canon John Grealy, was (probably by design of the archbishop) a Knock enthusiast. 'Whatever the clergy may think,' he remarked to Gilmartin at the end of August 1932, 'the laity have a firm belief in the reality of the apparitions.' The recent crowds had deeply impressed him: 'The piety of the people who came here on the night or morning of the 15th was something astonishing. Round the chapel they went all night – men & women – on their bare knees.'[13] As committed as Grealy was to Knock's revival, he was advanced in years when he became parish priest and administrator of the shrine, and there were clear limits to what he could accomplish by his own unaided efforts. It was his and Knock's good fortune that supremely dedicated, skilful and youthful lay leadership now asserted itself in the persons of the spousal team of William Coyne (Liam Ua Cadhain) and his wife, Judith Coyne.

Though they were to have many lay and clerical helpers over the years, it is difficult to exaggerate the importance of the Coynes in the twentieth-century history of Knock and especially in the story of its revival from the mid 1930s through the late 1950s. No other members of the laity associated with the shrine can be compared with the Coynes in significance or impact; they stand on the same distinct plane of importance as Archdeacon Cavanagh earlier and Monsignor James Horan later. Liam Coyne embodied in his person the three streams of nationalism, Catholicism and Gaelicism that flowed together so insistently in early-twentieth-century Ireland. Born to 'a respected Roscommon–Mayo family', he received some of his education abroad in Germany. While a student there during the First World War, he was briefly imprisoned 'because, like all Irishmen then, he was considered a British subject'. Trained in the law, he was practising as a solicitor in the town of Ballyhaunis by the time of the Irish War of Independence. Politics also beckoned, and while serving in the IRA, he gained a seat on the Mayo County Council. It no doubt aided his political career, as it did those of so many others, to be arrested by the British during the revolutionary period. He was later elected by his colleagues as chairman of the county council, and under the new Irish judicial system established by the Free

State after the Treaty, he was appointed the first district justice for south-west Mayo, a post which he retained for about three decades, until his death in September 1953.[14]

By the time that he first met his future wife, District Justice Coyne was already deeply religious, and he seems to have shared with her, from the beginning of their life together, a very strong devotion to the Blessed Virgin Mary. It could hardly have been accidental that they exchanged their marriage vows in 1925 on the feast of Our Lady of Lourdes. His Marian enthusiasm was also reflected in his dedication to the rosary. The author of his obituary in the 1954 *Knock Shrine Annual*, the Holy Ghost priest Father Michael O'Carroll, himself perhaps the greatest Irish Mariologist of the twentieth century, recalled that Liam Coyne 'recited at the very least the fifteen decades of the rosary twice each day'. But above all, of course, Coyne's Marian passion (and that of Judith Coyne as well) was exemplified in the work done for Knock shrine. As Father O'Carroll, who knew him well, rightly remarked, the shrine 'became the centre of his life, the focus of all his desires and ambitions'. Through his unceasing activity and publications on behalf of his beloved Cnoc Mhuire, he became the chief salesman for the shrine, rarely missing an opportunity to place it in the public limelight.

Although Liam Coyne was certainly to play the greater role, particularly in public, until his premature death in 1953, his wife Judith was, in her capacity as the honorary general secretary of the Knock Shrine Society, the organizing genius of the enterprise from their home (called 'Buissonnets') at Bridgemount near Castlebar. Until she finally stepped aside in 1996, when she was well into her nineties, Mrs Coyne always played an essential role in the publication of the hugely important *Knock Shrine Annual*. She apparently told Catherine Rynne in the late 1970s that her husband was its primary editor until his death in 1953,[15] but Mrs Coyne must have shouldered much of the editorial burden even then, and she carried nearly all of it after his demise.[16] A childless couple, the Coynes dedicated their lives individually and together to the cult of the Virgin Mary and to the enhancement of Knock as a worthy expression of their passionate Marian enthusiasm.

The Coynes were instrumental in the formation in August 1935 of the Society for Promoting the Cause of Knock Shrine, or what soon became known more simply as the Knock Shrine Society.[17] They and the other leaders of the new organization were exclusively laymen and laywomen – at a time when Irish bishops and priests were in general extremely jealous of their own prerogatives and not inclined to tolerate free-wheeling interference by members of the laity in religious matters. Despite its lay leadership, however, the new Knock Shrine Society fully accepted the reality of clerical control. When announcing its establishment in January 1936 in *Good Counsel*, the Irish Augustinian quarterly, Liam Coyne made a point of stressing that the society had been formed 'in order the more effectually to carry out the wishes of His Grace' Archbishop Gilmartin, and that the placement of the society under the Virgin Mary's protection had been done 'with the approval and under the patronage of the archbishop'.[18] In his private dealings with Gilmartin as well, Coyne was remarkably deferential. For example, when sending the archbishop in March 1936 a draft of a new official handbook for pilgrims to the shrine, Coyne observed: 'I should like to make it clear that the draft is merely a series of suggestions which have been made from time to time as the need arose. They are, of course, submitted to be altered by addition or subtraction, as Your Grace wishes.'[19] Similarly, when urging in June 1935 the setting up of a medical bureau for Knock, Coyne prompted the archbishop's secretary, Father James Fergus: 'It is essential to have some means of checking reported cures, and the only way it can be done is through some such recognized channel. I suggest that His Grace give approval to a named panel of doctors for that purpose. The names to be submitted [to Gilmartin].'[20] With the suitably diplomatic Coyne showing such deference, the Knock Shrine Society with him as its president was not likely to clash with the ecclesiastical authorities. Indeed, the lay and clerical leaders of this major effort to bring about Knock's revival appeared to work in nearly perfect harmony.

The primary aim of the society at its foundation and for the next five years was to secure the official 'recognition of Knock as an approved shrine to Our Lady if it be pleasing to God'. As a first step towards this goal, Gilmartin authorized for distribution in May 1935 a prayer leaflet soliciting support for a huge 'crusade of prayer' so that 'this great pilgrimage of devotion might be crowned with that ecclesiastical sanction from the Holy See which would include Knock among the privileged shrines of Our Lady'. Supporters enrolling in this crusade were asked to offer one Pater, Ave and Gloria and to say the Memorare for this intention.[21] The crusade constituted the first big publicity campaign mounted by the society. Its leaders arranged for 'the issue of nearly five hundred thousand prayer leaflets, and these have been distributed throughout the world'.[22] As early as January 1936, Liam Coyne asserted that a 'great army of 100,000 persons' had already joined the crusade, presumably by returning prayer cards to society headquarters.[23] Such supporters were regarded as associate members, and by 1938 the editor of the *Annual* boasted that these prayerful co-operators had come to number at least 500,000 persons.[24]

Among the other principal aims of the Knock Shrine Society were 'to assist in the organisation of pilgrimages where necessary, and particularly to help sick pilgrims', and 'to cooperate with the doctors in control of the Medical Bureau when required'.[25] Accomplishing these tasks led to the formation of two brigades of highly committed and self-disciplined members – an all-male body of stewards (also called at first *brancardiers* after the Lourdes example and usage) and an all-female body of handmaids. The handmaids, who numbered about 100 by 1938, had as their primary duty caring for sick or disabled pilgrims at Knock; the stewards, of whom there were approximately 200 in 1938, were mainly responsible for regulating crowds in and around the apparition church as well as for controlling processions, though they too shouldered part of the burden of caring for invalids at the shrine. It was specifically stated that the stewards were drawn 'from the towns and parishes adjoining the shrine', with certain Catholic lay bodies (the St Vincent de Paul Society, Confraternity of the Sacred Heart, Catholic Young Men's Society and Pioneer Total Abstinence Association) furnishing the bulk of recruits.[26] Essentially the same thing must also have held true for the handmaids, with such organizations as the Legion of Mary, Children of Mary and parish sodalities providing most of the members.

At its inception, as might be expected, the Knock Shrine Society had a leadership that was drawn almost exclusively from Co. Mayo, although as early as 1936 an active subcommittee was functioning in Dublin.[27] The Mayo leaders in these early years were invariably based in the towns and belonged to the middle class, especially its professional section. Besides its president, District Justice Liam Coyne, and its honorary general secretary, Judith Coyne, the leadership of the society in April 1936 included Michael Egan, secretary of the Mayo County Council in Castlebar; Miss K.M. Ronaldson, also of Castlebar, the Mayo county librarian, who chaired the handmaids' committee, paralleling Egan as head of the stewards' committee; and P.J. Houlihan, a bank official in Balla, who served successively as honorary secretary and treasurer of the society.[28] Associated with these leaders were several local medical doctors, including George Maguire of Claremorris, the secretary of the Knock Medical Bureau, and John Lyons of Kilkelly, whose interest in film-making was to prove of great value to the society.[29] Also closely connected to the leadership at the start were nine women who were designated as local 'representatives' for the towns of Balla, Ballyhaunis, Castlebar, Kiltimagh, Swinford and Tuam. They were charged with setting up local committees in each of these six urban centres.[30] In its social and gender profile the leadership of the Knock Shrine Society was quite similar to that of the Legion of Mary: in both the accent was on the towns, the middle class and women, though with a pronounced tendency for men to dominate leadership at the top.

The idea of having local representatives specializing in the recruitment of new members of the society was further refined with the establishment of a privileged category of membership known as 'promoters'. Promoters were those who enrolled at least five additional recruits. Besides enjoying the spiritual benefits attached to ordinary membership, promoters shared in the graces of the special Masses said on three Marian feasts celebrated at the shrine.[31] 'District promoters' directed the activity of others operating at the local level. What might be achieved by a single district promoter was dramatically demonstrated by Mrs J. O'Connell of Leitrim. By securing 'the services of over seventy promoters in her area', she was able to enrol as many as 1,200 new members by 1939.[32] Hundreds of volunteers offered themselves as promoters. The 1939 *Knock Shrine Annual* carried the names of about 1,000 promoters, and the number had swelled to approximately 1,700 by the time of the 1940 *Annual*.[33] The district promoters kept these local promoters involved in the enterprise by distributing prayer leaflets to them, issuing other religious and shrine-related literature, receiving lists of new members, and carrying out other duties specified by Mrs Coyne, who in some respects devolved to them responsibilities that had originally belonged to her as the honorary general secretary.[34] The membership campaign that was intelligently structured in this way produced impressive results. The 1938 *Annual* reported that by paying the required one-shilling yearly subscription, 'upwards' of 20,000 people had joined the Knock Shrine Society since its launching in August 1935. Its members could be found in all thirty-two counties and included 'many helpers in America, England, Scotland, and even in Switzerland'. Through its promoters, asserted Liam Coyne, 'the numbers interested and cooperating by their prayers as associates are not less than half a million in Ireland alone'.[35]

The Coynes were quick to appreciate the importance of Dublin to their ambitious plans for reviving the shrine, and within months of the formation of the Knock Shrine Society they set on foot a Dublin sub-committee to take charge of organizing pilgrimages and promoting the cause in and around the capital. Presiding over the work of the Dublin sub-committee was a remarkable woman named Countess Bernadette O'Byrne, who, besides being a vice-president of the Knock Shrine Society, served as president of its Dublin sub-committee from 1936 until her death in 1958. Described by her close friend Father Michael O'Carroll as 'one of the most devoted, convinced, zealous workers for Knock shrine that ever lived', Countess O'Byrne came from a well-to-do Irish family 'noted for its attachment to the highest ideals of faith and fatherland'. With her husband, Count Patrick O'Byrne (a papal count), she 'took an active part in the movement for national independence'. In the years 1921–2 Count O'Byrne represented the 'Irish Republic' as Envoy Extraordinary and Minister Plenipotentiary in Italy and at the Vatican. While stationed with her husband in Rome, Countess O'Byrne's main activity was helping to edit the *Official Bulletin*, a republican digest of news and information 'published monthly and distributed among influential circles in the Vatican, the Roman diplomatic corps, and the international press'. Thus, like other leading activists in the cause of Knock, she had a close association with Irish revolutionary nationalism in the recent past. Once she became president of the Dublin sub-committee in 1936, Countess O'Byrne committed her enormous energies wholeheartedly 'to the work of explaining and promoting the shrine'. She excelled as 'a most ardent propagandist' for Knock, but she was also a skilled administrator and for many years devoted herself to 'the organisation of pilgrimages, the composition and distribution of literature, [and] the direction and supervision of the Dublin office'.[36]

The Coynes and their allies were fiercely determined to make Knock shrine much better known throughout Ireland and abroad. Publications were one of their main vehicles. Late in 1935 Liam Coyne produced *Knock Shrine*, a book of over 200 pages containing many illustrations and available for only 3s.[37] The book told the story of the original apparition of 21 August 1879, reproduced much of the evidence given by the seers, highlighted the role of Archdeacon Cavanagh, and emphasized the many miraculous cures that had allegedly occurred at Knock by recounting a long list of them, including some notable recent ones. The first printing of 3,000 copies sold out in just two months and a second edition appeared in August 1936.[38] Indeed, gradually expanding in size and in its use of photographs and other illustrations, the book was to go through numerous editions in subsequent decades; its sales, though not exactly known, perhaps exceeded 100,000 copies in its various versions.

By far the most important publication of the Knock Shrine Society was its soft-covered *Annual*, which has impressively maintained an unbroken record of yearly publication since its first issue in 1938. The contents of the *Annual* were extremely well suited to publicizing the shrine and its revival as well as to attracting the interest of Marian enthusiasts in particular and Irish Catholics more generally. In the early issues, which largely set the tone for the future, there was an appealing mixture of shrine-related news and information, historical matter about Knock's first years, a circumstantial record of the larger pilgrimages each season, listings of 'favours received' (including alleged cures) through Our Lady's intercession, devotional materials, long lists of promoters and donors, and reasonably detailed financial statements. Regular readers of the *Annual* could easily understand the aims, plans, operations and achievements of the society as it avidly pursued the task of reviving the shrine. Members, promoters and other benefactors could easily discover what the shrine authorities were doing with their subscriptions and donations. In addition, readers of the *Annual* would often have had the very pleasant experience of seeing mentioned in this periodical either their own names, those of relatives, friends or neighbours, or at least the names of religious or social groups to which they belonged and which had undertaken pilgrimages to Knock.

Two notable changes made in the *Annual* in its early years were deliberately calculated to stimulate reader responsiveness and recognition. One was the increased space devoted to publishing letters (or extracts from them) about favours received through Mary's intercession. Below a brief series of such letters in the initial 1938 issue the editor announced: 'This page will be devoted to the recording and public acknowledgment of spiritual and temporal favours received through Our Blessed Lady. They will be inserted free of charge.'[39] There was a strong response in 1939, when the *Annual* carried almost fifty notices of such favours, and the size of the yearly list tended to grow with the passage of time: the 1944 *Annual* devoted some fifteen pages to an enumeration of the blessings reported by Knock enthusiasts.[40] The other notable change with obvious reader appeal was the increased use of photographs. This was particularly the case in the major section of the *Annual* devoted to the record of pilgrimages in the previous season. In 1938 no photographs at all appeared in that section, and in 1939 there were only three, but the pilgrimage section of the 1943 *Annual* was graced by more than forty photographs. Indeed, on certain pages photographs of pilgrims displaced or almost displaced the printed word entirely.[41]

Not only did the *Annual* become physically more attractive but it also remained cheap. Until 1941 it cost as little as sixpence – a price that reflected a partial subsidization of printing costs and a readiness to forego profits from the publication in return for increased distribution.[42] The *Annual* was sold at the shrine on pilgrimage days, and by 1941 it was also readily available for sale in the Dublin area from the stock newly kept at the Knock Central Bureau in that city.[43] According to the editor in 1943, the *Annual* enjoyed 'a general circulation in hospitals and amongst invalids, who are always anxious and grateful to get it'.[44] Even when in 1941 increased printing costs and the loss of advertising revenue owing to wartime conditions forced its price to be raised to nine pence a copy, the *Annual* – running to 136 pages and now including all those photographs – could still be considered a bargain, not to mention a great advertisement for the shrine.[45]

Its promoters advertised Knock not only through their publications but also by means of lectures, films and radio broadcasts. Among the earliest and most effective of the recruiting tools were the 16-mm films made of several Knock pilgrimages by Dr John Lyons of Kilkelly, Co. Mayo. As early as April 1936 the Knock Shrine Society made plans to show the films in neighbouring towns as part of its wider publicity campaign. By the time that the 1938 *Annual* appeared, parish committees and other interested parties had sponsored public viewings in at least ten western towns. In addition, Knock's supporters had arranged a series of 'private showings at different convents' in Dublin. Perhaps most significantly, with the permission of Monsignor John D'Alton, the new president of St Patrick's College, Maynooth (and future archbishop of Armagh and cardinal), the films were shown there in the Aula Maxima, apparently with both clerical students and professors in attendance. According to the *Annual*, 'there was a crowded hall and the students received the picture with enthusiasm'.[46]

But even greater use was made of the radio, with the Coynes gradually establishing excellent rapport with broadcasting officials at Radio Éireann.[47] Liam Coyne and the distinguished physician Dr J. Stafford Johnson took to the airwaves as early as August 1935. Coyne told the story of Knock, stressing 'the most remarkable continuity of cures' and mentioning in particular the case of Katherine Flynn, a 'hopeless invalid' suffering from the spinal disease known as Pott's Caries, who was allegedly cured at Knock in 1925.[48] Johnson, who had taken the lead in launching the Knock Medical Bureau, gave his radio address on that subject, explaining that participating doctors would be looking for 'genuinely organic disease' of a severe kind, with proof of both prior existence of the disease and the lasting nature of the cure.[49] A much greater publicity coup was the event organized by Liam Coyne and others at the Gaiety Theatre in Dublin in mid December 1936. The featured speaker on the topic of 'A Day at Cnoc Muire' was Thomas Derrig, Minister for Education in de Valera's government. Described earlier by Liam Coyne as 'deeply interested in [the] Knock cause', Derrig may have employed his political contacts to arrange for the event to be broadcast on Radio Éireann.[50] The proceedings were not only heard by thousands on radio but also published in pamphlet form by the *Connaught Telegraph*.[51]

Besides exploiting the magic of the wireless to dispense all sorts of information about Knock, its energetic promoters soon realized that Irish radio-listeners could in effect become vicarious pilgrims by tuning in broadcasts of major activities at the shrine. Thus, beginning in the late 1930s, it became customary for a suitable portion of the first large pilgrimage of the season to be broadcast from Knock. In May 1936 listeners to Radio Athlone heard a report describing the big Legion of Mary pilgrimage from Tuam archdiocese, with hymns provided by a local convent choir, commentary by Father Daniel Corcoran, curate of Knock, and a sermon by a Cork city Vincentian priest who boasted (without warrant) that the Pope 'was about to give Knock his solemn approbation'.[52] In July 1937, Radio Athlone broadcast some of the proceedings of one of the biggest mid-season pilgrimages to Knock, involving about 6,000 pilgrims from Limerick organized by the Third Order of St Francis (eight special trains and fifty buses were needed to transport them).[53] And in the third week of August 1939, on the occasion of the diamond jubilee of Knock shrine, radio captured the pinnacle of the two-day programme – High Mass for the throngs of pilgrims, most of them from St Michan's Conference of the St Vincent de Paul Society in Dublin.[54] Linked to this broadcast was another special programme from the Dublin studio of Radio Éireann 'giving a full account of the story of Knock shrine, including a radio drama written by Eily MacAdam'.[55]

In attracting attention to Knock, few things could match the power of a reputation for cures, and promoters of the revival of the shrine showed a lively awareness of this phenomenon from the beginning of their campaign. The prayer leaflet which inaugurated the campaign, and which Archbishop Gilmartin had authorized in May 1935, boasted that 'countless favours and blessings as well as cures of an extraordinary nature have been obtained at Knock through the intercession of Mary, Mother of God'.[56] The almost complete lack of official medical support for reported cures did not prevent Knock's promoters and their allies from making numerous claims. Addressing in August 1936 a throng of pilgrims in what the *Irish Catholic* headlined as 'a great national demonstration of faith', the Cistercian Father Jarlath Ronayne, a native of Brikens near Knock, recalled the miracle (a case of blindness cured) that he had personally witnessed at the shrine as a young man.[57] Speaking to 4,000 pilgrims from his own diocese in May 1937, Bishop Patrick Morrisroe of Achonry drew attention to the cures of two women at Knock in 1936, one from Co. Donegal and the second from Tuam.[58] Sometimes the cures claimed in accounts of Knock in the late 1930s had occurred many years earlier, as in the *Irish Catholic* story of October 1938 headlined '"God be Praised, I Can See": How Our Lady of Knock Heard an Old Woman's Prayer' – a tale told by an Irish-American septuagenarian who had witnessed this cure before emigrating as a young girl from Co. Roscommon.[59] Likely to have had a greater impact were accounts of invalids cured recently at Knock who later returned as healthy pilgrims. Reports in 1939 offered at least two such cases.[60] It was also difficult to gainsay the powerful personal testimony of the Dublin Carmelite Father J. A. Rabitte, who in September 1939 told over 4,000 child pilgrims from Connacht that when a little boy over forty years ago, he had come to Knock as an invalid and was eventually cured through the Virgin Mary's intervention.[61] Just as powerful, no doubt, was the effect on the first big group of pilgrims (over 10,000 people) in the 1940 season when during the ceremonies an old woman loudly cried out, 'I am cured, thank God! I am cured!'[62] The stress laid on all these claims of cures illustrates the importance attached by the shrine authorities to making Knock, just like Lourdes, a sacralized place where the care of the sick was a defining characteristic of its renown and its rituals.

What explains the marked intensification of the cult of Mary on which Knock shrine thrived during the 1930s? It is clear that Marian devotion met certain needs of Irish society in the inter-war period. One was the need to sublimate the sex drive on a rather massive scale because of Ireland's remarkably aberrant demographic behaviour. With a rigid system of impartible inheritance throughout the countryside, delaying the succession of a single heir to the family farm until the death or incapacity of the elderly family head, marriage was increasingly postponed in the post-Famine decades. By the 1930s the late age of marriage in Ireland (about 36 for men, 29 for women) put the country at the extreme end of the European scale. At the same time a very high proportion of Irish men and women – about a quarter in each case – went through life without ever marrying at all. Again, the Irish situation was highly exceptional. The 1926 census disclosed that 'there was a larger proportion of unmarried persons of all ages [in the twenty-six counties of Ireland] than in any other country for which records are kept'.[63] Under these circumstances it was culturally necessary to blunt the sexual appetites and everything that might stimulate them. Sexual purity was elevated to the highest of moral virtues, sexual transgression raised to the gravest of sins. In this relentless work of sexual repression and sublimation, no religious weapon was more useful than inculcation of devotion to the Virgin Mary, the very icon of purity.[64]

If Marianism was in part a response to rather extreme demographic trends, its intensification in the inter-war years was also a product of the cultural defensiveness of the new Irish state after 1921. The revolutionary élite and its supporters were acutely conscious that the degree of political independence wrested from Britain was not matched by cultural independence. Many Irish nationalists were still obsessed not only with the need to supplant the language of their ancient foes but also with the formidable task of countering their ideas and values – ideas that were held to be ever more subversive of religion, the family and sexual modesty. It was because of this widespread perception of moral pollution from Britain – through cheap novels and Sunday newspapers, films and radio – that the Free State quickly instituted a strict regime of censoring films (1923) and publications (1929). But in the eyes of the anti-modernist Irish moral police, clerical and lay, filth and corruption were constantly evading the official censors. What could not be achieved politically or bureaucratically could perhaps be accomplished religiously or supernaturally. Again, since the threats were so often framed in terms of moral pollution and especially sexual misconduct, a strengthening of allegiance to the Blessed Virgin Mary was invariably seen as the most fitting remedy.[65]

In Ireland as elsewhere, Marianism also played a central role in what was increasingly depicted as the war against communism and (what was almost as bad) socialism. The Bolshevik revolution of 1917 and the consolidation of Soviet power in the 1920s and 1930s, with the brutal repression of organized religion in the USSR, stood as a terrible warning of what might happen to Catholicism, and indeed Christianity in general, if the 'Red menace' were not contained. The 1930s have recently been described as 'a decade of unprecedented anti-communist fervour in Ireland'.[66] Anti-communism was already a potent enough force by the early 1930s, when it became the basis for a 'Red scare' used unsuccessfully against the Republican Fianna Fáil party by its pro-Treaty opponents in the prelude to the 1932 election, and it was the basis as well for the sharp attacks by the Catholic bishops on expressions of socialist Republicanism in 1931 and 1934.[67] But as the important recent study by Fearghal McGarry has emphatically demonstrated, anti-communism reached flood tide in Ireland in response to the Spanish Civil War of 1936–9. The atrocities committed by the Spanish Republican forces against the Catholic Church and its personnel in Spain were painted in the most lurid colours in the Irish secular and religious press; Franco and his right-wing nationalist insurgents found a vast reservoir of support, or at least sympathy, across almost the entire spectrum of Irish politics.[68] There was a pronounced tendency among members of the Catholic hierarchy and Fine Gael politicians to portray the Spanish Civil War in starkly religious and even apocalyptic terms. Those fanning the flames against the Soviet-supported Spanish Republic and for Franco's nationalists proclaimed that the choice was as simple and absolute as 'God or no God' (James Dillon), 'Christianity or atheism' (Daniel McMenamin), 'Christ or anti-Christ' (Patrick Belton).[69] As bishops, priests and mainstream politicians tirelessly repeated, the Spanish conflict was 'a consequence of the expansion of Russian communism', and if the communists succeeded in Spain, Britain and Ireland would not long be safe.[70]

Although Irish Catholic piety in numerous forms was mobilized in the war against communism, Marian devotion played a highly conspicuous role. This was especially true as the cult of Our Lady of Fatima came to occupy a dominant position in the devotional life of Irish Catholics during the 1940s, for in its central elements the Fatima cult was specifically anti-communist. Allegiance to the Immaculate Heart of Mary and to the rosary, as demanded by the Fatima virgin, was to be the impregnable bulwark against communist expansion and the key to the eventual conversion of Russia. But even during the 1930s the campaigns against communism and moral pollution stimulated an enormous upsurge of Marian devotion in Ireland. Its most characteristic form was the tremendous flowering of the cult of Our Lady of Lourdes. Though the Irish fascination with Lourdes was hardly a new phenomenon, it was during the 1930s that Lourdes became almost a national obsession among Irish Catholics. In the first two years after its formal opening in May 1930, the replica of the Lourdes grotto built by the Oblate Fathers of Mary Immaculate at Inchicore in Dublin attracted 'a million people', according to one estimate. (Though no doubt inflated, this number would still be impressive even if reduced by half or more.) But the most obvious and significant sign of the nationwide zeal for Lourdes in the 1930s was the dramatic multiplication of a whole series of large annual pilgrimages to the famous French shrine. Organized by a plethora of Catholic bodies, lay and clerical, these pilgrimages, and their many ramifications backward into further religious activity in parishes all over the country, raised the Lourdes cult to a level unprecedented in Ireland before or since.[71]

This Irish Catholic enthusiasm for Lourdes was part of a much broader set of religious and political developments. With the energetic support of the Vatican, the great French shrine was experiencing its own revival in the 1930s, as the papacy once again used Marianism morally to arm its followers against the menaces of modernism and communism. Pius XI capped the celebrations surrounding the seventy-fifth anniversary of the famous 1858 apparitions at Lourdes by canonizing Bernadette Soubirous in Rome on 8 December 1933, the feast of the Immaculate Conception. Her elevation to sainthood initiated another round of special religious events at Lourdes in 1934. The pinnacle, however, came a year later when the Vatican decreed that Lourdes should be the site of the extensive events marking the official end of the great Holy Year declared in 1933 by Pius XI in honour of the nineteenth centenary of Christ's crucifixion and redemption. Hundreds of thousands of pilgrims journeyed to Lourdes for a solemn triduum of Masses closing the Holy Year in April 1935. This vast turnout helped to push the total pilgrim traffic to Lourdes up to 1.1 million – a record for the shrine – in 1935 as a whole.[72]

It was thus hardly an accident that the revival of Knock shrine gained direction and momentum in the mid 1930s. Knock was certainly fortunate in the single-minded dedication, finely tuned diplomatic skills and endlessly resourceful promotional abilities of its two principal leaders, Liam and Judith Coyne. After visiting the great French shrine themselves with the Third Order of St Francis sometime before 1935, the Coynes openly wondered if Knock could ever be like Lourdes, as Judith Coyne told me in an interview in 1993.[73] Their struggle to make it so, begun auspiciously when Lourdes itself was enjoying a lusty resurgence, was to consume the rest of their lives. For them and for Irish Marianists in general, it was a struggle crowned in the Marian Year of 1954, when at a dramatic ceremony in St Peter's Basilica in Rome, Pius XII, the greatest of Marian popes, recognized Knock as one of the twenty major Marian shrines in the world;[74] and crowned again in 1979, when Pope John Paul II, whose Polish Catholicism is steeped in a perfervid Marianism, made his own famous pilgrimage to Knock, drawing in his wake perhaps as many as 450,000 people to the Mayo shrine on the day of his visit alone.[75] But if the Coynes and their close associates did much for Knock, what did far more for its revival was the extensive compatibility between the dynamics of Irish society and politics in the 1930s and what this physically undistinguished shrine in a remote corner of the country had to offer. There pilgrims could embrace an intense religious experience focused on the Virgin Mary that would morally arm them against sexual licentiousness (the 'cult of the body', as someone aptly called it) and atheistic communism, and that would affirm traditional Irish and Catholic cultural values in the face of the swelling tide of moral pollution from Britain.

Church or Nation
An Irish-American Dilemma

LAWRENCE J. McCAFFREY

Since January 2002, when the *Boston Globe* published a series of articles exposing priestly sexual abuse in the archdiocese, a malaise has gripped Catholic America. Exposure of the grisly situation in Boston led to revelations of similar incidents throughout the country, some going back forty years or more. The greatest degree of anger has been focused on Boston's Cardinal Law (since replaced), his auxiliary bishops and other prelates in the United States who transferred priests guilty of heinous sexual molestations from parish to parish where they preyed on other young victims, mostly male. Along with the reports of the sexual misconduct of priests and the irresponsibility of bishops came the news that millions of dollars were paid to victims as compensation or hush money. This information has hit hard when the Church is closing schools in many cities and needs funds to perform its social services. Insurance has borne the burden for many of the pay-offs, but that source is drying up and companies are increasingly reluctant to accept the Church as a client.

Abuse charges have defrocked priests or relieved them of parish duties. Casualties include members of the hierarchy, including Milwaukee's Archbishop Rembert Weakland. In May 2002, TV and newspaper journalists reported that in 1998 the archdiocese paid $450,000 to a man claiming the archbishop sexually abused him in the early 1980s. A few days later, Rome granted Weakland's request for retirement, submitted long before the reported incident. His fall severely jolted American Catholics, especially liberals. He was one of the most intellectual, certainly the most progressive, member in the upper reaches of the hierarchy. Weakland was sympathetic to ordaining women and married men and to the problems of homosexuals. He also offended the Vatican by meeting with and engaging in a discussion with abortion advocates.

After the *Globe* launched its series of articles on clerical sexual abuse, the subject became a major topic in many newspapers and magazines – inspiring cover stories in both *Time* and *Newsweek* – and on television information programs. Liberal as well as conservative voices, including

William Buckley and William Bennett, demanded resignations from bishops who shielded priest scoundrels. After much pressure, Rome in December 2002 accepted Cardinal Law's offer to depart. On 9 September 2003, his replacement, Archbishop Sean Patrick O'Malley, a Capuchin friar, offered abuse victims $85 million in compensation.

Requests from the press, television, the laity and priests who have lived up to the obligations of their vocation but feel tarnished by the conduct of those less principled, have persuaded many but not all bishops to open their files, free victims from confidentiality agreements, and to report distant and more recent abuse cases to civil authorities. The large number of abusers and victims and their lawsuits has increased the agony and stress of Catholic America. As the revelations mount and the costs rise, many of the faithful approach the brink of despair.

Many journalists and letters to newspaper refer to the abuse as paedophilia but in most instances ephebophilia is a more accurate description. A majority of victims have been post-pubescent youths, adolescents in secondary school or minor seminaries, or older males in major seminaries. Weakland's accuser was in his thirties when the seduction allegedly occurred. Since a large number of liberals fear that gays are scapegoats for clerical sexual abuse, the focus on paedophilia rather than ephebophilia is political correctness, an avoidance of any hint of homophobia. Recently, an increasing number of women have joined men in complaining of priestly sexual misconduct.

As indicated in the Law case, Rome slowly, and somewhat reluctantly, responded to the situation. Vatican authorities did meet with American cardinals and Bishop William Gregory of Bellevue, Illinois, president of the Bishops' Conference. After two days of dialogue – 23 and 24 April 2002 – a press release indicated division among the cardinals and no consensus on catering to majority American Catholic opinion's demand for a zero-tolerance response to clerical sex abuse. Sensitive to lay anger and impatience, and the need to restore confidence in their leadership, the hierarchy promised that its June meeting would provide an effective and satisfactory solution to the crisis. Reduced Mass attendance and contributions to parish collections and Catholic social services forced bishops to realize the consequences of lay fury. Quite a few Catholics believe that the only way they can influence the direction of an authoritarian church is by withholding money, a point well made by *Commonweal* editor, Margaret O'Brien Steinfels, in her address to the Bishops' Conference in Dallas on 13 June 2002.

But powerful Roman voices, insisting on the priority of canon law, have indicated Vatican disapproval of the American hierarchy identifying sexual abusers and turning them over to civil authorities. Gianfranco Ghirlanda, S.J., Dean of the Faculty of Canon Law at Gregorian University, in an article in the Jesuit journal *La Civilta Catholica*, denounced the idea of bishops revealing the indiscretions of priests, subjugating them to the consequences of civil law, or testing them for psychological disorders. He wrote:

'From a canon law perspective, the bishop and the superior are neither morally or judicially responsible for the act committed by one of their clergy.' Supposedly, *La Civilta Catholica* reflects Vatican thinking. A few weeks later, it insisted that American press coverage of clerical sexual abuse was motivated by satisfying its readers' 'morbid and scandalistic curiosity', and by bias against Catholicism and the papacy.[1] Honduran Cardinal Oscar Andres Rodriguez Maradiaga, supposedly a candidate to succeed Pope John Paul II, also blames a scandal-hungry press for exaggerating clerical sexual abuse. The distinguished historian Philip Jenkins, in *The New Anti-Catholicism: The Last American Prejudice,* endorses this charge. He offers evidence that over forty years only a miniscule percentage of priests in the United States sexually misbehaved and true cases of paedophilia have been rare. In fact, Jenkins insists that there is no evidence that Catholic clerics are more of a threat to children than other professions that come in contact with them.[2] However, Catholics expect more from their priests than they do from such caregivers as teachers, day-care attendants or boy-scout leaders. In April 2002, Archbishop Julian Herranz, head of the Vatican Council, said that bishops do not have to turn over the record of sexually abusive clergy to civil authorities.[3] Ghirlandi's and Herranz's positions and the attitude of *La Civilta Catholica* make it unlikely that people around the Pope look kindly on a policy of zero tolerance. Call to Action, a liberal Catholic lay group, has also voiced dissent from no-second-chance responses to clerical misconduct, arguing that while paedophilia might be incurable, other sexual falls from grace may not be.[4]

Newspapers throughout the country covered the Conference of American Bishops that opened in Dallas, Texas, on 12 June 2002 to discuss and solve the crisis. The next day's *Dallas Morning News* revealed three month's of research findings of two of its journalists, who charged that 'roughly two-thirds of the top US Catholic leaders have protected priests guilty of sexual abuse in a systematic practice that spans decades and continues today'. On that same day, the *Boston Globe* reported that 'lawyers, newspapers and interest groups have estimated that as many as 1,500 priests have molested children in the last five decades'. Of these, 250 were suspended or removed and four bishops resigned.

On 14 June 2002, the bishops concluded their Dallas meeting by agreeing that all past, present and future abusers would no longer function as priests. They are expected to live lives of penance, preferably in monasteries. The choice of defrocking is up to their bishops and ultimately Rome. Approved by a vote of 239 to 13, this policy also insists that all bishops must report allegations of priestly abuse of minors to public authorities. In general, the bishops were quite happy with the result, but many victims wanted offenders removed from the priesthood and not just from the ministry. They and others not completely satisfied with the Dallas results complained that the bishops most responsible for scandals and cover-ups escaped reprimands and resignations. Both Chicago papers, the *Sun-Times* on 16 June and the *Tribune* on the next day, pointed to the bishops' escape from any punishment as a conference failure. As the latter pointed out, proportionally members of the hierarchy were far more responsible for the scandal than the clergy. Chicago's Cardinal Francis George wanted to discipline negligent members of the hierarchy but decided that the meeting had accomplished as much as it could. He said that he would bring the matter up at later gathering of prelates.

In Dallas, the bishops created a national Office For Child and Youth Protection to interact with the bishops in enforcing the new policy. Its chair, Governor Frank Keating of Oklahoma, indicated that he would make sure that bishops responsible for transferring abusive priests and covering up their crimes would be held accountable for their contribution to the crisis.[5] On 16 June 2003, Keating resigned, complaining that some bishops were not fully co-operating in the disclosure of improper clerical conduct, and comparing their devious secrecy with that of the Cosa Nostra (Mafia).[6]

In addition to by-passing the bishop's role in abetting and covering up abuse, the Dallas meeting also avoided discussions of other key questions circulating around the scandal. Notorious priestly misdeeds have also occurred in Ireland and, like the United States, in other places where Catholicism has deep Irish roots, such as Newfoundland and Australia, leading to speculations that its sexually neurotic, puritanical Celtic version breeds perversion.[7] And many analysing the sources of clerical deviancy are asking if celibacy attracts the psychologically and sexually immature into the priesthood and discourages mentally stable men from considering a religious vocation? They also wonder if the massive and increasing shortage of priests in a sacramental religion necessitates the ordination of women and married men? Some want to know whether the Catholic priesthood has become a gay profession? If so, does the homosexual ambience of seminary and clerical life drive some heterosexuals out of religious life and discourage others from entering, and are the large numbers of gays in the clergy a factor in the abuse scandals? Liberals and conservatives have come to different conclusions. But another, more crucial, long-term question has not drawn the attention of those discussing the problem and future of American Catholicism. Can an authoritarian institution, structurally formed in the late Roman Empire and medieval period, adapt to a modern, liberal, democratic political culture?

Before the advent of Protestantism, western Christianity exhibited adaptability to a slowly changing world. This flexibility diminished during sixteenth- and seventeenth-century theological disputes, conflicts between church and state, and bloody wars of religion. Christianity unsuccessfully challenged the rationalism of the eighteenth-century Enlightenment, forfeiting the allegiance of middle-class intellectuals, and never really adjusted to the nineteenth-century Industrial Revolution and subsequent urbanization, resulting in the defection of a large segment of the working class.

With its late Roman Empire and medieval-based institutions and values, Catholicism's hierarchical and authoritarian structure has had a more hostile confrontation with the modern world than Protestantism, but has continued to command allegiances in underdeveloped, mostly agrarian societies. This was especially true for Ireland where Catholicism symbolized cultural identity in a contest with Protestant-represented English colonialism. Religion distinguished conqueror from conquered, powerful from powerless, alien from native. In the early nineteenth century, Daniel O'Connell laid the foundations of Irish nationalism on the agitation for Catholic civil liberties. As nationalism became an increasingly pervasive force in Irish life, so did the practice of religion. Relationships between faith and fatherland were important dimensions of what Emmet Larkin has frequently described as Ireland's 'Devotional Revolution'. From the 1820s through most of the twentieth century, Catholicism in the words of Patrick O'Farrell in *Ireland's English Question* (1972) has been in addition to worship 'a set of values, a culture, a historical tradition, a view on the world, a disposition of heart and mind, a loyalty, an emotion, a psychology – and a nationalism'.[8]

But Irish and Continental Catholicism differed in responses to a changing political culture. Except for Belgium, the latter, in its rejection of the French Revolution, industrialism and urbanization, was wedded to the Old Regime, denouncing liberalism, democracy and the integrity of private consciences. In Ireland, O'Connell's liberalism, as well as their country's bondage, encouraged Irish Catholic nationalists to embrace representative government, a wide suffrage, the separation of Church and state, and, on a comparative basis, religious tolerance. Irish Catholics developed a split personality, sharing loyalties to a liberal political ethos and the western world's most authoritarian religion. Not until the Church became embroiled in conflicts with the modern world under Pius IX and his successors, and Irish immigrants had to adapt to the liberal–democratic traditions of the rest of the English-speaking world, did this contradiction initiate troublesome dilemmas.

Inherited from its English parent, anti-Catholicism was at the core of American nativism.[9] Since the Irish were the first large Catholic group of immigrants to enter the United States, they became the principal targets of no-popery. Traumatic adjustments of agrarian, mostly illiterate newcomers to urban America resulted in massive social disorder that strained the resources of Anglo-Protestant communities. But the religious faith more than the behaviour of the Irish fuelled nativist wrath. Anglo and Scotch-Irish Americans were convinced that people loyal to Roman authoritarianism and superstitions could never be good citizens. They viewed them as a subversive threat to American liberal values and institutions, the opening wedge of papal aggression in the United States.

While a burden, Catholicism also consoled the American Irish. Latin Masses, the sacraments and a myriad of devotions built a bridge of familiarity between rural Ireland and urban America. Catholic liturgies provided immigrants and their descendents psychological as well as spiritual comfort and security in hostile environments. With their religious, educational and social dimensions, Catholic parishes defined city neighbourhoods and sheltered their occupants from Anglo- and Scotch-Irish hostility. In many ways, they functioned as transported peasant villages in an urban setting.[10]

Skill deficiencies and no-popery antagonism doomed at least two generations of Irish Americans to menial labour or domestic service. In compensation, they took advantage of openings for status and power in politics, organized labour, athletics, entertainment and religion. Using their familiarity with the English language and political culture, from the mid nineteenth century to its close the Irish rose from the lowest ranks of the Democratic Party to its dominant urban force. They also were active in the evolution of organized labour. In 1879, Terence V. Powderly became the first Grand Master of the Knights of Labor, the initial effort to unionize workers on a national scale. Two years later, when the American Federation of Labor came into existence, Irish and Jews were its most numerous leaders. In the first decade of the twentieth century, the former were presidents of fifty of the AFL's one hundred and ten locals. In the early years of baseball, the national game, the Irish supplied most of its stars. They also dominated boxing until the 1930s when Joe Louis came on the scene. Unlike baseball, with its American pastoral nuances, the brutality of boxing probably harmed more than it benefited the Irish image. While Irish comedians, singers, dancers and actors were featured in theatre and vaudeville, early stage-Irish images tended to be negative.

Catholicism best exhibited Irish influence and power.[11] In America, as in Ireland, it attracted the best and brightest talent. In both places, families took great pride and achieved distinction through priest sons and nun daughters. By the close of the nineteenth century, most of the hierarchy, clergy and other religious in the American Church were Irish. Since they controlled urban political machines, labour unions and, most importantly, the Catholic Church, the Irish adjusted other Catholic ethnics to the American environment and made them adjuncts of Irish-American power.

Ambiguity defined the attitude of Irish-American bishops to the life and culture surrounding their people. Typified by New York's Archbishop Michael Corrigan, east-coast prelates attempted to isolate them from materialism, secularism and Protestant proselytism. Although many Catholics were underprivileged, prelates were reluctant to condone social reform movements, branding them as secularism in some instances even socialism. Often distrust of change included opposition to labour unions. However, in the Midwest, where the Irish faced less prejudice and enjoyed more flexible social structures and dynamic economies, bishops were more tolerant of adaptations to local cultural, economic, political and social environments. They often spoke kindly of public schools and favoured organized labour so the Church could retain working-class loyalty. St Paul's Irish-born archbishop, John Ireland, was the leading Americanist in the hierarchy.[12]

In 1899, some French, Canadian and American bishops, fearing that Ireland and his colleagues were challenging the Church's traditional conservatism, prevailed on Leo XIII to condemn their optimistic linking of Catholicism and Americanism. In a *Testem Benevolentia* letter to Baltimore's Cardinal James Gibbons, primate of the Church in the United States and friendly to the Ireland faction, Leo condemned a distorted version of Americanist positions as secularism. This denunciation, followed by Pius X's campaign against modernism, stultified Catholic intellectualism throughout the world. However, interpreting Leo's encyclical *Rerum Novarum* (1891) and Pius XI's *Quadragesimo Anno* (1931) from American perspectives and situations, a majority of bishops and priests in the United States adopted a friendly stance toward labour unions.

By 1900, Irish Americans had ascended economic and social ladders. Many males were skilled workers with a significant number in the ranks of the middle class – businessmen, lawyers and doctors. Inspired by nuns, Irish women were over-represented in both the teaching and nursing professions. Because so many Irish people served in police and fire departments, held politically connected jobs, worked on railroads or for urban transport systems, taught in public schools and nursed in hospitals – occupations that survived during the Great Depression of the 1930s – the Irish probably weathered hard times better than many other citizens. Shared suffering during the Depression and Catholic America's patriotic response to the Second World War decreased religious prejudices; so did watching movies, the country's most influential form of mass entertainment. When popular stars such as Spencer Tracy, Pat O'Brien and Bing Crosby portrayed Irish-American clerics more as social workers than as sacramental ministers, and when most heroic chaplains in war films were Irish-American priests, Catholicism appeared in a more favourable light.[13]

Post-war, Irish-American and general Catholic economic progress continued to elevate the status of Irish Americans. Using the educational benefits of the Servicemen's Readjustment Act of 1944 (G.I. Bill of Rights), a multitude of Irish Americans earned college and university diplomas and graduate and professional school degrees, transforming themselves into an essentially middle-class community that became less urban and more suburban. White flight from expanding African-American neighbourhoods and the tensions of racial conflict, as well as a search for a better life, motivated this residential change.

Despite their prominence in American political, religious and social life, and in the world of entertainment, and their middle-class, often suburban, respectability, Irish-American Catholics remained psychologically insecure and culturally isolated from the American mainstream until the 1960s. They tended to avoid contact with other Americans, preferring to socialize in various religious societies such as the Knights of Columbus and the Daughters of Isabella. Rather than use the free or inexpensive services of public elementary and secondary schools and state universities, a large number spent considerable sums of money to educate their children in schools and colleges emphasizing Catholic distinctiveness and denouncing secular, materialistic and pragmatic American values. Neo-Thomism, at the core of Catholic higher education, better prepared students to live in the thirteenth than the twentieth century, and substituted defensive apologetics for creative and critical thinking. Catholic higher education was much more interested in producing successful middle-class businessmen and professionals to support and finance the Church than intellectuals who might criticize it, and doctors and lawyers to oppose birth control, abortion and divorce. In the 1950s, two Catholic scholars, John Tracy Ellis and Thomas F. O'Dea, complained that American Catholicism had failed to balance the economic and social success of its people with intellectual achievement.[14]

Anti-black racism that began in the nineteenth and persisted well into the twentieth century also illustrated remaining Irish Catholic insecurity. As part of an emphasis on social justice, since the 1930s many members of the hierarchy and clergy had championed the civil liberties of African Americans. Some Catholic colleges, such as St Ambrose in Davenport, Iowa, stressed labour and racial justice issues in their curricula and social atmospheres. But most Catholics, those who remained in the cities, often supported by their priests, expressed antagonism, vocally and sometimes physically, to housing and equal-education opportunities for blacks. Parishes that once sheltered Irish and other Catholic ethnics from Anglo- and Scotch-Irish Protestant discrimination became paranoid garrisons of bigotry.[15]

Although culturally and socially isolating themselves from other Americans, Catholics insisted on, and where they were in great numbers frequently succeeded in, imposing their moral values on the rest of the community, forbidding the sale of contraceptives, forcing censorship of movies and other popular entertainments. For some time, Massachusetts forbade married women to teach, fearing it might encourage them to practise birth control.[16]

In the 1930s and 40s, many Catholic newspapers irritated American liberals by defending dictatorial regimes in Portugal, Spain, Argentina and, for a while, Italy, as antidotes to communism. Although the anti-Semitic Father Charles Coughlin lost much of his Catholic following in 1936 when he turned against President Franklin D. Roosevelt, many working-class Irish and Germans, especially on the east coast, continued to follow the demagogue padre from Royal Oak, Michigan. During the Second World War, young Irish lads were physically assaulting Jews in Boston. Catholic sympathy for fascist rulers abroad and the impact of Father Coughlin and his satellite, the Christian Front, confirmed opinions that Catholicism was inappropriate to the American setting.

During the 1950s, Irish and general Catholic anti-communism, reflecting defensiveness and a need to demonstrate loyalty to the United States, led to excessive support for Wisconsin's Senator Joseph McCarthy's anti-Red and Pink crusade that libelled and ruined careers without really uncovering serious threats to American security. Not all McCarthy devotees came from within the Church, but a large number did, including New York's Cardinal Francis Spellman, and they fed Liberal anti-Catholicism.

American Catholics, unaware of the conflict between their religious and civil loyalties, drew clear separations between religion and social, economic and political issues. They failed to comprehend that contraception, abortion and censorship in a pluralistic society had social, medical and cultural nuances extending beyond Catholic interests and moral views.

While justified in resenting efforts to impose a Catholic will on the general population, critics underestimated positive Irish-American contributions. True, their urban political machines were often corrupt but their religious values pioneered the Democratic Party's change of direction from individual to communal liberalism. On the national political stage, Catholic politicians in Congress, mostly Irish, played key roles in making the New Deal, Fair Deal, New Frontier and Great Society instruments of social justice and racial equality and in transforming American foreign policy from isolationism to internationalism. Auxiliary Bishop Bernard Sheil of Chicago denounced Joe McCarthy as he previously had condemned Father Coughlin. Congressman Eugene McCarthy from St Paul, Minnesota, and other Catholics in the House and Senate joined in rejecting the hysterical libels of 'Tail Gunner' Joe.

In post-war America, Catholic isolationism and solidarity slowly crumbled. As indicated in the previous paragraph, Irish politics spread beyond local to national and international concerns. Second World War Catholic servicemen met and co-operated with Jews, Protestants and, to a limited extent, people of other races. They came home more cosmopolitan and tolerant. While Catholic colleges and universities were limited in intellectual perspectives, they increasingly improved, expanding student curiosity as well as knowledge. Numerous Catholics attended secular or Protestant-founded universities, especially their graduate and professional schools, experiencing the impact of new ideas and cultural attitudes. Migrations to city fringes and suburbs often meant leaving single-ethnic urban, and joining multi-ethnic suburban, parishes. Consequently, connections between religion and nationality became more fragile.

John F. Kennedy's victory in 1960 and the national and international popularity of his presidency actualized as well as symbolized the American Catholic passage from urban, working-class ghettos of mind and place to middle-class suburbs of acceptability and respectability. In his time, President Kennedy wasn't the only Irish-American Catholic at the apex of the power structure. John McCormack, also from Massachusetts, was speaker of the House of Representatives; Montana's Senator Mike Mansfield was

Senate majority leader; and John Bailey from Connecticut chaired the Democratic National Committee. Emancipated from their defensive, inferiority complex, secure in their American status, Catholics finally joined the totality of American life. Those still obsessed with communism contributed to the imprudent and demoralizing American involvement in Vietnam. But others, including many priests and nuns, vigorously campaigned for civil rights and racial equality and a conclusion of the war in south-east Asia. Attempting to free his country from the Vietnam quagmire, Senator Eugene McCarthy courageously challenged President Lyndon Johnson in the 1968 presidential primaries. His strong showing in New Hampshire and impending victory in Wisconsin persuaded the Texan to abandon his re-election bid. With the way cleared by McCarthy, New York's Senator Robert F. Kennedy also became a presidential candidate. After narrowly defeating the Minnesotan in the California primary, Kennedy seemed the obvious Democratic candidate but Sirhan Sirhan's assassination bullet might have put Richard Nixon in the White House.

Positive Irish-American involvements in the economic, social and political life of the country reduced fears among other Americans that they and other Catholics were an alien force. Catholic immersion in the American mainstream also had religious consequences. American assimilation and Kennedy's New Frontier idealism propelled young men and women into seminaries and convents as well as into the Peace Corp and civil rights agitations. During the 1940s, 50s and 60s, large numbers of Catholics attended Mass, received the sacraments, and contributed generous sums to parishes and Catholic causes and institutions. At Vatican II, in the early 1960s, American bishops played a negligible part in liturgical and theological discussions but were a force in persuading the Church to accept the freedom and sanctity of private consciences; ecumenical overtures to Jews, Protestants and Orthodox Christians; and the validity of separation of Church and state. Liturgical and some rule changes that emerged from the council – the use of the vernacular, the expanded role of the laity in services, more lenient Lenten and Friday abstinence and fasting obligations – raised expectations that the Church would become more flexible in regard to sexual and matrimonial matters.

For most of those anticipating change, contraception was the key issue. They believed it was time for Rome to abandon its pre-urban and pre-industrial view that the fundamental purpose of matrimony was to produce souls for God rather than to foster love between parents and children. Marriage as a birth factory imposed a lighter burden in times and places when sons were field-hands and daughters kitchen-maids and child-tenders. Even in the early Industrial Revolution, when children were in factories instead of school, they could contribute economically. But in Catholic, middle-class America, where parents were determined to raise families in comfort and economic security and send daughters and sons to colleges and universities, common sense dictated prudent child-bearing.

The Church's approved rhythm system failed to satisfy as either family limitation or as support for healthy sexual relationships. Making love by calendars and thermometers violated rather than sustained natural sexual desires and diminished affection between husbands and wives. Since it often failed to prevent unwanted pregnancies, the rhythm system earned the label 'Roman Roulette'.

When Paul VI appointed a commission to study and make recommendations on the family-planning issue, a majority of Catholics expected an acceptance of the contraceptive pill. The 1968 papal encyclical, *Humanae Vitae,* dashed these hopes by rejecting the commission's pro-contraception recommendations, reaffirming the traditional rejection of 'unnatural' means of birth control. Throughout the western world, most Catholics refused to abide by this decision, an authority-defying precedent that expanded into other areas, resulting in an unofficial schism in American and European Catholicism. Now there are two Churches, one for the hierarchy and clergy, another for a lay majority. According to a May 2002 *Newsweek* poll, 50 per cent of American Catholics felt at odds with Church teaching on sexuality. 59 per cent did not think that screening gays out of the priesthood would make much difference in reducing the problems of abuse. 51 per cent had no qualms about attending Mass in a parish with an openly gay priest. 73 per cent were ready to accept married priests and 65 per cent ordained women.[17] A number of Catholics are fanatical pro-life harassers of abortion clinics and doctors, but most seem to leave the decision to have or not have a child to private consciences. While conservatives ridicule 'cafeteria Catholics' picking and choosing what to believe, many of them ignore those papal and hierarchical positions on social justice, capital punishment and world disarmament that liberals embrace. Since they have little concern with the health, education and general welfare of poor children, many opponents of abortion seem to believe that the right to life ends with birth.

The Irish, the most affluent, well-educated and suburban of Catholic ethnics, once the most obedient and faithful members of the American Church, now lead opposition to its power and arrogance. Like other prosperous members of the Church, they no longer contribute their best and brightest to the religious life. Once full of dedicated young men and women, seminaries and convents are now thinly populated. There is a massive shortage of priests, nuns and brothers. Many of those remaining in their vocations are quite old. The Church's shortage involves quality as well as quantity. Intelligence doesn't appear to be a prime feature of seminarians or young priests.

Residing in the suburbs, socializing with a wide variety of people who do not share their religion, and sending their children to public schools and non-Catholic colleges and universities, have diminished the religious dimensions of Irish-American and other Catholic ethnicities. Bishops and priests no longer speak for the laity. Parishes have ceased to be the focal points of Catholic lives. Organizations such as the Knights Of Columbus, the Holy Name Society, the Daughters of Isabella and the Altar and Rosary Society cannot compete with local country clubs for Catholic membership. Irish Americans who once found the essential ingredient of their identity in religion now search for it in history and culture – music, literature and theatre.

Since the 1960s, American Catholics, confident and comfortable about their place in the United States, have confronted dichotomies in their loyalties to the most liberal political and the most authoritarian religious systems and have decided that their priority commitment is to the former. They still find spiritual and psychological comfort in the Mass, sacraments and devotions, and still believe in what they consider the essentials of their faith. These do not include unquestioning subservience to the authority of popes or bishops or what a celibate hierarchy and clergy have to say about sex or marriage. Obviously the current sexual abuse scandals have subverted confidence in Church leaders who have abetted and covered up crime, and were far more interested in avoiding scandal than upholding morality and more concerned with the institution than the people it was supposed to serve. Most of the laity insisting on reform demand openness, the end of secrecy and a voice for the laity in the governance of the Church.

As indicated at the beginning of this essay, the search for causes of the sexual abuse scandals and cover-ups and the creation of policies to prevent their repetition are, in the long run, secondary to understanding the place of the Catholic Church in the twenty-first-century western world. Is it only relevant in environments of poverty and ignorance or does it still have a vital role in politically, economically and socially more sophisticated societies? Can an institution structurally and mentally set in the distant past come to terms with the spiritual and secular needs of Catholics in liberal–democratic political cultures? Can bishops who receive their appointments from Rome and are subject to an absolute monarchy respond to lay voices? If they do, will the papacy endorse concessions that they make to liberalization? If Rome insists that canon law supersedes civil law and that the Church exists beyond the jurisdiction of civil authority, will the laity subordinate its political to its religious loyalties? Events in the United States since the 1960s suggest that a majority will decide that the Church, as now constructed, is inappropriate to its concept of freedom and human dignity, and will respond to Roman authoritarianism with increasing indifference to, and detachment from, the institutionalized Catholic Church. Seemingly, most Catholics in the United States and western Europe take pride in the history and mystery of their religion but would like to see it more in symmetry with the political institutions they treasure, a constitutional rather than an absolute form of religious governance, with a strong lay influence, and a pope as a symbolic rather than absolute monarch. In other words, they want their Church to become an integral part of the total lives they live.

Unionism and the Mass Media

EOGHAN HARRIS

John A. Murphy is always comfortable speaking to Unionists, which he does at every opportunity, without either condescending to them or concealing his own opinions. But he is equally good at speaking for Unionists. This essay is a tribute to his efforts in that field. It starts from the premise that Unionists themselves have not had a fair hearing in the mass media, asks why this should be so and proposes some remedies. As the essay deals in perceptions, it makes general statements that may grate on readers with a passion for the singular exception. In this case, mentally preface every general statement with those three valuable words: by and large.

Why do Unionists, who have such a powerful moral and political case, make such a poor showing in the mass media? Why is it a truth universally recognized that Northern Unionists are not as good as Northern Nationalists in getting their point across? Should these statements seem too simplistic or too sweeping, subject them to a simple test. Can you recall regular public commentary congratulating Unionist politicians on the skill with which they made their case, and calling attention to the failure of Nationalists in this field? No, you can't. Conversely, can you recall regular public comment about how well Sinn Féin use the media? Yes, you can.

The perception that Unionists come across badly in the media, particularly on television and radio, is a commonplace of public discourse, not only in the Irish Republic, in the UK and the US, but even in Unionist circles. And it dates back to the beginning of the Troubles. At the start of the Civil Rights campaign (1966–9), Unionists put their problems with the press and television down to media bias. But even then it was clear that, bias or no bias, Unionist politicians could not compete with the SDLP leader John Hume in a television or radio studio.

During the period of the armed struggle (1972–96), Unionism's problems in persuading a UK audience to accept their view of the Troubles became less important for a time. Media deficiencies were diluted by the sympathy the Northern Protestants rightly received for the dignity and courage with which they met the worst the IRA could do to them. But the prelude to the Good Friday Agreement (1993–8) saw the perception of poorish performance by Unionists become once again a matter of public comment. Indeed, in the immediate aftermath of the Agreement, some Unionists were openly critical of the UUP failure to present it as a political and moral victory. The Hume–Adams talks and the ceasefire that followed put Unionists under severe pressure in the media. A symptom of the new awareness that all was not well was when the Ulster Young Unionist Council commissioned me to contribute to an analysis of the problem which was subsequently published in the pamphlet *Selling Unionism*.[1]

As time went on, the perceived imbalance between Unionists and Nationalists in the mass media became more acute as Sinn Féin began to replace the SDLP as spokespersons for Northern Nationalism. As soon as John Hume backed out of the studio lights, Gerry Adams of Sinn Féin adroitly stepped into his media shoes, filling them comfortably and showing the same skill as John Hume in manipulating the medium of television.

Naturally there have always been individual Unionists who were masters of the mass media. Ken Maginnis, MP, made a good impression on audiences in the Irish Republic. So did David Ervine of the PUP. For some time after he received the Nobel Peace Prize, David Trimble enjoyed a brief popularity south of the border. But even these fine performers often gave the impression of swimming against a media tide.

The 11 September atrocity shone a hard light on Unionism's structural problems with the media. At first sight Unionism had a unique chance to make friends with America. The Bush Administration was against terrorism of any tint. And soon after 11 September, the IRA was linked to the Colombian guerrilla group FARC, which was no friend of the United States. Constitutional Unionism had a unique chance to present itself as a reliable ally of America in the international war against terrorism. But, far from making hay, Unionist politicians spent the time looking for rain. On trips to the USA, instead of focusing firmly on the IRA, they frittered away their advantage by making pointless attacks on the Irish Republic. Meantime, Sinn Féin masterfully misdirected the mass media away from Columbia and back to a series of metaphysical speculations on the possibility of an IRA gesture on arms.

Some of these mistakes arose partly from political ineptitude. But, since they surfaced in the mass media, they were symptomatic of a deeper structural problem that Unionism seems to have in meshing political actions with their projection in the form of political theatre at which television excels. Although David Trimble had done much to modernize the UUP's approach to media, Unionism still seems not to understand that, in the age of television, most politics is media politics.

In sum the problems that first surfaced in 1969 are still around. By and large, Unionism is still not as successful as Nationalism in making its case. Since Unionists are not inferior to Nationalists, intellectually or morally, this imbalance needs investigation. We need new answers to the question at the head of this essay: Why do Unionists find it hard to get a fair hearing? In the absence of academic research in this area, I should like to offer some firm opinions, drawing on my experience as a sometime media advisor to Unionist politicians, on twenty-five years as a television producer for RTÉ, on conducting media courses in EU countries, and on a theoretical document I published in 1987 called *Television and Terrorism*.[2]

Certainly in the Irish Republic, Unionist spokespersons start out with a tribal handicap. The consensus against armed struggle in opposition to the Northern state has always been a leaky one. On the other hand, the respectful hearing given to Ken Maginnis and David Ervine shows that a sizeable constituency in the south is willing to listen to a spokesperson from the other side who can tell the Unionist story. Of which more anon.

Likewise it must be conceded that Unionists have some real problems with the British media. In my own experience, the prevalence of post-colonial guilt in British media circles, particularly in the BCC, is matched only by an astonishing degree of antipathy against the Unionist community, most of it based on historical ignorance. As against that, the residual respect for balance in British media means that at least Unionist spokesmen are free to appear, even if they are treated somewhat frostily compared with Gerry Adams and Martin McGuinness. The real problem, however, is that when they appear they are not able to attract the support of a mass audience.

Finally, Unionists making a case in the USA are up against an active Irish-American lobby, with many links to the White House. But this bloc only posed a problem in the early days of the armed struggle. Today the US media are much more sophisticated. However, while there is a big market for the Unionist side of the story, they make no systematic effort to supply that market on a steady professional basis. Yet, from time to time, exceptional Unionist spokespersons easily push local prejudices aside and attract support from fair-minded people, in the Irish Republic, in the UK and in the USA. Accordingly, we must dig a little deeper for the source of Unionist difficulty. At the risk of reductionism (a risk I always think worth running), I would like to propose that the Unionist problems arise from what mass media audiences, either consciously or subconsciously, perceive as three fundamental flaws in the Unionist approach to both making a case and, much more importantly, to telling their story.

First, Unionist spokespersons are seen to be too wedded to text over tone, to what is said rather than who says it, to the song not the singer. Their preference for content, not form, means they come across on mass media as more concerned with the calorific value of the political meal than how it is cooked or presented on the plate, or whether it is served with goodwill or not.

Second, Unionist spokespersons are perceived by audiences *to lack an adequate and attractive theory of political change.* In Ireland and the UK (and I would argue in all western countries) change is conceived as a moral imperative and any attempt to avoid it arouses antipathy. And of course in a political culture such as that of the United States, where the concept of change is something close to sacred, what comes across as persistent Unionist unhappiness with change, however well founded, does dreadful damage to its political image.

Third, and of greater importance than the preceding two perceptions, is the sense that Unionist spokespersons seem *more concerned to make a case than tell a story*. They are seen to treat the television studio as a court of law, in which the plaintiff with the strongest factual evidence is entitled to win. By contrast, nationalists see the studio as a fireside around which various factions contend for victory by telling a story that is superior to that of other narrators in plot, character and dramatic conflict.

In passing, it hardly needs saying that the nationalist conception of the mass media as a theatre rather than a courtroom is more congenial to those who work in the media, and more congruent with the theatrical nature of the medium itself. Consequently nationalists start out with a huge natural advantage, in form, if not in content. Let's now look at each of these points at greater length, as well as in ascending order of importance.

1. Unionists come across as more concerned with text than tone.

There is no doubt that, deep down, this attitude causes more antipathy among media people than any other. The Unionist passion for pinning down the precise meaning of words, however admirable it may be in a literary critic, when practised by a politician in a television studio can often come across as fiddly and finicky reverence for facts at the expense of emotional truth. As an ancillary to putting text before tone, Unionists are also seen to be more interested in *what* is said than in *who* said it. Aristotle's *Rhetoric* rejects this order of importance and reminds us that the first thing that affects an audience is the authority of the speaker; that is, not so much *what* is said but *who* says it. And if Aristotle had lived in the age of mass media, he would almost certainly have added a third term, *how* you say it.

In my experience many Unionists have problems with that point of view. Again and again, during the peace process, cultural chasms opened when conflicts arose between text and tone, singer and song, articulation and inspiration. Again and again, when discussing a deal, Unionists picked up on *what* was said, whereas Nationalists noted *how* it was said. This cultural gap is clearly religious rather than political in origin. On the Protestant side it has its roots in the Reformation, in the centrality of the Bible and the primacy of text. Many Northern Protestants were brought up on Sunday services where a single sentence of the Bible was parsed and pondered. No wonder they parse and ponder the fine print and footnotes of any political deal.

But that meticulous parsing causes profound problems with the culture of Northern Catholicism, the other principal culture in Northern Ireland (and, I would argue, with the culture of the mass media). Roman Catholics, formed by rich rituals such as the Mass and repetitive devotional exercises like the Rosary, naturally value tone as well as text, and take note of the sound of words as well as the meaning of words. So do television audiences. In fact modern society always favours emotional integrity over exact but emotionally inert factualism. Accordingly the understandable Unionist passion for text – understandable in any community seeking security – comes across on television as a finicky preoccupation with footnotes and fine print.

This can make Unionist spokespersons sometimes sound prolix and even petty. Furthermore, Dr Johnson's observation that 'some degree of truth must be sacrificed to concision' strikes a strong chord with both mass audiences and the people who produce and present the programmes. Not for a moment am I suggesting that what is said does not matter to the mass media. It does, but it doesn't necessarily matter more than the tone in which it is said. The proposition that the package can be as important as the product sounds slippery to the nuts and bolts Northern Protestant mind. Arguing that tone is sometimes as important as text, that the singer is as important as the song, or that the style is as important as the substance – all that can be anathema to the Calvinist tradition.

But from a moral as well as a media point of view, I believe this kind of essentialist thinking makes for poor practical politics. Philosophically, it is rooted in Platonic idealism rather than Aristotelian realism. Applied to politics, essentialism of this sort produces pointless Unionist questions ('Yes, yes, I can see there's a ceasefire, but what do Sinn Féin really, really mean by the word "peace"?'), which serve to confuse rather than clarify. There is much sense in the mass media's respect for tone as well as text. We all know, for example, that an apology is as much about form as content, about how someone says sorry as much as what they say. Saying sorry in an insolent tone of voice makes matters worse, not better. On the other hand an inarticulate but heart-felt apology can heal any breach.

In sum: Unionists should take more trouble over tone.

2. Unionists need an adequate and attractive theory of political change.

Much of the poor press that Unionists get in the United Kingdom (and even more so in the US) arises from the perception that Unionists seem to think of politics as a product rather than a process, as a practice that can force firm conclusions, rather than a process of continual change involving inconclusive, intermediate and indeed indeterminate settlements. This perception is compounded by the different cultural approaches to the very idea of politics on the part of the Unionist and Nationalist communities. Unionists tend to see politics as a means to an end, a burden to be laid down as soon as possible. But Nationalists tend to see politics as an end in itself, and as a pleasure to be prolonged.

Until David Trimble took over, many prominent Unionist politicians came across as Candide-like creatures whose only wish was to retreat from the public sphere and cultivate their garden. Judging by the low turn-out at elections by the Protestant middle class, this attitude persists. At some level Protestants seem to be saying that they see the public sphere as a lesser place which can be left to others. Although the UUP cannot be accused of shirking hard work, this sense of an amateurish approach to politics is hard to leave behind. Northern nationalists have compared it to sharing a house with a bored teenager who believes somebody else, presumably the British government, will pick up. It is a part-time attitude whose presence is hard to conceal under the cold gaze of a camera.

But much worse is the impression some Unionists give, when talking on television, that politics need be pursued only until boundaries have been set in stone. But on this earth there is no such end-game. Politics has porous, not permanent, goals. Above all, since permanent political change is part of the European political consensus, politicians who seem to have a problem with change put themselves outside the consensus both of the western body politic and the mass media. And insofar as they give the impression of being impervious to changed circumstances, Unionists lose out in three areas.

In the first place, by coming across as chary of change, Unionists deprive themselves of one of the most useful dynamic devices in media politics. Changing your mind when facts change is now seen in the western world as a moral virtue. Allowing reality to interrogate your actions frees up many positive political forces. As Hegel observed: freedom is the recognition of necessity. Next, by holding onto the high moral ground for too long, they wear out their moral welcome. Unionists are not unique in believing that holding the high moral ground can become a permanent fortified position. But the Israelis are now learning what Unionists should have learned a long time ago: that holding the high moral ground only gets you media points as long as you announce that you are anxious to come down from the heights as soon as possible. Lastly, by not coming forward freely to meet change, Unionists lose the moral bonus which the western world pays out to those who do not wait for change, but rush forward to welcome it, and to abandon past positions. The bonus is bigger when the order to abandon ship is announced in the mass media.

As far back as 1993, Sinn Féin discovered the dynamic of doing these double-takes. The political status that Sinn Féin secured from the first ceasefire was not confined to standing on the steps of the White House and Downing Street. It also opened the doors to RTÉ, the BCC and CBS.

To sum up this section: Unionists need to accept that there is an iron media consensus that change is both necessary, inevitable and good in itself, and that saying sorry on television is a sure way to get a good hearing. Whether we find these performances tacky or not is beside the point. They are a fact of modern media life. And, as Michael Collins observed, we must be loyal to the facts. But facts will only take Unionists so far. To really make their mark on the mass media, Unionists must go beyond the raw facts, beyond making a case, and scale the heights of telling a story.

3. Unionists should stop making a case and start telling their story.

By and large, Protestants tend to make a case whereas Northern Roman Catholics tend to tell a story. This contrast between the two cultures is not confined to Northern Ireland. Any time I have conducted media courses in EU countries, the interpreters who were present at such courses, and who constituted a kind of impartial *ad hoc* jury, agreed that, with some individual exceptions, participants from 'Protestant' countries like Germany tended not to be as good on television as participants from 'Roman Catholic' countries like Malta.

Could it be that Catholic cultures turn out marginally better mass media performers than Protestant cultures? That they are naturally better at telling stories (which television rewards) rather than making cases (which turns off television)? Allowing for the fact that this generalization opens the gates to scores of objections, exceptions, amendments and footnotes, I still believe that it grasps more than it lets fall.

Consider the different fortunes of Irish immigrants in the USA. Why was it Irish Roman Catholic immigrants rather than Presbyterian Irish immigrants who seized control of the American politico-media machines in the nineteenth century? Part of the answer is that politics and media provided for upward mobility. But a bigger part of the answer may be that democratic politics in the American style is much closer to the theatre than to the courtroom – a closeness that became more pronounced with the rise of the mass media – and that Irish Roman Catholics showed a special flair for that flamboyant but effective style of politics. Likewise, the Catholic Irish have maintained a media dominance in British television out of all proportion to their natural numbers, and possibly their natural talents. This is not, as some Unionists believe, a conspiracy, but comes from the cultural tendency of Catholics to package politics as political theatre, thus tailoring it for instant consumption by television and radio.

This does not mean that Protestants are condemned to make a case whereas Catholics are confined to narration. It is more a matter of Protestants giving themselves permission to transgress the cultural constraints which make them favour case-making over narration. On the EU courses, as soon as the Germans applied the same storytelling principles, they impressed the interpreters as formidable participants in the televised discussions. The empirical evidence of these EU courses confirms the conventional wisdom among British broadcasters and critics – that, by and large, Northern Catholics come across as more sympathetic on television than Northern Protestants. But on closer scrutiny Northern Catholics turn out to be telling stories rather than scoring points.

John Hume's mastery of the mass media began when he told a story called An Agreed Ireland. For better or worse it moved the world in a way that Unionists' argumentation from the facts could not do. No case, no matter how well made, could compete with Hume's story. It could only be supplanted by a better story. From this it follows that, unless Unionists wish to be marginalized in the mass media, they must be prepared to package the heroic story of the people, their contribution to the complex tapestry of Ireland, their stoic struggle for survival in the face of IRA terrorism – to package this epic tale as political theatre. Alas, Unionists have been slow to do so. Politics, presented as political theatre, seems to pose particular problems for Northern Protestants. Like their Puritan forebears, they do not seem to trust theatre. In fact nothing points up the difference between Unionists and Nationalists so much as the different ways they approach political theatre.

By and large, Roman Catholics regard politics as taking place in a kind of public theatre that is covered by television cameras and where the rules of narration and drama are the norm. Conversely, Northern Protestants regard politics as taking place in a courtroom or a committee of parliament, and that the person favoured by the facts should come out on top. In this conflict between theatre and courtroom, between story and facts, although my political sympathies favour the Unionist case, my moral sympathies are strongly on the Roman Catholic side. Courts can have all the facts and still not come at the truth. But while Shakespeare can sometimes be shaky on the facts, his story always tells the truth.

At this point it might be useful to define what I mean by 'story' in the context of Northern Ireland. In brief, I think of it as an epic tale which concerns the journey of an historical community, be it Catholic or Protestant, Jewish or Palestinian, towards a Promised Land. The secret is to tell that story so well that the other community, eavesdropping, can empathize with the search for a secure haven. By now, thanks to John Hume, we know the nationalist story so well that in some ways it has worn a bit threadbare. But what is the Unionist story? So far we cannot say that we have heard it at all. But, at the risk of offending Unionists, I would like to offer a rough outline that I think would travel well on television.

The Unionist story is about how a heroic, hardworking people travelled to another country, and settled, sometimes in complex circumstances; how, with great courage and hard work, they put their own stamp on the soil of their adopted home, became Irish in the most indelible sense, and in spite of a cruel campaign to make them go away, or be less human, they stayed true to their decent beliefs, and stayed put, and have surely earned the right to be regarded as intrinsically Irish, and to be allowed to express their sense of Irish identity in their own way. No other story will do. No other story has so many points of contact with similar stories, particularly the stories of northern nationalist and southern nationalist emigrants to the United States. Some Irish Catholics settled on Indian lands, some of them treated blacks badly. But, on the whole, by courage and hard work, they were eventually entitled to call themselves Americans.

Unionists must stake their media claim to full Irish as well as British identity. They must learn from Northern nationalists how to appeal from history to politics. They must learn that all television invitations, no matter what their formal subject might be, are also invitations to tell their story. It is not so much that Unionists have to abandon case-making, as that they must add myth-making to their studio skills. They must learn to tell their epic story even as they make their case. So what are the elements of this epic? The same as those deployed by Homer and praised in Aristotle's *Poetics*. The Unionist epic must allow for empathy, heroic characters, a narrative of suffering and necessity, catharsis and a redemptive ending. The story should start with a flawed but heroic people (Northern Protestants) for whose predicament the audience must be persuaded to feel empathy by showing how they had the same human frailties and made the same mistakes as people on the other side. After that comes a noble narrative of necessity: the arrival, full of hope, in a strange land, the cruel sufferings of the early years in the massacres of 1641, the daring deeds that defined their people (the Siege of Derry, the Boyne), the years of triumph and triumphalism, and the openly admitted misdeeds and mistakes (the mistreatment of Northern nationalists), followed by the stoic endurance of the IRA's armed struggle and the catharsis and amazing grace of the Good Friday Agreement, with its powerful potential for reconciliation and renewal.

How is this epic story to be integrated with something so mundane as a political interview? Let me give an example. Let us imagine – alas, it is easy to imagine – some dark moment in the peace process. Public order, Northern Ireland is in peril, people are losing their heads, and a Unionist spokesperson finds herself on her own in a studio with thirty seconds to rally her own side and reach the other side.

This is how she does it. The interviewer asks if there is any light in the dark. She looks levelly at the interviewer, wraps the epic shawl around her shoulders, reaches deep into the root of her people's history and simply says: 'Yes, things are bad tonight. But it's only one night. We've been on this island a long time. We've seen a lot of nights, some good, some bad, but we always got up the next morning. In four hundred years and more we never lost hope. We're not going to lose hope now. We're not going to give in to those who say the two sides can never come together. We think they can. It may not look like it tonight. But tomorrow is another day.'

Every time Unionists come on radio or television they should tell some element of that epic story of endurance. It should be told with 'an humble and contrite heart'. This way it might cause the other side to take counsel with their own hearts, and, hopefully, help them make their own acts of contrition.

Notes on Contributors

MAURICE BRIC is Senior Lecturer in History, and Director of American Studies at University College Dublin.

DESMOND M. CLARKE is Professor of Philosophy at University College Cork.

MAURA CRONIN is Lecturer in History at Mary Immaculate College, University of Limerick.

TOM DUNNE is Professor Emeritus of History at University College Cork.

PAUL DURCAN is Ireland Professor of Poetry.

JAMES S. DONNELLY, JR. is Professor of History at the University of Wisconsin-Madison.

OWEN DUDLEY EDWARDS is Reader in History at the University of Edinburgh.

RUTH DUDLEY EDWARDS is an historian, journalist and crime writer.

LAURENCE M. GEARY is a Lecturer in History at University College Cork.

EOGHAN HARRIS is a journalist, and a media and political adviser.

LIAM IRWIN is Head of the Department of History, Mary Immaculate College, University of Limerick.

EMMET LARKIN is Professor of History at the University of Chicago.

J.J. LEE is Glucksman Professor of Irish Studies, New York University.

LAWRENCE M. MCCAFFREY is Emeritus Professor of History at Loyola University Chicago.

CLÍONA MURPHY is Professor of History at California State University, Bakersfield.

CONOR CRUISE O'BRIEN is a writer and journalist.

TOMÁS Ó CANAINN is an Uileann piper and writer.

SEÁN Ó COILEÁIN is Professor of Modern Irish at University College Cork.

ÚNA O'DONOGHUE is a TV researcher and former teacher.

Notes

J.J. Lee: A Personal Appreciation

1 John A. Murphy, 'Myself and "the Cruiser"', in Richard English and Joseph Morrison Skelly (eds), *Ideas Matter: Essays in Honour of Conor Cruise O'Brien* (Dublin, 1998), p .62.
2 Michael Glazier (ed.), *The Encyclopedia of the Irish in America* (Notre Dame, Ind., 1999), pp. 417–33.

Ruth Dudley Edwards and Úna O'Donoghue: John A. Murphy: The Singer and the Song

1 John A. Murphy, 'The Piano in Macroom', *The Cork Anthology*, ed. Seán Dunne (Cork, 1993), p. 235.
2 Ibid.
3 Ibid., p. 238.
4 Ibid., p. 239.
5 Ibid., p. 240.
6 Ibid., p. 241.
7 John A. Murphy, 'Eamon de Valera: Informal Reflections', in *The Recorder* (American Historical Society), 44 (1983).
8 Murphy, 'Eamon de Valera', p. 87.
9 Ibid., p. 86.
10 Quoted in Vincent Power, *Voices of Cork* (Dublin, 1997), p. 174.
11 Ibid., p. 90.
12 Email to Úna O'Donoghue.
13 Murphy, 'Eamon de Valera', p. 87.
14 John A. Murphy, 'Myself and "the Cruiser", in Richard English and Joseph Morrison Skelly (eds), *Ideas Matter: Essays in Honour of Conor Cruise O'Brien* (Dublin, 1998).
15 Ibid., p. 54.
16 Power, *Voices of Cork*, p. 179.
17 Ibid.
18 Ibid.
19 Ibid., p. 180.
20 Ibid.
21 Murphy, 'Myself and "the Cruiser"', p. 57.

22 Ruth Dudley Edwards, *Patrick Pearse: The Triumph of Failure* (London, 1977).
23 John A. Murphy, 'Further Reflections on Nationalism', in *The Crane Bag*, 2, 1 and 2 (1978), p. 158.
24 Murphy, 'Myself and "the Cruiser"', p. 57.
25 Letter to Úna O'Donogue, n.d. but *c.* autumn 2002.
26 Seanad debate, 4 July 1979.
27 Seanad debate, 3 June 1992.
28 Seanad debate, 20 December 1979.
29 Seanad debate, 18 December 1980.
30 Power, *Voices of Cork*, p. 172.
31 Emails to Ruth Dudley Edwards, 21 and 22 December 2002.
32 Email to Úna O'Donoghue, 23 January 2003.
33 Seanad debate, 8 December 1988.
34 Seanad debate, 28 May 1992.
35 Recollection of Ruth Dudley Edwards.
36 Murphy, 'The Piano in Macroom', p. 237.

Desmond M. Clarke: One Commonwealth, Three Nations: the Concept of a Nation in English Republican Thought 1640–80

1 Sidney's *Discourses* was published posthumously in 1698 by John Toland, but was probably written in 1681–3.
2 Both sides in the Civil War appealed to an ancient constitution or fundamental law. 'The case for the crown was not that the King rules as a sovereign and that there was no fundamental law, but that there was a fundamental law and that the King's prerogative formed part of it.' J. G. A. Pocock, *The Ancient Constitution and the Feudal Law*, 2nd edn (Cambridge, 1987), p. 51. This has also been acknowledged by Adrian Hastings, *The Construction of Nationhood: Ethnicity, Religion and Nationalism* (Cambridge, 1997), p. 50: 'Basically that principle [i.e. of the Great Charter] was common to both sides in the Civil War. It was a national presupposition.'
3 Much of the historical work involved in making this relation familiar is due to Quentin Skinner. See for example 'History and Ideology in the English Revolution', in *Historical Journal*, 8 (1965), pp. 151–78; 'The Ideological Context of Hobbes's Political Thought', in *Historical Journal*, 9 (1966), pp. 286–317; *Liberty before Liberalism* (Cambridge, 1998). See also Markku Peltonen, *Classical Humanism and Republicanism in English Political Thoughts 1570–1640* (Cambridge, 1999); David Underdown, *A Freeborn People: Politics and the Nation in Seventeenth-Century England* (Oxford, 1996).
4 Hastings, *The Construction of Nationhood*, p. 38.
5 Gellner's original thesis is found in *Nations and Nationalism* (Oxford, 1983). See for example Linda Colley, *Britons: Forging the Nation 1707–1837* (Yale, 1992).
6 Anthony D. Smith, *The Ethnic Origins of Nations* (Oxford, 1986), and *National Identity* (Harmondsworth, 1991).
7 For example, J.G.A. Pocock (ed.), *The Political Works of James Harrington* (Cambridge, 1977), p. 15; Martin Dzelzainis, 'Ideas in Conflict', in N.H. Keeble (ed.), *The Cambridge Companion to Writings on the English Revolution* (Cambridge, 2001), p. 36.
8 The problem of definition is addressed by, among others, David Miller, *On Nationality* (Oxford, 1995).

9 *The Writings and Speeches of Oliver Cromwell*, 4 vols., (ed.) Wilbur C. Abbott (Cambridge, 1937–47), I, 127. All references to Cromwell are to this edition, which is indicated as 'Abbott', followed by the volume and page. See also Abbott, II, 37, 'both in this Kingdom and the Kingdom of Scotland . . . and the Kingdom of Ireland'.

10 Abbot, I, 742. Cromwell frequently refers to the English nation; see for example, II, 68 ('the common enemy of this nation'); II, 186 ('the late great transactions of this nation'); II, 283 ('many godly people in Scotland are not satisfied with the proceedings of this nation [i.e. England] concerning the death of the late king'); II, 320 ('the inhabitants of this nation').

11 Abbot, II, 107. On 17 August 1654, Cromwell wrote to the Lord Deputy and Council in Ireland, informing them 'to cause the Act, entitled an Act for the settling of Ireland . . . to be published and dispersed in the several provinces of Ireland . . . to the end that all the people of that nation concerned therein may understand what the intentions of the Parliament are towards them' (Abbott, III, 407).

12 Abbott, II, 306. When the campaign was concluded, Cromwell met on 10 December 1651, with select members of parliament, army officers, and others 'to come to a settlement of the Nation' (Abbott, II, 505); in March 1656, the Protector sent instructions to the Lord Deputy and Council in Ireland, which included a pardon for 'all such of the Scottish nation who are now inhabiting or dwelling in any part of Ulster or in the County of Louth' (Abbott, IV, 126). The same expression, 'Scottish nation' is used on p. 127. On 10 June 1658, Cromwell sent 'Instructions from his Highness to the Council of Scotland, for the government of that nation' (Abbott, IV, 825).

13 Wales, however, seems to have been included with England as a single nation. For example, when the Protector invited 'the People of England and Wales, to a Day of Solemn Fasting and Humiliation' on 20 March 1653/4, he argued that 'God hath vouchsafed to appear very much in working the Deliverance of the Nation from their bondage and thraldome, both Spiritual and Civil' (Abbott, III, 225).

14 Abbott, III, 454. On the same occasion he claims to have had 'the approbation of the officers of the army in the three nations of England, Scotland, and Ireland' (ibid., 456). The oath taken by Cromwell on his appointment as Protector, 16 December 1653 included the following references to the three nations: 'Whereas the major part of the last Parliament . . . resigned unto me their Powers and authorities; and whereas it was necessary thereupon, that some speedy Course should be taken for the Settlement of these Nations upon such a Basis and Foundation as, by the Blessing of God, might be lasting, secure property, and answer those great ends of Religion and Liberty so long contended for; . . . and having also been desired . . . to take upon me the Protection and Government of these Nations . . . [I] shall, . . . to the best of my Understanding, govern these Nations according to the Laws, Statutes, and Customs thereof' (Abbott, III, 136–7). Following taking the oath, he claimed that 'he desired to rule and govern the three nations no longer' than God required (ibid., p. 138).

15 Abbott, III, 139, 140, 144.

16 Abbott, III, 144. In a speech to parliament on 23 January 1656/7, Cromwell tells them that 'God hath bestowed upon you, (and you are in possession of it,) three nations and all that appertains to them' (IV, 389).

17 Ibid. The same exclusive reference to 'the Common-wealth of England' occurs in Abbott, III, 897. When discussing peace with the Dutch on 17 and 18

November 1653, Cromwell 'spoke of the affection and the inclination of the Parliament for a good peace and a permanent union between the two republics, and said that they had earlier proposed a coalition between the two nations – one in which all the mutual interests of state and of the nations would be combined . . . [this would result in] a permanent one [i.e. peace] between the two states and nations' (Abbott, III, 122–3).

18 Abbott, III, 915. On 26 October 1655 Cromwell complains about the way the King of Spain and 'his subjects have all along, in those parts of America, treated the English nation' (Abbott, III, 878).

19 Abbott, IV, 39. The 'English nation' appears as one partner in other international negotiations. For example, Cromwell writes to the Duke of Muscovy, Alexius Romanoff, on 7 April 1657: 'As men knew how ancient the friendship and how vast the trade has been for a long train of years between the English nation and the people of our empire' (IV, 449).

20 Abbott, IV, 29.

21 See Cromwell to the Lord Deputy and Council in Ireland, 17 August 1654 (Abbott III, 407); Cromwell to his son, Henry Cromwell, 'Instructions for Ireland', 16 November 1657: 'It being necessary for the good government of our said dominion of Ireland in all our affairs there . . .' (Abbott, IV, 666).

22 J. R. Kenyon (ed.), *The Stuart Constitution 1603–1688*, 2nd edn (Cambridge, 1986), p. 18. Charles referred later, in the same text, to the 'excellent constitution of this kingdom which hath made this nation so many years both famous and happy to a great degree of envy' (p. 19). The Nineteen Propositions, 1 June 1642, are found on pp. 222–6.

23 Abbott, II, 11.

24 See Quentin Skinner, 'Classical Liberty, Renaissance Translation and the English Civil War', in *Visions of Politics*: vol. 2, *Renaissance Virtues* (Cambridge, 2002), pp. 308–43.

25 For a contemporary expression of this philosophy, see Philip Pettit, *Republican Freedom* (Oxford, 1997).

26 Abbott, III, 290. The declaration was dated 9 May 1654.

27 For example, after the decisive battle at Worcester, Cromwell wrote to the Speaker of Parliament: 'I am not able yet to give you an exact account of the great things the Lord hath wrought for this Commonwealth and for His people' (Abbott, II, 462). A similar letter to the Speaker after the battle of Dunbar includes: 'If He that strengthens your servants to fight, pleases to give you hearts to set upon these things, in order to His glory, and the glory of your Commonwealth, besides the benefit England shall feel thereby, you shall shine forth to other nations, who shall emulate the glory of such a pattern, and through the power of God turn into the like' (Abbott, II, 325).

28 Abbott, III, 5–6. Cromwell made a similar speech to the Nominated Parliament, 4 July 1653: 'You may well know, after divers turnings of affairs, it pleased God, much about the middle of this war, to winnow (if I may so say) the forces of this nation, and to put them into the hands of other men of other principles than those that did engage at the first' (Abbott, III, 53). Cromwell had written a lengthy justification of his cause, and that of the army, in reply to Colonel Robert Hammond, 25 November 1648, when Hammond was tempted to retire from the army because of a conflict of loyalty to king and parliament. The ultimate justification was '*Salus Populi*' and the people in question were also 'God's people' (Abbott, I, 697).

29 Don M. Wolfe (ed.), *Complete Prose Works of John Milton* (New Haven and London, 1962), III, 190. Subsequent references to *CPW*. The peculiar evil of

tyrants is that they 'hazard the welfare of the whole Nation' (*CPW*, III, 193).

30 *CPW*, III, 199.
31 *CPW*, III,202.
32 *CPW*, III, 236, 237.
33 *CPW*, III, 215.
34 *CPW*, III, 451.
35 *CPW*, III,315.
36 *CPW*, III, 368.
37 *CPW*, III, 303, 305.
38 *A True State of the Case of the Commonwealth* (London, 1654), p. 1. Subsequent references to *True State.*
39 *True State*, p. 2.
40 *True State*, pp. 43, 47. On p. 44 he refers to the 'settled forces . . . within the three Nations' and the 'publick business in all the three Nations'.
41 *True State*, p. 5.
42 *True State*, p. 6. He returns to this argument later in the book, where he argues that 'the kings of this Nation pretended always, and maintained an Interest of their own, as they were Kings, distinct and superior to that of the People' (p. 28).
43 *True State.* p. 19.
44 *True State*, p. 48. When describing the some of the disputes in parliament before it was disbanded by Cromwell, Nedham says that it was 'as much divided, as if they had been people of two distinct nations' (p. 21).
45 *True State*, p. 49.
46 *True State*, p. 50.
47 *True State*, p. 52.
48 J G.A. Pocock (ed.), *The Political Works of James Harrington*, (Cambridge, 1977), p. 157. All subsequent references to Harrington are to this edition, identified as *Harrington.*
49 *Harrington*, pp. 231, 238.
50 *Harrington*, p. 159.
51 *Harrington*, p. 160. Harrington had argued that 'the situation of these countries [i.e. Ireland and Scotland] being islands . . . seemeth to have been designed by God for a commonwealth. And yet that, through the straitness of the place and defect of proper arms, can be no more a commonwealth for preservation; whereas this, reduced unto the like government, is a commonwealth for increase, and upon the rightest foundation that any hath been laid from the beginning of the world unto this day' (pp. 159–60).
52 *Aphorisms Political*, 2nd. edn (London, 1659), in *Harrington*, Aphorism LVII (p. 769).
53 *Harrington*, p. 167.
54 *Harrington*, p. 168.
55 'discovered unto mankind by God himself in the fabric of the commonwealth of Israel, and afterwards picked out of his footsteps in nature and unanimously followed by the Greeks and Romans' *Harrington*, 161. Cf. *Oceana*, p. 174: 'I shall appeal unto God and to the World. Unto God in the fabric of the commonwealth of Israel.' On pp. 174–7 he outlines as a model the 'natural' commonwealth of Israel. Cf. Aphorism CXX, p. 778: 'The highest earthly felicity that a people can ask, or God can give, is an equal and well-ordered commonwealth. Such a one among the Israelites was the reign of God.'
56 *Harrington*, p. 170.
57 *Harrington*, p. 191. 'But the Teutons [i.e. Normans] . . . divided the whole nation

into three sorts of feuds; that of earldorman . . .' (p. 192).

58 *Harrington,* p. 173, where he claims that 'the interest of the commonwealth is in the whole body of the people, and whereas this, in case the commonwealth consist of an whole nation, is too unwieldy a body to be assembled' and therefore there should be a council sufficiently representative of the whole people that it 'can never contract any other interest than that of the whole people' (p. 173).

59 *Harrington,* p. 185. Harrington refers to the 'national religion' at p. 204, and to the 'national religion of Israel' at p. 268. The argument involves what is usually called the fallacy of composition, i.e. the mistake of concluding that, since parts of a composite reality (such as a nation) have some feature, then the whole composite must have the same feature.

60 *Harrington,* p. 251. Harrington reflects contemporary discussion in England about re–admitting Jews. He suggests that Ireland be planted with Jews, but that they not be admitted to England. 'To receive the Jews after any other manner into a commonwealth were to maim it; for they of all nations never incorporate but, taking up the room of a limb, are of no use or office unto the body, while they suck the nourishment which would sustain a natural and useful member' (p. 159). Cromwell had also addressed the same question, but much more favourably.

61 *Harrington,* p. 165, where 'the hand which holdeth the sword is the militia of the nation', and p. 158, where 'the genius of this nation hath ever had some resemblance with that of ancient Italy, which was wholly addicted unto commonwealths'.

62 *Political Discourses: viz. Patriarcha, or the Natural Power of Kings. The Free-holders Grand-Inquest. Observations upon Aristotles Politicks. Directions for Obedience to Government* (London, 1680).

63 pp. 482–3.

64 Filmer, *Patriarchial,* p. 14: 'it is a common Opinion, that at the confusion of tongues, all of which were not Confused Multitudes, without heads or Governors, and at liberty to choose what Governours or Government they please'; and pp. 15–16: 'But howsoever the manner of this Division [into distinct families] be uncertain, yet it is most certain the Division it self by Families from Noah and his Children, over which the Parents were Heads and Princes.'

65 *Patriarcha,* p. 41–2: 'But let us Condescend a while to the Opinion of Bellarmine and Suarez, and all those, who place Supreme power in the Whole People; and ask them if their meaning be, That there is but one and the same power in All the people of the World; so that no power can be granted, except All the Men upon the Earth meet and agree, to choose a Governour.' Filmer argues that, if all the people of the world had been given political authority collectively, as republican theorists assume, it would be impossible to prevent a legitimate secession by any group of people who wish to separate from an established commonwealth, 'thereby a Gap is opened up for every petty Factious Multitude, to raise a New Commonwealth, and to make more Commonwealths than there be Families in the World' (p. 43).

66 'For tho' it were granted, that some of the Saxon kings came in by inheritance . . . yet William the Norman did not, for he was a bastard, and could inherit nothing.' *Discourses concerning Government,* 3rd edn (London, 1751), p. 88.

67 Ibid., p. 244.

68 Ibid., p. 12.

69 While Filmer does not question 'the rights or liberties of this or any other

nation', Sidney points out that Filmer's theory implied that nations cannot have 'any such in subjecting them necessarily and universally to the will of one man; and says not a word that is not applicable to every nation in the world, as well as to our own' (ibid., p. 11).

70 Ibid., p. 24.

71 Ibid., p. 75.

72 Ibid., p. 90. Sidney rejects Filmer's assumption that we know what a kingdom is, because 'it is one thing in one place, and very different in others' (p. 87). He later refers to the numerous 'nations governing themselves by their own will' (p. 207) in Italy. Cf. p. 231: 'The practice of most nations, and (I may truly say) of all that deserve imitation, has been as directly contrary to the absolute power of one man, as their constitutions.'

73 Ibid., pp. 151–2.

74 Ibid., p. 211. Sidney argues that, where there is already some form of hereditary monarchy in place, there are frequent wars and disputes about who should inherit the crown unless the consent of the people is taken as the decisive factor. Cf. pp. 196, 331, 333.

75 Ibid., p. 399.

76 Ibid., p. 403.

77 Ibid., p. 406.

78 Ibid., p. 196, where he refers to England as a 'nation [that] was rent in pieces' by William the Norman's son, Robert; on p. 196 he also refers to Scotland as a nation. The 'Polanders, Danes, Swedes, Germans, and such as were under the Roman empire' were nations (p. 333). On p. 211 Ireland is given as an example of a 'foreign nation' that was used by a king to wage war on his own people.

79 Ibid., p. 413.

80 Before looking at the texts, John Pocock suggested to me that I would be more likely to find England described as a nation than to find the concept of national identity applied equally to what we think of today as distinct national groups.

81 Sydney, *Discourses*, p. 59.

82 'Agreement Reached in the Multi-Party Negotiations', Constitutional Issues, 1, and Annex A, 1.

83 The research on which this essay is based was partly supported by the Programme for Research in Third-Level Institutions (2), in a collaborative project based at University College Cork, under the title 'Identity'.

Liam Irwin: Personalities and Politics: The Presidency of Munster and the Lords Lieutenant 1660–72

1 The first president was appointed in Connacht in 1569 and in Munster the following year. The plan for a presidency of Ulster was never implemented. For the role of the presidencies in Tudor Ireland, see N. Canny, *The English Conquest of Ireland: A Pattern Established 1565–1576* (Sussex, 1976); see also Denis J. Kennedy 'The Presidency of Munster under Elizabeth and James I', unpublished MA thesis, UCC, 1973.

2 Boyle's career in the 1640s is discussed in J.A. Murphy, 'The Politics of the Munster Protestants 1641–9' in *Journal of the Cork Historical and Archaeological Society*, lxxvi, no. 23 (1971), pp. 1–20; there are also an unsatisfactory biography, Kathleen Lynch, *Roger Boyle, First Earl of Orrery* (Knoxville, 1965) and an unpublished MA thesis, J.B. Olden, 'The Public Life of Roger Boyle', UCC, 1956.

3 For Orrery's pivotal role in that decision, see Liam Irwin,'The Suppression of the Irish Presidency System' in *Irish Historical Studies,* xxii, no. 85 (March 1980), pp. 21–33.
4 Royal Warrant, 26 October 1660 (SP63//304/89).
5 British Library, Egerton Ms. 2551, ff. 69–70.
6 Aidan Clarke, *Prelude to Restoration: End of Commonwealth* (Cambridge, 1999); J.I. McGuire, 'The Dublin Convention, the Protestant Community and the Emergence of an Ecclesiastical Settlement in 1660' in Art Cosgrove and J.I. McGuire (eds), *Parliament and Community* (Belfast, 1983), pp. 121–46.
7 Karl S. Bottigheimer,'The Restoration Land Settlement in Ireland: A Structural View' in *I.H.S.,* xviii, no. 69 (March 1972), pp. 1–21.
8 Royal warrant 4 November 1661 (*Calendar of State Papers relating to Ireland, 1660–62,* p. 454).
9 Ibid., p. 578. He arrived on 27 July 1662.
10 Charles II to the lords justices, *State Papers Ireland,* 23 November 1661 (SP63//308/110), NLI microfilm.
11 Nicholas to Lord Chancellor, 9 November 1661 (SP63//308/79).
12 Orrery to Ormond, 20 November 1661, British Library, Add. MSS. 37,206, f. 27.
13 Orrery to Ormond, 26 December 1661, T. Morrice, *A Collection of the State Letters of the Right Hon. Roger Boyle* (2 vols., Dublin, 1743), vol. i, pp. 48–9.
14 Orrery to Secretary Nicholas, 29 November 1661 (SP63//307/264); Orrery to Archbishop Bramhall, 22 November 1661 (HMC, *Hastings Manuscripts,* iv, 1947, p. 120).
15 BL, Add. MSS. 37,206, f. 107; NAI, M2449, f. 62; see also Kathleen Lynch, *Roger Boyle,* p. 120 *et passim.*
16 The relationship between both men is treated at length in D. Deignan, *The Ormond–Orrery Conflict, 1640–1680: A Study in Mid Seventeenth-Century Irish Society and Politics,* Ph.D. dissertation, Brown University, 1982.
17 Orrery to the king, 23 May 1663 (*Cal. SP Ire., 1663–5,* p. 100). Orrery also complained Ormond to influential people at court, see HMC, *Report 6,* 1847, appendix p. 317.
18 Ormond to Orrery, 5 December 1663 (HMC, *Ormonde Manuscripts,* NS3, 1904, pp. 115–16).
19 Patrick Moore to Ormond, 2 July 1664 (ibid., pp. 176–7).
20 Orrery to Ormond, 19 December 1665 (*Orrery State Letters,* i, p. 202); 12 January 1666 (BL, Add. MSS 37,206, f. 185); Orrery to Sovereign of Kinsale, 19 December 1665 ('MSS of the Old Corporation of Kinsale', *Analecta Hibernica,* 15, 1944, p. 208); Letter to Orrery from Cork city seeking directions, 8 January 1666 (BL, Add. MSS 37,206, f. 191); Sovr. of Kinsale to Orrery, 17 January 1666 (BL, Add. MSS 37,206, f. 190).
21 *Orrery State Letters,* i, pp. 219–20, BL, Add. MSS 37,206, f. 213.
22 *Orrery State Letters,* i, p. 254, BL, Add. MSS 37,206, ff. 29, 42–3.
23 Orrery to Arlington, 12 October 1666 (*Cal. SP Ire., 1666–9,* p. 223).
24 Orrery to Byron, 16 June 1666 (HMC, *Ormonde Manuscripts,* NS3, 1904, pp. 228–9; BL, Add. MSS 37,207, f. 63; *Orrery State Letters,* ii, p. 15.
25 Orrery to Ormond, 9 September 1667 (BL, Add. MSS 37,207, ff 144–5.
26 Orrery to Sovr. And Burgesses of Kinsale in *Analecta Hibernica,* 15, 1944, p. 214.
27 Ormond to Orrery, 20 September 1667, printed in T. Carte, *Life of James, Duke of Ormond* (vol. v, Oxford, 1851), pp. 51–3.
28 Orrery to Ormond, 24 September 1667(*Orrery State Letters,* ii, p. 305).
29 Ormond to Orrery, 12 June 1666 (Carte MSS 48, f. 50, NLI microfilm).
30 Orrery to Ormond, 17 June 1666 (BL, Add. MSS 37,207 f. 74), to which is

appended the deposition of the spy whom Orrery employed, ibid., ff. 75–6.
31 Ormond to Secretary Bennett, 13 May 1663 (SP63//313/147).
32 Ormond to Arlington, August 1666 (SP63//321/134).
33 Ormond to Bennett, 10 February 1664 (*Cal. S.P. Ire., 1663–5*, p. 363); Ormond to Arlington, 1 March 167 (*Cal. S.P. Ire., 1666–9*, p. 311).
34 Ormond to Orrery, 24 February 1666 (BL, Add. MSS 37,207, ff 10–11).
35 Ormond to Arlington, 18 April 1666 (SP63//320/95).
36 Ormond to Ossory, 19 October 1668 (Carte MS 147, f. 90).
37 *32nd Annual Report of Deputy Keeper Public Records* (London, 1871), App. 1, p. 219.
38 An account of Ormond's progress from Kilkenny to Munster, 4 September 1666 (*Cal. S.P.Ire., 1666–9*, p. 205).
39 Orrery to Arlington, 22 September 1666 ibid., p. 214).
40 Orrery to Arlington, 8 October 1666 (*Orrery State Letters*, ii, pp. 66–7)
41 Morrice, *Memoirs*, p. 82.
42 He states that it occurred before Orrery's impeachment in 1669 rather than in 1672, ibid., pp. 82–3.
43 Ormond to Ossory, 24 September 1668 (Carte MS 147, ff. 86–7).
44 BL, Add MSS 37,208, f. 191.
45 Carte MS 69, f. 415, 70, f. 419.
46 Ibid., 69, f. 415.
47 Ormond to Ossory, 9 Feb. 1669, printed in Carte, *Life of Ormond*, v, p. 101.
48 J.I. McGuire, 'Why was Ormond Dismissed in 1669?', *I.H.S.*, xviii, no. 71 (March 1973), pp. 295–312.
49 Orrery to Ormond, 13 March 1667 (Carte MS 147, f. 52), Orrery to Ormond, 17 March 1667 (*Orrery State Letters*, ii, pp. 343–6).
50 Ormond to Orrery, 10 March 1667 (Carte MS 147, f. 51); see also Carte, *Life of Ormond*, v, pp. 52, 83 and Lynch, *Roger Boyle*, p. 133.
51 Orrery to Lord Chancellor Boyle, 13 March 1667 (Carte MS 147, ff. 191–3).
52 Orrery to Ormond, 16 March 1668 (BL, Add. MSS 37,208, ff. 196–8).
53 *Orrery State Letters*, ii, pp. 149–56 *et passim*.
54 Morrice, *Memoir of Orrery*, p. 99; Aungier to Williamson, 22 November 1670 (SP63//329/112).
55 Orrery to Conway, 27 February 1669 (SP63//325/20).
56 Lynch, *Roger Boyle*, p. 134.
57 Ormond to Orrery, 20 September 1667 (Carte, *Life of Ormond*, v, p. 52).
58 Orrery to Boyle, 31 December 1667 and 20 February 1668 (Carte MS 147, f. 189 and ff. 215–17).
59 Duchess of Ormond to George Mathew, March 1669 (HMC, *Ormonde Manuscripts*, NS3, 1904, p. 443).
60 Orrery to Conway, 1 March 1670 (SP63//327/37).
61 Conway to Rawdon, 17 December 1670, (HMC, *Hastings Manuscripts*, ii, 1930, p. 378).
62 Lynch, *Roger Boyle*, p. 222.
63 Carte MS 70, f. 476.
64 Ormond to Ossory, 4 October 1679, (HMC, *Report 6*, app. (1877), p. 724).
65 The details of the charges are in the Orrery papers at Petworth, MS 13,188, folder 12, NLI microfilm; see also *Cal. S.P. Ire., 1669–70*, pp. 725–6.
66 'Formular of Instructions', 14 December 1570, in A. Collins (ed), *Letters and Memorials of State: Sydney State Papers* (London, 1746), vol. i, pp. 48–59.
67 P. Williams, *The Council in the Marches of Wales under Elizabeth I* (Cardiff, 1958), p. 56.

68 R. R. Reid, *The King's Council in the North* (London, 1923), p. 262, n. 5.
69 *Cal. S.P. Ire., 1666–69*, p. 477.
70 Ossory to Arlington, 18 May 1669 (*Cal. S.P. Ire., 1669–70*, p. 725).
71 Orrery's memorandum on his impeachment is printed in *Cal. S.P. Ire., 1669–70*, p. 30.
72 However during his stay in London Orrery did, it would appear, get involved in the court intrigues surrounding Robartes (SP63//325/20 & 27).
73 Berkeley to Orrery, 20 September 1670 (SP63//329/28).
74 Berkeley to Arlington, 23 September 1670 (SP63//329/32).
75 Orrery to Conway, 28 July 1671, *Cal. S.P. Dom. 1671*, p. 411; the King's commission, dated 10 June 1671, appointing Henry Boyle a lieutenant in Orrery's troop of horse is in *Cal. S.P. Dom. 1671*, p. 314.
76 Orrery to Conway, 20 September 1670 (SP63//329/28).
77 Lord Aungier to Williamson, 16 August 1670 (SP63//328/145.)

Maurice J. Bric: Daniel O'Connell and the Debate on Anti-Slavery, 1820–50

1 Much of the research for this paper was conducted while I was the Burns Fellow at Boston College during the summer months of 2002. I would like to thank the staff at Connolly House and the Burns Library for their support and kindness to me during my stay with them. I would also like to thank Tom Garvin and Timothy P. O'Neill for their comments on an earlier draft of this paper.
2 Hannah Maria Wigham, *A Christian Philanthropist of Dublin* (London, 1886), p. 14. For the wider world of reform, see also Betty Fladeland,'"Our Cause being One and the Same": Abolitionists and Chartism', in James Walvin (ed.), *Slavery and British Society. 1776–1846* (London, 1982), pp. 69–99 and J.T. Ward, *Popular Movements c.1830–1850* (London, 1970).
3 See however, Nini Rodgers,'Equiano in Belfast: A Study of the Anti-Slavery Ethos in a Northern Town', in *Slavery and Abolition*, 18 (1997), pp. 73–89 and 'Two Quakers and a Utilitarian: The Reaction of Three Irish Women Writers to the Problem of Slavery, 1789–1807', in *Proceedings of the Royal Irish Academy*, 100C, no. 4 (2000). For context, see also W.A. Hart,'Africans in Eighteenth-Century Ireland', in *Irish Historical Studies*, 33, no. 2 (2002), pp. 19–33.
4 Oliver Warner, *William Wilberforce and His Times* (London, 1962), p. 95; Douglas Riaich, 'Ireland and the Campaign against American Slavery, 1830–1860', Ph.D. dissertation, University of Edinburgh, 1975, pp. 29–30; and Oliver McDonagh,'O'Connell in the House of Commons', in Donal McCartney (ed.), *The World of Daniel O'Connell* (Dublin & Cork, 1980), p. 46. It should also be noted that one of the earliest leaders of the anti-slavery movement, Granville Sharp (1735–1813), also took a moral view of colonial slavery, which he linked with 'domestic corruptions', and, as a result, also supported the independence and reform of the Irish parliament; see David Brion Davis, *The Problem of Slavery in the Age of Revolution, 1770–1823* (Ithaca, 1975), p. 394. For the earlier phase of the British anti-slavery movement, see Roger Anstey, *The Atlantic Slave Trade and British Abolition, 1760–1810* (London, 1975).
5 For these organizations and their world, see Walvin, *Slavery and British Society*; Robin Blackburn, *The Overthrow of Colonial Slavery. 1776–1848* (London & New York, 1988); and Reginald Coupland, *The British Anti-Slavery Movement* (new edn, London, 1964).

6 For the broad significance of petitions, as well as their complexity and the 'soaring numbers' involved, see Seymour Drescher, 'Public Opinion and the Destruction of British Colonial Slavery' and James Walvin, 'The Propaganda of Anti-Slavery', in Walvin, *Slavery and British Society*, pp. 24–5 and 49–68 respectively, and Walvin, 'The Public Campaign in England against Slavery, 1787–1834', in David Eltis and James Walvin (eds), *The Abolition of the Atlantic Slave Trade* (Madison & London, 1981), pp. 63–79.

7 Riaich, 'Ireland and the Campaign against American Slavery', pp. 25, 22; Christine Bolt, *The Anti-Slavery Movement and Reconstruction. A Study in Anglo-American Co-operation* (Oxford, 1992), p. 16. In 1824, for example, 81 Dublin Friends signed a petition to the House of Commons 'to expedite the ultimate object of complete emancipation . . . by every wise and prudent means' (Riaich, p. 22). See also Richard S. Harrison, 'Irish Quaker Perspectives on the Anti-Slavery Movement,' in *Journal of the Friends' Historical Society*, 66 (1990–93), pp. 106–25.

8 O'Connell's parliamentary resolution is cited in Anthony J. Barker, *Captain Charles Stuart. Anglo-American Abolitionist* (Baton Rouge & London, 1986), p. 41. The mast-head of *The Liberator*, which was first published on 1 Jan. 1831, is quoted from Fladeland, 'Our Cause being One and the Same', p. 78. O'Connell's opinions are taken from speeches to anti-slavery societies between 1829 and 1831, as in *Daniel O'Connell upon American Slavery with other Irish Testimonies* (American Anti-Slavery Society, New York, 1860), pp. 8–9.

9 Aileen S. Kraditor, *Means and Ends in American Abolitionism* (Chicago, 1989), pp. 5–6. The AASS sought to 'complete' the 'enterprise' of the Founding Fathers: to admit 'all persons of color, who possess the qualifications which are demanded of others, ought to be admitted forthwith to the enjoyment of the same privileges, and the exercise of the same prerogatives, as others' *Constitution and Declaration of Sentiments* (ASS, Philadelphia, 1833).

10 C. Duncan Rice, *The Scots Abolitionists. 1863–1861* (Baton Rouge & London, 1981), p. 83 *et passim;* Samuel May to Mary Carpenter, 28 October 1844, and Phillips to George Thompson, 29 July 1839, as in Clare Taylor, *British and American Abolitionists: An Episode in Transatlantic Understanding* (Edinburgh, 1974), pp. 230, 238, 74, respectively. May's remarks were made in a lengthy review of the history of the anti-slavery movement in America. Taylor has edited the more important letters between the leading abolitionists in Britain, Ireland and the United States from the rich anti-slavery collections in Boston Public Library and as such, her work is an important source for this study. For the issues which divided the American anti-slavery movement, see Kraditor, *Means and Ends;* and Betty Fladeland, *Men and Brothers, Anglo-American Anti-Slavery Co-operation* (Chicago, 1972). For Phillips, see 'The Patrician as Agitator', in Richard Hofstadter, *The American Political Tradition and the Men Who Made it* (New York, 1989), pp. 175–210.

11 Walvin, 'Propaganda of Anti-Slavery', pp. 52–3. See also the *Dublin Association for Endeavouring to Promote the Mitigation and Gradual Abolition of Slavery in the British Colonies* (Dublin, 1824); Dublin Negro's Friend Society, *Objects of the Society* (Dublin, 1829); and Charles E.H Orpen, *The Principles, Plans, and Objects of the Hibernian Negro's Friend Society* (Dublin, 1831). In Cork, the anti-slavery movement shared rooms with the local temperance society when the latter was founded there in 1831. See Colm Kerrigan, *Father Mathew and the Irish Temperance Movement 1838–1949* (Baldoyle, 1992), p. 27.

12 Barker, *Captain Charles Stuart*, p. 51. See also Stewart J. Brown, 'The New Reformation in the Church of Ireland, 1801–29', in Stewart J. Brown and David W.

Miller (eds), *Piety and Power in Ireland, 1760–1960: Essays in Honour of Emmet Larkin* (South Bend, Ind., 2000), pp. 180–208; Irene M. Whelan, 'Evangelical Religion and the Polarization of Protestant-Catholic Relations in Ireland, 1780–1840', Ph.D., University of Wisconsin-Madison, 1994; and Desmond Bowen, *The Protestant Crusade in Ireland, 1800–70. A Study of Protestant–Catholic Relations between the Act of Union and Disestablishment* (Dublin, 1978).

13 This theme was often suggested during the enquiries of the 1830s and 1840s. For example, see the evidence presented to the enquiry on tithes in 1831–2, as in Edward Brynn, *The Church of Ireland in the Age of Catholic Emancipation* (London & New York, 1982), p. 192. Stuart also discovered during his visit to Ireland in 1830–31 that abolitionism was seen as a 'Protestant' cause and as such, was presumed to ignore 'Irish sufferings' (Barker, *Captain James Stuart*, pp. 51–2). For the correlation between the development of the British anti-slavery movement and evangelical nonconformity, see Drescher, 'Public Opinion', p. 34.

14 Rice, *Scots Abolitionists*, pp. 83–5; Bolt, *Anti-Slavery Movement and Reconstruction*, p. 6. For reservations about the emerging public influence of Fr. Mathew and his temperance movement, not least because his crusade was seen as entertaining 'sentiments too liberal towards Protestants', see Elizabeth Malcolm, *'Ireland Sober, Ireland Free': Drink and Temperance in Nineteenth-Century Ireland* (Dublin, 1986), pp. 135–40. The quotation is from p. 136.

15 Howard Temperley, *British Antislavery, 1833–1870* (London, 1972), pp. 1–3, *et passim;* Wigham, *Christian Philanthropist*, ch. 2, *et passim*. For the wider Quaker world, see 'The Quaker Ethic and the Antislavery International', in Davis, *Problem of Slavery*, pp. 213–54; J. William Frost, *The Quaker Origins of Antislavery*, (Norwood, Pa., 1980); Anstey, *Atlantic Slave Trade*, ch. 9, *et passim;* and Frederick B. Tolles, *Quakers and the Atlantic Culture* (New York, 1960).

16 Maria Luddy, *Women and Philanthropy in Nineteenth-Century Ireland* (Cambridge, 1995), pp. 64–7; Rodgers, 'Two Quakers and a Utilitarian'. For the influence which early-nineteenth-century American women had as 'republican mothers' and inculcators of civic virtue, see Linda Kerber, *Women of the Republic: Intellect and Ideology in Revolutionary America* (Chapel Hill, 1980). Webb was one of the more influential anti-slavery leaders and his bookshop and printing business involved him in a wide range of contacts within the movement; see Richard S. Harrison, *Richard Davis Webb: Dublin Quaker Printer (1805–72)* (Cork, 1993), and Marie-Louise Legg (ed.), *Alfred Webb. The Autobiography of a Quaker Natonalist* (Cork, 1999). For Allen, see Wigham, *Christian Philanthropist*.

17 Clare Midgley, *Women against Slavery* (London, 1992), pp. 3–4. Hannah Webb is quoted in a letter from Richard to Sarah Webb, 3 August 1840, as in Taylor, *Abolitionists*, p. 100. For a short discussion of female anti-slavery societies in Ireland, see Midgley, *Women against Slavery*, pp. 50–51. See also *Report of the Hibernian Ladies' Negroes' Friend Society* (Dublin, 1833) and 'A Letter from the Ladies' Anti-Slavery Society to their Countrywomen', in *The Irish Temperance and Literary Gazette*, 2, no. 77 (28 April 1838), p. 310. For the broader context, see Louis and Rosamund Billington, '"A Burning Zeal for Righteousness": Women in the British Anti-Slavery Movement', in Jane Rendall (ed.), *Equal or Different: Women's Politics, 1800–1914* (Oxford, 1987), pp. 82–111.

18 'Speech of Daniel O'Connell at a Meeting of the Loyal National Repeal Association, Dublin, 29 September 1845 in *Daniel O'Connell upon American Slavery*, p. 31; Barker, *Captain James Stuart*, pp. 41–5; Temperley, *British Anti-Slavery*, pp. 12–18; Izhak Gross, 'The Abolition of Negro Slavery and British

Parliamentary Politics, 1832–3', in *Historical Journal,* 23, no. 1 (1980), pp. 63–85. For O'Connell's involvements in wider reform networks, see Fergus D'Arcy, 'O'Connell and English Radicals', in McCartney, *World of Daniel O'Connell,* pp. 54–71. See also J.R. Ward, (ed.), *British West Indian Slavery, 1750–1834: The Process of Amelioration* (Oxford, 1988) and William Laurence Burn, *Emancipation and Apprenticeship in the British West Indies* (London, 1937). For the support which Irish MPs gave to this measure, see Coupland, *British Anti-Slavery Movement,* p. 138.

19 Joseph Sturge and Thomas Harvey, *The West Indies in 1837* (London, 1837); Wigham, *Christian Philanthropist,* pp. 25–33; Harrison, 'Irish Quaker Perspectives', p. 115; Barker, *Captain James Stuart,* pp. 155–6; Rice, *Scots Abolitionists,* pp. 62–3. For Sligo's term in Jamaica, see Burn, *Emancipation and Apprenticeship,* pp. 290–318, *et passim.* For his views, see his *Jamaica under the Apprenticeship System* (London, 1838). O'Connell's warning to the government was made in the context of his alliance with the governing Whigs, known as the 'Lichfield House Compact', for which see Angus Macintyre, *The Liberator* (London, 1965), pp. 139–46, 152–66.

20 O'Connell's to Sturge, 7 July 1838, in Henry Richard, *Memoirs of Joseph Sturge* (London, 1865), pp. 174–6; Howard Temperley, 'The O'Connell–Stevenson *Contretemps*: A Reflection of the Anglo–American Slavery Issue', in *Journal of Negro History* (*JNH*), 47 (1962), pp. 217, 221; Rice, *Scots Abolitionists,* ch. 3. For the convention, see Temperley, *British Antislavery,* pp. 85–92.

21 These people were active in a number of benevolent and reform associations, including those which focused on temperance and slavery. Madden, the historian of the United Irishmen, had also been a magistrate in the West Indies and appeared before the parliamentary enquiry into the impact of the Emancipation Act; see his *A Twelvemonth's Residence in the West Indies during the Transition from Slavery to Apprenticeship,* 2 vols. (1835), and Annie Heloise Abel and Frank J. Klingberg (eds), *A Side-Light on Anglo-American Relations, 1839–1858, Furnished by the Correspondence of Lewis Tappan and Others with the British and Foreign Anti-Slavery Society* (Lancaster, Pa., 1927), pp. 57–66, *et passim.* The (Dublin) *Register,* 1 February 1840, also printed Madden's address on 'Irish antipathy to the free black'; as cited in Abel and Klingberg, p. 30, n. 27. For Martin and Mathew, see Kerrigan, *Father Mathew.* Among the members of the Webb family who attended the convention were Richard Webb and his wife Hannah (1809–62), James Webb Snr. (1776–1854) and his sons, Thomas (1806–84) and James H. Jr (1810–68) and his wife, Ann.

22 The memoranda of Garrison and Webb are quoted from Taylor, *Abolitionists,* pp. 94 and 92 respectively.

23 Waring and Webb were sisters. Edmundson was daughter of John Wigham of Edinburgh and step-daughter of Jane Smeal, two prominent personalities within the British anti-slavery movement. Through her marriage to Joshua Edmundson of Dublin, she was also connected to Hannah Webb; see Legg, p 1, 83, n. 30. For the wider importance of these family networks, see Rice, *Scots Abolitionists,* pp. 41–5 and Temperley, *British Abolitionists,* p. 213.

24 The reference to Haydon's portrait is taken from Midgley, *Women against Slavery,* p. 2. The other quotations are respectively from Maria Waring's memorandum of the convention and from Lucretia Mott to Maria Weston Chapman, 29 July 1840, as in Taylor, *Abolitionists,* pp. 95 and 103–4. Mott had been appointed to attend the convention as one of the delegates from New

York. See also James Mott, *Three Months in Great Britain* (Philadelphia, 1841); Rice, *Scots Abolitionists*, p. 93; and Benjamin Quarles, *Black Abolitionists* (New York, 1969), pp. 131–3. Redmond later brought O'Connell's *Address* with him to America in December 1841. For the memoranda of several Irish delegates to the London convention, see Taylor, *Abolitionists*, pp. 94–101. For the defeat of the motion to admit women delegates, see *Freemans Journal*, 16 June 1840. For reports on the convention, including a report of O'Connell's speech of 'great length', see *Freemans Journal*, 18 June 1840. The *FJ* carried further reports on 20, 26 and 27 June 1840.

25 Wigham, *Christian Philanthropist*, p. 225. Garrison and Waring are quoted in Taylor, *Abolitionists*, pp. 116 and 98. In a similar vein to Garrison, Harriet Martineau informed Maria Chapman that 'Garrison was quite right, I think, to sit in the gallery at Convention . . . It has done much for the woman question, I am persuaded. You will live to see a great enlargement of our scope, I trust' (Gayle Graham Yates (ed.), *Harriet Martineau on Women* (New Brunswick, 1985), pp. 159–60. See also Frederick B. Tolles (ed.), '*Slavery and 'The Woman Question': Lucretia Mott's Diary of her Visit to Great Britain to Attend the World's Anti-Slavery Convention of 1840* (Haverford, Pa., 1952). For a short survey of the women's movement in America before 1850, see Christine Bolt, *The Women's Movement in the United States and Britain* (Brighton, 1993), pp. 12–95; Jean Fagan Yrellin, *Women and Sisters: The Antislavery Feminists in American Culture* (New Haven & London, 1989); and Jane Rendall, *The Origins of Modern Feminism: Women in Britain, France and the United States, 1780–1860* (Basingstoke & London, 1985).

26 Jacqueline Van Voris (ed.), 'Daniel O'Connell and Women's Rights, One Letter', in *Eire-Ireland*, vol. 17, no. 3 (1982), pp. 35–9. Thompson's pamphlet is quoted in Riaich, 'Ireland and the Campaign against American Slavery', p. 119. For sentiments similar to those expressed to Mott, see Elizabeth Cady Stanton, *Eighty Years and More. Reminiscences 1815–1897* (New York, 1971), p. 89. It might also be noted that at the annual meeting of the ASS of 1832, O'Connell had called for 'female petitions' on slavery while the following year, he defended the right of women to petition parliament during the debate on anti-slavery in the House of Commons; see Midgley, *Women against Slavery*, p. 64. For O'Connell's influence on the women's movement in contemporary France, see Claire Goldberg Moses, *French Feminism in the 19th Century* (Albany, 1984), pp. 109–110, *et passim*.

27 The quotations are from the letters of Webb to Maria Weston Chapman, 22 February 1842, Webb to Quincy, 16 October and 16 August 1843, Webb to Maria Weston Chapman, 22 February 1842, and Webb to Quincy, 2 February 1844, in Taylor, *Abolitionists*, pp. 168, 201–2, 193–4, 169 and 215.

28 Jane Jennings & Ladies of the Cork Anti-Slavery Society to Maria Weston Chapman, 1 December 1841, as in Taylor, *Abolitionists*, p. 158. For the view of anti-slavery within the Repeal movement, see Webb to Quincy, 2 February 1844, for example, where he observed that 'amongst the active Repealers there is not a genuine anti-slavery man, as far as I know, but O'Connell. The rest are angry with him for what he has said and written against proslavery Americans. They cling to the ultimate idea of receiving help from America, and don't like to affront Brother Jonathan' (ibid., p. 215).

29 Before being appointed ambassador to London in 1834, Stevenson had represented Richmond, Virginia in the US Congress where the anti-Adams faction had also engineered his election as Speaker in 1827. O'Connell's charge that he was also 'a slave-breeder – one of those beings who rear up slaves for the

purposes of traffic', caused considerable controversy on both sides of the Atlantic. See Temperley, 'O'Connell–Stevenson *Contretemps*', pp. 217–33; the quotation is from p. 223.

30 The quotations are from *Daniel O'Connell upon American Slavery*, pp. 7, 5, 21, 12, 13. Washington is quoted from his letter to the Dublin MP, Edward Newenham, in Jared Sparks (ed.), *The Writings of Washington*, 12 vols. (Boston, 1834–7), vol. 9, p. 398.

31 C. Duncan Rice, 'The Anti-Slavery Mission of George Thompson to the United States, 1834–1837', in *Journal of American Studies*, 2 (1968), pp. 13–31; Barker, *Charles Stuart*, pp. 192–3. See also Max Berger, 'American Slavery as Seen by British Visitors, 1836–1860', in *Journal of Negro History*, 30, no. 2 (April 1945). As Fladeland has pointed out, discomfort about visiting lectures was not confined to America. When John A. Collins visited Britain in early 1840, for example, he 'believed that Americans travelling in Britain were as much obliged to speak out against class prejudice as British travellers were to attack slavery in America' (Fladeland, 'Our Cause', p. 76). As such, Bolt has suggested that the 1840 Convention 'was in fact the highpoint of co-operation between the two nations' see (*Anti-Slavery Movement and Reconstruction*, p. 24).

32 Garrison to George Benson, 22 March 1842, as in Taylor, *Abolitionists*, p. 170. For this address, see *Daniel O'Connell upon American Slavery*, pp. 38–40. John O'Connell is quoted from his letter to Haughton, 23 November 1840, in ibid. pp. 35–6. For Irish attitudes to anti-slavery, see Maurice J. Bric, 'Daniel O'Connell and America' in Michael Glazier, (ed.), *The Encyclopedia of the Irish in America*, (South Bend, Ind., pp. 712–4); Gilbert Osofsky, 'Abolitionists, Irish Immigrants, and the Dilemmas of Romantic Nationalism', in *American Historical Review*, (October 1975), pp. 889–912; and Douglas Riaich, 'Daniel O'Connell and American Anti-Slavery', in *Irish Historical Studies*, 20, no. 77 (March 1976), pp. 3–25.

33 Garrison to George Benson, 22 March 1842, as in Taylor, *Abolitionists*, p. 171; Oscar Sherwin, *Prophet of Liberty. The Life and Times of Wendell Phillips* (New York, 1958), pp. 127–31.

34 Garrison to R.D. Webb, 27 February 1842, and to George Benson, 22 March 1842, as in Taylor, *Abolitionists*, pp. 169 and 171 respectively. In a similar letter to Allen, Garrison reported that the address had been 'spurned and denounced by the Irish papers in Boston' Wigham, p. 61 (*Christian Philanthropist*).

35 Riaich, 'Ireland and the Campaign against American Slavery', pp. 188–9. For the address of the Pennsylvania Anti-Slavery Society, see *Freemans Journal*, 12 May 1843. O'Connell's reply to the 'Executive Committee of the Cincinnati Repeal Association' is in The Loyal National Repeal Association, *The Following is a Copy of the Address* . . . 11th October 1843, (New England Anti-Slavery Tract Association, Boston, 1843?), Tract No. 2. The quotation is from p. 1.

36 '*Address* . . . 11th October 1843', pp. 1, 2, 5, 9, 12; Edmund Quincy to R.D. Webb, 27 November 1843, as in Taylor, *Abolitionists*, p. 207; Riaich, 'Daniel O'Connell and American Anti-Slavery', p. 17. For background, see Anthony J. Barker, *The African Link. British Attitudes towards the Negro in the Era of the Atlantic Slave Trade, 1550–1807* (London, 1978), esp. part II which examines the eighteenth-century roots of 'the theory of Negro inferiority'. See also Winthrop D. Jordan, *White over Black: American Attitudes towards the Negro, 1550–1812* (Chapel Hill, 1968) and W. Baker, 'William Wilberforce and the Idea of Negro Inferiority', in *Journal of the History of Ideas*, 31, no. 3 (1970), pp. 433–40.

37 Kevin Kenny, *The American Irish: A History*, (Harlow, UK, 2000), pp. 84–6;

Riaich, 'Ireland and the Campaign against American Slavery', pp. 165, 182, 184–6; Madeleine Hooke Rice, *American Catholic Opinion in the Slavery Controversy* (New York, 1964), reprinted from 1944.

38 Osofsky, 'Abolitionists, Irish Immigrants', pp. 892, 905; Maurice O'Connell, 'Daniel O'Connell and Irish-Americans', pp. 14–5. The MASS is quoted from the society's annual report for 1847, as *Daniel O'Connell upon American Slavery*, p. 48.

Emmet Larkin: The Beginning of the Irish Effort to Provide for the Roman Catholic Foreign Missions before the Famine

1 William Forbes Adams, *Ireland and Irish Emigration to the New World from 1815 to the Famine* (New Haven, 1932); David Fitzpatrick, *Irish Emigration, 1801–1921* (Dublin, 1994).
2 *Irish Catholic Directory*, 1846, p. 359.
3 Kevin Condon, *The Missionary College of All Hallows, 1842–1891* (Dublin, 1986), p. 32.
4 William B. Ullathorne, *The Autobiography of Archbishop Ullathorne*, (London, n.d.). See pp. 133–45 for an interesting account of the *ad hoc* nature of recruiting clergy for a foreign mission.
5 Cullen Papers, Archives of the Irish College, Rome.
6 Ibid., 17/9/1839, 12/12/1839.
7 Ibid., 2/2/1840.
8 Kirby Papers, Archives of the Irish College, Rome.
9 Ibid.
10 Cullen Papers.
11 *Scritture Riferite nei Congressi, Irlanda*, v. 27, f. 560. Archives of the Society for the Evangelization of the People, Rome.
12 Ibid.
13 Kirby Papers, 8/1/1842.
14 Ibid.
15 *Scritture Riferite nei Congressi, Irlanda*, v. 27: ff. 605–6
16 Kirby Papers, Foley to Kirby, 9/16/1841.
17 *Irish Catholic Directory*, 1839.
18 Peter Clarke, *A Free Church in a Free Society*, (Hartsville, SC, 1982), p. 427.
19 Ibid., p. 429.
20 Ibid., p. 427.
21 Ullathorne, *Autobiography*, p. 134.
22 Condon, *All Hallows*, p. 221, fn. 8.
23 Ibid., p. 18.
24 *Irish Catholic Directory*, 1839–1844, *passim*.
25 Condon, *All Hallows*, p. 18.
26 Ibid., pp. 19–20.
27 Ibid., p. 21.
28 Ibid., p. 22
29 Ibid.
30 Ibid., p. 35.
31 Ibid., pp. 37–42.
32 Ibid., p. 43.
33 Ibid., p. 53.
34 Ibid., p. 45.

35 Cullen Papers, 19/3/1842.
36 Kirby Papers, 27/7/1842.
37 Ibid., 15/10/1842.
38 Ibid., 24/1/43.
39 *Scritture Riferite nei Congressi, Irlanda*, v. 28, ff. 56–7.
40 Kirby Papers, 12/2/1843.
41 *Scritture Riferite nei Congressi, Irlanda*, v. 28, ff. 59–60; Kirby Papers, 1/4/43.
42 Ibid.
43 Crotty Papers, Archives of Cloyne, Cobh, Ireland. 'Diary of Very Rev. Richard Canon Smiddy', p. 4.
44 Kirby Papers, 15/5/1843.
45 *Scritture Riferite nei Congressi, Irlanda*, v. 28, ff. 12–13, 2 October 1843.
46 Ibid., ff. 116–17.
47 Kirby Papers, 2/11/1843.
48 Ibid., 16/4/1843.
49 Condon, *All Hallows*, '*Matricula*: 1842–1850', pp. 290–300. See also pp. 61, 63, 83, 86.
50 Ibid., p. 69.
51 Ibid., p. 61.
52 Ibid., p. 63
53 Ibid., p. 231, fn. 21.
54 Ibid., p. 129, 134. Between 1873 and 1896, moreover, of the 634 priests ordained at All Hallows for the foreign missions 617, or more than 97%, went to the English-speaking missions, and about half (295) of those 617 went to the United States.

Clíona Murphy: Nova Scotia, Ireland and the British Empire in the Writings of Charlotte Elizabeth Tonna, 1829–46

1 Judith Fingard, *The Anglican Design in Loyalist Nova Scotia, 1783–1816* (London, 1972), p. vii.
2 As her life progressed she was known by different names: Charlotte Elizabeth Browne (maiden name); Charlotte Elizabeth Phelan (first marriage); Charlotte Elizabeth Tonna (second marriage); many of her publications were simply under the name Charlotte Elizabeth.
3 *Letters from Ireland* (London, 1838) hereafter, *Letters*. Harriet Martineau, too, had a book of the same name published in 1852, reprinted: Glenn Hooper (ed.), *Letters from Ireland, Harriet Martineau* (Dublin, 2001). Martineau's thoughts on 'Political Economy' and 'mesmerism' were published in *The Christian Lady's Magazine*, hereafter, *CLM*. Both women were from Norwich and while Tonna was totally deaf, Harriet Martineau was partially deaf. Here the comparisons stop. Tonna was more conservative.
4 *Personal Recollections* (first published in London in 1841. Edition cited here was published by John Taylor, New York, 1844), hereafter, *Recollections*. The novels are *The Rockite: An Irish Story* (London, 1829), *Derry: A Tale of Revolution* (London, 1833), *The Deserter* (Dublin, 1836) and *Combination: A Tale, Founded on Facts* (Dublin, 1832).
5 Monica Correa Fryckstedt estimates she was the author of 130 titles, 'Charlotte Elizabeth Tonna: A Forgotten Evangelical Writer', in *Studia Neurophilologica*, 52 (1980), pp. 79–102 (hereafter, Fryckstedt (1)), p. 79.
6 *Helen Fleetwood* (London, 1841), *The Perils of the Nation* (London, 1843), *The Wrongs of Woman* (London, 1843). Scholars concerned with her industrial

writings have little to say about her Irish writings. See Susan Zlotnick, *Women, Writing and the Industrial Revolution* (Baltimore, 1998), pp. 123–67 *et passim.* Ivanka Kovacevic and S. Barbara Kanner, 'Blue Book into Novel: The Forgotten Industrial Fiction of Charlotte Elizabeth Tonna', in *Nineteenth Century Fiction,* 25 (1970–71), pp. 152–73, Joseph Kestner, 'Charlotte Elizabeth Tonna's *The Wrongs of Woman*: Female Industrial Protest', in *Tulsa Studies in Women's Literature,* 2 (1982), pp. 193–224.

7 The 1844 Factory Act, which banned night work for women, the Ten Hour Bill (Fielden's Factory Act) and the Public Health Act (1848) are said to have been influenced by *The Perils of the Nation* (1843). L.H.J. Tonna, *A Memoir of Charlotte Elizabeth; Embracing the Period from the Close of Personal Recollections to her Death* (New York, 1847), p. iii. See Kestner, p. 200.

8 'She was well known in this country, as well as in England', Obituary, *Rome Citizen,* (upstate New York), 18 August 1846. See also Harriet Beecher Stowe's introduction to the American edition of *The Works of Charlotte Elizabeth* (New York, 1844, 7th edn by 1849).

9 Upon Tonna's death, she was described as 'this very successful religious writer', in *Gentleman's Magazine,* (October 1846), pp. 433–4. See Linda H. Peterson, *Traditions of Victorian Women's Autobiography* (Charlottesville, 1999), *passim.* Vineta Colby, *Yesterday's Woman* (Princeton, 1974), pp. 174–8, Elizabeth Jay, *The Religion of the Heart* (Oxford, 1979), pp. 198–9. Elizabeth Kowaleski, "The Heroine of Some Strange Romance": The *Personal Recollections* of Charlotte Elizabeth Tonna', in *Tulsa Studies in Women's Literature,* 1 (Fall 1982), pp. 141–53.

10 One exception is Fryckstedt (1).

11 Extracts from Tonna's *Letters from Ireland* have been cited in Glenn Hooper (ed.), *The Tourist's Gaze, Travellers to Ireland, 1800–2000* (Cork, 2001), pp. 60–64 and Patricia Craig (ed.), *The Belfast Anthology* (Belfast, 1999), p. 307 and pp. 340–41.

12 It was approximately 100–150 pages each month. See Monica Correa Fryckstedt, 'Charlotte Elizabeth Tonna and *The Christian Lady's Magazine*', in *Victorian Periodical Review,* 14 (1981), pp. 43–9.

13 Kestner, 'Charlotte Elizabeth', p. 205.

14 Ibid., *passim.*

15 For poems see fn.125. There is no mention of her in Tony Gray, *The Orange Order* (London, 1972) or in Ruth Dudley Edwards, *The Faithful Tribe* (London, 1999).

16 Judith Fingard, 'English Humanitarianism and the Colonial Mind: Walter Bromley in Nova Scotia, 1813–25', *The Canadian Historical Review,* LIV. No. 2 (1973), pp. 138–9, p. 139, fn. 68. L.S. Loomer, *Canadian Notes and Queries,* 1974, pp. 9–10. Isabella A. Owen, 'Charlotte Elizabeth', *Acadiensis,* 1, (1901), pp. 228–35. This article is mostly a synopsis of Tonna's life based on her publications. There are only a few comments based upon the folk memory of Tonna's visit. The *Nova Scotia Historical Review* (discontinued, 1995) has no article on Tonna.

17 Loomer, *Canadian Notes and Queries,* p. 9.

18 See Paulette M. Chiasson, 'As Others Saw Us: Nova Scotian Travel Literature from the 1770s to the 1860s', in *Nova Scotia Historical Review,* 2, no. 2 (1982), pp. 9–24.

19 I have focused in more detail on *The Rockite* and Tonna's reflections on the Second Reformation, Catholic Emancipation and the National Schools in Cliona Murphy, '"The Destruction of the Protestant Church and the Dismem-

berment of the British Empire": Charlotte Elizabeth, Evangelical Anglican in Pre-Famine Ireland', in *Women's Studies: An Interdisciplinary Journal*, 30, no. 6 (2001), pp. 741–62.

20 Clara Lucas Balfour, *A Sketch of Charlotte Elizabeth* (London, 1854), p. 27.

21 Ibid., p. 28.

22 Ibid., pp. 31–2.

23 'I felt it a sort of degradation to have an Irish name' *Recollections*, p. 102. See Murphy,'The Destruction of the Protestant Church', p. 745.

24 See Owen and Loomer. They also state that Phelan went'progressively insane' but do not give a source. Loomer, *Canadian Notes and Queries*, p. 10, Owen, Charlotte Elizabeth', pp. 231–2.

25 Hugh Anderson, *The Life and Letters of Christopher Anderson* (Edinburgh, *c.* 1854), p. 152.

26 The following publications refer to the year she left Ireland (1824). Tonna, *The Happy Mute: or the Dumb Child's Appeal* (London, 1835). Anon., *Memoir of Jack Britt: The Happy Mute* (London, 1850), p. 47. Balfour, *Sketch*, p. 35. She tells Christopher Anderson in a letter in 1830 that she was in Ireland from 1819 to 1824, *Life of Christopher Anderson*, p. 146.

27 *Recollections*, pp. 88–99.

28 My attention was drawn to Bromley by Nova Scotian historian, Judith Fingard (see fns. 1 and 17). Walter Bromley, *An Appeal to the Virtue and Good Sense of the Inhabitants of Great Britain on Behalf of the Indians of North America* (Halifax, 1820). Fryckstedt (1) states she could trace less than a dozen letters in Irish, British and American libraries, p. 80, fn. 5. Tonna told friends that if they allowed any of her letters to be published'even as elucidation on her life' she would regard it as a'gross breach of confidence'. Balfour, *Sketch*, p. 22.

29 *CLM*, February 1836, p. 98. Kowaleski argues this account was influenced by art Tonna saw later.'Heroine', p. 145. According to Shirley Foster, most crossings were from Liverpool and went to Boston or New York, usually stopping first at Halifax, to disembark Canadian immigrants. Sail ships took about thirty days to cross the Atlantic to Nova Scotia. (Tonna mentions a storm, perhaps, that is why her trip was longer). With the advent of steam (1838), the passage was shortened to ten days. Shirley Foster, *Across New Worlds, Nineteenth Century Women Travellers and Their Writings* (Hempsted, 1990), p. 75.

30 *CLM*, October 1838, p. 293.

31 An old French soldier saved her from frostbite and on another occasion she could not write because her ink was frozen. *Recollections*, p. 95.

32 *CLM*, August 1839, p. 98. See also Chiasson,'As Others Saw Us', p. 13.

33 See her novel on slavery, *The System; A Tale of the West Indies* (London, 1827).

34 *CLM*, July 1839, p. 8.

35 Ibid., November 1838, p. 386. Charles Inglis was bishop from 1787 to 1816 and was originally from Donegal. He was the first Anglican bishop in Nova Scotia and the first bishop in the British overseas Empire See R.V. Harris, *Charles Inglis, Missionary, Loyalist, Bishop* (Toronto, 1937).

36 Bromley, *An Appeal*, p. 35.

37 *Recollections*, p. 142. *The Rockite* was dedicated to Lord Mountsandford.

38 Ibid., p. 197.

39 L.H.J. Tonna, *Memoir*, p. 9.

40 *Letters*, p. 90.

41 They went into many editions. See *Recollections*, 136–7. Tonna writes about how much she valued the Society in *Letters*, pp. 90–92 and in *Recollections*, p. 142.

42 See Murphy,'Destruction', pp. 749–52. Also James Donnelly, Jr.,'Pastorini and

Captain Rock: Millenarianism and Sectarianism in the Rockite Movement 1821–4', James Donnelly Jr. and Samuel Clark (eds.), *Irish Peasants: Violence and Unrest, 1780–1914*(Madison, 1983), pp. 102–37.

43 The literature on the Second Reformation continues to grow. See especially, Alan Acheson, 'The Evangelicals in the Church of Ireland, 1691–1996', Ph.D. Thesis, Queens University Belfast, 1967. Desmond Bowen, *The Protestant Crusade in Ireland* (Dublin, 1978), *Souperism; Myth or Reality* (Montreal, 1971). Stewart J. Brown, 'The New Reformation Movement in the Church of Ireland, 1801–1829', in Stewart J. Brown and David Miller, (eds.), *Piety and Power in Ireland, 1760–1960*, pp. 180–208. Brian McNamee, 'Second Reformation in Ireland', *Irish Theological Quarterly*, xxxiii (1966), pp. 39–64.

44 *Recollections*, pp. 348–9.

45 She was aware of Gayer's work on the Dingle Peninsula. After his infamous trial in 1845, when he sued the *Kerry Examiner* for libel, he wrote to *The Christian Lady's Magazine* to state that his converts were still being persecuted by the local community. See *The Protestant Magazine*, June 1842, p. 178 for references to Gayer and Nangle. See also July 1842, p. 241 on the 'Poor Converts at Dingle' and extracts from 'Report of the Achill Mission', pp. 246–7.

46 His pamphlet *Doctrines of the Church of Rome and Disorders of Ireland. An Address to the Protestants of Great Britain* (Mortimer, 1836) was reviewed in *CLM*, April 1836, p. 376.

47 *CLM*, July 1838, p. 93.

48 She wrote the introduction to *Twenty Six Sermons by the Late Reverend Charles Seymour* (Dublin, 1835).

49 *CLM*, pp. 386–7.

50 *Recollections*, p. 350.

51 O'Connell's speech (3 April 1838) included the question 'Would the bones of Derry lie worse because those of old Mrs. Cathcart lay among them?' The poem, dated 5 April 1838, was published in the *CLM*, June 1838, pp. 533–4.

52 See Murphy, 'Destruction', p. 754.

53 *Recollections*, p. 349.

54 Ibid., p. 203.

55 She agreed with Colonel Acton's speech, in parliament, when he stated that the movement was likely to 'rivet more firmly the fetters of Popery on the deluded victims of that soul–destroying superstition'. Quoted in *PM*, July 1842, p. 247.

56 *CLM*, October 1838, p. 293.

57 Ibid. February 1839, p. 100.

58 Ibid., November 1840, p. 457. According to Glenn Hooper this exasperation about the ignorance of the English with regard to Ireland was common. Some saw it as one of the reasons behind the rebellion of 1798, and was, thus, a justification of travel writing as a preventative measure against trouble in the future. See Leon Litvack and Glenn Hooper (eds.) 'Searching for Ireland after the Union', *Ireland in the Nineteenth Century: Regional Identity*, (Dublin, 2000), pp. 215–32. See pp. 216–17.

59 *PM*, 1 February 1842, p. 51.

60 *Letters*, preface.

61 *Recollections*, p. 197.

62 *Letters*, p. 64.

63 Thomas Leland, *History of Ireland from the Invasion of Henry II* (London, 1775) referred to in *CLM*, September 1834, p. 257. Sylvester O'Halloran, *A General History of Ireland from the Earliest Accounts to the Close of the Twelfth Century*

(London, 1778) referred to in *CLM*, February 1836, p. 25.

64 Christopher Anderson, *Historical Sketches of the Native Irish and Their Descendants*, 2nd edn (Edinburgh, 1830), CLM, February 1836, p. 125. See also *CLM*, October 1834, pp. 377–8.

65 *CLM*, October, 1834, p. 384.

66 Anderson, *Life of Christopher Anderson*, pp. 145–53. See p. 148.

67 *CLM*, October 1839, p. 358.

68 Henry D. Inglis, *Ireland in 1834, A Journey throughout Ireland* (London, 1835).

69 Baptist Wriothesley Noel, *Notes of a Short Tour through the Midland Counties of Ireland, in the Summer of 1836* (London, 1837), see CLM, May 1837, Book Review, pp. 464–9. Plagiarism was not uncommon. See Percy G. Adams, *Travel and Travel Liars, 1660–1800* (Berkeley, 1962).

70 See Kovacevic and Kanner, 'Blue Book into Novel', fn. 7.

71 *CLM*, March 1836, pp. 248–52.

72 Ibid., February 1838, p. 119–24.

73 The work she was referring to was probably his *Two Addresses on the Deplorable State of the Indians* (London, 1815).

74 *Recollections*, p. 94.

75 *CLM*, October 1838, p. 292.

76 Ibid., December 1838, p. 485, fn. 1. Thomas Chandler Haliburton, *Historical and Statistical Account of Nova Scotia* (Halifax, 1829). He was also a judge and published humourist. He moved to England and was elected to parliament in 1858.

77 J. Crosskill, *A Comprehensive Outline of the Geography and History of Nova Scotia from the Discovery of America to the Reign of Victoria* (Halifax, 1838).

78 *CLM*, March 1838, p. 258.

79 Ibid., January 1838, p. 7.

80 According to Hooper, 'After 1800 many English travellers . . . [were] determined to read Ireland as a natural offshore extension of the British state, as yet uneasily yoked in Union, but possessing great potential nevertheless', *The Tourist's Gaze*, p. xx. He elaborates on this idea in his essays 'Anne Plumtre: An Independent Traveller', in Margaret Kelleher and James H. Murphy (eds.), *Gender Perspectives in Nineteenth–Century Ireland* (Dublin, 1997) and 'Searching for Ireland after the Union', already cited.

81 This idea has been explored by Edward Said in *Orientalism* (New York, 1978) and has been applied to the Irish context by John McAuliffe in 'Women's Travel Writing in Mid-Nineteenth Century Ireland' in *Gender Perspectives in Nineteenth-Century Ireland*, pp. 140–47, by Kevin Whelan in 'Writing Ireland: Reading England', *Ireland in the Nineteenth Century: Regional Identity*, Leon Litvack and Glenn Hooper (eds.), (Dublin, 2000), pp. 184–98, and by Joep Leersson in *Remembrance and Imagination: Patterns in the Historical and Literary Representation of Ireland in the Nineteenth-Century* (Cork, 1996), p. 33. See Whelan, p. 190. He speaks of 'the estranging effect of the lack of a national Irish audience or publishing industry – the lack of a middle class . . .'. See also Niall Ó Ciosáin, *Print and Popular Culture in Ireland, 1750–1850* (New York, 1997), ch. 2.

82 *CLM*, October, 1838, pp. 291–2.

83 Preface to bound volume 3 of *CLM* (January–June 1835). Preface is dated June 1835.

84 Ibid., October 1838, p 293.

85 Ibid., January 1839, p. 3.

86 Bromley, *An Appeal*, p. 26.

87 Chiasson, 'As Others Saw Us', p. 10.
88 *Recollections*, p. 96.
89 *CLM*, October 1838, p. 294.
90 See Bromley, *An Appeal*, p. 33. Bromley agrees with Tonna and, in a footnote to her letter he cites William Penn as having similar views. See also *CLM*, December 1838, p. 484.
91 See introduction to Charles Even, *The Lost Tribes of Israel: or, The First of the Red Men*, (Philadelphia, 1861) and Stanford M. Lyman, 'Postmodernism and the Construction of Ethnocultural Identity: The Indian Theory and the Lost Tribes of Israel', in *Sociological Spectrum*, 17, issue 3 (July–September 1997).
92 *CLM*, October 1838, p. 295.
93 *CLM*, March 1839, p. 201.
94 Ibid., pp. 195–7.
95 *Recollections*, p. 97. More detail in *CLM*, January 1839, pp. 6–12.
96 *The Rockite*, pp. 90–91.
97 *Recollections*, pp. 113–14.
98 Ibid., pp. 108–110.
99 *CLM*, September 1834, p. 281.
100 Ibid., January 1839, p. 92.
101 Henry Monck Mason, *History of the Origins and Progress of the Irish Society* (Dublin, 1844) and J.G. MacWalter, *The Irish Reformation Movement* (Dublin, 1851).
102 *Jack the Dumb Boy* and *Memoir of John Britt: The Happy Mute*. See fn. 26.
103 One campaign raised £1,300. Balfour, *Sketch*, p. 39. A series of articles on St Giles were published in the *CLM* in 1837.
104 *CLM*, October 1839, p. 299.
105 Ibid. February 1838, p. 151.
106 *The Deserter*, pp. 74–8. *The Deserter* was among many of her works to be translated. It was published in French (*par* P.F.J. Braue, Dulau and Cie, *Londres*,1853).
107 *CLM*, October 1837, pp. 355–62.
108 *CLM*, February 1834, pp. 155–8. *CLM*, March 1830, p. 282.
109 *Recollections*, p. 142.
110 *CLM*, March 1839 p. 282.
111 Letter dated 3 November 1831 posted on: www.autographs.demon.co.uk/lit1/body_lit1.html
112 *CLM*, January 1834, p. 2.
113 Ibid., January 1838, p. 96.
114 Ibid., February 1840, p. 179.
115 *Recollections*, p. 97.
116 *CLM*, October 1838 p. 296.
117 *Recollections* p. 96.
118 *CLM*, January 1839, p. 2. See also July 1839, p. 7.
119 Quoted in Chiasson, 'As Others Saw Us', p. 21.
120 *CLM*, July 1843, p. 59.
121 Ibid., January 1839, p. 92.
122 Ibid., July 1843, p. 91.
123 *Life and Letters of Christopher Anderson*, p. 147
124 *CLM*, October 1834, p. 376.
125 Ibid., September 1834, p. 279.
126 'Orangeman's Submission', *CLM*, January 1838, p. 37. 'Maiden City' and 'No Surrender' printed in John Cooke (ed.), *Dublin Book of Irish Verse*,

1728–1909(London, 1909), poems, 45 and 46. For'Grave-Yard', see fn. 51 above.
127 *Letters*, p. 305.
128 She launched a scathing campaign against *The Tablet* and its editors in *The Protestant Magazine* in the early 1840s.

Maura Cronin: Young Ireland in Cork, 1840–49

1 T.F. O'Sullivan, *The Young Irelanders* (Tralee, 1944), p. 14.
2 Ian d'Alton, *Protestant Society and Politics in Cork 1812–1844* (Cork, 1980), p. 200; Maura Murphy, 'Municipal Reform and the Repeal Movement in Cork, 1833–1844' in *Journal of the Cork Historical and Archaeological Society*, p. lxxxi, 1976.
3 Denis Gwynn, 'Denny Lane and Thomas Davis' *Studies*, xxxviii, (March 1949), pp. 16–18.
4 Richard Davis, *The Young Ireland Movement* (Dublin, 1988), p. 264; Kevin B. Nowlan, *The Politics of Repeal* (London, 1965), pp. 46–57; *Cork Examiner*, 17 May 1876.
5 From 1842 until 1848, all these individuals, with the possible exception of Ralph Varian, Felix Mullan and Charles Murphy, contributed to the *Nation* or to its more militant successors, the *United Irishman* and *Irish Felon.* Ellen Mary Downing was 'Mary'; Michael Joseph Barry was 'M.J.B', 'Beta' and 'Brutus'; Denny Lane was Domhnall na Glanna.
6 Smith O'Brien Papers, Ms. 434, letter 1258, Barry to Smith O'Brien, 27 October 1844; National Library of Ireland Ms. 2644, letters 149, 153, Lane to Smith O'Brien, 16 June 1845.
7 *Cork Examiner*, 14, 19 May, 23 June, 9, 16 July, 5 November 1845; Slattery Papers, Cashel Diocesan Archives, 1845/9, Crotty to Slattery, 15 September 1845.
8 *Cork Examiner*, 26 November 1845.
9 *Southern Reporter*, 26 October, 2 December 1830; *Cork Mercantile Chronicle*, 19 March 1832.
10 Maura Cronin, *Country, Class or Craft: The Politicisation of the Skilled Artisan in Nineteenth-Century Cork* (Cork, 1994), pp. 97–100; *Cork Mercantile Chronicle*, 19 March 1832.
11 Daniel Owen Maddyn, *Ireland and Its Rulers* (London, 1844), i, p. 194.
12 *Cork Examiner*, 27 October 1841. For a valuable analysis of the complexities of Cork reform and O'Connellite politics in the 1820s and early 1830s, see Fintan Lane, *In Search of Thomas Sheahan: Radical Politics in Cork 1824–1836* (Dublin, 2001).
13 Samuel Lewis, *Topographical Dictionary of Ireland* (2nd edn, XXX, 1842), I, 404; *Aldwell's Cork Post Office Directory* 1844–5, (Cork, 1844) p. 80; Chief Secretary's Office, Registered Papers, Outrage Reports, 1835, 6/63; *Southern Reporter*, 14 December 1839.
14 *Southern Reporter* 25, 28 August 1841; *Report of the Select Committee on Minister's Money, Ireland*, H.C., 1847–8, xvii, cols. 46–7; *Cork Examiner*, 20 December 1841, 3 January 1842, 1 June 1846.
15 Maurice O'Connell (ed.), *The Correspondence of Daniel O'Connell* (Dublin, 1972), vi, letter 2735, Joseph Hayes of Cork to O'Connell, 14 August 1840.
16 *Cork Examiner*, 12 November, 1 December 1841, 21 October 1842.
17 *Cork Examiner*, 20, 22 April, 15 May, 21 November 1844, 5 February, 31 October 1845; *Report of the Repeal Association: Report on Reading Rooms* 1844–5, ii, pp. 331–2, 338–46; Day Papers, Cork Archives, 80/123; *Cork Constitution*, 23 November 1844; William Smith O'Brien Papers, NLI: Ms. 2644, letter 163, Denny Lane to Thomas Davis, 10 April 1845: 'What I long anticipated and mentioned to you long since is coming about: [Francis S.] Murphy

[one of the city's MPs] is about taking up some namby-pamby federalism; Ms. 434, letter 1258, M. J. Barry to Smith O'Brien, 27 October 1844.

18 *Cork Constitution*, 29 April, 13 May 1843; *Cork Examiner*, 4, 15 September 1843.

19 *First Report of the Commissioners Appointed to Enquire into Municipal Corporations in Ireland*, H.C., 1835, xxvii, Appendix, p. 48; *Cork Examiner*, 16 June 1845.

20 *Cork Constitution*, 6 June 1846.

21 O'Connell, *O'Connell Correspondence*, vii, letter 3244, Thomas Lyons to O'Connell, 11 July 1846.

22 *Cork Constitution*, 20 June 1846.

23 *Cork Examiner*, 7, 14 August 1846; *Cork Constitution*, 4 August 1846.

24 One of the most vociferous critics of the Chamber of Commerce and Town Council was Joseph Hayes, a veteran of the Emancipation campaign and of the other reforming drives of the 1830s and 40s. By 1846 Lane and Barry were in their late twenties, while the more militant element emerging in the following two years included, for instance, the nineteen-year-old Joseph Brennan.

25 *Cork Examiner*, 2 December 1846, quoting a speech by Isaac Varian.

26 *Cork Examiner*, 15 January 1847. Luke Shea, JP of Carrigaline, Denny Lane, Michael Joseph Barry, Edward Brady, and Isaac Varian were all committee members.

27 Irish Confederation Minute Book, Royal Irish Academy, Ms. 23.H.40. This showed a total of only ninety-six members from Co. Cork, and listed none at all for the city, though this was probably due to inefficient communication between centre and provincial branch. Membership was most common among farmers, professional men (doctors and solicitors), Catholic clergy and shopkeepers, though artisans, teachers and a few labourers were also present on the lists.

28 *Cork Examiner*, 2 December 1846.

29 *Cork Examiner*, 22 September 1847.

30 Smith O'Brien Papers, Ms. 438, letter 1936. Barry to Smith O'Brien, 23 July 1847.

31 John Mitchel Papers (Hickey Collection), NLI, Ms. 3225, pp. 9–11; *Cork Examiner* 6, 20 October, 6, 20, 31 December 1847; *Southern Reporter*, 25 January 1848. The publications available in the reading room were: *The Daily News, Douglas Jarrold's Newspaper* and *Magazine, The Packet, The Limerick Reporter, Peter Carroll's Register, The Dublin University Magazine, The Cork Magazine, Howit's Journal, Sharpe's London Magazine, The North American Review, The Builder,* 'some northern newspapers', the *Cork Examiner, Southern Reporter* and *Cork Constitution*and the *Nation.* The Irish classes, held twice weekly at a charge of sixpence, were arranged by the antiquarian Thomas Windele.

32 Within a month, it had 135 members, but only the list of the first subscribers remains, so identification is difficult. *Cork Examiner,* 13 September 1847.

33 *Southern Reporter,* 25 January 1848. Smith O'Brien Papers, Ms. 442, letter 2374, Barry to Smith O'Brien, 22 February 1848.

34 *Southern Reporter,* 20, 25 January, 24 February 1848.

35 Smith O'Brien Papers, Ms. 441, letter 2349, Barry to Smith O'Brien, 5 January 1848.

36 John Mitchel Papers, Ms. 3225, pp. 8, 9, 22–5; *United Irishman*, 18 March 1848; *Southern Reporter,* 16, 8 March 1848.

37 *Southern Reporter*, 30 March, 27 April 1848.

38 *United Irishman*, 15 April 1848; Chief Secretary's Office, Registered Papers, Outrage Reports, 1848, 6/506.

39 *Irish Felon*, 24 June 1848; *Cork Constitution*, 13 July 1848; *Southern Reporter*, 13 July 1848; Smith O'Brien Papers, Ms. 442, letter 2490, Smith O'Brien to his wife, July 1848.CSORP.OR. 1848, 6/905, 935. Address to government from the

loyal traders of Patrick Street.

40 *Cork Constitution*, 4, 11, 13, 18 April, 23 May 1848; *United Irishman*, 5 May 1848; *Southern Reporter* 23, 30 May, 1 June 1848; CSORP.OR 1848, 6/397, 405, 424, 464, 447, 489, 505, 574, 634.

41 *Southern Reporter*, 15 July 1848.

42 *Southern Reporter*, 23 May 1848. Each club was to be founded with the co-operation of four members of the Citizens' Club, regular reports of progress were to be made to that club, and the district clubs were to abide by a set of rules issued by the Citizens' Club. The rules of the clubs were as follows: (1) Members were to devote themselves to achieving National Independence by every practicable means. (2) Discussion of sectarian and party topics was to be prohibited. (3) The club was to be governed by a committee of twelve, and a president and vice-president were to be elected for six months and enabled to frame necessary bye-laws. (4) Clubs were to remain open from 11 a.m. to 1 p.m. (5) A chairman (the president, vice-president or committee member) was to preside at discussions and silence was to be observed at all other times. (6) Smoking 'or any other objectionable practice' was to be forbidden, and infringement of this rule to be reported to the committee.

43 *Southern Reporter*, 6 January, 7, 18 March, 23, 30 May, 1 June 1848.

44 Smith O'Brien Papers, Ms. 442, letter 2374, Barry to Smith O'Brien, 22 February 1848; letter 2429, Barry to Smith O'Brien, May 1848.

45 *Southern Reporter*, 14 March 1848.

46 *Southern Reporter*, 30 March, 25 April, 3 June 1848; *Cork Examiner*, 18 March, 30 May 1848; Smith O'Brien Papers, Ms. 442, letter 2476, Denny Lane to Smith O'Brien.

47 CSORP.OR. 1848, 6/872, 973, 990, 998; *Cork Constitution*, 6, 25 July 1848; *Southern Reporter*, 18 July 1848.

48 CSORP.OR. 1848, 6/866; *Cork Constitution*, 27 July 1848.

49 *Cork Constitution*, 20, 27 July, 8 August 1848.

50 *Cork Constitution*, 27 July 1848; CSORP.OR. 1848, 6/1025–6.

51 *Southern Reporter*, 15 August, 7 September, 14 November 1848.

52 *Southern Reporter*, 2 January, 20 March 1849; Slattery Papers, Cashel Diocesan Archives 1849/29, Delaney to Slattery, 10 May 1849.

53 CSORP.OR. 1849, 6/575, 582.

54 *Cork Constitution*, 5, 14, 25 July, 4 August 1849.

55 *Cork Constitution*, 2, 16, 18, 23, 30 October, 10, 13 November 1849.

56 Davis, *Young Ireland Movement*, p. 244.

57 O'Sullivan, *Young Irelanders*, pp. 117–18.

58 Maura Murphy, 'The Ballad Singer and the Role of the Seditious Ballad in Nineteenth-Century Ireland: Dublin Castle's View', in *Ulster Folklife*, 25 (1979), pp. 97–8; O'Sullivan, *Young Irelanders*, p. 312.

59 *The Spirit of the Nation, or Ballads and Songs of the Writers of 'The Nation'* (Dublin, 1911), pp. 220, 228, 278, 326; Ab t-Athair Padruig Breathnach, *Songs of the Gael* (Dublin, 1922); T.F. O'Sullivan, *Young Irelanders*, pp. 572–3, 546,

60 Charles Gavan Duffy, *Thomas Davis: Literary and Historical Essays* (Dublin, 1846); *Young Ireland: A Fragment of Irish History 1840–45* (Dublin, 1884); *Young Ireland: Four Years of Irish History 1845–49* (Dublin, 1887); Michael Doheny, *The Felon's Track* (Dublin, 1918).

61 Padraig Eric Mac Fhinn, *An tAthair Mícheál P.Ó hIceadha* (Baile Atha Cliath, 1974), pp. 22–3.

62 Barry M. Coldrey, *The Christian Brothers and the Development of Irish Nationalism* (Dublin, 1988).

63 Denis Gwynn, *Thomas Davis and Young Ireland* (Cork, 1949); Gwynn, 'Denny Lane and Thomas Davis; M.J. McManus (ed.), *Thomas Davis and Young Ireland* (Dublin, 1945).
64 *The Educational History of Ireland*, Parts I and II (Dublin, 1960).
65 Cronin, *Country, Class or Craft*, pp. 156–7.
66 Maura Cronin, 'Denny Lane' *Journal of the Cork Historical and Archaeological Society*, 100 (1995), pp. 1–15; 101 (1996), pp. 143–57.
67 O'Sullivan, *Young Irelanders*, pp. 318–19.
68 *Cork Constitution*, 20 July 1848; Fr. Mat Horgan Papers, Royal Irish Academy, Ms. 12.G.15, November 1850.
69 *Cork Examiner*, 22, 23 May 1876, 24 January 1889, 30 November 1895.

Lawrence M. Geary: Anticipating Memory: Landlordism, Agrarianism and Deference in Late-Nineteenth-Century Ireland

1 Michael Davitt, *The Fall of Feudalism in Ireland* (London and New York, 1904), pp. 164–5.
2 P.A. Canon Sheehan, *Luke Delmage* (Dublin, 1901), p. 397. I am grateful to Patrick Maume for this reference.
3 Joseph Lee, *The Modernisation of Irish Society, 1848–1918* (Dublin, 1973), pp. 89–90.
4 W.E. Vaughan, *Landlords and Tenants in Mid-Victorian Ireland* (Oxford, 1994), p. 226.
5 For Davitt and Moore, see Adrian Frazier, 'Davitt at Moore's Door', pp. 47–59, in *The Dublin Review*, 9 (2002–3).
6 Victoria Glendinning, *Trollope* (London, 1992); for Trollope and hunting in Ireland, see pp. 12–14, 126, 151, 172, 219. For a brief account of the origins and social trappings of fox-hunting in Ireland, see Terence Dooley, *The Decline of the Big House in Ireland. A Study of Irish Landed Families 1860–1960* (Dublin, 2001), pp. 56–9, 260–64.
7 Cited in Dooley, *The Decline of the Big House in Ireland*, p. 56. For Mahaffy, see W.B. Stanford and R.B. McDowell, *Mahaffy. A Biography of an Anglo-Irishman* (London, 1971).
8 William O'Brien, *Recollections* (London, 1905), p. 376.
9 For a detailed analysis of this type of protest, see L.P. Curtis, Jr., 'Stopping the Hunt 1881–2: An Aspect of the Irish Land War', in C.H.E. Philbin (ed.), *Nationalism and Popular Protest in Ireland* (Cambridge, 1987), pp. 349–401.
10 Anthony Trollope, *The Landleaguers* (Oxford, 1993), pp. 95–7.
11 George Moore, *Hail and Farewell* (London, 3 vols., 1911–1914), vol. 1 *Ave*, pp. 260–64. See also Idem., *A Drama in Muslin* (London, 1886). For Moore, see Adrian Frazier, *George Moore 1852–1933* (New Haven and London, 2000).
12 *Freeman's Journal*, 9 September 1887.
13 *Cork Examiner*, 10, 12 August 1887, cited in my MA thesis, 'The Land War on the Kingston Estate 1879–1888' (UCC, 1979), which was completed under John A. Murphy's direction. He also supervised my Ph.D. thesis, 'The Plan of Campaign, 1886–1891' (UCC, 1985), which was published under the same title by Cork University Press in the following year. I have consciously drawn on material and ideas from both theses in this essay.
14 50 & 51 Vict., C 20, 'An act to make better provision for the prevention and punishment of crime in Ireland, and for other purposes relating thereto', 19 July 1887.

15 *Freeman's Journal*, 9 September 1887.
16 Ibid.
17 William O'Brien, 'The lost opportunities of the Irish Gentry', in William O'Brien, *Irish Ideas* (New York and London, 1970), pp. 13–29, at pp. 16–17.
18 Ibid., pp. 14, 22–3.
19 James S. Donnelly Jr., *The Land and the People of Nineteenth-Century Cork: The Rural Economy and the Land Question* (London and Boston, 1975), p. 251.
20 *Ballinrobe Chronicle*, 6 January 1877. I am grateful to Gerard Moran for this reference. See Gerard Moran, *A Radical Priest in Mayo. Fr. Patrick Lavelle: The Rise and Fall of an Irish Nationalist 1825–86* (Dublin, 1994), pp. 158–9.
21 Dooley, *The Decline of the Big House in Ireland*, pp. 33–4, 51–2. See also Vaughan, *Landlords and Tenants in Mid-Victorian Ireland*, p. 106.
22 *Cork Examiner*, 23 July 1868.
23 Michael Davitt, *The Fall of Feudalism in Ireland or the Story of the Land League Revolution* (London and New York, 1904), pp. 164–5.
24 CSORP 1891/28047, National Archives of Ireland.
25 See, for instance, speeches by John Dillon at Kenagh, Co. Longford and Gorey, Co. Wexford, *Freeman's Journal*, 8 November 1886, 4 January 1887, and at Castlerea, Co. Roscommon, *United Ireland*, 11 December 1886; William O'Brien at Keadue, Co. Roscommon, *Freeman's Journal*, 22 November 1886.
26 *Freeman's Journal*, 19 November 1886.
27 Anna Parnell, *The Tale of a Great Sham*, edited and introduced by Dana Hearne (Dublin, 1986), pp. 61–2.
28 CSORP 1887/1519, National Archives of Ireland.
29 Marie-Louise Legg, *Newspapers and Nationalism. The Irish Provincial Press, 1850–1892* (Dublin, 1999), pp. 77, 125.
30 Quoted in ibid., p. 158.
31 Davitt, *The Fall of Feudalism in Ireland*, p. 165.
32 Laurence M. Geary, 'The Land War on the Kingston Estate, 1879–1888' (unpublished MA thesis, UCC, 1979), pp. 64, 68–73.
33 E.C. Hamilton, *The Woodford Evictions* (Dublin, 1886).
34 Laurence M. Geary, *The Plan of Campaign, 1886–1891* (Cork, 1986), p. 94.
35 Ibid., pp. 105–7. L. Perry Curtis has recently argued that the landlords' response to the activities of the Land League and the National League was more robust than that generally portrayed by historians of the land war. L. Perry Curtis Jr., 'Landlord Responses to the Irish Land War, 1879–87', *Eire Ireland*, 38, 2–4 (2003), pp. 134–88.
36 William L. Feingold, 'The Tenants' Movement to Capture the Irish Poor Law Boards, 1877–1886', *Albion*, 7/3 (1975), pp. 216–31. Idem., *The Revolt of the Tenantry: The Transformation of Local Government in Ireland, 1872–1886* (Boston, 1984).
37 *Cork Constitution*, 16 March 1888.
38 *Cork Constitution*, 23, 30 December 1887; 2, 3, 10 August 1889; CSORP 1888/684, National Archives of Ireland.
39 *Cork Constitution*, 19 October 1888; CSORP 1888/21816, National Archives of Ireland. See also Colman O'Mahony, *In the Shadows. Life in Cork, 1750–1930* (Cork, 1997), pp. 289–92.
40 Susanne R. Day, *The Amazing Philanthropists, being Extracts from the Letters of Lester Martin, PLG* (London, 1916), p. 155. This work was based on her own experiences of the Cork board of guardians, to which she was elected some twenty–five years after the incident recounted here.
41 *Cork Constitution*, 17, 24, 28, 29 January 1890.

42 *Daily Chronicle*, quoted in *Cork Constitution*, 20 January 1890.
43 *The Times*, 25 January 1890.
44 William O'Brien, 'The lost opportunities of the Irish Gentry', p. 24.
45 Elizabeth Bowen, *Bowen's Court* (London, 1942), pp. 322–5.

Owen Dudley Edwards: Whence Parnell?

1 Firstly, although this essay is mine alone, it goes to John A. Murphy as representative of the love held for him by my parents (R. Dudley Edwards and Síle Ni Shúilleabháin), my wife, Bonnie, and my sisters, Mary and Ruth, as well as myself, and reflects influences from all. It also shows my debts to my mother's county, as well as to the historians of its College (most recent of which are due to the present long-suffering editors). Mr Gerry Long of the National Library of Ireland has supplied me with an invaluable source with his customary generous efficiency, and the staff of the National Library of Scotland have been invaluable as always. Dr Gabriel Flynn has most courteously provided me with the text of his articles on Bishop Thomas Nulty, the major treatment by a modern professional historian. My thanks are also due to Dr Pauric Travers and to Professor Alvin Jackson.
2 F.S.L. Lyons, *Charles Stewart Parnell* (New York, 1977), p. 15.
3 R.F. Foster, *Charles Stewart Parnell: The Man and His Family* (Brighton, 1976), p. 61.
4 St John Ervine, *Parnell* (London, [1925], 1944) p. 19; Norman Vance, *Irish Literature – A Social History* (Oxford, 1990), constructively assesses Ervine with slight mention of his *Parnell*, for whose ferocious demolition see Henry Harrison, *Parnell Vindicated* (London, 1931).
5 Ervine, *Parnell*, pp. 19, 26, 47, 31.
6 Robert M. McWade, *The Uncrowned King. The Life and Public Services of Hon. Charles Stewart Parnell Comprising a Graphic Account of His Ancestry; also Family Reminiscences, Related by his Aged Mother, Delia Tudor Stewart Parnell* (Philadelphia, 1891), p. 38. Her version of her father's life had been incorporated in Thomas Sherlock, *Charles Stewart Parnell* ([1880], 1882), pp. 14–31, a useful indication of what Parnell would have known of his grandfather. It is the stuff of elation, not of resentment. Michael Davitt, *The Fall of Feudalism in Ireland* (London and New York, 1904), p. 175 is instructive here:

> There was something that might be called Cromwellian in Parnell's dislike of the House of Commons. Neither at this [1879] nor at any other period of his career had he any genuine racial or personal hatred of England or of Englishmen. Statements to the contrary are more legend than fact, and have been invented to support some theory of incurable hostility to the nation from which he sprang by overzealous eulogists, with the object of justifying his attitude of personal antipathy to those who opposed him after the catastrophe of 1890. But he had a strong feeling against the House of Commons, possibly due to its browbeating conduct towards himself during stormy scenes in the chamber.

7 On Stewart, apart from Sherlock, Barry O'Brien, *Life of Charles Stewart Parnell* (London, [1898], 1910), Foster, Lyons, see R.W. Irwin, in *Dictionary of American Biography*, and Samuel Willard Crompton, in *American National Biography*; *ANB* (1999) has an up-to-date list of sources, and perhaps unconsciously sets up its own parallel with the career of namesake-grandson in terming his career 'splendid and uneven'.
8 Barry O'Brien, *Parnell* pp. 48–9.
9 John Howard Parnell, *Charles Stewart Parnell* (London, [1898], 1910), pp. 85–6, 125. Parnell quoted Froude very much to his purpose in addressing the US House of Representatives on 2 February 1880, using Froude's 'Romanism and

the Irish Race' in *North American Review* (December 1879 and January 1880) to support his own arguments, whereas Irish nationalist responses to the article up to then simply sought to gainsay it. See also Davitt, *Fall of Feudalism*, p. 114: 'Those who have descried Mr Parnell as being ignorant of Irish history have repeated an opinion expressed by some one who possibly never heard him on any subject which made a wide demand on historic reading.'

10 T.P. O'Connor, *Charles Stewart Parnell* (London, 1891), p. 19.

11 Melville E. Stone, *Fifty Years a Journalist* (New York, 1921), pp. 84–5.

12 Lyons's judgement of Barry O'Brien was in a letter to myself, thanking me for a warm review of his book in the *Glasgow Herald* where I said it was one of the greatest biographies written in our century but not the greatest biography of Parnell, which was Barry O'Brien's. Lyons described Barry O'Brien's book as incomparable. Robbins's book was *Parnell: The Last Five Years* (London, 1926); Robert Kee, *The Laurel and the Ivy* (1993); for Wilde see his 'The Soul of Man under Socialism', *Fortnightly Review* (February 1891); and review of Froude, *The Two Chiefs of Dunboy, Pall Mall Gazette,* (13 April 1889).

13 A.M. Sullivan, *New Ireland* (1877: 1882 ed.), pp. 420, 409. Sullivan's wife, Frances Genevieve was from Louisana in the Confederate States of American when they married in 1861.

14 For Gavan Duffy's authoritative dealings with the Irish Literary Society of London in the 1890s see R.F. Foster, *W.B. Yeats. I. The Apprentice Mage* (Oxford and New York, 1997), pp. 118–24. O'Reilly telegram to Gavan Duffy, n.d., Gavan Duffy, *My Life in Two Hemispheres* (New York, 1898), II, p. 347. Martin died 29 March 1875, which was a Monday, so the priests wasted no time before assembling, evidently feeling a Protestant demise in Newry did not inhibit a Catholic conclave in Kells. In all probability the priests' meeting had been convened long before on less secular matters, but someone – probably O'Reilly himself – struck while the iron was hot, or the corpse not yet cold. It was not a very representative meeting, even of priests, with less than one-sixth of the diocese present – about half the constituency's priests, at best. Kells is ten miles north-west of Navan, which is 29 miles north-west of Dublin. The move may have been taken to forestall an attempt to bring back the Cullenite Repealer Alderman Peter Paul McSwiney, now Lord Mayor of Dublin, who had had strong clerical support as possible candidate in the 1874 General Election but who had been squeezed out by John Martin and the tenant-farmer Nicholas Ennis. The Bishop, Thomas Nulty, probably preferred Martin and Ennis to McSwiney, all the more if he were Cardinal Cullen's man. That did not commit Nulty to the Home Rule League, but he was less hostile to it than Cullen – or McSwiney. Gavan Duffy, like McSwiney, saw himself as a Repealer but where McSwiney used the label to keep clear of Home Rule in the interest of Cullen, Gavan Duffy did so to give himself a free hand – and the back of that hand to Cullen.

15 *The Times*, 3 April 1875, 5 April 1875.

16 Frank Hugh O'Donnell, *Irish Parliamentary Party* (London, 1910), p. 124. There is no reason to think that O'Reilly's Gavan Duffy crusade was crypto-Cullenite, as this suggests. Some of its initial support may have been. Gavan Duffy was later caught between Cullenites led by McSwiney and Home Rulers, finding to his disgust that what he had taken to be the more intransigent position of refusing to compromise on Repeal – in which he was, no doubt consciously, repeating the pre-election professions of Mitchel – had been hijacked in the purely sectarian Catholic clericalist interest with the birth centenary of Daniel O'Connell in August 1875, manipulated by Lord Mayor McSwiney and

Cardinal Cullen to imply O'Connell's life and services had ended with Catholic Emancipation in 1829, all subsequent politics removed. Gavan Duffy, by now publicly identified with hostility to Home Rule, was chosen to give the Dublin banquet toast of Irish legislative independence, and his speech was drowned out with cries of 'Butt, Butt!', on which the proceedings closed. McSwiney got a Papal knighthood out of it, and Duffy returned to Australia where he was made Speaker of the Victoria Assembly 1876–80, after which he retired to London literary life. See David Thornley, *Isaac Butt and Home Rule* (London, 1964), pp. 265–8. As Duffy lay dying in Nice in 1903, his children heard him singing John O'Hagan's song from his *Nation* (his daughter Louise told my father):

> My native heath is brown beneath,
> My native waters blue;
> But crimson red o'er both shall spread,
> Ere I am false to you,
> Dear Land!
> Ere I am false to you.

17 Gavan Duffy, *The League of North and South* (London, 1886), v–xiii: 'Dedication by way of Preface' to Justin McCarthy, where he attacks McCarthy for assuming that a 'policy of Independence' at Westminster was introduced by Parnell 'now tried in action for the first time'; Parnell subsequently told the Special Commission that he had been led to the policy by the precedent Duffy accused McCarthy of ignoring. ('I had some knowledge, not a very deep knowledge, of Irish history, and had read about the independent opposition movement of Sir Charles Gavan Duffy and the late Mr Frederick Lucas in 1852: and whenever I thought about politics I always thought that this would be an ideal movement for the benefit of Ireland.' Evidence 30 April 1889, Parnell, thirteenth answer.)

18 Gavan Duffy, *My Life*, II, pp. 348–9.

19 Barry O'Brien, *Parnell*, pp. 66–7. Gavan Duffy, *My Life*, II, pp. 349–51. Thornley, *Butt*, p. 231.

20 James F. Meenan (ed.), *Centenary History of the Literary and Historical Society of University College Dublin* (Tralee, 1956), chapter 1 and appendices. F.S.L. Lyons, *John Dillon* (London, 1968), pp. 15–18. Lyons mentions Parnell's election for Meath but says nothing of the Dillons' roles in it (though he does note (p. 201) that when Irish Parliamentary Party reunion was negotiated in 1899–1900 and 'when arbitration by Sir Charles Gavan Duffy . . . was suggested, [John Dillon] . . . rejected the proposal'). Thornley, *Butt*, pp. 251–4. A.M. Sullivan, *New Ireland* (Philadelphia, 1878), pp. 400–405. Lyons, *Parnell* (New York, 1977), pp. 47–50. Foster, *Parnell*, p. 141, quotes William Dillon to John Madden, 27 March 1875, mentioning his several long talks with Parnell, deciding he was 'a very thorough and sincere Home Ruler' having at first been 'inclined to distrust him rather, as I thought his publishing that letter sending £25 towards the expenses of Mr Mitchel's election looked very like an election dodge'. John Dillon may have attended one or more of these talks but must have been away from Dublin attending the dying Mitchel up to 20 March and then perhaps helping his elderly relatives with estate and funeral arrangements. His presence at the deathbed suggests that status.

21 Gavan Duffy, *My Life*, II, pp. 350–51. The conclusion is bitterly Gibbonian:

> Mr Butt was much elated by the Meath election. It disembarrassed him of an associate with theories of his own, and who insisted on the dangerous novelty of Independent Opposition. In his place he got a young man who accepted the

> entire programme of the League without demur, and who it might be hoped would prove a steady and deferential supporter. Alas for the futility of human hopes; in a brief time the new recruit completely overthrew the power of the leader, succeeded to his place, and established Independent Opposition as one of the permanent principles of the National programme in Ireland.

On Parnell's distrust of Dillon, see Conor Cruise O'Brien, *Parnell and his Party 1880 – 1890* (London, 1957), pp. 248, 250–51.

22 Thomas Nulty's account of Parnell appeared in his appeal for the National Indemnity Fund to the clergy and laity of the Diocese of Meath, reported *United Ireland,* 6 October 1888. *The Times,* 3, 5 April 1875. *The Times,* as always pretentious in error, called the Donaghmore minister the Revd George Elliott, but on this and all other nomenclature problems I prefer Thom's *Almanac and Official Directory 1875.* Lyons, *Parnell,* p. 50. Emmet Larkin, *The Consolidation of the Roman Catholic Church in Ireland, 1860–1870* (Dublin, 1987), pp. 214–18.

23 *United Ireland,* 6 October 1888.

24 Parnell, *Parnell,* pp. 139–40.

25 Emmet Larkin, *The Roman Catholic Church and the Emergence of the Modern Irish Political System 1874–1878* (Dublin and Washington, 1996), pp. 394–6.

26 T.P. O'Connor, *The Parnell Movement* ([New York, Cincinatti, 1886], 1888), 114n, quoting Nulty, the date given as September 1847. Gabriel Flynn,'Bishop Nulty and the Irish Land Question', *Ríocht na Mídhe,* VII, no. 3 (1984: concluded no. 4 (1985–1986)), p. 15, fn. 6, citing *Drogheda Argus,* 22 August 1881, quoting interview with James Redpath for what seems the same incident ascribed to September 1848. (See also James Redpath, *Talks About Ireland* (New York, 1881).) Nulty (1818–98) was ordained 1846 but his first appointment as Curate (Trim) was in 1847. This inclines one to the 1847 date, taking him to have been on relief work in the small Cavan portion of the diocese, but he could have been later briefly given a *locum* to supply for a vacation or (it was the Famine, and priests were not immune) a death.

27 Andrew Kettle, *Material for Victory,* ed. L.J. Kettle (Dublin, 1958), p. 19. *The Times,* 5, 7, 10, 13, 15 April 1875. Foster, *Parnell,* pp. 141–5. Nulty's vetting arrangements may not have been as formidable at this short notice than they were found by J.A. Dease on 13 June 1871 in Mullingar when he unsuccessfully sought the Westmeath nomination: 'I was put through my catechism by Dr. Nulty in the presence of some 40"sacreds"' (Thornley, *Butt,* p. 118). Dease thought Nulty was for him but the meeting declared for his opponent, the 'Repealer' P.J. Smyth. In Parnell's case the meeting clearly refused to take a decision beyond issuing a communiqué as to an agreeable meeting, but there is a clear implication of the nomination being his if he could campaign convincingly: at the same time, there was no directive and Tormley was clearly surprised at the feeling engendered by the time of the strategically delayed nomination meeting (O'Reilly and Tormey at Kingscourt, in Cavan, were at considerable distance from Navan).

28 There may also have been an element of revengeful piety for Mitchel, who had broken bitterly from his fellow-Carlylean Young Irelander Gavan Duffy in winter 1847–8, had left Australasia as a fugitive convict where Gavan Duffy had done so as statesman and knight of the Empire, and who hardly wanted to pioneer an electoral strategy whose realization would replace his high-principled absenteeism with an apotheosis for Sir Charles at the heart of the British Establishment. But perhaps Dillon did see in Parnell the hope of the future. If so, he then did nothing about cultivating the hope for two

years: this might have been consistent with both parties personally and politically finding it best to give each other leeway after the Gavan Duffy sabotage. The Dillon papers show Parnell consulting Dillon on nominations of possible activities from April 1877 (where he may have sought Dillon's services in an unsuccessful attempt to forestall the nomination of a potential leadership rival, Edmund Dwyer Gray of the *Freeman's Journal*, duly elected MP for Tipperary: Lyons, *Dillon*, p. 22).

29 *The Times* did Naper proud ('will give fresh life and interest to this election . . . his long residence, in the county, his high personal character, his practical knowledge of agricultural matters, and his sympathy with the people and desire to improve their social conditions are qualifications superior to any that his competitors can advance . . . He thinks . . . that "the revision of Irish business measures by an Irish tribunal before they are submitted to the Imperial Parliament would be most beneficial"' [which seems an interesting precursor of Joe Chamberlain's 'Central Board' scheme of 1885]). Naper pledged to work for agricultural buildings and labourers' dwellings 'to which he has given much attention' (this time anticipating the Gerald Balfour administration twenty years later). *The Times* was less happy in continuing 'he appeals to the electors as a landlord' (13 April 1875). Kettle, ibid.

30 Foster, *Parnell*, pp. 142–3. *The Times*, 15 April 1875.

31 Foster, *Parnell*, p. 143. For Moody on Davitt's version of the Irishtown meeting which inaugurated the Land War of 1879, demolishing his reiterated accusations against Canon Geoffrey Bourke, see his *Davitt and Irish Revolution* (Oxford, 1982), pp. 292–5.

32 Davitt, *Fall of Feudalism*, p. 175.

33 Thomas Nulty, *The Land Agitation in Ireland* (i.e. his Letter of February 1881 to clergy and laity of Meath diocese), p. 5. Nulty had taught economics at St Mary's College, Mullingar, 1857–64.

34 Davitt, *Leaves from a Prison Diary* (London, 1885), II, pp. 106–12. Davitt, *Fall of Fedualism*, p. 174.

35 Edward Norman, *The Catholic Church and Ireland in the Age of Rebellion 1859–73* (New York, 1965), pp. 170–71, 161–3, 403. Thomas Flanagan, *The Tenants of Time* (New York, 1988), p. 313. (The judgement is made by a schoolmaster in the novel.) Thornley, *Butt*, pp. 187, 200–201, 227, 234, 253. Nulty's 'returned Yank' acquaintance would have been almost entirely from Irish-American communities. Parnell told the Special Commission on 1 May 1889 that in 1871–72 [accidentally rendered in court as '1873'], 'I did not mix with the Irish people in America. I had no connexion with politics.' The MacEvilly story came from my father whose informants would have been elderly Galway priests.

36 Revd Bernard J. Canning, *Bishops of Ireland* (Ballyshannon, 1987), p. 145. John A. Murphy, 'Religion and Irish Identity', Princess Grace Irish Library, *Irishmen in a Changing Society* (Gerard's Cross, 1989), pp. 133–4.

37 Flynn, 'Nulty', pp. 106–7. The successful petitions against the North and South elections in 1892 were emotively rehearsed by an old Unionist, Philip Henry Bagenal, in *The Priest in Politics* (London, 1893), which cul_minated with a report of the Belfast Convention. This book in fact illustrated perfectly the conviction of Unionists that Home Rule meant clerical bullying, moral pressure and violence of the kind that flourished under Nulty in 1892. Anti-Parnellism deserves much more study as a well-spring of Unionism.

Tom Dunne: Daniel Corkery's *The Hidden Ireland* and the Politics of the Gaelic World

1 Patrick Maume, *'Life That is Exile': Daniel Corkery and the Search for Irish Ireland* (Belfast, 1993), p. 92. Hereafter, Maume, *Life*.
2 Seán Ó Tuama, 'Donal Ó Corcora', in S. Ó Mórdha (ed.), *Scríobh IV*, pp. 94–108. The words quoted are Ó Tuama's version of what Murphy said.
3 L.M. Cullen, 'The Hidden Ireland: Reassessment of a Concept', in *Studia Hibernica*, no. 9 (1969). Reprinted as a pamphlet, with a postscript. (Dublin, 1988), the quote is from p. 25 of the reprint.
4 Ibid., p. 52.
5 Patrick Maume,'Life That is exile: Daniel Corkery (1878–1964) and The Search for Irish Ireland' MA Thesis, UCC, 1990. Hereafter, Maume, *Thesis*
6 Francis McManus,'The Literature of the Period', in Francis McManus (ed.), *The Years of the Great Test* (Cork, 1967), pp. 115–27; p. 117.
7 Ó Tuama, 'Donal Ó Corcora', p. 97.
8 Daniel Corkery, *The Hidden Ireland* (Dublin, 1924; paperback edn, 1967), pp. 12, 14–15, 149–50, 252–3. For a debate in Irish on the Renaissance between Corkery and Pádraig de Brún, see *Humanitas* (1930–31).
9 Maume, *Life*, pp. 19, 41, 50–51.
10 Ibid., p. 21.
11 Ibid., p. 25.
12 Ibid., p. 19.
13 Ibid., p. 30.
14 Albert Memmi, *The Coloniser and the Colonised* (London, 1974; first published in French 1957), pp. 108–9.
15 Ibid., p. 137.
16 Maume, *Life*, pp. 50–51.
17 Maume, *Thesis*, p. 369. His opposition focused on'the clauses . . . that concern your king' (Maume, *Life*, p. 82).
18 Joep Leerssen, *Mere Irish and Fíor–Ghael: Studies in the Idea of Irish Nationality, Its Development and Literary Expression prior to the Nineteenth Century*. (Amsterdam, 1986; paperback edn, Cork, 1996), p. 372.
19 See Clare O'Halloran, *Golden Ages and Barbarous Nations: Antiquarianism and Cultural Politics in Ireland c. 1750–1800*. (Cork, 2004).
20 Joseph C. Walker, *Historical Memoirs of the Irish Bards* [1786] (2nd edn, 2 vols., Dublin, 1818), vol. 1, p. 87. Charlotte Brooke, *Reliques of Irish Poetry* [1789] (2nd edn, Dublin, 1816), pp. 229–30.
21 James Hardiman, *Irish Minstrelsy or Bardic Remains of Ireland with English Poetical Translations* (London, 1831), 2 vols.
22 Joep Leerssen, *Remembrance and Imagination: Patterns in the Historical and Literary Representation of Ireland in the Nineteenth Century* (Cork, 1996), pp. 178–9.
23 Hardiman, *Irish Minstrelsy*, vol. II, pp. 36–41, pp. 3–9.
24 Edward Walsh, *Reliques of Irish Jacobite Poetry, with Metrical Translations* (2nd edn, Dublin, 1866), p. iii.
25 Thomas Davis, *Essays and Poems* (Dublin, 1945), pp. 96–7.
26 B. Ó Conaire (ed.), *Douglas Hyde, Language, Love and Lyrics: Essays and Lectures* (Dublin, 1986), p. 68. See also p. 113.
27 Corkery, *Hidden Ireland*, pp. 134–5.
28 Ibid., e.g. pp. 121,132, 137, 269. See T. Dunne, 'The Gaelic Response to Conquest and Colonisation: The Evidence of the Poetry', in *Studia Hibernica*, no. 20 (1980), pp. 7–30.

29 Corkery, *Hidden Ireland*, pp. 6, 8, 19, 285.
30 Hardiman, *Irish Minstrelsy*, vol. I, p.xxx, 336 (note).
31 John O'Daly, *The Poets and Poetry of Munster* (2nd series, Dublin, 1860), pp. vii–viii; Walsh, *Reliques*, p. 2.
32 Ó Conaire, *Hyde*, pp. 156–7.
33 Pádraig Ó Duinnín (ed.), *Amhráin Eoghain Ruaidh Uí Súilleabháin* (Dublin, 1901), p. xxvi.
34 Pádraig Ó Duinnín (ed.), *Filídhe na Máighe* (Dublin, 1906), p. xvii.
35 Maume, *Thesis*, p. 413.
36 Corkery, *Hidden Ireland*, pp. 21, 23–4, 143, 185.
37 Ibid., pp. 143–4, 148.
38 Ibid., p.144. Also pp. 36, 42, 63, 185.
39 See D. Ó Céileachair and P. Ó Conluain, *An Duinníneach* (Dublin 1958).
40 Corkery, *Hidden Ireland*, p. 42.
41 Ibid., p. 41.
42 Ibid., pp. 144, 148.
43 Ibid., pp. 26–30.
44 Collected and edited by David Greene and Fergus Kelly as *Irish Bardic Poetry. Texts and Translations Together with an Introductory Lecture by Osborne Bergin* (Dublin, 1970).
45 Corkery, *Hidden Ireland*, pp. 109–21. Tadhg Ó Donnchadha (ed.), *Amhráin Dhiarmada Mac Sheáin Bhuidhe Mac Cárrthaigh* (Dublin, 1916) and *Dánta Sheáin Uí Mhurchadha na Ráithíneach* (Dublin, 1907).
46 Eleanor Knott, *The Bardic Poems of Tadhtg Dall Ó Huiginn 1550–1591* (2 vols., London, 1920, 1922), i, pp. xiv–xlix.
47 Corkery, *Hidden Ireland*, pp. 83–5.
48 Ibid., pp. 72–5. Bergin, *Bardic Poetry*, p. 9.
49 Corkery, *Hidden Ireland*, p. 76. Also pp. 127, 154, etc.
50 Ibid., ch. 4, especially pp. 95, 124.
51 Ibid., pp. 107, 100.
52 Ibid., p. 120.
53 Ibid., p. 106. For an important recent survey of the evidence see Breandán Ó Conchúir, S. Ó Coileáin (eds), *Saoi na hÉigse* (B.A.C., 2000), pp. 55–81.
54 Ibid., p. 102.
55 Ó Donnchadha, *MacCárthaigh*, pp. 33, ff.; Corkery, *Hidden Ireland*, pp. 117–20.
56 Corkery, *Hidden Ireland*, pp. 111–17.
57 Ibid., p. 241. See Ó Duinnín, *Filídhe na Máighe.*
58 Corkery, *Hidden Ireland*, p. 107.
59 E.g. Ó Duinnín, *Amhráin Eoghain Ruaidh*, p. xxx; Seán Ó Faoláin, *King of the Beggers* [1938] (paperback edn, Dublin 1980), p. 35; Cullen,'Reassessment', pp. 48–9.
60 Breandán Ó Buachalla, *Aisling Ghéar. Na Stiorbhartaigh agus an tAos Léinn 1603–1788* (Dublin, 1996); Éamon Ó Ciardha, *Ireland and the Jacobite Cause, 1685–1766* (Dublin, 2002), p. 38.
61 Breandán Ó Buachalla, 'Irish Jacoboite Poetry', in *The Irish Review*, no. 12 (1992), pp. 40–49.
62 See Tom Dunne,'Subaltern Voices? Poetry in Irish, Popular Insurgency and the 1798 Rebellion', in *Eighteenth-Century Life*, vol. 22, no. 3 (November, 1998), pp. 31–44; and'"Tá Gaedhil Bhocht Cráidhte"': Memory, Tradition and the Politics of the Poor in Gaelic Poetry and Song', in L.M. Geary (ed.), *Rebellion and Remembrance in Modern Ireland* (Dublin, 2001), pp. 93–111.
63 Ó Ciardha, *Jacobite Cause*, p. 46.

64 Corkery, *Hidden Ireland*, pp. 126–7.
65 Ibid., pp. 129–35.
66 Ibid., pp. 137–9.
67 Ibid., p. 142.
68 Ibid., pp. 156, 162, 157.
69 P.S. Dineen and T. O'Donoghue (eds), *Dánta Aodhagáin Uí Rathaille. The Poems of Egan O'Rahilly* (2nd edn, London, 1911), pp. xxiii, xx. Corkery, *Hidden Ireland*, p. 158.
70 Dineen and O'Donoghue, *Dánta Aodhagáin*, xxi. Corkery, *Hidden Ireland*, pp. 158–9.
71 Dineen and O'Donoghue, *Dánta Aodhagáin*, poem 5, lines 15–16.
72 Corkery, *Hidden Ireland*, pp. 164, 174–5.
73 Ibid., p. 171.
74 Ibid., pp. 129, 162, 179, 182.
75 Ó Duinnín, *Amhráin Eoghain Ruaidh*, p. xxxvii and preface.
76 Ibid., pp. vii–xxxviii. Quote from 'preface'. Corkery, *Hidden Ireland*, pp. 154–203.
77 Ó Duinnín, *Amhráin Eoghain Ruaidh*, pp. xxvii–xxx. Corkery, *Hidden* Ireland, pp. 204–5.
78 Corkery, *Hidden Ireland*, pp. 184, 190, 212.
79 Ibid., pp. 190, 194.
80 Ibid., pp. 197–9.
81 Ibid., p. 23. See e.g. pp. 21–2 for his recognition of bilingualism in Irish cities; pp. 18, 58 on it being a feature of the surviving Catholic Big Houses; p. 163 for Ó Rathaille's use of English.
82 Ibid., pp. 23, 182–3, 201.
83 Ibid., pp. 194–200.
84 Ibid., p. 219.
85 Piaras Béaslaí, 'Merriman's Secret: An Interpretation', in Risteárd Ó Foghludha (ed.), *Cúirt an Mheadhon Oídhche by Brian Merriman* (Dublin, 1912), pp. 1–19, 6, 10, 1.
86 Corkery, *Hidden Ireland*, pp. 217–18.
87 Ibid., pp. 228, 222, 233, 219, 238–9, 235.
88 Ó Tuama, 'Dónal Ó Corcora', p. 106.
89 Béaslaí, 'Merriman's secret', pp. 3, 14, 2–3.
90 Corkery, *Hidden Ireland*, pp. 222, 234.

Tomás Ó Canainn: To the New World and Back with Pipes, Fiddle and Flute: The Transmission of Irish Traditional Music

Works Cited:
Ó hAnnrachain (ed.), *Go Meiriceá Siar* (An Clóchomhar Tta., 1979).
Irish Folkways, R & KP, 1957. Irish Heritage, 1942
Liam Ó Dochartaigh, *Notaí ar Ghluaiseacht na Gaeilge i Meiriceá 1872-1892.*
O'Neill's Music of Ireland (Chicago, 1903).
Pat Mitchell and Jackie Small, *The Piping of Patsy Touhey* (Na Píobairí Uilleann, 1986).
Harry Bradshaw, *Michael Coleman, 1891–1945* (Viva Voce, 1991).
Capt. Francis O'Neill, *Irish Folk Music: A Fascinating Hobby* (1910).
Capt. Francis O'Neill, *The Dance Music of Ireland, 1001 Gems* (1907).

James S. Donnelly Jnr.: The Revival of Knock Shrine

1 See my article 'The Marian Shrine of Knock: The First Decade', in *Eire-Ireland*, xxviii, no. 2 (summer 1993), pp. 55–99.

2 David Blackbourn, *Marpingen: Apparitions of the Virgin Mary in Nineteenth-Century Germany* (New York, 1994), pp. 29–30 and ch. 1 generally.
3 'Notes Taken during the Process' of the Episcopal Commission by Father James S. Fergus, undated, *c.*1939 (Knock Papers, Tuam Diocesan Archives); Revd Michael Walsh, *The Apparition at Knock: A Survey of Facts and Evidence* (Naas, 1955), p. 119.
4 *Irish Catholic* (hereafter cited as *IC*), 24 August 1929.
5 *IC*, 17 October 1940.
6 See James S. Donnelly, Jr., 'The Peak of Marianism in Ireland, 1930–60', in Stewart J. Brown and David W. Miller (eds), *Piety and Power in Ireland, 1760–1960: Essays in Honour of Emmet Larkin* (Belfast and Notre Dame, Indiana, 2000), pp. 253–8.
7 Father John Tuffy to Archbishop Thomas Gilmartin, 23 April 1926 (Knock Papers, Tuam Diocesan Archives). See also Tuffy to Gilmartin, 17 March 1926 (ibid.).
8 Revd Dr. J. Kinnane to Gilmartin, 18 April 1926 (ibid.).
9 Letter to Gilmartin, 2 June 1926 (ibid.).
10 *IC*, 24 August 1929.
11 Interview with Mrs Judith Coyne at Knock Shrine, 15 August 1993.
12 *IC*, 24 August 1929.
13 Canon John Grealy to Archbishop Thomas Gilmartin, 30 August 1932 (Knock Papers, Tuam Diocesan Archives).
14 In this and the succeeding paragraph I rely on the highly informative and thoughtful obituary of W.D. Coyne written by the distinguished theologian and Marian scholar Father Michael O'Carroll, C.S.Sp., for the *Knock Shrine Annual* (hereafter cited as *KSA*). See *KSA* (1954), pp. 63–6.
15 Catherine Rynne, *Knock, 1879–1979* (Dublin, 1979), p. 153.
16 In a special ceremony honouring her in the basilica at Knock in September 1997, Archbishop Michael Neary of Tuam publicly declared that Mrs Coyne had edited the journal herself for the first fifty-seven years of its existence. See *KSA* (1998), p. 14.
17 A formal petition seeking ecclesiastical sanction for the establishment of such a body was drawn up on 19 July 1935. Canon Grealy signed the petition on 21 July and Archbishop Gilmartin signified his approval on 23 July. The first meeting of the society took place at Knock on 21 August 1935 – the fifty-sixth anniversary of the original apparition. The popular title of 'Knock Shrine Society' was adopted as the official title in December 1959. See Revd Michael I. Mooney, 'Knock Shrine Society, 1935–1960', in *KSA* (1960), p. 13.
18 W.D. Coyne, 'Knock Shrine', in *Good Counsel: An Irish Augustinian Quarterly*, i, no. 4 (January 1936), p. 152.
19 W.D. Coyne to Archbishop Thomas Gilmartin, 19 March 1936 (Knock Papers, Tuam Diocesan Archives).
20 W.D. Coyne to Father James S. Fergus, 18 June 1935 (ibid.).
21 Prayer Leaflet, printed *'cum permissu superiorem*, 2/5/35' (ibid.). See also *IC*, 27 April, 20 July 1935.
22 *KSA* (1938), p. 5.
23 W.D. Coyne, 'Knock Shrine', p. 152; *IC*, 27 April 1935.
24 *KSA* (1938), p. 6.
25 W.D. Coyne, 'Knock Shrine', p. 152.
26 *KSA* (1938), pp. 45–52; *KSA* (1944), p. 105; *IC*, 2 May 1936, 25 August 1938.
27 *KSA* (1960), p. 14.

28 *IC*, 2 May 1936; *KSA* (1938), p. 67; *KSA* (1939), p. 99; *KSA* (1940), p. 123.
29 *KSA* (1938), pp. 8–9, 31.
30 *IC*, 2 May 1936.
31 *KSA* (1939), p. 93.
32 *KSA* (1939), p. 9.
33 *KSA* (1939), pp. 93–9; *KSA* (1940), pp. 107–18. It is especially notable that in both of these lists the names are overwhelmingly those of women rather than men.
34 *KSA* (1939), p. 9.
35 *KSA* (1938), p. 6. It is unclear whether a sound basis existed for this far-reaching claim, apart from the fact that the Coynes had apparently succeeded in distributing approximately 500,000 prayer leaflets designed to advance the cause of the shrine. Even the figures for dues-paying members should be treated with some caution. On the other hand, during the diamond-jubilee year of 1939, the society reduced the annual dues from a shilling to just sixpence in an effort 'to multiply our membership and thereby ensure increased interest and consequently more prayer'. This stratagem succeeded admirably. The sum of £732 collected in subscriptions of sixpence for the year ending in early December 1939 indicates a total membership for that year not far short of 30,000. See *KSA* (1938), p. 5; *KSA* (1939), pp. 9, 99; *KSA* (1940), p. 123.
36 Revd Michael O'Carroll, *A Priest in Changing Times: Memories and Opinions of Michael O'Carroll, C.S.Sp.* (Blackrock, 1998), pp. 56–7.
37 W.D. Coyne, ''Knock Shrine', p. 152. Coyne was said to have worked on the book for five years in the early 1930s, largely in response to Archbishop Gilmartin's statement at Knock in August 1929 that 'the story of the apparition required further examination before ecclesiastical approval could be given'. Coyne presented to Gilmartin the fruits of his five-year labour in the form of a manuscript or typescript on 3 June 1935, presumably with a view to securing the archbishop's prior approval for its publication. Printed copies of the book first became available on 27 November 1935. See Mooney, 'Knock Shrine Society', p. 12.
38 *IC*, 2 May 1936.
39 *KSA* (1938), p. 25.
40 Although many of the favours recorded had to do with recovery from serious physical illness or disease, a little note in italics (beginning in 1939) at the head of these yearly listings stated that the reported blessings were 'not within the class of cure submitted to the Medical Bureau'. See *KSA* (1939), p. 57. See also *KSA* (1939), pp. 57–61; *KSA* ((1940), pp. 81–8; *KSA* (1941), pp. 117–23; *KSA* (1942), pp. 48–53; *KSA* (1943), pp. 67–75; *KSA* (1944), pp. 58–72.
41 *KSA* (1938), pp. 10–13; *KSA* (1939), pp. 15, 26–7; *KSA* (1941), pp. 9–74; *KSA* (1943), pp. 5–40.
42 *KSA* (1940), pp. 6–7.
43 *KSA* (1941), p. 6.
44 *KSA* (1943), p. 3.
45 *KSA* (1941), p. 6.
46 *KSA* (1938), pp. 8–9. See also *IC*, 2 May 1936.
47 Liam Coyne thanked the Director of Broadcasting T.J. Kiernan in the 1938 *Annual* for including Knock Shrine devotions in his programming and for finding time for other broadcasts about the shrine from the Dublin studio of the service, sometimes on short notice. See *KSA* (1938), p. 15.
48 *IC*, 17 August 1935. For a discussion of Flynn's case, see W.D. Coyne,' Knock Shrine', pp. 151–2.

49 *IC*, 24 August 1935.
50 W.D. Coyne to Father James S. Fergus, 18 June 1935 (Knock Papers, Tuam Diocesan Archives).
51 *'A Day at Cnoc Muire': Lecture Delivered at the Gaiety Theatre, Dublin, on Sunday, 13th December 1936, by Tomás Ó Deirg, T.D. . . .* (Castlebar, 1937).
52 *IC*, 9 May 1936. See also *IC*, 2 May 1936.
53 *IC*, 1, 15 July 1937.
54 *IC*, 17 August 1939.
55 Ibid. The text of Eily MacAdam's radio play 'The Apparitions at Knock' – a highly effective piece of publicity for the shrine – was published in the 1939 *Annual* with permission from the Director of Radio Éireann. See *KSA* (1939), pp. 84–90.
56 Prayer Leaflet, printed '*cum permissu superiorem*, 2/5/35' (Knock Papers, Tuam Diocesan Archives).
57 *IC*, 22 August 1936.
58 *IC*, 20 May 1937.
59 *IC*, 20 October 1938.
60 One was that of Garda H. Conroy, brought to Knock on a stretcher in 1938 because of 'spinal trouble' but now serving as a steward and to all appearances cured. The other involved a young woman of twenty who had 'laid in a metal frame' for fourteen months, but who was now serving as a handmaid with responsibility for stretcher cases herself. See *IC*, 11 May, 1 June 1939.
61 *IC*, 28 September 1939.
62 *IC*, 9 May 1940.
63 Conrad M. Arensberg and Solon T. Kimball, *Family and Community in Ireland*, 2nd edn (Cambridge, Mass., 1968), p. 99. See also ibid., pp. 100–117. See also Brendan M. Walsh, 'Marriage in Ireland in the Twentieth Century', in Art Cosgrove (ed.), *Marriage in Ireland* (Dublin, 1985), pp. 132–50.
64 Among many examples of Irish Catholic literature emphasizing the utter depravity of illicit sexual behaviour and portraying the Virgin Mary as the perfection of purity, see the booklet entitled *Grown Up* (Dublin, 1957) for young women by the Redemptorist priest Father John Carr, especially his chapter on 'companionships' (pp. 44–56). 'There are two roads to marriage', declared Father Carr, 'the one mapped out by God, the other mapped out by the devil; the one white and fragrant with the flowers of Christian chastity, the other choked with the rank and poisonous growth of a thousand sins; the one leading those that walk it to the best of blessings, the other leading – as is only too often evident – to the penalty of God's own curse' (p. 75).
65 Donnelly, 'Peak of Marianism', pp. 272–81.
66 Fearghal McGarry, *Irish Politics and the Spanish Civil War* (Cork, 1999), p. 35.
67 Dermot Keogh, *The Vatican, the Bishops, and Irish Politics, 1919–1939* (Cambridge, 1986), pp. 180–81; F.S.L. Lyons, *Ireland since the Famine* (New York, 1971), pp. 527–8; Richard English, 'Socialism and Republican Schism in Ireland: The Emergence of the Republican Congress in 1934', in *Irish Historical Studies*, xxvii, no. 105 (May 1990), pp. 48–65; Richard English, *Radicals and the Republic: Socialist Republicanism and the Irish Free State, 1925–1937* (Oxford, 1994), especially chs 3 and 4 (pp. 124–215).
68 McGarry, *Irish Politics and Spanish Civil War*, especially chs 5 and 6 (pp. 135–205).
69 Ibid., p. 194. For examples of the striking of apocalyptic notes by Catholic priests and bishops, see Donnelly, 'Peak of Marianism', p. 269.
70 McGarry admirably surveys the responses of different elements of the Irish

Catholic Church to the Spanish Civil War. Catholic bishops showed the strongest tendency to view and project the war in Spain as a struggle between Christianity and communism. See McGarry, *Irish Politics and Spanish Civil War*, pp. 140–51.

71 Donnelly,'Peak of Marianism', pp. 253–8. For the claim about the overwhelming popular response in the years 1930–32 to the opening of the Lourdes grotto at Inchicore, see Peter Costello, *Dublin Churches* (Dublin, 1989), p. 156.

72 *IC*, 2 February, 2, 9 March, 4 May, 22 June 1935, 9 May 1936; Donnelly,'Peak of Marianism', pp. 255–6.

73 Interview with Mrs Judith Coyne at Knock Shrine, 15 August 1993.

74 Liam Ua Cadain, *Cnoc Muire*, pp. 297–305, 308–10. See also *KSA* (1956), page facing table of contents.

75 *The Irish Times*, 1, 2 October 1979; *KSA* (1980), pp. 3–19; Monsignor James Horan, *Memoirs, 1911–1986*, edn Father Micheál MacGréil, S.J. (Dingle, 1992), pp. 155–72.

Lawrence J. McCaffrey: Church or Nation: An Irish-American Dilemma

1 *Boston Globe*, 31 May 2002.

2 Kathleen Parker's column, *Chicago Tribune*, 12 June 2002.

3 CBS News, 20 May 2002.

4 *Boston Globe*, 30 May 2002.

5 *Boston Globe*, 12 June 2002.

6 *Los Angeles Times*, 12 June 2003, MSN, 16 June.

7 Louise Fuller's *Irish Catholicism since 1950: The Undoing of a Culture* (Dublin, 2002) provides an excellent analysis of the impact of sexual abuse scandals on the Church in Ireland.

8 Patrick O'Farrell, *Ireland's English Question* (New York, 1972), p. 304

9 Ray Allen Billington, *The Protestant Crusade, 1800–1860* (Chicago, 1964); John Higham, *Strangers in the Land: Patterns of American Nativism, 1860–1925* (Chicago, 1965); and Philip Jenkins, *The New Anti-Catholicism: The Last Acceptable Prejudice* (New York, 2003).

10 For examinations of the Irish-American experience, see Patrick Blessing, in Stephan Thernstrom (ed.), 'The Irish', *Harvard Encyclopedia of American Ethnic Groups* (Cambridge, Mass., 1980); Maureen Dezell, *Irish America Coming Into Clover: The Evolution of a People and a Culture* (New York, 2001); Marjorie Fallows, *Irish-Americans: Identity and Assimilation* (Englewood Cliffs, N.J., 1977); Andrew M. Greeley, *The Irish-Americans: The Rise to Money and Power* (New York, 1981); Kevin Kenny, *The American Irish: A History* (New York, 2000); Lawrence J. McCaffrey, *The Irish Catholic Diaspora in America* (Washington, D.C., 1997) and *Textures of Irish America* (Syracuse, 1998); Kerby Miller, *Emigrants and Exiles: The Irish Exodus to North America* (New York, 1985); William V. Shannon, *The American Irish* (New York, 1964); and Carl Wittke, *The Irish in America* (New York, 1970).

11 The three most comprehensive studies of American Catholicism, including the Irish impact, are Charles R. Morris, *American Catholicism: The Saints and Sinners Who Built America's Most Powerful Church* (New York, 1997); Jay P. Dolan, *The American Catholic Experience* (New York, 1985); and James Hennessey, S.J., *American Catholics: A History of the American Catholic Community in the United States* (New York, 1981).

12 Information on the Americanist issue can be found in Gerald P. Fogarty, *The*

Vatican and the American Hierarchy from 1870 to 1965 (Wilmington, Del., 1985); Robert D. Cross, *The Emergence of Catholic Liberalism in America* (Chicago, 1967); Robert Emmet Curran, *Michael Augustine Corrigan and the Shaping of Conservative Catholicism in America, 1878–1902* (New York, 1978); and Marvin O'Connell, *John Ireland and the American Catholic Church* (St Paul, 1988). In a recent book, *American Catholic Lay Groups and Transatlantic Reform in the Progressive Era* (Chapel Hill, N.C., 2002), Deirdre M. Moloney explains the complexities of the Americanist issue. Rochester's Bishop Bernard McQuaid, while an ally of Corrigan favored separation of Church and state and organized labour.

13 The impact of the Irish film image is discussed in Joseph M. Curran, *Hibernian Green on the Silver Screen: The Irish and American Movies* (Westport, Conn., 1989); Lawrence J. McCaffrey, '*Going My Way* and Irish-American Catholicism: Myth and Reality', in *New Hibernia Review* 4:3 (autumn, 2000), pp. 119–27.

14 John Tracy Ellis, *American Catholics and the Intellectual Life* (Chicago, 1955); and Thomas O'Dea, *The American Catholic Dilemma* (New York, 1958).

15 'Paranoid garrisons of bigotry' is the thesis of John T. McGreevy, *Parish Boundaries: The Catholic Encounter With Race in the Twentieth Century North* (Chicago, 1996).

16 Catholic pressures against birth control and married teachers are discussed in John A. Farrell, *Tip O'Neil and the Democratic Century* (Boston, 2001), pp. 102, 103, 104.

17 *Newsweek*, 6 May 2002.

Eoghan Harris: Unionism and the Mass Media

1 Arlene Kelly (ed.), *Selling Unionism* (Belfast, 1995).

2 Eoghan Harris, *Television and Terrorism* (RTÉ, 1987).

Index

Tabula Gratulatoria

Maurice Ahern, Univeristy College Cork
Donald Akenson, Queen's University, Ontario
Toby C. Barnard, University of Oxford
Thomas Bartlett, University College Dublin
Brendan Bradshaw S.M., Dublin
Diarmuid Breathnach, Bray, Co. Wicklow
Elizabeth Brosnan, Waterfall, Cork
Nora Browne, Cork
Patrick Buckley, Royal Irish Academy Library
C.G. Buttimer, *Journal of the Cork Historical and Archaeological Society*
Kent Carty, Dublin
Jeremiah Casey, Cork
Aidan Clarke, Trinity College Dublin
Bob Collins, Dun Laoghaire, Co. Dublin
R.V. Comerford Esq., NUI Maynooth
Art Cosgrove, Dublin
Donal J. Counihan, University College Cork
Seamus Crowley, Mallow, Co. Cork
J.P. Crowley, Waterfall, Co. Cork
Louis M. Cullen, Co. Dublin
Ian d'Alton, Dublin
Mary A. Daly, University College Dublin
Pat Deasy, Tower Books, Cork
Barry Duggan, Carrigrohane, Cork
Dymphna Dunlea McCormack, Athlone

Jeremiah Falvey, Cloyne, Co. Cork
Aengus Fanning, Dublin
Connell and Mary Fanning, University College Cork
Brian Farrell, Bray, Co. Wicklow
Honora Faul, National Library of Ireland
Ignatius Fennessy OFM, Co. Dublin
Finola Finlay, Vancouver, BC
B.P. Fitzgerald, Dublin
John Fitzgerald, University College Cork
Ruth Fleischmann, England
Roy Foster, University of Oxford
Michael Galvin Esq., Lissarda, Co. Cork
James Good, Cork
David Goodall, England
Roger Grufferty, Dublin
Padraig Hamilton, Cork
Martin Hayes, University College Cork
Nora M. Hickey, Kinsale
Michael Holland, Heritage Office, University College Cork
Patrick Holohan, Clogheen, Co. Cork
Maurice F. Hurley, Bandon, Co. Cork
Cal Hyland, Rosscarbery, Co. Cork
James James Good, Douglas, Cork
Francis M. Johnson, Sligo
M.H. Keen, Oxford
Thomas Kelleher, Ballinspittal, Co. Cork
Sheila Kelly, Presentation Convent, Cork
James Kelly, St Patricks College, Dublin
Éamon Lankford Esq., Cork
Margaret Lantry, Cork
Seamus Lantry, Cork
Peter Leonard, Castlebar, Co. Mayo
Patricia Lucy, Cork
Maria Luddy, University of Warwick
Margaret MacCurtain, Co. Dublin
John Maguire, University College Cork
Michael and Mary Maguire, University College Cork

Martin Mansergh, Co. Tipperary
Kathleen Martin, Cork
Ged Martin, Youghal, Co. Cork
Mairead Maume, Cork
Patrick Maume, Dublin
Frank Mc Carthy, Colaiste an Spioraid Naoimh, Cork
Mark Mc Carthy, Galway
Declan McCormack, Co. Dublin
Donal McIlraith, Fiji
Michael Mortell, University College Cork
Rita Moynihan, Cork
Connie Mulcahy, University College Cork
Peter Murray, Crawford Municipal Art Gallery
Amelia Murray, Crookstown, Co. Cork
Kevin Murray, University College Cork
Grace Neville, Univeristy College Cork
Eibhlin Ni Chriodain, Cork
David Nolan, Cessy, France
Sean Nyhan, Cork
Catherine O'Brien, National University of Ireland, Galway
Kevin O'Byrne, Skibereen
Colin O Callaghan, Buttevant, Co. Cork
Leachlain O Cathain, Corcaigh
Seán O Coileáin, University College Cork
Tomás Ó Con Cheanainn, Co. Cill Mhartain
Breandán Ó Conchúir, University College Cork
Donnchadh O Corrain, University College Cork
Gearoid O Crualaoich, University College Cork
Caitríona Ó Dochartaigh, University College Cork
Liam Ó Dochartaigh, Cumann Merriman
Finola O'Donovan, Cork
Patrick O Donovan, University College Cork
Proinsias O Drisceoil, Kilkenny
Fineen O Driscoll, Cork
Mary Pius O'Farrell Sr., Presentation Centre, Cork
Clare O'Halloran, University College Cork
Eunan O'Halpin, Trinity College Dublin

Eoghan Ó hAnluain, Co. Dublin
Roibeárd Ó hÚrdail, Glanmire, Co. Cork
Sean O Laoithe, Charleville
Frank O Mahony, Bantry, Co. Cork
Colman O Mahony, Cork
D.P.J. O'Mahony, Cork
Seán Ó Mordha, Dublin
Diarmuid Ó Murchadha, Cork
Joan Ó Murchú, Cork
Liam P. Ó Murchú, University College Cork
John O Neill, Cork
Eileen O Neill, Cork
Pádraig Ó Riain, University College Cork
Aidan and Deirdre O Shea, Cork
Seamus O Tuama, University College Cork
Finola O'Donovan, Cork
Eunan O'Halpin, Trinity College Dublin
Mary Pius O'Farrell Sr., Presentation Centre, Cork
Clare O'Halloran, University College Cork
Willie Parker, Youghal, Co. Cork
David Pembrey, Greenes Bookshop, Dublin
Hugh P. Pollock, Cork
Máirín Quill, Cork
Carmel Quinlan, University College Cork
Pól T. Ruiséal, Univeristy College Cork
Michael Sexton, University College Cork
Lee Snodgrass, Ballydehob, Co. Cork
Mary Steele, University College Cork
Virginia Teehan, Hunt Museum, Limerick
John R. Thuillier, Kinsale, Co. Cork
Seán Ua Súilleabháin,University College Cork
Jean van Sinderen-Law, University College Cork
Madeline Ward O'Sullivan, Cloghroe, Co. Cork
Noel Whelan, Dublin
Gerard T. Wrixon, University College Cork